The Apache Diaspora

AMERICA IN THE NINETEENTH CENTURY

Series editors
Brian DeLay
Steven Hahn
Amy Dru Stanley

America in the Nineteenth Century proposes a rigorous rethinking of this most formative period in U.S. history. Books in the series will be wide-ranging and eclectic, with an interest in politics at all levels, culture and capitalism, race and slavery, law, gender, and the environment, and regional and transnational history. The series aims to expand the scope of nineteenth-century historiography by bringing classic questions into dialogue with innovative perspectives, approaches, and methodologies.

The Apache Diaspora

Four Centuries of Displacement and Survival

Paul Conrad

Published in Cooperation with the
William P. Clements Center for Southwest Studies,
Southern Methodist University

PENN

UNIVERSITY OF PENNSYLVANIA PRESS

PHILADELPHIA

Published by
University of Pennsylvania Press
Philadelphia, Pennsylvania 19104-4112
www.upenn.edu/pennpress

Printed in the United States of America on acid-free paper
1 3 5 7 9 10 8 6 4 2

Library of Congress Cataloging-in-Publication Data
Names: Conrad, Paul, author.
Title: The Apache diaspora : four centuries of displacement and survival / Paul Conrad.
Other titles: America in the nineteenth century.
Description: 1st edition. | Philadelphia : University of Pennsylvania Press, 2021. |
Series: America in the nineteenth century | "Published in Cooperation with
the William P. Clements Center for Southwest Studies, Southern Methodist University" |
Includes bibliographical references and index.
Identifiers: LCCN 2020037029 | ISBN 9780812253016 (hardcover)
Subjects: LCSH: Apache Indians—History. | Apache Indians—Migrations. | Apache Indians—
Relocation. | Apache Indians—Government policy. | Apache Indians—Ethnic indentity.
Classification: LCC E99.A6 C595 2021 | DDC 979.004/9725—dc23
LC record available at https://lccn.loc.gov/2020037029

CONTENTS

Fantastic and Terrible Stories

Everyone laughed at the impossibility of it,
but also the truth. Because who would believe
the fantastic and terrible story of all of our survival
those who were never meant
to survive?

—Joy Harjo, "Anchorage"

A young man walked the grounds of a school counting graves. He had been sent to Carlisle, Pennsylvania, in 1898 for an education, to be trained in welding, construction, and other industrial skills. As he passed through rows of gravestones, counting to 105 before he got "mixed up," he learned other lessons. "Very few came back," he observed.[1]

Sam Kenoi was one who did, however. He slipped away one night on a westbound train and returned to his people. At this time, his Apache Indian relatives were U.S. prisoners of war and had been since the army rounded them up from their Arizona reservation in 1886 and shipped them into exile in Florida, Alabama, and then Oklahoma. Kenoi married and started a family. He settled on the Mescalero reservation in New Mexico after Apache POWs were finally freed in 1913 and given a choice of where to live. After his first wife died of pneumonia, he remarried and had more children. He organized his people in a bold effort to seek reparations for their twenty-seven-year internment.[2]

Most lives are full of tragedy and triumph, and Kenoi's was no exception. But his life was also particular, shaped by who he was as an Apache. Kenoi confronted challenges that his ancestors had faced for generations. How does one exist in a world that does not want you to exist as you are? How does one survive that which so many are not surviving? How does one start over in a foreign land or on land made foreign by colonialism? Kenoi responded to these questions creatively, pushed back on those who mistreated him, and lived boldly within the constraints of his circumstances.[3]

Pulling back from Kenoi's particular story, a broader portrait of Apache life and death across North America and the Caribbean comes into view. Apache men and women throw themselves into the Gulf of Mexico, desperate to escape the boat waiting to carry them overseas. A priest pens an entry in a leather-bound ledger near the Pacific coast of Sonora—another Apache girl buried after months of forced labor. Apache boys run errands for the governor of Quebec, and Apache women gather water for their masters at a neighborhood well in Mexico City. Apache men pull a pine tree out of the chimney of an old U.S. fort in Florida and apply mortar to Spanish fortifications in the port of Havana. An Apache servant and a black slave marry in a church in a Mexican mining town as a crowd of their friends looks on. Their children have children, who have children, their descendants still living across North America today.[4]

*   *   *

"What can we say that would make us understand better than we do already?" Joy Harjo asks in her classic poem "Anchorage." She proceeds to encapsulate in a few stanzas core themes of American Indian history: rootedness and displacement, pain and laughter, a seemingly impossible but true survival. In researching this book, I have often come back to Harjo's question. What might I say that would make you understand better than you already do the history of Native people confronting colonialism? As an outsider, I will never understand what it means to be Apache in America in the way Kenoi did, and many writers have already offered powerful lenses through which we might understand stories like his. Evoking their insights, I could see Kenoi's history as rooted in "cycles of conquest" or "resistance to forced colonization." I could frame his tale as a story of "surviving genocide" or as a story of "survivance," among other possibilities. There is deep insight in all of these formulations, but there is also something not fully captured by them: the far-flung geography of Kenoi's life and the lives of Apaches like him.[5]

These are lives of resistance, survival, and more, but they are also lives that map the diaspora of a people. The use of the term "diaspora" has expanded in recent years, and it has sometimes been employed simply as a synonym of "migration" in order to describe any dispersal of a people from their homeland. Scholars employing a more rigid conception have argued that diasporas are characterized by the following: migration, collective memory of an ancestral home, a continued connection to that home, a sustained group consciousness, and a sense of kinship with group members living in different places. All five of these elements are evident in Apache history, even if some characteristics have been more pronounced at certain moments than at others. Recognizing that there was (and is) an Apache diaspora helps us understand Apache and North American history better.[6]

"Diaspora" is not a word in common usage among contemporary Apache communities, and for this reason I long hesitated to name what I was observing as such. Over time, however, I became convinced that I could not avoid the concept, in no small measure because Apaches so clearly expressed its significance in their stories even if they did not use the word. They told of remembering when "such and such child was lost over in that country" and of wanting to have "all our children together where I can see them." They spoke in exile about longing to return to "my land, my home, my father's land." They repeated valiant tales of displaced Apache captives' escapes and returns to kin against the odds.[7] "Diaspora" is useful not only as a descriptor of such stories but also as a concept for analyzing them. It requires following migrating people and considering their circumstances and choices wherever they ended up. Those uprooted from their place among Apaches struggled to survive in the absence of the societal recognition of belonging and kinship structures central to well-being in Apache lands. They responded to this existential problem by banding together with each other and also by forming new relationships with outsiders. They often retained an "Apache" identity, but they also sometimes built new self-understandings as they navigated life in colonial societies across multiple generations. They were not only affected by the experience of diaspora, but they also influenced the societies in which they found themselves, especially when they were large in number, but sometimes even when they were relatively few.[8]

The experience of diaspora also had implications for Apache people who managed to remain in ancestral lands but felt the loss of their kin. This loss was most frequently rooted in affection, in the void felt by no longer being able to speak to or see a relative. In the era Sam Kenoi lived, Apache parents sent care packages and letters to their children at U.S.-run boarding schools through the government mail system, soliciting news and telling them to come home soon. Past generations of Apaches had regularly petitioned Spanish, Mexican, or U.S. officials to return to them their loved ones who labored in Chihuahua, Mexico City, and beyond in the eighteenth and nineteenth centuries. These concerns also reflected material interests, because the loss of kin—sometimes on a large scale—could challenge the ability of a group to protect itself from enemies, obtain sufficient food, or even reproduce. The Chihene Apache leader Victorio indicated as much when he explained in 1872 that U.S. efforts to force Apaches to reside on an undesirable reservation had scattered his people, and few babies had been born since. He told U.S. officials that if they instead allowed them to return to their homeland where they wanted to live, "we shall have many with us, and we shall increase." Such remarks illustrate how genocide, the elimination of a group of people as such in whole or in part, was a central factor in the history of the Apache diaspora, either as an intent or as a consequence of imperial forced migrations and as a motivation for Apache mobility.[9]

If diaspora represents the key analytical lens of this book, Apache history and identity also warrant further introduction. Scholars have usually applied the term "Apache" to encompass those groups across the North American Southwest who speak dialects of a language in the Athapaskan family. They explain the coherence of the category as being based on a shared ancestral language, similarities in belief systems and historical subsistence strategies, or ties of kinship across groups that facilitated alliances in times of war or for raiding or trading expeditions. It nevertheless remains the case that these designated "Apache" groups have recognized themselves as distinct, with identities defined most by belonging in extended families whose ties of kinship linked together larger collectives. There was not historically (nor is there in the present day) one overarching Apache "tribe" or nation.[10]

Like many terms for Native American groups in common usage, "Apache" is what scholars call an exonym. It is a term originally used by outsiders to refer to a given group, rather than its name for itself in its own language. Historically, they distinguished themselves from others in the broadest sense through variants of the term "Ndé" (the people). Yet "Ndé" did not itself reflect a collective category of identity or a "nation." It was instead modified by more particular understandings of belonging and loyalty that were closer-knit. There was the extended family to whom you belonged, the cluster of families with whom you lived, and the links through marriage and other forms of kinship that tied you to neighboring groups of people that formed clans or bands depending on the Apache group. The nineteenth-century Apache leader Cochise, for example, knew himself as the chief or spokesperson, *nantan*, for the families that formed his local group, or *gotah*. This group had a name based on its favorite camping spot in the Dragoon Mountains of what is now southeastern Arizona, "bi-at-siga," or "there is a clearing on its summit." Together with other local groups linked through kinship in the broader region, Cochise's people formed a larger band, the Chokonen, or "juniper people." While the Chokonen had relatives among and might sometimes call upon the aid of other neighboring Apache bands, such as the Chihene (red paint people) or Nedni (enemy people), they owed the greatest loyalty and possessed the greatest sense of obligation to other Chokonens.[11]

While some exonyms are relatively neutral in their connotations—referring to a people's way of life, place of residence, or cultural traits—many are derogatory: Sioux, "little snakes"; Comanche, "people who want to fight all the time"; Apache, "enemy." The English glosses on Apaches' own names for outsiders illustrate as much: Mexicans, "people with brown eyes"; Pueblos, "people living close to the water"; Navajos, "little gee-string people"; white people, "enemy." Many of the exonyms for Native groups with which readers are probably familiar were inherited from Indigenous languages, but European colonizers had a penchant for generalizing and redefining them further. While sometimes this practice was rooted in ignorance, it was also often strategic. The use of the term "Apache" in the seventeenth and eighteenth centuries was in part fueled by colonists' interests in obtaining slave labor. Declaring that "the entire Apache nation" had resisted Spanish rule, and was therefore "an enemy" to colonial society, served to justify their enslavement. By labeling a wide array of surrounding Indigenous peoples as Apache, the Spaniards and their Native allies could ensure their supply of enslaved laborers would be abundant.[12]

A focus on diaspora casts Apache histories in a new light. "Every tribe had a trail of tears," the Lumbee activist Helen Scheirbeck once said, capturing a basic truth often underappreciated by non-Natives. Forced migrations were unusually common within Apache history, however—because Apache homelands bordered competing nations and empires, and also because of the ways Apache mobility challenged the interests of imperial invaders. The importance of diaspora and mobility in Apache history predated colonialism. Athaspaskan-speaking communities have resided and continue to reside not only in what is currently known as the U.S. Southwest and Mexico but also in the Pacific Northwest and northern Canada. This linguistic connection suggests migration over time, as ancestral Apaches moved from the north through the Rocky Mountains into new southwestern homelands by the sixteenth century. Prior to the arrival of Spaniards in the late sixteenth century, Apache groups had developed a symbiotic relationship with village-dwelling agriculturists, such as the Pueblos of present-day New Mexico. Though most Apache groups practiced some agriculture, through the mobility of hunting, gathering, and long-distance trade they also came to possess resources useful to their Pueblo neighbors—hides, meat, tools, pottery—which they might exchange for products they desired, such as corn and cloth. While Apache and Pueblo peoples sometimes came into conflict, especially in times of drought and resource scarcity, their ways of life were usually not in tension with each other but rather were mutually beneficial.[13]

Apache mobility proved more challenging to European and Euro-American empires and nation-states and their citizens. Southern Apaches, for example, viewed their homelands as a chain of diverse landscapes with valuable resources that they moved between seasonally to plant crops, hunt, or harvest wild fruits throughout the year. This chain of places ensured that they had a diversified source of food and varied climates well suited to life during particular times of the year—cool highlands in the summer, warmer lowlands in the winter. Yet such mobility was anathema to European and Euro-American understandings of exclusive property rights; or to their understandings of fixed settlement and farming as linked to civilization and Christianity; or by the nineteenth century, to their belief that exclusive jurisdiction over a defined territory was at the core of what it meant to be a nation.[14]

Apache mobility was not in and of itself timeless or unchanging. It was often sparked by adaptation to a colonial world in which capture, enslavement, and forced migration loomed. Ironically, the displacement of kin to distant places also served as an impetus for further Apache mobility, in attempts to recover those in diaspora. Past generations of scholars sometimes explained this mobility and warfare in racial terms as "innate" and unchangeable characteristics. Apache wars with Mexico and the United States, in those analyses, represented an inevitable clash between "races." Yet following the Apache diaspora across four centuries highlights a different explanation. If they fought vigorously for self-determination in familiar lands, it is in part because they and their ancestors had so often experienced the opposite: subjugation and forced removal to foreign places in which survival in diaspora was difficult.[15]

Over time, diaspora played an important role in influencing not just outsiders' understandings of who was Apache but also internal political divisions, identities, and places of residence among Native groups. One illustration of this in the present day is the presence of federally or state-recognized Apache tribes in Arizona, New Mexico, Oklahoma, Texas, and Louisiana.[16] In part because the term "Apache" became meaningful to many Natives themselves through colonialism and diaspora, I use this term throughout the book. I also make clear the specific band names of groups wherever possible, using the Apache language terms most familiar to contemporary Apache communities and scholars, such as "Chihene" or "Chokenen" rather than English or

Spanish referents like "Warm Springs" or "Mimbreño." While some readers may be familiar with "Chiricahua" as a cover term for Chihene, Chokonen, Nedni, and Bedonkohe Apaches, I follow recent scholarly usage and the preferences of some contemporary Apache groups in using the term "Southern Apache" instead. This is in recognition of the fact that it was generally only Chokonens who were considered true Chiricahuas historically.[17]

While many Apaches have conceived of their own history and identity as rooted in part in the far-flung places to which their ancestors were displaced over time, outsiders have tended to be most captivated by Apache histories of resistance to colonialism. For some readers, the very name Apache is probably inseparable from another—Geronimo. Though Geronimo hailed from a particular Apache band, the Bedonkohe, his overarching association with resistance to U.S. expansion has saturated understandings of Apache history at large. In his penchant for having his photo taken brandishing a gun on horseback, in his drive to continue a life of raiding for livestock long after most Apaches had settled on reservations, and in his participation in the creation of his own biography highlighting his martial feats, Geronimo played a role in building his celebrity and in shaping his image and that of other Apache people. As Geronimo has gone from villain to freedom fighter to controversial problem causer, depending on the era and the author, so too in many respects have understandings of Apache history more broadly.[18] Many Apaches, including Geronimo, did in fact resist the United States and other empires militarily, but what is too often lost in the focus on daring raids and clever ambushes is what they were fighting for. Geronimo was unusual in the degree to which his actions were rooted in a desire for glory, property, or retribution. But even Geronimo exemplifies the importance of diaspora in Apache history. In the 1870s and 1880s, he fled the Arizona reservations to which he had been assigned multiple times because of rumors of being imprisoned and sent far away. He and his companions finally surrendered in part because they had tired of the difficulties of life evading Mexican and U.S. troops in mountain strongholds in both nations, but also because they longed to be reunited with their kin. One American tourist who visited the Florida fort where Geronimo was held after his 1886 surrender wrote with surprise about seeing him "nursing a baby." Even a man deemed by many fellow Apaches to be a selfish troublemaker was not immune to the tug of kin in the face of separation from them.[19]

Two images from roughly the same time period serve to illustrate the connections between displacement and resistance in Apache history. The first is an 1886 photograph taken by Camillus Sidney Fly, an early photojournalist of

Figure 1. Scene in Geronimo's camp, 1886.

sorts. Titled *Scene in Geronimo's Camp Before Surrender*, it portrays a group of armed Apache men outside a brush shelter, or wickiup, on a rocky ridge, eyes locked on the camera. The idea for the pose may have come from the men themselves, but more likely it was from Fly. The overarching message to U.S. viewers at the time is not difficult to discern. The visibility of an Apache home might at first glance suggest a domestic scene, but the focus is clearly on the people outside the home: formidable, armed men and, perhaps most unsettlingly, very young, armed boys. At the time, this photograph would have served as confirmation of viewers' worst fears: whatever the success of U.S. soldiers in battle against Apache men, the next generation of "Geronimos" was being raised up to take their place. It would also have assuaged any concerns about the killing of Native women and children in military campaigns. After all, the image suggested, they were belligerents too.[20]

This propagandistic image contrasts with another from less than two decades earlier. The French mining engineer Louis Simonin traveled widely to observe the mines of North America, and in an 1867 synthesis of his findings, he included an illustration recreating a scene he may have witnessed, which he titled *Apache Prisoners Condemned to the Mines of Mexico*. It paints a striking contrast to the photograph of Geronimo's camp. Here an armed Mexican overseer stands over Apaches pounding away at ore. The overseer leans on his gun in a relaxed posed, puffing on a cigarette. The walled enclosure and distant cannon pointing at the group signify their subjugation, their

Figure 2. Apaches condemned to the mines of Mexico, 1867.

backbreaking labor evident in the heavy load one prisoner carries off toward a doorway, muscles straining. The text of the book praises the riches of Mexican mines while noting that Apaches posed a key impediment to mines' even greater productivity even as they also provided a source of hard labor to break up ore when captured in war.[21]

Attention to the frequency with which Apaches experienced forced dependence far from home as prisoners, slaves, or students helps explain Apaches' drive for self-determination through mobility, diplomacy, and violence. The portrait of armed Apache men resisting empires that dominates popular and historical understandings cannot be understood without the other image, which reminds viewers of the Apache men, women, and children who strove to live out their lives in diaspora in unfamiliar lands as markets, empires, and nations sought to control them for their own ends. After all, in the era when these images were created, armed Apache men frequently traveled into Mexico precisely with the aim of recovering their displaced kin.[22]

The diasporic displacements and existential struggles of Apache people for survival have implications beyond the bounds of Apache history as well. Apaches influenced the places and peoples they encountered through their lives and labors and also through colonial attempts to manage their resistance to the forms of race- and gender-based servitude that marked colonialism.

Their history reveals surprising ebbs and flows in the practice of Indian slavery. It illustrates the intersection of African and Native diasporas and the influence of both on societies in North America and the Caribbean. It highlights parallels between U.S. officials and their Hispanic predecessors in southwestern America in their approaches to Native people, sometimes out of emulation and admiration, at other times out of ignorance. It shows how deportation and incarceration became key strategies of state control, long before the twentieth century, when such histories are usually rooted.[23]

The broadest aim of this book, however, is to better illuminate the "fantastic and terrible" story of the colonization of Indigenous peoples in North America. Much recent writing on the history of the North American West, in particular, has focused on either the fantastic or the terrible, on either Indigenous power or Indigenous pain. Historians of the "fantastic" have examined the spaces where Indigenous peoples retained significant power and autonomy: the plains and river systems that were home not just to frontiers but also to Indigenous empires. A key value of this approach has been in telling unexpected stories that challenge the teleology of inevitable conquest and decline and in highlighting Native understandings and decision-making rather than casting Europeans as the primary agents of historical change. Another illuminating approach has emphasized new explanations of the "terrible," especially by drawing upon settler colonialism as a framework of analysis. This work sees the logic of elimination as a core process driving the formation of societies like the United States. While attuned to Native survival, these studies focus on the often-genocidal processes driving colonialism in societies where European settlers and their descendants sought to replace Native people living on Native lands.[24]

These apparently contrasting visions are not necessarily incompatible, but they are significantly shaped by scholars' chosen parameters. Histories emphasizing Native autonomy and power focus mostly on the period before the nineteenth century and the interior of continents, whereas histories of settler colonialism and genocide focus on the nineteenth century and after and on the spaces where settler and Native communities met. A change in chronology or geography significantly alters the story historians uncover.[25]

Following people in motion across a broad chronology and geography challenges the bifurcated portraits of Native American and colonial histories. It is true, for example, that Apache groups retained political autonomy through much of the nineteenth century, but it also the case that this autonomy was connected to the forced dependence of thousands of men, women, and children captured and exploited by outsiders who pointed to their kin's resistance to colonial rule as justification. It is true that the United States' approach to Indigenous peoples often centered on the elimination of Natives, which differs from traditional colonialism's emphasis on exploiting the colonized for their labor. Yet it is striking that Spain, Mexico, and the United States alike often exploited Apaches for their labor as a strategy of elimination, including putting them to especially dangerous tasks because they viewed them as expendable. While relatively few histories of the North American West have examined the intersection of African American and Indigenous histories, attention to the Apache diaspora brings the West into a broader conversation about the relationship between Native and African diasporas. After all, diasporic and exploited Apaches and Africans both lived and died—often in the same communities—across North America and the Caribbean.[26] The *longue durée* of Apache history also challenges a still-common distinction drawn between a Hispanic American colonialism of forced inclusion and an Anglo-American colonialism of elimination. For more than three hundred years, enslavement, warfare, and forced migrations failed to bring a final solution to the supposed problem of Apache independence and mobility. Spain, Mexico, and the United States overestimated their own power and underestimated Apache resistance and creativity, though they significantly influenced Native societies—and their own societies—in the process.[27]

*   *   *

The history of the Apache diaspora is laid out in this book in eight roughly chronological chapters. Each chapter also possesses a thematic focus on a key location to which Apaches were displaced over time: palaces, prisons, schools. The first part of the book, "Becoming Apache in Colonial North America," begins by tracing precolonial histories of captivity and migration before examining the formation of Apache diasporas in the context of Spanish, Comanche, and French colonialism. The labor demands of colonial societies significantly altered life for virtually all Indigenous peoples in southwestern America, but especially that of mobile Native people who resisted colonialism and were cast as enslaveable "Apaches" and circulated through Native and European societies across North America. The chapters in this part of the book consider how these displaced Apaches navigated lives in bondage in New Mexico, New Spain, and New France by forging connections with other exploited people, including servants and slaves of African descent. In places where a significant number of Native captives were shipped over time, Apache identities proved surprisingly enduring. The groups from which these people were taken, meanwhile, often fled from their former homelands in search of a safe place to live. By the late eighteenth century, slavery and diaspora had played a key role in the migration and coalescence of the Apache groups that remained in southwestern America, while simultaneously scattering Apache people into colonial societies across the continent.

Part II explores the role that empires and nation-states played in the history of Apache diasporas in the centuries to come. Although enslavement did not end, imperial policies more than labor demands increasingly uprooted Apaches in the late eighteenth and nineteenth centuries. Here the focus narrows to the mobile Apache groups that most challenged imperial aims and lived closest to colonial societies over the longest period of time: Southern, or Chiricahua, Apaches, who encompassed the Chihene, Chokonen, Nedni, and Bedonkohe bands. To a lesser extent, Mescalero and Western Apache histories are also addressed here, particularly in the context of their relations with Southern Apaches. A central theme of the chapters in this section are the imperial efforts to control Apache mobility and end Apache resistance to colonial rule, especially through forced migration, confinement in reservations, or deportation to distant places for forced labor or incarceration, including the Caribbean. Through the Spanish, Mexican, and U.S. periods, surprisingly similar, unsuccessful but also destructive schemes often served more to change Apache mobility and spark new strategies of resistance than they did to subjugate Apache groups. In the late nineteenth and early twentieth centuries, for example, the railroad, mail, banks, and newspapers all played a role in the forced exile of hundreds of Apaches to the U.S. Southeast and the removal of their children to distant boarding schools in Pennsylvania and Virginia after their arrival. Yet these same technologies also furthered Apache efforts to thwart the U.S. imperial policies intended to divide them. Displaced Apaches proved able to stay connected with each other, with children away at boarding school, and with relatives who had remained on or had been able to return to the reservations in Arizona or New Mexico. Students who survived boarding school, meanwhile, almost universally returned to relatives rather than remaining in white society. Like generations before them, Apaches adapted creatively to circumstances not of their own choosing, but more than in the past, they were also able to remain linked to kin and community despite displacement.

The epilogue examines the legacies of diaspora in the ensuing decades of the twentieth century. It begins by following Apache pilgrimages in the 1980s to places where their ancestors had been displaced in the past. The difficulties—and perseverance—reflected in such histories had become part of what it meant to be Apache in the present. Apache pilgrimages as free citizens of their own tribal nations and the United States would have been unthinkable to non-Natives a century before, who often spoke of exterminating them all. The return of Apaches to key sites of diaspora also serves as a touchstone for reflecting on the fact that separation from kin and homeland nonetheless remained ongoing problems without final resolution. Hard-fought battles in the twentieth century for reparations for wrongful internment and the unilateral dissolution of reservation lands proved decidedly mixed in their outcomes, in part because of political divisions among Apache groups that were related to past forced migrations. In the present, contemporary Apache nations, like other Indigenous peoples, face continued struggles for sovereignty, disproportionate incarceration, and an epidemic of murdered and missing women. Diaspora and colonization continue.

*   *   *

Sam Kenoi never forgave the United States for the struggles of his life. "Ever since I was taken prisoner when I was 11 years old, I have known nothing but mistreatment for the Indians," he said as an old man living through the Great Depression in New Mexico. "The white people talked about how they got us out of savagery," he added, "but they got us into worse, into slavery." For Kenoi, "slavery" meant a lack of self-determination, it meant important choices being made for a people that led to their suffering and death. It was to Kenoi a powerful word that named the oppression he had lived through—the early death of his mother in Alabama, the graves of his kin at Carlisle.[28]

As Kenoi knew so well, the history of colonialism for Native people was one of pain and loss, slavery and dispossession, but it was also a history of resistance, adaptation, and return. These fantastic and terrible stories are Apache history, Native history, all of our histories.

PART I

Becoming Apache in Colonial North America

Having issued a definitive sentence of death in just war in
this Kingdom against the entire nation of Apache Indians,
and those that join with them, infidel, irreducible, common
enemies of our Holy Catholic Faith and of all the Christian
Indians of this Kingdom . . . they may be taken out of the
Kingdom and distributed [to labor] for a period of 15
years . . . these in no time shall be allowed to return to the
kingdom.

—Governor Don Juan Manso, Santa Fe,
New Mexico, 1658

The Indians said through the interpreters . . . that they were
very sad and discouraged because of the repeated attacks
which their enemies, the Utes and Comanches, make upon
them. These had killed many of their nation and carried off
their women and children captives until they now no longer
knew where to go to live in safety.

—General Don Antonio Valverde Cosio at the Plains
Ndé village of La Jicarilla, 1719

[She] told María to shut up, that she was an *Apacha*, which
means a descendant of Apache Indians.

—Testimony in the Inquisition trial of Doña Teresa de
Aguilera y Roche, Mexico City, 1664

CHAPTER 1

The Palace

The Palace of the Governors is not a dramatic building. Its beige adobe walls and wood-beamed portal that face the central plaza of Santa Fe blend with the surrounding streetscape. The history of the palace, though, belies its sedate exterior. It was probably built around 1618 by Governor Juan de Eulate and, through the coming decades, was the site of much intrigue—affairs, charges of heresy, robberies—until the Pueblo Indians revolted against Spanish rule and kicked the colonists out of New Mexico in 1680. The Indians moved into the palace for the next decade, until they were evicted upon the return of the Spanish. The coming centuries would bring new administrators, new scandals, and new political machinations, including Mexican independence and the invasion of the United States.[1]

It was not just the political elites of different empires and nations who called this building home, however. Hundreds of Native men, women, and children spent their lives in the Palace of the Governors and places like it in the years after Don Juan de Oñate established the enduring Spanish presence in New Mexico in 1598. While Oñate and others complained that they had not found the riches they had hoped for, others learned that the gold of New Mexico was its people, and the ability to exploit them was a means to build wealth. Some scandalized observers criticized New Mexico residents for treating Natives like slaves or livestock, but most colonists participated in and welcomed the forced labor of Native people, whether a single captive acquired in a military campaign or two dozen wrangled for export to the mining district of New Spain.[2]

Spaniards and Natives alike shared certain beliefs about who could justifiably be held in bondage and exploited, views that facilitated slave trading in seventeenth-century New Mexico. This traffic was rooted in both Indigenous and European traditions and justified by certain shared principles: enemies taken in war could be made slaves, and so could someone already

held in bondage by someone else. The Spanish colonists added another category: rebels, or "apostates," those deemed to have already been subjugated by
or submitted to Spanish rule who subsequently rose up in rebellion or were
found to be engaging in pagan rituals. While colonists had various potential
sources for slaves, including Africans and Asians transported through the
transoceanic slave trade and their descendants, the Native population surrounding New Mexico represented a particularly accessible supply.[3]

Yet not all residents of New Mexico and its surroundings were equally
vulnerable. From a Spanish perspective, for example, not all Natives were
equally enslaveable. Military conquest and religious instruction had turned
some into insiders—Christian Indian vassals who were required to pay tribute and were often exploited for their labor but were also generally viewed
as off limits for enslavement unless they rebelled. Pueblos who received religious instruction from gray-robed Franciscan missionaries were contrasted
with the pagan "Apaches" who surrounded them. Though these latter groups
actually engaged with colonial newcomers in varied ways, including trade,
diplomacy, and intermarriage, the Spanish interest in slave labor led them to
simplify and generalize. They argued that nearly all mobile Indigenous people who surrounded New Mexico were "Apaches," despite the reality of ethnic
and political diversity. Belying evidence to the contrary, they also argued that
all Apaches were at war with the Christian Kingdom of New Mexico and
thus could justifiably be enslaved. Various bands of Ndé (Apache) and Diné
(Navajo) people thus became "an entire Apache nation," common enemies
along with "those that join with them" of the Spanish and "Christian Indians."
The actions of any one group could be mobilized as supporting evidence to
justify campaigns to acquire slaves from all in a "Just War."[4]

If such generalization helped assuage Spanish moral and legal concerns
about a burgeoning slave trade, it also had enduring historical consequences.
By the mid-seventeenth century, the very terms "Apache" and "slave" in Spanish New Mexico had become almost synonymous. This was merely the latest
regional example of a ubiquitous phenomenon. The term "esclavo" (slave)
had its origins in the reduction of conquered Slavic peoples to bondage in
medieval times. After 1492, slavery became associated with new peoples in
particular places: Carib in the Caribbean and Chichimec on the frontiers of
central New Spain. This was not a phenomenon unique to Spanish colonization, as the association between "Pani" and slave in New France reveals.[5]

Though it took decades for the threat to be felt in full, New Mexico's thirst
for Indian slaves ultimately posed a significant challenge to Apache groups.
Some turned to slaving in order to protect their own communities, offering

up Ute, Wichita, or Pawnee enemies at trading fairs. Others experimented with appeals to Spanish missionaries, perhaps out of genuine interest but also probably in the hopes that it might shield them from slave raids. Communities felt the enduring loss of kin captured and taken into bondage.[6]

Yet displacement and exploitation were experienced most viscerally by the hundreds of Native men, women, and children transported to places like the Palace of the Governors. Here diverse Native people were categorized as Apache slaves, confronted by masters who sought not only to put them to work but also to turn them into valuable human commodities that might be used to pay off debts or sold in distant markets at a premium price. Though the context of their exploitation was particular, in other respects the experience of these residents of the Palace of the Governors in Santa Fe evoke slavery in other colonial contexts. Exploited people, alienated to a significant degree from the protection of kin and community and often confined within locked chambers, learned the language of their masters, engaged with new religious and cultural traditions, and sought to better their circumstances within colonial society or by fleeing beyond it. Told day after day they were "Apaches," subjugated enemies, they adapted to new lives not of their own choosing by forging alliances with each other and with those more powerful than they. The diaspora that they faced is one that would endure for generations.[7]

Captivity, Mobility, and Colonization

Captivity, "isda' nliiní"—"they have to live with them," as the phrase in Apache translates into English—is an experience that predated the arrival of Europeans. Before the Spanish came, the ancestors of Apaches had migrated south from what is now Alaska and Canada, learning to hunt new game, to gather new plants, and to sow and harvest crops in new environments. Captives have always represented a useful way of learning things, of acquiring knowledge about a foreign place or people. Captive exchange fosters cultural change. Similarities in brush-covered homes, rituals, and origin stories in the very least suggest intimate contact between the Shoshonean people of the Great Basin and Rocky Mountains and the ancestral Apaches who had traveled through their lands.[8]

A slave, "na' ł' a," was someone "sent around," "he who is commanded." One related Mescalero expression meant to "slave till death."[9] This was an experience that also predated the arrival of the Spanish in the Southwest. Native oral traditions and archeological evidence point to the physical domination of outsiders for their labor, especially at particular times and places, such as at Chaco Canyon. Ancestral Apaches, however, lacked the need or desire for slaves in any significant numbers. They had no large-scale public works projects or temples to build. Their own families provided sufficient labor to produce the hides, pemmican, baskets, or pottery that dog trains hauled to trade. By the time Spanish invaders began trekking north, the same was largely true for Apaches' neighbors as well.[10]

Though war and captive taking were not the norm, they were always possible when drought made food scarce. In such times, corn was no longer traded willingly and might be taken by force instead. Descending out of the mountains to a Pueblo village, a small group of Apache men might snatch the young man guarding the storehouse rather than kill him, a choice that could lead to a counterattack, or facilitate a return to peaceful relations when he was offered up and returned to his people in exchange for something they desired later.[11]

Following the potential life trajectory of such a captive provides a means to introduce Apache societies, their ways of life, and understandings of captivity and exploitation. Among Apaches, a captive would be put to use, forced to do menial work for a time—to tend the dogs and their halters used for transport or to bring water or wood. He might be traded or given to another group before he was given a name or before he even learned enough of their language to converse. If kept among them, he might seek to prove himself as a man. He would do the work assigned to him dutifully to earn trust, to show his loyalty and valor in hunting or against an enemy, to gain the favor of a family.[12]

A captive was no longer a captive when he became a relative, such as when he was adopted as someone's son or married into the group, thus becoming obligated to others and obligating others to him. Kin to a new people, he might also still be recognized as kin to his natal community. This would be a further enticement to exchange resources or to provide aid in war in the future.[13]

Transformed into an Apache (Ndé) man, a former captive would join his wife's extended family. This family joined together with other extended family households to form a local group under the leadership of a *nantan* (spokesman, headman). The Spanish later called these local groups *rancherias*, or small settlements. The local group, or *gotah*, was the heart of an Apache person's world, encompassing the relationships—and obligations—that defined their humanity and ensured their survival.[14]

Captives would have learned that women and men each made distinctive contributions. Men mastered the manufacture and use of the bow, arrow, and war club for hunting and fighting, crafting them from the resources of the landscapes in which they lived, from rocky deserts to cool mountain forests. Women built homes, tended children and crops, and also knew all about the edible wild plants of the region. They gathered wild potatoes, walnuts, piñon nuts, grapes, mulberries, and mesquite beans. The century plant, or agave, was especially important for Apache groups residing in the southernmost lands. From it they obtained mescal crowns, which could be roasted overnight in pit ovens and eaten, or ground into a pulp and buried to ferment into a potent alcoholic beverage.[15]

Captives among Apaches would also have learned about the seasonal movement of their encampments—to harvest crops, gather and process plants, hunt, and trade. They would come to know that they were anchored to particular places, however. The names of local groups indicated as much: "ni-ki-ya-dé-ne" (people of the land that is their native land) was the name of one Apache local group in the nineteenth century. The names of the networks of local groups that together composed bands also usually referenced the lands in which they lived or the resources they harvested from them, for example: Cúelcahén Ndé, "people of the tall grass."[16]

Only later, if they remained with Apaches for a longer time, would a captive have become familiar with their stories and belief in the creator, Ussen, who had made the universe, and White Painted Woman, mother of Child of the Water, who had then created people. Only later would they come to understand the power of the mountain spirits, or *gahe*, and ceremonies like the Crown Dance, in which masked dancers invoked the gahe, usually joined by a clown who entertained the crowd but also possessed curative power. Only later would they have come to fully understand the moral code that divided insiders from outsiders, sanctioning the taking of enemy property through raids designed to avoid pursuit and making it imperative to retaliate for loss of kin by mobilizing war parties.[17]

If captivity and mobility had played a role in the Apache past, they would play an even more important role in the future, beginning in the sixteenth century, when the Spanish began entering into Apache territories periodically. Although these expeditions failed to establish a permanent Spanish colony, they succeeded in taking a number of captives. The Chamuscado-Rodriguez Expedition of 1581 was not the first such incursion, and it was not atypical when its members seized a captive to serve as a guide from an Apache settlement they encountered on the banks of the Pecos River, in what is now southeastern New Mexico. After traveling further out onto the plains, they decided to return to the Rio Grande but now had to decide what to do with their captive. They freed him and gave him some meat, a parting gift for goodwill. They continued east without him very cautiously, however, "fearing that the natives might try to avenge the seizure of the guide."[18]

A few years later, Spanish wrangling over "Querecho" captives, likely either Chihene Apaches or Navajos, sparked a series of raids and counterraids in the vicinity of Acoma Pueblo. One Spaniard, Francisco Barreto, had acquired a Querecho woman before she managed to escape back to her people. He was not willing to let her go easily. He and other members of his expedition devised a plan to orchestrate a surprise attack on her people's settlement to recover her. It failed to recapture the woman but destroyed a field of corn.[19]

In another raid the next day, the Spanish destroyed another field of corn, captured a different woman, and negotiated a parley to exchange her for Barreto's slave. They did not realize that the interpreter negotiating on their behalf—another captive woman—was secretly in collusion with the Apache/Navajo group in question. She convinced the group they could avoid having to give up any of their people. They dressed a woman up to look like Barreto's slave, whom they had already sent back to her family. Meanwhile, they planned to surprise the Spaniards with a volley of arrows at the meeting arranged to exchange captives. In the chaos, they hoped that both the impersonator and the interpreter would be able to escape. Ultimately this plan succeeded in wounding Barreto but not in recovering the women. They remained among the Spanish, though the interpreter reportedly fought "like a lioness" for her freedom.[20]

News of kidnapped guides and stolen women probably raised concerns among Apaches, but during the sixteenth century these Spanish expeditions retreated like flash floods that wreak havoc but recede quickly with the sun. Even the conquest of New Mexico led by Don Juan de Oñate, in 1598, did not have a significant impact on Apache groups initially. In this period they continued to draw upon the precedent of their relationships with Puebloans and neighboring Plains groups to guide them. Are they hostile to us? What do they want from us? What do they have that might be useful to us? If dealing with outsiders was not a new experience for Apaches, these "Spaniards" must have in the very least appeared as an unusual bunch, a kaleidoscope of peoples: mestizos and mulattos and their families, African and Indian slaves, Tlaxcalan Indian allies, robed friars, and a few Spanish-born men.[21] After the long journey north from Mexico City, many of these settlers proved disappointed in what they discovered, including Don Juan de Oñate himself. Before he was forced out of New Mexico by charges of excessive violence against Indians and general misgovernance, he noted that "what we have thus far discovered is nothing but poverty."[22]

Despite disappointment, most of the colonizers stayed. After 1598, they slowly built farms, ranches, and one lone town at Santa Fe, an isolated outpost in a landscape still controlled by Indians. The construction of the Palace of the Governors, probably begun during Juan de Eulate's tenure as governor around 1618, is symbolic of the small but growing footprint of the newcomers on the social landscape of the Native Southwest.[23]

The Spanish kingdom that surrounded Santa Fe grew slowly. A decade later, a visitor to New Mexico explained that the "great Apache nation" continued to encircle Spanish New Mexico. It was no exaggeration that New Mexico was surrounded by Native peoples, though they did not in fact constitute one nation as this friar suggested. Traveling east from Santa Fe in the 1620s or 1630s, a Spaniard would have entered the lands of the wealthiest of Apache groups: the Plains peoples, ancestors of today's Jicarillas and Lipans. Bison herds were the central source of their wealth. Their town-dwelling Pueblo neighbors valued the hides and meat that Apache men hunted and the women processed for food and clothing. That Plains Apache traders also offered tools, shell ornaments, and pottery acquired through other suppliers added to their appeal.[24]

Traveling south from Santa Fe, a Spaniard would have entered into the lands of the ancestors of the so-called Chiricahuas, or Southern Apaches of later times, as well as some Mescalero bands. Trade was less central to these groups' lives than it was to the Apache people of the plains, because the former practiced more agriculture and were less reliant on outsiders as a result. If they did sometimes exchange deer hides for corn, they also planted their own crops and gathered plants from their mountain homelands, like their Western Apache neighbors, who were the most isolated from contact with the Spanish during the colonial period.[25]

A Spaniard traveling north and west from Santa Fe would have spoken of encountering another Apache group, the "Apaches de Navaju" or Diné, as they called themselves. Until the eighteenth century, by which time the Diné had become a sheepherding pastoral people, Spaniards usually labeled them as an Apache group not only because they spoke closely related languages but also because doing so facilitated their enslavement. Outsiders did note that in comparison with other Apache groups, they were the most agricultural and lived in fixed villages as opposed to seasonal encampments, a cultural distinction referenced through the use of the term "navaju," a Tewa word meaning "arroyo with cultivated fields."[26]

During the first half of the seventeenth century, Spaniards' opinions on their relations with these so-called Apaches varied. Fray Francisco de Velasco

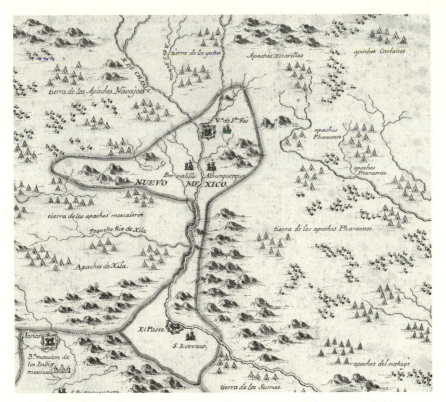

Figure 3. Detail of copy of 1728 map showing New Mexico surrounded by
Apaches. Courtesy of the British Library Board, Add. MS 17650b.

wrote in 1609 that all the "heathen Indians" surrounding Spanish New Mexico thought that Spaniards were self-interested "scoundrels." He alleged that
Apaches were responsible for unrest among Pueblo Indians because they tried
to persuade them that no benefit came from associating with Spaniards and
they should "throw off the heavy Spanish yoke." By the 1620s, some observers
reported that Spanish campaigns to seize Apache slaves had caused enmity
toward the Spanish and retaliatory attacks.[27]

References to trade also abound, however. Apache groups, especially
those on the plains, drew upon whatever they found of value in their lands to
engage in commerce with Spaniards. By 1617, if not earlier, Spaniards were
engaging in trade with Plains Apache traders at Pecos Pueblo. Like Puebloan
peoples before them, Spaniards learned that the plains trade was a key means
of getting by in this region. Apaches' dogs hauled in their hides, meat, tallow,
and salt. Puebloans brought blankets, pottery, maize, and turquoise to trade.

Spaniards added livestock, axes, spears, and firearms to the mix. One Spanish governor later noted that going to the plains to trade was what "colonists most hunger for." One indication of how central this trade was to New Mexico colonial society was the fact bison hides had become the "dress commonly worn," and Spanish colonists used them "also for sacks, tents . . . footwear, and many other purposes."[28]

Although Plains Apache groups were not immune from Spanish slave raiding and violence during this early period, they maintained good relations with Spaniards through trade. In fact, one way they sought to deflect Spanish slave raids from their own communities was by becoming slave suppliers. The Apache and Navajo people represented the most common source of slaves for colonial society in New Mexico during the seventeenth century. Yet Apaches also proved willing to capture and trade their Wichita and Pawnee enemies to the Spanish in exchange for horses, tools, and some measure of security from becoming the victims of Spanish labor demands themselves. This relationship is reflected in the presence in New Mexico and the mining districts of northern New Spain of "Quivira" slaves, the name Spanish explorer Francisco Vásquez de Coronado had given to the portion of the plains these enemies of the Apache called home.[29]

Apaches initiated Spaniards into trade using some of the same methods they had used with their Pueblo neighbors before. The most reliable people were kin, and thus one strategy was to turn foreign trading partners into relatives. One striking example of this came to light because of an Inquisition trial it prompted. One Spanish soldier in the 1660s was tried for bigamy for marrying an Apache woman in a ceremony at her plains village and having "left a child among the heathens." His father had reportedly done the same, suggesting that the practice was neither unusual nor new to the 1660s. Such traditions provided a means for Apaches to transform outsiders into insiders, leaving a Spaniard with kin among them, and they with kin among the Spanish. This relationship would have furthered trade relations, diplomatic negotiations, and requests for military aid.[30]

Apaches also learned to appeal to unique elements of the Spanish worldview. Expressing interest in baptism gained them favor with Spanish friars and could protect them from Spanish governors and colonists. For at least some Apache leaders, engagement with Catholicism went beyond its practical benefits. The Chihene Apache headman Sanaba provides an illustration. Friar Benavides reported that he attended Mass at Senecu pueblo weekly, traveling fourteen leagues (about thirty-five miles) each way from his peoples' village, west of the Rio Grande. Benavides also believed that Sanaba

carried the Spanish message back to his own people, preaching and converting them to Catholicism.[31]

Yet such engagement with the Spanish could also prove risky. When a
Plains Apache leader expressed interest in becoming a Catholic in the late
1620s, for example, the governor of New Mexico reportedly followed up by
ordering a slave raid on his very group. The response of Apaches and their
neighbors to such duplicity illustrates another strategy of engagement with
the Spanish newcomers: mobilizing allies to threaten retaliation. The actions
of Governor Felipe de Sotelo Osorio created such a negative response among
both Plains Apaches and their neighbors that it sparked "a revolt throughout
the entire province." While the Spanish governor had hoped to sell the captives his raid had taken as slaves in New Spain, in the end he had to agree not
to in order to quell the outrage, though the ultimate fates of the captives are
unclear. Other evidence of Apache raids or attacks suggests that they often
followed a Spanish slave raid and were not long lasting or indiscriminate.
Such was the case in February 1639, when Captain Juan Gómez de Luna led
a slave raid disguised as a trade expedition to the lands of the "Long Hair
Apaches" and captured some of them, to which they responded by attacking
wagon trains on the road south from Santa Fe in the coming months.[32]

At least for the first forty years of the sustained Spanish presence in
New Mexico, Apache groups adapted to the newcomers through strategies
of trade and kinship, appeals to Catholicism, and targeted retaliations that
helped them to avoid mass enslavement. Some Plains Apache groups became
slave suppliers themselves, offering up enemy captives in the hopes of keeping their own communities secure. But as Spaniards increasingly turned to
Indian slavery as a source of labor and profit, no one would prove immune
to its effects.[33]

Slavery and the Roots of Diaspora

Spanish friars and the governors were two key factions in New Mexico colonial society that helped make the threat of enslavement and diaspora a constant for Apaches in the coming years. And yet it is an understatement to
say that they did not always see eye to eye in the endeavor. Much of what we
know about the practice of Indian slavery in New Mexico during the seventeenth century comes from the power struggles between church and civil
officials that led to legal inquiries and trials. Friars claimed that governors
"come with an insatiable thirst to return rich [to New Spain]," which led them

to exploit Indians "as if they were black slaves" or "calves or colts."[34] It is certainly the case that governors sought to supplement their relatively meager two-thousand-peso-per-year salary, but they countered that friars were no different: they seized "orphans" from Indian households and sometimes sold them in New Spain to support mission finances or "rescued" them from their families in order to put them to work for the church without pay. Governors were far more likely than friars to call what they were doing slavery, but both exploited a class of producers maintained primarily through acquisition; they practiced the violent domination of people separated from their kin and socially shamed—two modern conceptualizations of slavery.[35]

None of this, however, would have been possible without a third group: Pueblo Indian allies. If campaigns against Native peoples were often ordered or directed by Spanish governors, they relied heavily upon Indian men to actually capture the enslaveable. It was common for a few dozen Spanish militiamen to be accompanied by hundreds of Pueblo Indians who proved willing to aid the Spanish in part for the reward of carrying some captives back to their own communities. While specific Pueblos may have sought to avoid attacking groups that were their traditional allies, ultimately the Spanish reliance on Pueblo military labor to supply the Indian slave trade strained Pueblo-Apache relations.[36]

Indian slaves were not the only source of labor in Spanish New Mexico. As conquered vassals of the Spanish crown, the population of eighty thousand or so Pueblo Indians at the time of Oñate's conquest were subject to the *encomienda* system. In theory, a conquered pueblo was granted to their conqueror, or *encomendero*, who was responsible for maintaining arms for their protection and for helping to facilitate their Christianization. In return, the encomendero received tribute from them. In New Mexico, this tribute consisted of cotton cloth or hides, which were collected from each Indian household in May, and a few bushels of corn, which were collected in October. As long as the Pueblo population remained large, this tribute helped to support the leisure and wealth of the encomendero class. The encomenderos also supplemented official tribute by also extracting labor from their encomienda to work their farms and ranches. While in theory this labor was paid at one-half real per day, currency was limited, and Pueblo laborers complained that Spaniards sometimes failed to pay them, either in currency or in kind.[37] Friars, colonists, and governors quickly learned to supplement the labor of their encomienda Indians as well. Having asserted Spanish jurisdiction, they sentenced Pueblo people to terms of temporary enslavement for criminal acts. They took Pueblo Indian children from their homes to be "educated," an education that appears to have consisted primarily of labor. "Voluntary" labor on behalf of the church was usually unpaid also, as friars claimed that it was a reflection of the new converts' devotion and that it furthered their religious education.[38]

Such illegal exploitation had real consequences, however. Governors faced audits, called *residencias*, at the end of their terms of office in which abuse of Pueblo Indians or illegal enslavement of Indians was often a charge investigated. As legal insiders, Pueblo Indians could appeal to Spanish officials for the redress of grievances. Moreover, the immediate presence of their kin and communities could lead to uprisings when exploitation was deemed too burdensome. While the Spanish maintained power through the display or threat of violence, the Spanish hold on a Pueblo population that outnumbered them was tenuous and vulnerable, helping to limit the outright enslavement of large numbers of Pueblo people.[39]

With limits on the uses of Pueblo labor and a declining Pueblo population—from perhaps eighty thousand in 1598 to seventeen thousand or so by 1680—the Spaniards turned in new directions. Governor Luis de Rosas's period in office in the late 1630s and early 1640s illustrates well the role that New Mexico governors played in furthering the importance of captive taking and enslavement. Governor Rosas was accused of journeying to the plains to kill a great number of friendly Apache people and taking others captive. During the audit that followed his term of office, one witness testified that "the Christian natives of the pueblo of Pecos [had] made a great demonstration of feeling in regard to this, because they were living with them [the Apache] and with them they had their commerce, by means of which they clothed themselves and paid their tributes."[40] The response in Pecos Pueblo to the governor's action illustrates the depth of relations between particular Pueblo and Apache groups and the risks Puebloans would take to support their Apache allies, because "collusion" with heathen Apache or Navajo bands could lead the Pueblo Indians to be sentenced to enslavement themselves.[41]

While commerce on the plains continued, the increased volume of captive taking and the fates captives were being subjected to—enslavement and hard labor—were beginning to influence Spanish relations with Apaches. After the 1630s, Plains Apache groups sometimes conducted trading fairs in their own lands, rather than in pueblos closer to Spanish settlements, while also establishing settlements further north and east on the plains. Retaliatory campaigns became more common as well, as did Plains Apache efforts to sell enemy Wichita or Pawnees as captives to seek to satisfy Spanish demands. As for Governor Rosas, slavery was not his only vice. In 1641, he was murdered by the husband of a woman he had an affair with.[42]

One of Rosas's successors was a slave trader even before he took office. Don Juan Manso was distinct from other governors in that he and his family were long-term residents of the North American Southwest. Before he assumed the governorship in 1656, he was a successful merchant in trade between New Mexico and Parral, a key silver mining town in Northern New Spain that had boomed after silver strikes there in the early 1630s. Apache or Navajo slaves who garnered thirty or forty pesos in New Mexico could sell for three times that amount in Parral, and Manso and others had sensed opportunity. Pine nuts, salt, hides, and other resources of the region also garnered buyers in the mining town—slave trading was one part of a bigger business that flourished in the decade before he took office.[43]

There was a problem, however. Slave traders like Manso had generated controversy and come under legal scrutiny in New Spain because they did not always bring proof with them that the Indians they were selling were legally enslaved. To garner the highest prices, buyers in New Spain wanted titles and bills of sale, the kinds of legal documents one would receive in purchasing an enslaved African. To purchase a slave without such documents could put one at risk for having one's slave declared free when the Spanish courts periodically cracked down on the illegal enslavement of Indians. In 1649, for example, when the royal court (*audiencia*) in Guadalajara caught wind of the ubiquity with which New Mexico merchants and governors were engaged in these activities, they ordered that all Apaches in Parral be manifested and those without legitimate "justification" be freed. Theoretically, there should not have been any justification—no royal decree had provided an exception for New Mexico or Nueva Vizcaya, as was sometimes done elsewhere, to the general prohibition on Indian slavery in the Spanish empire since the mid-sixteenth century. In practice, however, old arguments proved enduring: the idea that Indians could be enslaved if they had been captured in a just war, sentenced to hard labor for a crime or rebellion, or had been "rescued" from captivity among other Indians.[44]

Perhaps it was to further his slave-trading business that Juan Manso sought appointment to become governor of New Mexico. As governor, he followed in the footsteps of his predecessors and declared a "sentence of death" against the Apache nation for resisting Spanish rule and authorized a "just war" against them. The logic went as follows: while Apaches justified death for resisting Spanish rule, the Spaniards were willing to be merciful. In lieu of death, captives could be held "in deposit" (for safekeeping) by Spanish masters for fifteen years of unpaid labor, which for children would begin to be counted at the age of twelve. Manso's order also invoked the other key category of enslaveable captives: those rescued from captivity among other Indians. In exchange for the payment of their ransom, this group could be put to work for fifteen years as well.[45]

With this order as justification, Manso carried out a campaign in the mountain ranges near Zuni Pueblo, likely targeting Chihene Apache groups. He killed some of them and captured the others. He drew up documents to allow for the transfer and sale of these captives outside of New Mexico, and he even noted that "under no condition could they return to New Mexico." If their enslavement was theoretically temporary (a kind of involuntary indentured servitude), exile was to be permanent. This policy helped assuage buyers' concerns in New Spain and helped ensure there would be demand for Apache slaves in towns like Parral.[46]

Some scholars have noted that all of this was nothing more than "legal gibberish." Governors like Manso were essentially making their own law in violation of royal decrees, and they faced charges against them for doing so in residencias conducted at the ends of their terms of office. Yet their legal improvisation was not necessarily viewed as "gibberish" by contemporaries, including prospective masters, and thus had real consequences for captives' lives. It also reveals the logic that propelled Spanish practices of Indian slavery in the first place, not just in New Mexico but elsewhere in the empire as well.[47]

Whether sanctioned by the Spanish Crown or simply by the creative law-making of local residents and governors, popular support for the idea that particular Indigenous groups were enslaveable was widespread and enduring. The sheer number of royal orders concerning Indian slavery—and the frequency with which some exceptions to the blanket prohibition were made—makes this clear, as do the findings of recent scholarship indicating that hundreds of thousands of Indians were enslaved in colonial Spanish America. As late as 1756, after countless decrees by predecessors, King Ferdinand VI was still reminding his subjects that "no Indians except Caribs could be enslaved," an order that both illustrates the controversy of enslaving Indians and the lingering belief that for some Indigenous groups an exception had been warranted.[48]

The Caribs of Northern New Spain and the North American Southwest were Apaches, whom Spaniards contrasted with settled Christian Indians, whom they might exploit but who were generally viewed as off limits for outright enslavement. In New Mexico, as elsewhere, an interest in procuring slaves drove the Spaniards to simplify their surroundings. The various groups that constituted what Spaniards called an "entire Apache nation" had not always been at war with them, as we have already seen, nor were they in fact politically united. This argument, however, signaled an open season on any group the Spaniards claimed to be Apache for capture and enslavement and helped lead to the liberal ascription of that term. Governors' "sentences of death" became self-fulfilling prophecies: by indiscriminately targeting various mobile Native groups, governors like Manso helped spark reprisals that justified the acquisition of additional Native captives. The existence of a sentence of death against the "Apache" nation probably led captors to claim captives were Apache regardless of their actual origins.[49]

Juan Manso's immediate successor in the governor's palace did as much as any governor to fuel this slave trade when he traveled north from Mexico City to take up his post in Santa Fe in the Palace of the Governors. Like his predecessors, Don Bernardo López de Mendizábal came into conflict with church officials, had a penchant for extramarital affairs, and sought to enrich himself, including by trading in Apache slaves. He and his wife, Doña Teresa de Aguilera, are probably best known for the charge that they were secret Jews, which eventually helped lead to their arrest and trial by the Mexican Inquisition. While Mendizábal and Aguilera's legal troubles reveal much about their love of drinking chocolate, their tastes in fancy furniture, their disdain for New Mexican colonists, and their general lack of political savvy, they also provide perhaps the most descriptive extant documentation regarding Indian slavery in New Mexico.[50]

The journey by wagon from Mexico City to the southern border of New Mexico typically took three months or more. As their carts kicked up dust on their way north from El Paso along the royal road in the summer of 1659, Mendizábal and Aguilera would have observed simple farmsteads dotting the banks of the Rio Grande, with the mountain homelands of Apache (Ndé) groups looming in the distance. Only a few of the more affluent Spanish families had founded prosperous, larger haciendas. Such Spanish families dwelt near the Native towns that had been distributed to them as encomiendas. From these Pueblo towns, the Spaniards continued to receive annual tribute in cotton and corn. The most important benefit they received was the labor they could require of Indians on their farms and ranches. Echoing the broader distinctions Spaniards made between "Christian" and "barbarian" Indians, Mendizábal sought to improve the circumstances of Pueblo Indian laborers by raising their daily wage to one real while simultaneously proving an avid enslaver of Apache and other "heathen" Indians. Before arriving in Santa Fe, Mendizábal and Aguilera may have already been introduced to Indian slavery as a potential source of wealth and labor for themselves. They almost certainly observed the significant presence of Apache, Navajo, and other Native slaves who worked on farms and ranches and in Spanish homes by the 1650s.[51]

If their own actions are any indication, Mendizábal and Aguilera also quickly learned about the varied means through which New Mexico residents acquired their slaves. In the fall of 1659, weeks after assuming office, Mendizábal ordered military campaigns against the "Apache nation," sending forty colonists and eight hundred Pueblo Indians to raid Natives' camps and take seventy captives as slaves. As had previous governors, he claimed that all Apaches had risen up in war against the Spanish. Mendizábal was quickly making enemies, and not just among neighboring Apaches. His shocking statements, such as that "the *cabildo* [city council], his negress, and his bull were all the same thing," and his Indian policies, especially raising Pueblo wages and allowing traditional dances, turned local officials, priests, and colonists against him. He was not without allies, however, including a man who would later face an Inquisition trial himself for his marriage to a Plains Apache woman: Nicolás Aguilar. Mendizábal sent Aguilar around New Mexico with colonists and Pueblo Indian militiamen to campaign against the Natives who surrounded the Spanish kingdom. Plains Apache groups appear to have been largely spared, perhaps owing to Aguilar's close ties with them, yet Mendizábal drew up more than ninety decrees legalizing the seizure of captives from other Apache groups during his first months in office. Indian allies and militiamen, meanwhile, complained that he had seized their captives rather than allowing them to keep them. Mendizábal's list of enemies continued to grow.[52]

Direct capture in slave raids disguised as military campaigns was only one way in which a Native man or woman could end up in the governor's palace or a wealthy Spaniard's textile factory. After Mendizábal and Aguilera established a store in the governor's palace to sell a range of luxury goods they had brought with them from Mexico City, they quickly learned that there was little currency in New Mexico and that colonists were as likely to make payment in Apaches as they were in pine nuts, buffalo hides, or blankets. For example, Mendizábal advanced 189 pesos worth of goods to one resident of New Mexico, Felipe de Albisu, who worked down his debt by giving him Apache slaves: first a woman, then a fifteen-year-old boy, then another boy. But Mendizábal appears to have been dissatisfied by the pace of repayment. Albisu complained that Mendizábal simply took another Apache slave from him, a girl of fourteen or fifteen. When he pleaded with him to return her "because he did not have any other Apaches to serve him," the governor reportedly threatened to hang him. In other words, the powerful and wealthy rarely did the dangerous work of capturing their own slaves and could amass a large contingent simply by advancing goods to their poorer neighbors at inflated prices or strong-arming them. Some local citizens amassed large debts. Miguel de Inojos at one point owed the governor more than four hundred pesos, which at the time of Mendizábal's arrest by the Inquisition he was still paying periodically by sending the governor pine nuts, steers, mules, rams, and stockings, as well as at least three Apache Indian women, valued at thirty pesos each.[53]

It was not just common colonists who were at risk from slave-hungry governors. Weeks into his term of office in Santa Fe, Mendizábal seized eighteen Apache captives taken in a recent slave raid by Picuri Puebloans and a couple of Spaniards. The previous governor, Don Juan Manso, had commissioned this raid and argued that the slaves in fact belonged to him. Mendizábal countered that he had purchased the captives from the Indians in exchange for cows. Whatever the truth of the matter, it should be noted that the seizure of a previous governor's contingent of Indian slave seems to have been a typical act of an incoming governor during this period. Mendizábal's successor, Diego de Peñalosa, would do the same to him, seizing at least forty of his Apache slaves.[54]

While Mendizábal's labor needs explain in part his desire to purchase or seize so many Apaches, he also had his eye on Northern New Spain's Indian slave market. If he could export his Apache slaves to the mining district of Parral, they could be sold for about a hundred pesos each. This could represent a significant profit, given that they were worth only thirty or so pesos in New Mexico. Mendizábal did eventually attempt to sell multiple shipments of Apaches in Northern New Spain, but he kept a significant contingent for himself in Santa Fe. At least some of the slaves who were eventually exported probably also spent time in the governor's place first, as had slaves seized by previous Spanish governors throughout the first half of the seventeenth century. If Mendizábal was not unique in his actions, his particularly severe legal troubles open an unusually clear window onto the lives of Native servants and slaves, including through their own testimony.[55]

Experiencing Diaspora in the Palace of the Governors and Beyond

What did it mean to become "Apache" in seventeenth century Santa Fe? It was not the name Ndé or Diné people called themselves, even if it was a term with which they became familiar. "Apache" thus had distinct, layered meanings.

It remained a name used by outsiders to refer to independent Apache and Navajo groups in the region, but it also developed additional connotations rooted in the frequency with which such groups suffered enslavement and the claims that the enslavement of any "Apache" was justified by their resistance to Spanish rule. A master might therefore use the expression "my Apache" to talk about any Indian slave, regardless of their tribal origins. The term also had variants, such as "Apacha," a woman descending from Apache Indians, an epithet one might hear in a quarrel.[56]

In the frightening confusion of capture, shipment, and forced incorporation into a new society, naming was an important symbol of one's status as an exploited outsider. To be called Apache day in and day out reminded persons that they were being kept among an enemy, that they were being forced to stay in circumstances not of their own choosing. Apache slaves lacked basic autonomy in their daily lives. They could be sold at any time and were likely to be locked in their master's house at night, or most of the time, especially if they were women. They lacked protection. While Spanish law restricted masters' treatment of their slaves, in practice abuses were rarely investigated or punished. In fact, Spaniards like Don Bernardo and Doña Teresa drew upon their experience with their African slaves in their dealings with and understandings of Apaches, especially their belief that all slaves "are enemies of their masters," as Aguilera put it, and that whippings were key to controlling their behavior. In one particularly macabre example, a Spanish master was accused of flaying an Apache Indian servant and tanning his skin, claiming that "it was strong enough to be made into a doublet." Mendizábal's successor caught wind of the accusation but did nothing, perhaps because the incident had not occurred and only was malicious gossip. At the very least, however, the story suggests the callousness with which some Spanish masters joked about the disposable lives and bodies of their servants and slaves.[57]

The experience of the Apache slaves and servants of New Mexico governors was to some extent unique. An Apache woman serving the family of a militiaman in a settlement on the outskirts of her own homeland was more likely to escape, to be ransomed, or to be able to maintain social relations with her kin than were the dozens of slaves locked inside the governor's palace or the vast grounds of a wealthy Spaniard's estate in the Rio Grande valley south of the capital.[58] Muster rolls taken immediately after the Pueblo revolt in 1680 indicate that the confinement and congregation Native slaves experienced in palaces and estates became more the norm than an exception over time. A few examples help to illustrate. Captain Ignacio Vaca reported a household that included four small children and twenty Indians; Sergeant Major

Pedro Durán y Chávez reported that he was married, with eleven children and thirty Indians. Twelve such households contained at least 60 percent of all non-Pueblo Indian servants and slaves. In all, non-Pueblo Indian slaves and servants constituted more than 20 percent of the colony's population by 1680—around two hundred Spanish households were served by seven hundred or so Indian servants and slaves.[59]

While some of the governor's Apache slaves had spent time in captivity elsewhere before arriving in the governor's palace, the governor and his wife noted that a significant number of them did not yet speak Spanish. Aguilera referred to this group as the "uncivilized" and noted that they "could not understand what was going on" in household affairs. Aguilera was particularly fearful that they might escape, and she therefore often kept them locked up and did not let them attend Mass or saint's days festivals. For these masters, at least, preventing the escape of Apache slaves was more important than putting into practice the idea that Christianization was the reason for their enslavement.[60]

This is not to say that Apaches slaves did not learn Spanish or engage with Catholicism, but most of the instruction was carried out by other servants and slaves, not their masters. In fact, one unique characteristic of life in a place like the Palace of the Governors versus a small house on the frontier was the presence of a large group of bondspeople who might serve as a source of support, news and gossip, and also conflict. The constant inflow of newly acquired Apaches as payment for debts or through acquisition in new campaigns is worth noting. Perhaps this arrival of newcomers provided news of relatives from whom others had been separated, providing some solace or fueling hopes of escape and return. If such conversations occurred, they would not have been of interest to the Mexican Inquisition and the trial records upon which much of what we do know is based. What we know with greater certainty is that existing servants and slaves taught new arrivals what was expected of them—helping them learn Spanish, become familiar with Catholicism, and learn the routine of the palace. They taught the newcomers how to make chocolate the way the couple liked it, to clean and tend their beds, to fetch food from the cook in the kitchen, and even just to help keep Aguilera company since she did not leave the grounds much. As a result, they also learned to deal with her every whim and mood.[61]

The fact that virtually all Apaches mentioned in trial records are women also highlights the gendered logic that shaped the couple's acquisition of particular Apaches and the tasks to which they put them. Household labor was women's work, and they believed that Apache women could learn it more capably and easily than any man. While Apache boys are mentioned in the trial records, Mendizábal and Aguilera used them for other purposes, such as tending livestock or delivering merchandise or messages.[62] Male Apaches were also more likely than women to be shipped to New Spain for sale. Women and children predominated among war captives, but the number of men arriving in Northern New Spain for sale was roughly equal to the number of women, suggesting that they were in greater demand for mining and ranching work there and also that captors had concerns about keeping them secure in New Mexico.[63]

The gendered division in Apaches' experiences was a product of their captors' worldview. Aguilera, for example, viewed the mingling of unmarried men and women as unthinkable and dangerous. Apache "maidens" warranted careful protection, she noted, explaining that she kept them in one of the most interior rooms of the palace. The degree to which they were confined was in part a product of her fears of them escaping, but it also reflected particular concerns about her husband's behavior.[64] Don Bernardo's sexual abuse of servants and slaves became notorious and was met by resentment, anger, and violence on the part of Aguilera herself. She blamed her husband for his behavior, eventually claiming that his affairs had tormented her to the point that she viewed herself as having essentially been kept in a kind of slavery. Whatever her own suffering, she also blamed her servants and slaves for her husband's actions after he called for them to join him in the kitchen or another chamber of the palace. While Aguilera argued in public that the Indian women who served her were well treated and "she loved them like daughters," behind closed doors she called them "deceitful bitches" and alleged that they were essentially prostitutes, flogging them regularly for their alleged misbehavior.[65]

The servants and slaves of the palace, including Apaches, turned to each other in the face of their masters' violence. Many sought temporary refuge with one of Aguilera's paid servants, a woman named Doña Josefa, who had accompanied her north from Mexico City, was married to a young soldier, and had a house of her own in town. In her trial, Aguilera described multiple Indian servants or slaves whom she sought to throw out after learning of what she saw as her husband's sexual relations with them but what we might more accurately term his sexual violence against them. If one or more of these women may have used Aguilera's rage as a vehicle for their freedom, others apparently did not know where else to go, perhaps because of their young age and years in captivity. As a free Spanish woman, Doña Josefa apparently had the power to harbor them until Aguilera calmed down and sought their return.[66]

Ritual events in Spanish society may have provided some distraction from the mundane work and violence of daily life, when Apaches were allowed by their masters to attend them. Life in their societies of birth was also full of meaningful rituals, thus providing Natives a basis by which to interpret Spanish baptisms, weddings, and processions associated with religious holidays, even if their more nuanced meaning was not immediately clear. Apaches reportedly watched such public displays with interest, and while Aguilera sought to restrict her servants' and slaves' mobility, they did sometimes attend Mass. How soon the Apache slaves were baptized after capture is, unfortunately, not clear, because with few exceptions it goes unmentioned in the trial records, and New Mexico's baptismal records from this period are not extant.[67]

Friendships among servants and slaves were also common and played a role in their day-to-day survival. The conversations about which Aguilera complained she could not always hear or understand may have been no more than everyday gossip, but they may also have involved plans to escape or, in the case of free servants, to find employment elsewhere. Any demonstration of affection between her servants and slaves also could be met by violence, suggesting that the Aguilera found it worrisome or dangerous—or was perhaps simply jealous.[68]

She became particularly enraged when she saw evidence that friendships had become something more. When she caught Doña Josefa and one of her enslaved Africans named Ana embracing and kissing, she "scolded them severely." In part because of the frequency of Aguilera's physical and verbal attacks, Ana reportedly then feigned a pregnancy by wrapping herself with rags in order to gain better treatment. The household staff, including the Apache servants and slaves, helped keep up the ruse for a time until it was discovered and set Aguilera off on another tantrum, given that she had "even prepared what was needed for [Ana] and her baby."[69]

Pregnancy made for a good ruse because it was so plausible in a setting in which pregnancy and births among servants and slave were commonplace. It was fellow slaves who sought to aid a woman when she became pregnant. While many births occurred during the two years that the couple occupied the governor's palace, the most dramatic involved an Apache woman locked with others in a chamber inside the palace. Aided by the other women inside, this woman gave birth to a boy, whose health worsened after delivery. When their masters caught wind of what was going on, they knew that the proper action to take when death was imminent was baptism, suggesting they had at least some degree of religious belief, despite accusations to the contrary. Don Bernardo baptized the Apache boy himself, noting that his baptism would "surely be better than those of any of the poor priests of New Mexico." Clearly showing that he was not a humble man, this statement also reflected the broader contempt for church officials that was increasingly bringing him to the attention of the Mexican Inquisition. The Apache woman in question, meanwhile, faced layered challenges: pregnancy and labor in captivity in a foreign place without relatives to attend to her or help bring her child into the world and the death of her baby, which she was unable to mourn in customary fashion.[70]

Captivity, enslavement, and labor in Santa Fe, as on the farms and ranches in the countryside, was not always permanent, not always a one-way process of incorporation into or death within colonial society. Some Indian women who ended up in the governor's palace managed to escape and return home when a master or guest let down their guard and forgot to lock the door, as occurred when two Apache girls, one nine years old, the other ten, escaped with another Indian and her baby. Doña Teresa complained that it took "a lot of diligence" for her to track them down, but she finally found them in Cochiti Pueblo. Were these women being harbored in Cochiti? Was it common for some Pueblo Indians to help Apache slaves escape back to their people? Or was it with the aid of Puebloans that Doña Teresa managed to recover them, especially given the role that they played in the slave raids that captured so many Apaches in the first place? All are likely possibilities.[71]

It was not only through escape that slave status could be shed, however. The presence of free Apaches in the governor's palace illustrates as much. Those described as paid servants all performed more skilled work: for example, lace making and cooking. Perhaps these were the daughters of women enslaved earlier, suggesting that at least some New Mexicans took seriously their own claims that Indian slavery was temporary and not hereditary. For those Apaches who managed to become free over time, this was meaningful: it meant you could return to your own house at night—or at least try to do so, since the Doña did not like even her free servants to leave the palace. It also meant you could choose your own employers and leave their service if it was not to your liking. The hope embodied by the presence of free Apaches, promises of freedom after some period of time, and awareness that your own children might not be enslaved would surely have been cherished when Apaches came to learn of them. For those for whom such possibilities became a reality, however, the dishonor of the original enslavement was not easily cast aside. A quarrel between the servants of Doña Teresa and another family illustrates as much. While the roots of the fight are unclear, it ended with one servant being told she was no more than an "Apacha, a descendant of Apache Indians."[72]

While evidence suggests that Apaches could transition from slavery to freedom, how this process worked and how common it was for Spaniards to free their Indian slaves after ten- or fifteen-year periods of enslavement are unanswerable based on the extant documentary record from seventeenth-century New Mexico. Spanish understandings of "temporary slavery" suggest parallels to indentured servitude or debt peonage, but one obvious distinction is that Natives had no choice about entering into servitude or incurring the "debt" of their "rescue" from other Indians. Yet this is not the only difference. No extant documents reveal Spanish masters tracking terms of labor in the way that was done with indentured-servant contracts elsewhere in the Americas or Europe. While there are archival references to Indian men in the region having "paid off" their ransoms during the eighteenth century, I have seen no similar references for this earlier period.[73]

Indian slavery in New Mexico was conceptualized and justified as an open-ended system of incorporating and transforming non-Christian Indians, but Spanish masters' actions suggest that boundaries between slavery and freedom were not as porous as official rhetoric suggested. As later legal wrangling illustrated, Aguilera and her contemporaries fought official efforts to categorize their Apaches as "free" and make them pay them wages. Masters sought to retain or regain their Apaches' unpaid labor for as long as they possibly could.[74]

Perhaps the most distinct aspect of Indian enslavement in Santa Fe, as opposed to being in a militiamen's family at Taos, was the threat of transport to places so distant from home that escape and return would be difficult. For many Apaches, life in the governor's palace or a Spanish hacienda or textile factory was only temporary—until their master's agents carried them south into Sonora or Nueva Vizcaya to sell (as we will explore further in Chapter 2). Mendizábal alone sent seventy or eighty Indians to sell as slaves in New Spain, one means through which he sought to profit personally from his term in office. His calculation was straightforward: selling seventy Apache slaves in New Spain could yield a profit of five thousand pesos, more than two years of salary, and this is assuming that he paid the original purchase cost, which he probably did not.[75] The problem is that he had already come under legal scrutiny. His slave trading was probably not at the top of royal officials' concerns when they ultimately heeded the advice pouring out of New Mexico to depose Mendizábal. At the very least, however, it led officials to act to free the Indian slaves in question and authorize their masters to recover the purchase price in Parral and Sonora in the spring of 1660.[76]

Yet it was not simply through sale that Apaches could end up in diaspora in New Spain. Whether they were treated as dependents or as the property of New Mexico governors, their fates were linked to the governors when they fell into legal trouble, which was surprisingly common for New Mexico elites throughout the seventeenth century. For Mendizábal and Aguilera, their worst legal troubles came at the hands of the Mexican Inquisition, which had been building a case against them based on rumors and reports that had flowed out of New Mexico from the moment they arrived. This evidence included testimony gathered from their servants and slaves about what went on behind palace walls: Friday grooming rituals that some suspected seemed Jewish; a lack of religious devotion; malicious statements against church and civil officials; secret locked drawers; and more.[77]

By August 1661, the viceroy had appointed a replacement for Mendizábal, Diego Dionisio de Peñalosa Briceño y Berdugo. Peñalosa was initially received warmly, especially by the church officials who so despised Mendizábal, but in the end Peñalosa proved little different. After he arrived in Santa Fe, he tried to bribe the former governor and allow him to write his own audit; he seized much of his property, including Apache slaves; and like Mendizábal, he eventually came under legal scrutiny himself and was banished from New Spain. Peñalosa died in France, but not before he had given some of Mendizábal's Apache slaves to his friends in Mexico City as gifts and carried out campaigns of his own against Native groups to acquire additional slaves.[78]

Mendizábal and Aguilera were arrested in August 1662 and departed for Mexico a few months later, along with the Indian and African slaves they had managed to keep in their possession. While Peñalosa had seized as many of their slaves as he could, Aguilera had managed to retain at least seven of her Apache and Quivira (likely Wichita or Pawnee) slaves. They accompanied the couple, along with their enslaved Africans, on their long journey south and were put to work in the kitchen of the convoy serving the group. One of the Indians died along the way, while two of them were sold or distributed at stopping points. Popular support for Native slavery, even on the part of Inquisition officials, is illustrated by the fact that these women were not freed or returned to their original homelands or even allowed to simply remain in New Mexico as servants. By April 1663, both Aguilera and Mendizábal were locked in separate cells of the secret jail of the Inquisition, while their Apache and Plains Indian slaves were embargoed and placed in new homes.[79]

The fates of Natives brought to and embargoed in Mexico City illustrate how exploiting Indians came almost as easily to residents in New Spain's center as it did to residents of frontier New Mexico. In theory, these Indians were not owned by their new masters but rather simply being held in their care ("in deposit") until the Inquisition could resolve their case and, if necessary, liquidate the couple's assets to cover the costs of their imprisonment and trial. Aguilera's Apaches and Quiviras faced this fate. So too did other Native captives who Peñalosa had sent to Mexico City and the Inquisition had then embargoed because of the broader sea of legal troubles enveloping all parties involved. Peñolosa's "gifts" to area residents included girls like ten-year-old Ana, whom he described as an "angelical beauty in the form of an Apache" in a letter accompanying her and two bushels of pine nuts originally intended for one of his friends.[80]

The language used to discuss Native captives echoed a recent court order in the fall of 1659 by the audiencia of Guadalajara generated in part by news of Mendizábal's slave trading in Sonora and Nueva Vizcaya. This order required residents to manifest their Indians slaves for emancipation, and it is likely because of renewed legal scrutiny that individuals now spoke of Native captives as "gifts" rather than "slaves" and testified to their "complete liberty," even though it was in fact the Inquisition that now had ultimate say over their lives. Even Mendizábal, for instance, explained to the Inquisition that he had only sold Native captives "when it had been permitted" and that those in his service were entirely free and "without any charge of slavery." In fact, the recent court order had merely clarified that Indian slavery had been illegal all along, as noted in repeated royal decrees going back more than a century.[81]

Attention to the fates of captives distributed by the Inquisition in Mexico City qualifies the significance of "free" status for Native captives alienated from kin and homeland. When Mexico City residents petitioned to receive embargoed Indians, they provided the formulaic promise "to instruct them and indoctrinate them" but clearly also hoped that they might fulfill immediate labor needs. Doña Ana Muñez de Rojas, for instance, petitioned in June 1663 to receive an Apache woman "to teach and indoctrinate." While she promised to pay the girl one peso per month, she returned a month later and explained that since María was naked, it was necessary to buy her clothing, and she had also had to pay for a blanket for her to sleep on. Moreover, until she was further "instructed," her service was not worth anything, and Doña Ana thus hoped that the inquisitors would see fit to relieve her of having to pay María for the next six months. They granted this request, and a year later Doña Ana returned again with the same request—to not have to pay María because of the cost of clothing her. This time she noted that "she had baptized her, and set to work on instructing her in Christian doctrines."[82]

For a Native woman like María, the new line that the Spaniards drew between "free" and "slave" status probably meant little as she slept on a blanket at night while performing domestic service without pay. At the very least, her life in Doña Ana's household was temporary. When Doña Ana entered into the service of the viceroy, she took María with her to the royal palace and then left her there. What happened to María in the end is revealed in a later petition from Doña Ana to be relieved of any obligation to pay the required one peso per month salary, which she seems to have avoided paying all along anyway. The Inquisition's investigation revealed that María had spent years in the service of the viceroy, but he had later sent her to a nunnery. In 1672, almost ten years after arriving in Mexico City, María died there of smallpox. Like so many similar women, questions linger. The archival record does not reveal whether the viceroy paid María, in contrast to her former master who had not. No record notes whether it was María's decision to go to the nunnery or if this was a decision made for her. No account from María's perspective describes what solace, companionship, or religious devotion she may have felt in her life with other women.[83]

Some masters may have taken more seriously the obligations they entered into and their claims that they would care for Indian captives and even treat them like their own children. One New Mexico military officer whose Indian captives were swept up in the legal mayhem of these years and embargoed by the Inquisition suggested as much when he went to great lengths to ensure their return. Captain Toribio de la Huerta noted in a petition to the Inquisition that he was especially concerned about Juanchillo Toribio, "a heathen of seven or eight years old" who had been taken from him in New Mexico and transported to Mexico City, where he had been assigned to a new master. He noted that he had rescued the boy from "the civil wars that the Natives of New Mexico had with each other" and having "raised him," he feared that the boy might be heartbroken in his absence. The Inquisition returned both Juanchillo and his other Indian captive named Juan to the captain from the temporary masters they had been assigned to in Mexico City.[84]

Like Captain Huerta, Doña Teresa de Aguilera petitioned for the return of her Indian captives after her case ended and she finally secured her release from jail in 1665. Her husband—the former governor—had died in the Inquisition's jail, and Doña Teresa wrangled for the return of their property. The Inquisition ultimately returned four Indian women to her, including two Apache women, named Ines and Isabela. She too claimed they were treated like her own children, though as we have seen, past evidence suggests otherwise. In Mexico City, as in Santa Fe, they were integrated into a world of bondage that included enslaved Africans. They gossiped around a neighborhood well about their masters on good days, when she let them out of the house, but she also continued to seek to keep them locked up as much as possible. Legal troubles and past experience had made the Doña more paranoid than ever.[85]

Her paranoia proved warranted. In January 1666, less than a year after her release, Doña Teresa sought a hearing at the office of the Mexican Inquisition to present serious allegations against the now former viceroy, the Count of Baños. She explained that he had scaled the walls of her estate, entered through the back corral, and stolen three of her Indian servants: "Maria Quivira, Michaela Quivira, and Ines Apache." She demanded that they be returned to her and that the perpetrators of this "grave" plot—the count and his wife, Doña María de Córdova—be given punishment fitting the severity of their crime.[86]

At first glance, Doña Teresa's scandalous accusations are almost laughable, perhaps calling to mind the plot of a historical telenovela. We can imagine the scene: a middle-aged viceroy of New Spain huffing and puffing as he scales a wall, drops into the estate, and proceeds to plead with Indian women to leave with him. For some reason they decide to join him, and the group tumbles back over the wall and then slips into the night.

The Inquisition's investigation ultimately proved more disturbing than comedic, however. The viceroy's wife, testimony revealed, had in fact been trying to lure the Indian women back into her service. One of her black slaves had delivered them a message when the servants and slaves of the neighborhood collected water from a neighborhood well. The Doña's message was twofold. She said she would send a carriage to get them and that she would treat them better than Doña Teresa if they would come to her. If they decided not to, she would send someone with a knife to attack them.[87] One friend and neighbor of Aguilera then explained what had happened the night that the women had gone missing. A group of friends, including Doña Teresa, had come home late to her estate that night. When they could not find the Indian women, the first possibility that they had considered was that they "must have hung themselves." It was only later, when they did not find bodies but instead noticed a shoe outside the wall of the estate, that they reached the conclusion that they were alive and the viceroy must have taken them.[88]

That suicide was the first thought that crossed their minds strikes at the relationship Doña Teresa and her elite friends had with their servants or slaves. Claims of concern about them were belied by the casualness with which they could imagine their deaths. It suggests that they may have experienced the suicide of servants or slaves before and indicates that something about the women's demeanor—or treatment—had made this seem to those they served like a possibility. An important component of their thinking is revealed in another possibility that Doña Teresa and her friends did not raise—that the women had simply escaped of their own accord. Whatever the Doña's feelings about her servants, whether they were "like daughters" or "deceitful bitches," she could not bring herself to imagine that the women might not care about her at all.[89]

Another complaint to the Inquisition captures well both Spaniards' efforts to maintain control of Indians' unpaid labor and their slaves' challenges to their authority. In March 1673, María de la Concepción, a native of New Mexico, appeared at the office to petition for her freedom. She explained that as a child she had entered into the possession of Governor Diego de Peñalosa. Like his immediate predecessor, Peñalosa's blasphemy and sexual misconduct had eventually led him to face an Inquisition trial. Carried to Mexico City among his possessions, she had been placed "in deposit" in the home of Don Francisco Valdés, a citizen of Mexico City. Life in his house had "not been to her convenience," however, and she had recently escaped. Now Valdés "was after her," and she feared that he intended to "force her to serve him against her will." Describing her own understanding of the law, she noted that she should not be subject to bondage for any longer than ten years. She had already served this term, and more, and pleaded that the inquisitors "grant her the freedom she should enjoy." A month later, the Inquisition decided that María should not be freed because there were still matters pending in the case against her former master, Diego de Peñalosa.[90]

This story of a Native woman from New Mexico on the run from her master in Mexico City captures in a microcosm the experience of bondage and diaspora that Native men, women, and children faced in the seventeenth century as a result of Spanish colonization. Whether Natives were captured and enslaved in households, workshops, or the governor's palace in Santa Fe, sold into New Spain, or carried there and put "in deposit" in strangers' homes because of their masters' misdeeds, Spanish enslavement fundamentally altered life for hundreds of Apache and other Native people. Uprooted from kin and home and assigned a new place as "Apache" slaves in colonial society, their lives were shaped by the ongoing challenges posed by displacement and exploitation amid their relative powerlessness. Contrasted with the hereditary chattel slavery that enslaved Africans faced, the supposedly "temporary" nature of Apache enslavement suggests a parallel with the treatment of captives within Apache and other Native societies. But the scale of the slave trade and the frequency with which Apaches might be carried far from home deep into the Spanish Empire point to distinctions. So too do the challenges they faced in actually realizing belonging or some degree of self-determination. María de la Concepción's hope was quite modest—she claimed the right to choose to labor in a household more to her liking. In her quest, however, she faced formidable challenges from masters who employed every tool at their disposal to keep her in bondage: making up laws, inventing new ways of describing what was going on, or threatening violence.[91]

For Apache slaves, legal crackdowns too often failed to address the fundamental power relation at the heart of their enslavement. They could challenge their masters directly, they could escape and runaway, and they could petition courts if they managed to secure the aid of a sympathetic notary or priest. But if they remained in captivity, it was often their master's choice whether they recognized them as "free Indians" and treated them differently or continued to exploit their unpaid labor and treat them as slaves. The Inquisition illustrates how they were often aided and abetted by the very institutions that we might expect to seek justice for wrongfully enslaved and displaced Indians. While rooted in the idiosyncratic lives of their powerful masters, the experiences of Apaches like María and Juanchillo in foreign places far from home would soon become more common than ever.[92]

*   *   *

As hundreds of men, women, and children became "Apaches" in colonial society, the communities from which they had been separated debated the future. They did so in a context in which many had lost relatives to Spanish slaving. While slave trading was not the only cause of concern among them— drought, food scarcity, and commercial competition had all added to their worries—it undoubtedly played a key role in influencing a new approach to their neighbors in the months and years to come: war. Given that Spaniards relied upon hundreds of Pueblo allies to acquire the captives they enslaved, it is not surprising that Apache and Navajo alliances with Puebloan groups became strained to the breaking point, and the Puebloans faced the brunt of Apache and Navajo warfare.[93]

We know more about the Apache and Navajo groups' actions than about the internal debates that helped produce them. Suffering from famine and enslavement, they targeted what they perceived to be the cause of their troubles: Pueblo allies of the Spanish, horse and mule herds, and the wagon trains that carried their relatives into slavery in New Spain. In April 1669, Fray Juan Bernal declared that "the whole land is at war with the widespread heathen nation of the Apache Indians." He reported, furthermore, that "no road was safe" and that Apaches would "kill all the Christian Indians they can find and encounter." Fray Francisco de Ayeta would later recall the year 1672 as a turning point, when "the hostile Apaches who were still at peace rebelled and rose up, and the said province was totally sacked and robbed."[94]

Ironically, these efforts at least initially provided further justification for the Spaniards to pursue retaliatory raids in which they collected larger numbers of captives than ever before to enslave as Apaches. Given that colonists already possessed large numbers of slaves, it is not surprising that many decided to export war captives to the mining districts of Northern New Spain rather than keep them in bondage locally. Suffering from famine and Native attacks, they may have felt that they were struggling to support their existing households. The fact that men in particular were exported, as indicated by the relative balance in gender of baptisms in Parral, also suggests that security concerns in the context of war played a role.[95]

The diaspora of Apache captives south to the mining district of Parral and surrounding communities in the ensuing years altered the demographic makeup of Northern New Spain while providing Spanish residents there with a key source of labor. Many Apaches did their best to adjust to life in new circumstances not of their choosing: starting families with enslaved Africans, having children, or stealing from, attacking, or escaping from their masters. For others, the "sentence of death" against the Apache nation that continued to justify their export would prove real—usually because of dangerous work conditions that made life expectancy short, but occasionally because they decided that a life of exile and exploitation was no better than death and took their own lives, realizing one of Doña Teresa's many fears.

CHAPTER 2

The Mining District

On a spring morning in 1671, the chief magistrate in Parral, New Spain, was called to investigate the death of an Apache woman named Francisca. Traveling down the valley and across the river to the outskirts of town, Don Luis Valdés arrived at the estate of a longtime area resident and storekeeper, Nicolás Balderrama. Valdés discovered Francisca inside a corral, where she had hung herself with a belt. By collecting testimony from the servants and slaves living at the estate, he hoped to understand Francisca's motivations and whether some malfeasance was at the root of her apparent suicide. The women he interrogated told him that Balderrama regularly abused his servants and slaves, noting that an Apache woman had died from a lashing the year before. Francisca was a new addition to the household, and they said she had suffered from similar maltreatment, but not in recent days, because she had been ill.

If the magistrate harbored any serious concerns based on these reports, he kept them to himself, as he took no further action. Francisca's suicide may have been noteworthy, a point of conversation, a memory that lingered, especially among other servants and slaves. Perhaps their decision to testify openly about their treatment was also a source of conflict, because it might spark retaliation from their master and new punishments. Or maybe the whole affair was unremarkable in a context in which the death of servants and slaves was commonplace. Balderrama, a widower, was soon celebrating a second marriage and welcoming new children—and new Apaches to take care of them—into his home.[1]

The household of a Parral storekeeper serves as a touchstone for considering the broader history of Apaches in diaspora in Northern New Spain in the seventeenth century. Merchants transported Apache slaves to the Parral district beginning soon after the silver strikes turned it into a boomtown in the 1630s. For thirty years or so, Parral represented one node in the larger slave trade that governors and merchants from New Mexico helped to create.

Typically, merchants would bring a few Indian slaves with hides, textiles, and pine nuts to sell to Parral residents. Balderrama was a typical buyer. Well-off but far from the richest man in town, he purchased his first Apache as a slave in the 1650s to help in the store and home that he had built after coming north from Mexico City. The focus of the slave trade remained in New Mexico itself, though, where larger numbers of Apache slaves worked on ranches and farms and in homes, textile factories, and the governor's palace.[2]

The dynamics of the slave trade and the experience of Apache captives shifted as New Mexico descended into violence and famine in the 1660s and 1670s. Apaches had turned to war to recover kin, take horses and livestock, and end their victimization in the Indian slave trade. Their approach initially had paradoxical effects, however. Rather than shutting off the slave trade, Apache warfare and Spanish and Pueblo Indian reprisals created a new bonanza of captives, and Spanish residents shipped them south into New Spain more regularly than they had in the past. This decision was likely fueled by the reality of limited resources to support a large slave population, security concerns about keeping them at home and luring Apache attacks, and hopes that they might profit off their transport and sale in destinations like Parral, a populated mining district with wealthy residents and a diversified economy with a great demand for labor.[3]

Unfortunately for aspirant slave traders, this mass exile of Apache men, women, and children coincided with a new Spanish campaign to end Indian and Asian slavery across its empire. This campaign influenced Apaches' lives in Parral, but it did not prevent their transport there in the first place, indicating that conditions in New Mexico, more than commercial interests, were at the root of the diaspora.[4] As groups of Apaches were repeatedly hauled before officials and told that they were free, it became more common for some Apaches to be paid wages. As free servants, they could live in their own homes, where they could create a space apart from their employers, and they could change employers if the latter were not to their liking, as least in theory. For many Apache captives, however, exile to Parral proved a sentence to a quick death, as they were put to work in dangerous tasks, exposed to crowd diseases, and mistreated by masters who may have felt they had no investment to lose. Other Apaches experienced life somewhere in between these poles: told they were servants rather than slaves, but kept in their masters' homes, paid through room and board, and lashed and chained like the enslaved Africans they labored alongside. This was the case for Francisca.[5]

Whatever the degree of freedom Apaches attained in New Spain, it did not resolve the challenges produced by their exile there in the first place. Because they were barred from returning to New Mexico, it was up to the displaced

Apaches to forge new social bonds and rebuild a network of kin in diaspora that would help them to survive in new circumstances they had not selected.[6] Back in Apache homelands, meanwhile, leaders faced a dilemma: years of war by themselves had not ended the capture and exploitation of their kin but had instead fueled their mass exile hundreds of miles to the south. Setting aside the animosities that Pueblo aid to Spanish military campaigns had helped generate, some Apache groups ultimately joined with Pueblo Indian communities to assist them in August 1680 in executing the most successful Indian rebellion in North American history, partly in the hope of liberating their kin from enslavement. In the end, however, Apaches in exile in Parral were not returned to their communities of birth but continued to form a diasporic community in Northern New Spain that endured even after the transport of Native captives to places like Parral was temporarily cut off.[7]

The strange maelstrom of war, famine, labor demands, and Spanish anti-slavery sentiment fueled practices of forced migration, labor, and exile that presaged the fate of future generations of Apaches in diaspora. Spaniards associated slavery with profit and property but argued that moving captives in order to work in "nice families" and become Catholic was something else. After all, the idea that forced migration for the public good was justified had long undergirded labor draft systems that moved Natives from their mission towns to sites dozens of miles away to work. Such ideas would continue to undergird the forced migration of "enemy" Indians in the coming decades.[8]

While Apache captives—and many modern scholars—might argue that it was a distinction without a difference, it ultimately was a historically important one. Eventually, empires and nation-states labeled Apaches as prisoners of war and paid to exile them to tropical lands and put them to work or incarcerate them, claiming they were treating them well and not as slaves. Apaches' varied experiences in Parral in this earlier period illustrate how anti-slavery sentiment could lead Euro-Americans to disentangle "slavery" from "exile in order to work" on the basis that those transporting them were not profiting from the sale of captives. Yet for displaced Apaches, life in diaspora as discarded prisoners of war did not necessarily prove better than enslavement, either in this era or in the future.[9]

The Roots of Diaspora to New Spain

Decades before the Pueblo Revolt or Francisca's death, Spaniards in New Mexico learned that they could sell Apache and Plains Indian slaves in the mining towns of Northern New Spain at a significant profit. This trade was initially relatively small scale, however. Merchants like Juan Manso brought a few Indian slaves along with the hides, salt, and pine nuts that they also sold. As we have seen, governors attempted to send larger shipments with their agents to towns across Northern New Spain, such as those in Nueva Vizcaya or Sonora, but royal officials sometimes caught wind of such efforts and freed the Indians involved.[10]

Nicolás Balderrama's household illustrates this broader context, allowing us to consider both Spanish motivations for acquiring Apache Indians and the experiences of Apaches themselves. Balderrama first appears in the Parral archives about twenty years before Francisca's death, when he was thirty-seven years old. How long he had lived in town is unclear, but he was born in Mexico City in 1615, and like many men of his day, the silver mines had probably lured him north. Balderrama's relative success and wealth was based on a storefront, not on a mine. As has often proved true in mining booms, it can be more profitable to sell goods at inflated prices to those with silver or gold fever than to seek mineral riches yourself.[11]

By August 1653, Balderrama still had no children of his own, but that month he had an Apache slave baptized in the Parral parish and named him after himself. Though the priest did not specify Nicolás's age, the fact that he did not label him either "infant" or "adult" suggests that he may have been somewhere in between, which was typical of Apache captives transported to Parral. Of the ninety-seven baptismal entries of Apaches or Indians "from New Mexico" that include a specific age, the average age was just under ten. It can be jarring to view the entries of many Apaches whom we would view as quite young children: like Joseph, the four-year-old Apache servant of Diego Pérez de Villanueva; or María, the five-year-old Apache servant of Don Phelipe de la Cueva Montaño; or Juana, the Apache "adult servant" of Juan Luis Castelui who was seven or eight years old. That Parral priests sometimes described such young Apaches as adults indicates how seventeenth-century views of childhood differed from our own: they viewed the Indian in question as grown enough to work.[12]

Nicolás's route into Parral can be traced with more certainty than his age. Prior to becoming governor of New Mexico, Juan Manso was one of the primary sellers of Apache slaves in Parral in the early 1650s. Unable to order campaigns against Apaches himself, he relied in large part during this period upon indigenous suppliers, such as the Manso Indians of what is now southern New Mexico. The term "Manso" means "tame" in Spanish, indicating their views of this particular Indigenous group, and it is merely a coincidence that this particular Spanish merchant carried the same surname. Relations between Mansos and Apaches varied over time. Later, in the 1680s and 1690s, Apache groups and Mansos joined together in region-wide rebellions that one scholar has termed the Great Southwestern Revolt, but the early 1650s was a time of enmity between them. Spanish merchants took advantage of campaigns between the Mansos and Apache groups—likely ancestral Chihenes or Mescaleros—in order to acquire captives for sale in Parral under the rubric of *rescate*. In other words, they argued that they were "rescuing" these captives from lives of slavery among other non-Christian Indians.[13]

For the best resale value, merchants would want to travel first to Santa Fe to obtain titles and transfer documents from the governor authorizing the sale of captives as rescued Indians. This was particularly true after 1648, when officials concerned about the illegal enslavement of Indians ordered that all masters manifest their Apache slaves and provide justification that they were legally held. Because the lands of the Manso Indians were quite distant from Santa Fe, close to the royal road near El Paso, merchants sometimes traveled without them or requested that a governor in Nueva Vizcaya issue permission himself. Nicolás likely had a title, as his baptismal record describes him as a "slave," rather than using other common terms of the period, such as *criado*—"one who is raised up," or simply *sirviente*—"servant."[14]

While Nicolás's title is not extant, others from the time period are illustrative. Titles described the slave in question by their name, age, and distinctive features. In December 1654, for example, Francisco Lima transferred the title to a seven- or eight-year-old Plains Indian girl named Angelina—thin in body, "not yet a Christian," with a blue line down her face and nose and both hands painted with lines—to Doña Antonia de Alarcón Faxardo, the wife of Juan Lorenzo Bernardo. She then transferred the title to Don Andrés de Fargo, a citizen of Mexico City, who gave her one hundred pesos.[15] In July of that year, Francisco de Lima had transferred the title to an Apache Indian woman named Gracia, "37 years old more or less," and an Apache boy, seven or eight years old named Domingo Niculas, to Bartolome Hernandez for a hundred pesos. The title noted that Gracia had "three marks, one in the middle of the face and one on each cheek." Domingo Niculas had a square marking made on his stomach "with fire." These and similar descriptions in Parral slave sales suggest that some New Mexican Indians may have been branded prior to export, though traditional tattooing practices likely explain at least some of the markings described as well.[16]

In the mid-1600s, travel from southern New Mexico to Parral was an arduous journey that could take several months by wagon. If he was around ten years old, Nicolás likely would have known something about his fate,

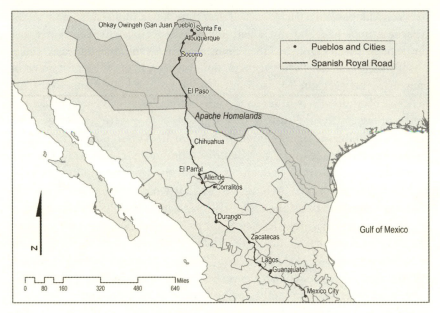

Map 1. The Royal Road (Camino Real).

aware that to be taken away in a wagon by the Spanish meant that he was going to be put to work. Perhaps he even knew by the direction in which he was traveling that he was not headed for Santa Fe or the farms and ranches of the Rio Grande but to more distant country.[17]

Nicolás was probably not alone in the cart in which he traveled, because a merchant usually purchased multiple captives from the Manso Indians in any one visit to make it worth his trouble. If this was the case for Nicolás, perhaps it eased his fears. They almost certainly would have known each other or even been relatives, given that they were acquired in the same campaign and were probably from the same Apache local group. They might have shared ideas about where they were headed or weighed the possibility of escaping. They would have known that the closer they got to Parral—had they tried to escape—the more likely it was that someone would catch them before they made it home. There were even rumors that Apaches caught reentering New Mexico might be shot on sight.[18]

Parral residents like Balderrama had various means of acquiring an Apache slave like Nicolás once they arrived in the district after several months en route. Local Indian "rebels" were sometimes offered as slaves in public auctions and sold to the highest bidder, but Indians from New Mexico were more typically acquired through inquiry with a merchant or friend involved in trade with New Mexico.[19] Such sales sometimes occurred outside of town, suggesting that the merchants or buyers had concerns about the legality of the trade. A few years before Nicolás's baptism, Antonio de Villalengua, a Parral resident, had received word that the wagons that traveled into New Mexico to gather salt had returned with some Indian boys and girls. Villalengua had met the traders outside town where their wagons were camped. When he asked to see the merchandise, they showed him three "naked and maltreated" Apache girls, who he guessed were seven or eight years old. After haggling the price—they were asking one hundred pesos each—Villalengua asked them about the titles that allowed for their transport and sale. When they responded that they had no titles, Villalengua went on his way, "recognizing the risk" of buying Indian girls without this guarantee.[20]

Villalengua's testimony, part of a broader inquiry into illegal slave trading, illustrates well the dynamics of the trade. Merchants arrived with a few Indian slaves as a part of their broader commercial endeavors. Potential buyers dickered over pricing and demonstrated awareness of the controversial legal status of Indian slavery and concern about the security of their potential investments. A royal decree the previous year that had imposed a fine of five hundred pesos on anyone caught illegally enslaving Indians was undoubtedly on some potential buyers' minds.[21]

While purchasing an Indian as a slave was not without risk, controversy also helped lower prices. Cost was probably a factor for someone like Balderrama to purchase an Apache instead of an African slave or a paid Indian servant. While Balderrama did eventually purchase enslaved Africans worth more than four hundred pesos each on average, Nicolás would have cost him a fourth or less of that price, between eighty and one hundred pesos. While for the merchants this represented a significant profit off of whatever price they had paid their Indians suppliers in kind, or what they could have sold him for in New Mexico—around thirty pesos—we should be careful to note that this relatively low cost made Apache slaves accessible to Parral residents. Similar in cost to Nicolás were two of his master's mattresses and their associated beddings, or six old chairs and some stools, or two desks his master used to handle store records—all items that Balderrama later reported on an inventory of his possessions. Locals welcomed Apaches as a labor source as epidemics affected the local indigenous population, African slaves remained extraordinarily expensive, and Apaches captives were taken in increasing numbers in war in New Mexico.[22]

Whatever the worries of buyers and sellers, Apache captives undoubtedly had their own concerns. Having traveled by wagon for weeks, guarded at night, perhaps chained, these three Apaches girls in 1649 were not dressed for the cold nights of late winter and early spring in the Rio Grande valley of New Mexico or the desert basins and hills they traversed on their way to the mining district of Northern New Spain. Parral itself lies at around six thousand feet, and temperatures as low as three degrees Fahrenheit have been recorded in March.[23] Perhaps it was because of the cold that the girls' condition stuck in Villalengua's mind: "naked and maltreated." The condition of the girls may have reflected slave traders' efforts to maximize profits, with clothing being a cost they were unwilling to undertake. They may have also been engaging in a practice common in other times and places—stripping captives so that buyers could poke and prod and ascertain for themselves what they perceived the captives' value to be. Having endured such treatment, the girls were subsequently separated between Parral households. The town magistrate tried to track down the girls as a part of his investigation into illegal slave trading, but it is unclear if he ever found them. The slave traders feigned ignorance as to their whereabouts, and when town officials brought various Apache girls before them to ask if these were the ones they had traded, they claimed to not recognize them.[24]

Did Nicolás Balderrama journey out of town to shop for his Indian slave? Did he peer inside a wagon full of Apache children before deciding upon the boy who would become his "Nicolás"? Was he looking specifically for a boy, perhaps because of ideas he had about how a useful a boy or girl might be in helping fulfill his specific labor needs? While the archival record does not answer these questions, it does make clear that forced incorporation into Balderrama's household represented a fundamental turning point in Nicolás's life that had begun at the moment of his capture. Among his Apache kin, he would have looked forward to initiation into manhood and experimenting with the bow. Perhaps he had already gone out on a raid to retaliate against Manso Indians for their attacks. He would have become familiar with the beliefs of Apaches and a world that was full of spiritual forces. He would have learned to name key features of the landscape using descriptive names. He would have learned about his ancestors and his family's lineage in order to understand who he was. Long winter nights would often have been enlivened by storytelling sessions that taught children how they were to act toward each other and toward neighboring peoples, stories about Coyote and his trickster pranks, about the mountain spirits inhabiting sacred peaks, and about culture hero and his victorious encounters with monsters.[25]

Nicolás's sense of security and understanding of his place in this world were fractured by his transport to Parral. He learned a daily work regimen there that bore little resemblance to life in his community of birth. For some Apaches, the difference was even more dramatic than for Nicolás. The demand for labor in Parral emanated from the mining industry and all of the industries that supported it: farming, cattle raising, charcoal making, salt production, lumber hauling, and more. Some Apaches worked in the mines themselves as ore pickers, others in some aspect of the broader process of hauling the ore to refining plants, where silver was actually recovered. While transporting ore was hardly an easy task, it also offered opportunities. In September 1655, for example, two slaves were implicated in a ring of petty thefts. Juan Cortés, an Apache Indian, and Nicolás Bargas, a mulatto, both helped manufacture bars of silver at one of Parral's silver smelters. In the process, they had apparently stolen "many pieces of silver on different occasions," or so alleged Captain Valerio Cortés, Juan's master. In subsequent investigations, Juan admitted everything, saying that he had stolen pieces of silver seven times and that Nicolás, the mulatto slave, had done so another four times. They took the silver pieces to various merchants and pawn shops around town, where they received a few pesos for each. One of the merchants who had bought silver from Juan explained his reasoning: it was simply an old custom to buy little pieces of silver from poor workers.[26]

Yet such opportunities proved a mixed blessing for those directly involved in the refining process. Silver refiners were clearly concerned about workers escaping from their haciendas, since they kept them chained at night or, at the very least, behind closed doors. The ore-processing plant of someone like Valerio Cortés, one of the most avid purchasers of Apaches in Parral, would have included multiple single-story buildings that completely enclosed patios where the ore was crushed and processed. The most efficient means used in Parral to extract metal from ore was the "patio process." First, workers laid out silver-bearing ore on the floor of a circular pit. The grinding process was driven by mules, which turned a central rotating post that forced blocks of stone down upon the ore and reduced it to a fine dust. After adding water to it, the Apache slaves would have then spread the muddy ore over a paved patio or courtyard, sprinkled it with mercury, salt, and copper sulfate, and drove the mules across it to mix it together. Sometimes, shackled workers were forced to walk over it themselves to be sure it was thoroughly mixed and the elemental silver divided from the mixture. Handling it greatly reduced the life expectancy of anyone involved. That this was an occupation for which Natives displaced from New Mexico and the plains were used in the district may help to explain their ubiquitous presence in the burial records of the district.[27]

Ranchers also purchased Apaches to supplement enslaved African and free Indian labor over time. Apache men were more likely than women to be gathered together on haciendas to tend sheep, mules, cows, or horses, in part because of the Spanish notion that ranch work was men's work. The degree to which Native groups around New Mexico had incorporated horses and other livestock into their daily lives by this time is debated, but references to livestock raiding at the very least suggest that this generation of Native men would have been familiar enough with animal husbandry to have been able to draw upon preexisting skills. Farm owners whose crops helped feed the Parral district also sometimes sought Apache men, even though women and children typically did the farming in Apache societies. Demand for male workers may help to explain why the gender breakdown of Apache baptisms in Parral is roughly even in both baptismal and burial records. In fact, of captives specifically described as "Apache," instead of the more generic "Indian from New Mexico," men outnumber women slightly. In addition to slaveowners' preferences, this gender ratio probably also reflected the fact that New Mexicans were keen on exporting men, especially after war became more common in the 1660s.[28]

Nicolás may have used some of his previous skills in tending Balderrama's horses and mules on his estate, but other tasks would have been new: transporting and delivering merchandise to customers, tending Balderrama's store. The most important break from Nicolás's past, however, and for any Apache transported to Parral, was separation from kin and the network of protection it represented. Their baptisms symbolized this erasure of past ties. While priests did sometime inquire about Apaches' parents, they often noted either that they were simply "heathens" or that Apaches "did not know how to give account of them," which suggests that they simply did not know enough Spanish yet to communicate. In Nicolás's case, the priest made no reference to parents at all. This was part of what it meant to become "Apache" in diaspora in Parral: to be initially a kinless person, an exploitable "heathen" Indian from elsewhere, someone with no lineage that was given recognition or legitimacy. Yet Spanish society also offered a rebirth of sorts that allowed captives to emerge from this symbolic social death: not only a new name, Nicolás, but also a Catholic godparent, who was tasked with looking after him and attending to his spiritual education. In Nicolás's case, this was a woman named María de la Cruz, probably the black slave woman by the same name who served as a godmother for a number of Apaches brought to Parral during this period.[29]

While the ceremony of Catholic baptism may have seemed strange to Nicolás, it was not incomprehensible. Many Apache groups had witnessed Spanish baptisms firsthand by the 1650s. He could also have drawn upon his own people's customs and ceremonies designed to ensure children's safety, survival, and proper education for perspective. Nicolás would not have remembered his own cradle ceremony, for example, but perhaps he had observed those of siblings, when a shaman said prayers and marked a child with pollen, making four dots on the face of a boy, tracing a line on the bridge of a nose of a girl, sometimes then holding the child to the four directions before placing the child into the cradle. This ceremony would have been followed by food and celebration. Reminiscent of the Spanish practice of godparenthood, it was common for Apache children to sometimes use "a parental term to [address] the person who lifted him into the cradle."[30]

In lieu of growing up in a camp among their kin or in a town adjacent to homelands they might reasonably hope to escape to, Nicolás and other Apaches were being brought to one of the largest towns in North America at the time. It had grown rapidly in the 1630s, after an aspiring miner got lucky and discovered a remarkable silver vein. Within a few years a town had grown up around the hill as the miner, his friends, family, and servants began to work the site and others learned of it and joined them. By 1640 there were more than eight thousand people living around Parral, more than triple the Hispanic population of all of New Mexico.[31]

Traveling through town on the way to Mass or running errands for his master, Nicolás would have observed the mines and ramshackle adobe huts that clung to the hillsides. He would have come to recognize the ore-processing haciendas, ranches, and farms that stretched along the Rio Parral into the countryside, perhaps even by the names of the owners who also patronized his master's store. Perhaps he also had a chance to admire the more opulent homes that residents had started to build in the 1640s, which were clustered near the center plaza and the church. Wealth made from silver helped pay for them to import fine furniture hundreds of miles north from Mexico City, along the royal road, and also to bring in enslaved African labor. Of the thousand or so slaves of African descent living in Parral by 1640, about half were imported directly from Africa, especially from Angola. The other half had been born in Spanish America and brought by their masters north to Parral. Nicolás's labor may have played a role in his master eventually earning enough to acquire several of these expensive slaves for himself.[32]

Nicolás would also have met Indians from varied places of origin speaking different languages. These represented the majority of Parral's population during its first few decades, as well as the majority of the labor force engaged in mining specifically. Some of them came of their own accord to Parral, including a significant number of Yaquis from the Pacific Coast who formed their own neighborhood. Two thousand or so Indians were wage workers, who not only earned a salary but under what was known as the *pepena* system could also gather rock after their workday was done to sell or attempt to refine on their own. Many Indians worked under a greater degree of coercion, however, whether because they were indebted (wages were sometimes advanced in kind at exorbitant prices rather than in specie) or under the *repartimiento* system. Repartimiento, a forced-labor draft system, was especially important in the Parral district: drawing laborers from missions as far as a hundred miles away for work stints that were not supposed to last more than six weeks. In theory, workers were supposed to be paid a wage, though in practice pay in overvalued clothes was more common than cash. Such exploitation echoed Spanish practices in New Mexico and elsewhere.[33]

Dressed in Spanish fashion, Indians from New Mexico may not have looked so visibly different from the other Natives dominating the town, but other signs may have marked them as "foreign" or "Apache": their scars or brands, their traditional tattoos. Such bodily markings distinguished them physically from the free Indian and mestizo laborers whom they worked alongside, just as skin color distinguished enslaved Africans. It is striking, for example, that Parral records almost always note whether a "black" or "mulatto" was free or enslaved, indicating the degree to which blackness was associated with slavery by the mid-seventeenth century.[34]

Back at home with Balderrama, Nicolás may have been well treated. Perhaps there was affection between them, perhaps Nicolás was regarded—as so many Spaniards claimed about their Indian slaves—like his own child. Whatever the nature of their relationship, it was not long lasting. Death records are not extant in the Parral parish for the 1650s, but he probably died within a few years of arrival, since he is not referenced in Balderrama's household in any later documents or in any other Parral archival records. Other possibilities exist: Balderrama may have sold or traded him as a part of his routine business, transporting Nicolás to a new life elsewhere in New Spain, or perhaps Nicolás escaped and returned to New Mexico, rejoining kin and spreading news of the experience of enslavement in exile.[35]

From Balderrama's standpoint, Nicolás was replaceable. By 1656 Balderrama had added additional Apaches to his home. We learn of a woman in his household named Juana because she christened her infant son "Carlos" in November of that year. Like Nicolás, Juana's life in diaspora in Parral was unrecognizable compared to what her life would have been in Apache country, particularly when it came to raising her child. There she would have given birth around other women, including skilled midwives who had proven success at bringing healthy babies into this world, and together they would have prayed and sung over the newborn.[36] She would have raised her son around an extended family as well, joking and laughing with other women as they prepared food and watched the children play in camp around them. Together they would have ensured that the proper ceremonies were conducted to bring up a healthy Apache boy, such as the haircutting ceremony they repeated in four successive spring seasons. For Juana and her child, Catholic ceremonies may have replaced these, or she may have combined them with Apache ways, at least behind closed doors.[37]

Juana's life illustrates how women's fates in diaspora differed from those of men in other ways as well. We might imagine household labor, which was typically women's work, to be less dangerous than mining or ore processing, but the dangers simply differed. Birthing children with a supposedly "unknown" father, for example, was quite common for Apache women in Parral. Who was Carlos's father, for instance? The priest listed him as unknown in the baptismal record, but it may have been another servant or slave, or it could have been Balderrama himself. The circumstances that gave rise to so many Indian and African slave women giving birth to children labeled mestizo or mulatto must be examined with the power dynamics between women like Juana and their masters in the foreground. How could a woman like Juana freely consent in a context in which her master possessed so much control over her life? If masters like Balderrama felt any affection for the women they raped, it is striking that they rarely acknowledged the children they fathered or freed them from lives of labor.[38]

Carlos may have been Juana's first child, or she may also have had other children who had remained behind in her native land. Undoubtedly, any mother separated from her children would have thought of them as she tended her master's home. While Balderrama's estate later bustled with his own children and other servants and slaves, in this period Juana was largely alone. Perhaps she received aid or companionship from the godparent she or Balderrama had chosen for Carlos: María, the black slave of one of her master's neighbors. As in the case of Nicolás, the close connections between Apaches and enslaved Africans illustrate the new social ties—some biological, some not—that helped make survival possible among people in diaspora.[39]

Balderrama's own household soon grew—with a wife and children and new Apaches displaced from their kin to serve his. By the spring of 1664, Balderrama had married a woman named Josepha Ramires, who gave birth to a girl they named María. In addition to caring for their own children, Apache women in Balderrama's home probably cared for his children as well. The baptism of another Indian woman from New Mexico, Phelipa, several months later suggests that she may have been purchased specifically to help care for María.[40] In the next five years, Josepha gave birth to two more girls and two boys, and the household incorporated at least five more Apache Indian women during this same period. It is unclear when Juana died, but perhaps she found some solace, some camaraderie in these other women's presence, even if none of them had chosen to live with Balderrama in the first place.[41]

The growth of Balderrama's household and his choice of Apaches to serve it coincided with broader shifts in Native-Spanish relations in New Mexico and, in turn, in the Apache slave trade to Parral. Between 1631 and 1665, only 115 Apaches and Indians described as "from New Mexico" were baptized in the district. This number underrepresents the actual number brought to Parral as referenced in correspondence or other records. Nonetheless, as a measure of the volume of the trade, the relatively low number of baptisms in Parral during this period suggests that most Indians enslaved in campaigns launched from New Mexico or purchased via trade with other Indians before 1665 were kept in New Mexico and put to work there in individual households, farms and ranches, missions and churches, textile factories, and the Palace of the Governors. This was about to change, because more than seven hundred Apaches and "Indians from New Mexico" appeared in the Parral parish registers in the next fifteen years alone.[42]

Diaspora and Emancipation

One key impediment to the establishment of a large-scale slave trade between New Mexico and New Spain warrants further consideration. Residents and officials took the illegality of Indian slavery seriously enough that the business could be quite risky. Recall the experiences of Governor Mendizábal and Governor Peñalosa of New Mexico considered in Chapter 1. The *audiencia* of Guadalajara thwarted their efforts to sell Apache slaves in Parral and Sonora and authorized masters to recover purchase prices from the merchants involved. When the merchants complained, they received permission to deduct the labor the masters had already received from the Indian slaves from the costs, though they did not succeed in avoiding repayment entirely. Although they warned governors that masters were not actually freeing all of the Indians in question, at least some were.[43] The descriptive titles extant in the Parral archives lend a human face to the enslaved, but they also sometimes note that slaves were freed as a result of judicial decrees against slavery.

Such was the case for Sebastián, an Apache slave "rescued" from captivity among other Indians, who had big eyes and an angular face marked by smallpox. At the time of his initial sale in Parral, he had not yet been baptized and was about seven years old. A note on his title extant in the Parral archives attests to his emancipation in Parral on May 28, 1660. The title of another Apache named Margarita describes her as a strong-bodied Indian woman about twenty-four years old, with a mole and a scar on the left side of her face; it also notes that she was freed the same day as Sebastián.[44]

These were not isolated cases. Orders to manifest and emancipate all Indians illegally enslaved in Parral occurred regularly: in 1648, 1659, 1660, 1671, and 1679. The mere fact that emancipation orders had to be repeated illustrates the persistence of Indian enslavement, but these efforts did have an impact. Officials thwarted several shipments of Apaches during the 1650s and 1660s and even jailed and fined the merchants involved. Don Juan Manso tried to bribe an official in Sonora to allow him to sell Apache slaves there, but the bribe was refused. When the Spanish campaign against Indian and Asian slavery reached a new empire-wide scale in the early 1670s, Parral residents brought forward 202 Apache Indians who were declared free.[45] When the governor caught wind that a shipment of Apaches the following year might have been sold as slaves, he ordered them brought forward to be reminded they were free as well. These twenty Apaches, ranging in age from five to twenty-eight, were told in Spanish that they were free persons without any charge of slavery. Perhaps some of them did not understand what was going on, but certainly that was not the case for all of them, because the governor claimed he had confirmed that they spoke Spanish. Given what we know about the spread of information in other slave societies, it seems highly implausible that slaves in Parral would not have discussed emancipation campaigns or circulated news of them to each other.[46]

It is striking that the numbers of Apache captives flowing into the Parral district reached a new high amid these efforts. Between 1666 and 1680, nearly four hundred baptisms of Apaches and other Indians from New Mexico occurred in Parral. Burial records suggest that this number should be viewed as an indication of an increased volume of traffic rather than as a comprehensive census of arrivals. It was common, for example, for Apaches to appear in the burial records with notes that they had only been baptized in the moments before death "out of necessity," indicating that they were relatively recent arrivals, had not been baptized previously, and were not among those Apaches appearing in the baptismal registers. More than three hundred burials of Apaches and "Indians from New Mexico" were noted during this

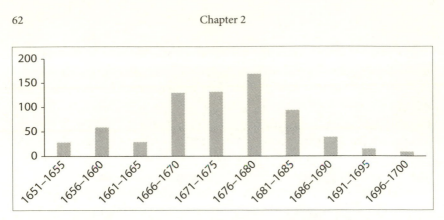

Figure 4. Baptisms of "Apaches" or "Indians from New Mexico" in Parral.

fifteen-year period alone. Given the costs of burial—seven or eight pesos—
there were probably others who were not granted Christian burial and thus
did not appear in Parral parish records at all.[47]

Why did New Mexico residents continue to bring Apache captives to the
district when the commercial prospects of the trade had worsened? Without
a doubt, New Mexico officials and residents preferred to profit if they could
by attempting to sell Apaches in the Parral district, and they still sometimes
succeeded. This was most evident in the ranching industry. In the 1670s, the
bishop of Durango ordered an investigation into the purchase of Indian slaves
by ranchers in Nueva Vizcaya. New Mexico residents were bringing Apaches
slaves to ranches in Northern New Spain, trading them for livestock, and
returning north with their newly acquired herds. The church taxed livestock
but not illegally enslaved Indians. Concerned that church tithes were dwin-
dling as result, the bishop interviewed merchants and slave traders in order
to understand whether Indian slavery was to blame for diminishing tithes.
What he discovered, notes the historian Andrés Reséndez, is that "Indians
amounted to a tax shelter." The bishop believed the amount of sheltered tax
revenue was enough to explain a decline in the tithes of the bishopric.[48]

Merchants and traders were not always able to circumvent Spanish anti-
slavery decrees, however, and they sometimes simply left groups of Apaches
behind. In 1662, for example, when the Nueva Vizcaya governor caught wind
of 120 Indian slaves arriving soon from Parral, he posted notices reminding
residents that no Indians could be bought or sold. When the shipment arrived,
the governor had the Indian slaves manifested in the center of Parral, and he
informed them "they were free to go wherever they wished and could not be
bought or sold by anyone."[49] When another shipment was interrupted a few
years later, the New Mexico resident involved, Captain Alonso García, argued

that he was not in fact selling the Indians in question; rather, he claimed that he had been commissioned by the governor and various friars to "extract" the Apache captives in question and "entrust them" to live with nice families and become Christians. He alleged that on the journey he had "told the Indians repeatedly that they were free, and they were happy to be traveling with him." The larger investigation painted a more complicated picture, because other testimony revealed that García had bartered with potential masters and had suggested they give him something in exchange for receiving an Indian, at least to cover transportation costs. Although these Indians "were not slaves," he told them, perhaps a piece of furniture or two fine hats, for example, might be a nice token of appreciation.[50]

Parral officials saw through García's charade, and he was ordered to return any payments he had received. The Indians in question were brought before Parral officials and told they were free, and García was fined court costs and warned that if he tried to sell Natives again he would be sentenced to six years of hard labor in the Philippines. It is striking, however, that the basic argument he and other contemporaries were making is one that was not without precedent and would gain even greater acceptance in the future: the idea that "extracting" heathen Indians for the purposes of their Christianization elsewhere did not circumvent royal decrees as long as those transporting them were not profiting from their sale. After all, the policy of forcibly transferring Indians to work for the public good had long been central to the repartimiento and encomienda labor draft and tribute systems. Even as these systems were gradually abolished, the basic justifications underpinning them endured.[51]

The weight of the evidence suggests that by the 1660s, many Indians from New Mexico arriving in the Parral district were not being sold as slaves. The fact that only a handful of Indians are described as slaves in parish records during this period could be explained as intentional concealment on the part of priests, but other data suggests this was not always the case. Extant financial records from mining enterprises and ranching operations indicate Apache laborers being paid wages, either because masters had taken seriously the emancipation decrees and warnings that illegally enslaving Indians would be met with significant fines, or perhaps because they had never viewed the Indians they had acquired arriving in shipments from New Mexico as slaves in the first place. At Felipe Catalán's silver refinery, for example, Apache laborers were paid between four and ten pesos per month. They worked as pickmen, ore carriers, and ore millers. At least some Apache ranch hands, meanwhile, earned about six pesos monthly—hardly high wages but not less than the free mulatto, Indian, or mestizo ranch hands they worked alongside.

The fact that Apaches were sometimes buried out of a charity and described as having "served no one," or alternatively, described as *vecinos* (citizens of town), indicates a range of experiences distinct from slavery, though not necessarily always a change for the better.[52]

The war in New Mexico that helped fuel economic decline and famine helps to explain why the Apache diaspora peaked despite emancipation campaigns. For example, Apache and Navajo warfare exacerbated the drought-induced famine that led to the abandonment of many pueblos. More than eleven hundred Pueblo families relocated from the lower Rio Grande region of New Mexico during the early 1670s, amid complaints of Apache attacks. While Spaniards and their Pueblo allies could still mobilize a response to such attacks and took large numbers of captives, there was a limit on how many captives New Mexico households, farms, missions, and ranches could absorb.

Spaniards were learning how risky it could be to enslave people near their own homelands. While masters could try to secure their captives behind locked doors, they could not prevent their slaves' kin in nearby homelands from attacking Spanish and Pueblo settlements, driving away their horse and sheep herds, and recovering their captive kin in the process. Given that Apaches who were freed in 1673 already spoke Spanish and had Christian names after only two months in Parral district, it is likely that they had spent time in New Mexico before their captors decided to export them out of concerns that they could not keep them secure or simply because they could no longer feed them.[53]

Whatever the motivations and hopes of New Mexico residents in exporting Native captives, it is not difficult to explain why Spaniards in the Parral district proved willing to accept the large numbers of them arriving in the district in the 1660s and 1670s. From the standpoint of potential masters in Parral, emancipation campaigns were not particularly problematic if it meant they paid little or nothing to receive an Apache captive or that they could recover the original purchase price of those they had purchased, as courts allowed. Even in cases where masters still paid for Apaches clandestinely, they almost certainly would have used the public controversy in haggling for a better price, if past precedent is any indication.[54]

Ultimately, many masters seem to have cared little whether an Apache was deemed a servant instead of a slave, as long as "pay" could be counted as the room, board, and clothing that they would have provided otherwise. In theory, greater restrictions existed on the treatment of servants versus slaves: the number of hours they could work, for example. Free Indian workers at mining enterprises were supposed to work only from sunrise until three or four in the afternoon, while slaves were to continue to work until sunset.

But officials rarely policed such matters or intervened in individual masters' household affairs.[55]

Emancipation decrees also often provided loopholes for the continued exploitation of Native captives: especially age. While an emancipated twenty-four-year-old adult might plausibly live on his own or travel elsewhere, this was not likely for a six- or seven-year-old. The 1671 royal order, for example, stated that freed slaves under fourteen could be kept in families and "be educated and well treated." They could go unpaid for at least five years, at which point they should be manifested to officials again so they could check in on them. This element of the decree may help to explain why the number of child baptisms in Parral spiked the following year, as masters brought young Apaches out of the shadows and registered them under new conditions of temporary enslavement. Ironically, the Spanish campaign against Indian slavery across the empire provided official legal sanction to the previously informally sanctioned practice of forced Indian child labor.[56]

One thing remained constant for Apaches, whether they were traded for livestock, furniture, or pesos; were freed and paid wages; or were simply left in town—they remained exiled from kin and homeland. This is noteworthy in this particular context, because the Spanish crown did mandate in other contexts that freed slaves be returned to their native lands. This was unthinkable to Spaniards in New Mexico, however, not only given the cost and logistical difficulties involved but also because they were at war with Apaches there.

In Spaniards' minds, slavery and profit were associated. The idea that people might be forced to move to labor but were not slaves was well established. This was the basic premise of institutions like repartimiento and encomienda, in which Native people were mandated to move long distances to work temporarily in order to serve the public good. In this context, colonial agents extended that rationale further in pursuit of the idea that enslavement and "permanent exile in order to work" were distinct categories. In doing so they presaged the actions of other imperial officials and colonists in the decades and centuries to come. The meaning of this rhetorical distinction for displaced Apaches' lives, however, warrants closer examination.[57]

Apache Life and Death in Parral at the Height of the Diaspora

Balderrama's household evokes broader trends in Apache experiences in Parral in the 1660s and beyond. Served by at least four Apaches in the 1650s and early 1660s, at least one of whom Balderrama described as a slave, after

1666 at least fourteen more "servants" would live and, in some cases, die on his estate. The estate consisted of his store, several houses, and a corral on the outskirts of Parral. The main house was decorated with a bust of Saint Nicolás and six painted hides from New Mexico, and furnished relatively modestly with a table and chairs, beds and mattresses, and his writing desks. His wealth was not insignificant, about ten thousand pesos total, but neither did it place him among the wealthiest class of Parral residents. Notably, in a 1672 inventory of his possessions conducted after the most recent announcement of emancipation, he did not list his Apaches as possessions, suggesting either that he in fact viewed them as free servants or that he simply knew enough to conceal his views of their status in public documents.[58]

Balderrama's household reflects other characteristics of Apaches' experiences in Parral as well: especially the ways in which Indigenous and African diasporas intersected here, as in other contexts in the Americas and Caribbean. By the 1670s, the population of Indians from New Mexico and the Great Plains roughly equaled the sizeable enslaved African population of about a thousand. While Balderrama initially may have acquired Apaches due to their lower cost, the success of his store had also enabled him to purchase four enslaved Africans: a black slave woman named Ignacia and her daughter, a little mulatto girl, who cost him 600 pesos; a mulatto woman named Nicolása, who cost him 430 pesos; and a black woman named Elena, for whom he had paid 450 pesos. Within Balderrama's estate, it was Elena who served as an overseer of sorts, directing the other servants and slaves to their tasks and taking precautions to prevent escapes. If servants and slaves in Parral were anything like those elsewhere, they were aware of their status, and perhaps even their value. The purchase price may have served as a source of pride for a woman like Elena, something she drew upon to distinguish herself from the Indians whom she helped her master manage and whom he had purchased for far less than Elena, if he had paid for them at all.[59]

One woman whom Elena managed and cared for was the Apache woman whose story began this chapter: Francisca, whom Balderrama acquired around 1670, when shipments of Apache captives from New Mexico to Parral were becoming more regular than ever. Francisca entered Balderrama's household around the time that his first wife died, perhaps during childbirth with their last child, Antonio, born in September 1670. Perhaps, as in the past, Francisca had been acquired to help with the infant, because she was baptized only weeks before. The priest noted that Francisca was an Apache woman of about thirty years old and born to non-Catholic parents in New Mexico. Francisca demonstrated no knowledge of Catholicism, but the priest gave special permission to baptize her because she was "sick and swollen." Serving as her godmother was a woman named María de Luxa, whom Balderrama would marry soon after his first wife's death and who would become Francisca's mistress.[60]

What we know about Francisca's life during her limited time in Parral owes in large part to the way she ended it. It is impossible to know for certain why she eventually decided to commit suicide in a corral, but the testimony the Parral magistrate gathered as a result of it in March 1671 tells us much about life in this household and offers clues. A mulatto slave named Nicolása explained that the past night, "like many nights before," Elena—the black slave and household manager—had chained her to a pole in the kitchen, where she slept next to Francisca and two other Apaches, named Magdalena and Mariquita. They fell asleep, but Francisca was not feeling well, and before dawn she had left the other women. In the morning, upon rising, Elena unchained Nicolása and she began to prepare chocolate for her masters as usual. Going to give a little stew to Francisca, she finally found her dead in the corral. Asked if her masters had whipped her and how they treated their servants, whether slave or free, she noted that she was chained because she had tried to escape recently after being whipped. Her master and mistress lashed her and the other servants frequently, "both the Apaches and the blacks." Mariquita similarly noted that she had been enclosed in the kitchen with the other servants the night before and explained that her mistress lashed all of them frequently, but she and the master had not lashed Francisca the night before because she was sick. She also explained that an Indian woman named Jazinta had died from an especially severe whipping several years before.[61]

This grim look inside Balderrama's home echoes evidence from elsewhere that the experience of many Apaches in Parral belied the language of kinship with which Spaniards described the Indians they were "raising up" as if they were their own children. It illustrates how much power masters could exercise over supposedly free Indians like Francisca, whose lived experience seems to have differed little from that of her legally enslaved counterparts. They slept in the same place, did the same work, and suffered the same punishments.

It also reveals that for many Apaches, exile to Parral was a "sentence of death" rather than an act of mercy—as the Spaniards claimed—whatever their informally or formally sanctioned statuses. If suicides like Francisca's were rare, hundreds of Apaches died because of disease, starvation, or workplace dangers. Even in the seemingly less harsh environment of a Spaniard's estate, death was commonplace. Of the eighteen Apache Indians associated with Balderrama's household in Parral records, eight are known only through

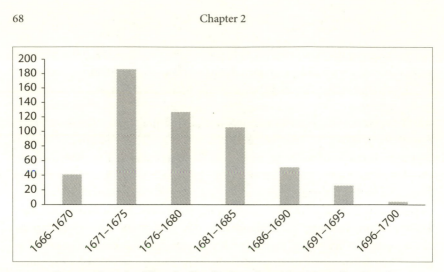

Figure 5. Burials of "Apaches" or "Indians from New Mexico" in Parral.

their death records. In the two cases for this household where both baptism and death records are extant, an admittedly small sample, death occurred within a year of baptism.[62]

Why did so many Apaches die in Parral? Some ended up in settings with dangerous work conditions that did not depend on the idiosyncrasies of their masters, as noted above. When Juan Fernández de Carrión acquired five or six Indian captives from the plains in 1667, for example, three had died within four years, probably because of the effects of mercury poisoning, which is absorbed through the skin, debilitates the joints, and degrades the kidneys and other internal organs. The choice of Apache or Plains Indians for dangerous tasks may have reflected their low or even free cost, providing a sense that they were essentially disposable. This was certainly true for Apaches convicted of crimes, who were put to the most difficult and dangerous tasks.[63]

For Apaches crowded in the servants' quarters of mining or ranching haciendas where disease spread easily, sickness could be equally as deadly as mercury. To be sure, Apaches were not the only group affected by periodic plagues during the 1660s and 1670s, but they were certainly well represented among the victims. A few specific examples illustrate the point, the fragmentary details of their burial records hinting at the individuals and families affected: María, the Apache wife of Manuel, a black slave, who had no belongings or will; Lucia, the Apache wife of Nicolás, a black slave, who had not even been baptized because she died so suddenly; Isabel, an Apache Indian woman who was not able to confess before she died because "she did not know how";

Lorenzo, an Apache man who was married but "no one knew who his wife was"; Antonia, "who did not serve anyone" and was buried out of charity.[64]

Apache servants and slaves confronted the constraints and injustices of their world in varied ways, like exploited people elsewhere. They attempted and sometimes succeeded in escaping, a fact that may have led New Mexico governors to order that they be taken "beyond Parral." Some turned to petty crime, banding with other servants and slaves to steal ore or livestock. In December 1672, for example, an Apache employee of Francisco Lima named Francisco, alias El Tortuga (the tortoise), came to the attention of Parral officials because of his involvement in a gang of thieves that included another Apache and a mulatto. He confessed to having broken into a number of houses and stolen jewelry, clothing, shoes, a rosary, and more. He was sentenced to two hundred lashes, public embarrassment by having his crimes called out, and six years of hard labor in chains in an ore-processing plant, a sentence he probably would not have survived. Somehow, he managed to break his chains and escape before he was ultimately apprehended for new thefts and sentenced to public execution. In December 1673, he was taken from his jail cell to the town gallows and hanged before a crowd of witnesses. In his early thirties at the time, Francisco died in exile hundreds of miles from the Apache camp where he had been born.[65]

Other servants and slaves responded to their circumstances by attacking their masters directly, rather than their property. In April 1670, two Apache women named Angelina and María attacked their mistress and her daughter and then fled the ranch where they worked in the Parral district. Although their mistress had survived, the daughter had died of her wounds. Their appointed attorney mounted a vigorous defense. While he did not deny that the women had committed the crime, he pleaded for consideration of mitigating circumstances in the sentencing process. These were two Apache women who spoke little Spanish, had not even been baptized, and had been subjected to illegal enslavement under harsh conditions. Surely their actions should be considered as "resistance," he argued, as an effort to escape the harsh conditions that they should not have been subjected to in the first place. This mistreatment, he added, was further illustrated by the fact that they were practically naked when they were apprehended.[66]

Appeals to sympathy and wrongs done to the women do not seem to have swayed the judge in this case, given the severity of their crime. He sentenced the women to hard labor in chains for the rest of their lives, though the court did note that they should be allowed to be taught the Catholic doctrines while working out their sentences. Sentences related to Apache crimes in

Parral illustrate the various means of labor coercion available in seventeenth-century Spanish colonial society: captured in war or ransomed from enslavement among other Indians, María and Angelina's attempt to escape slavery ultimately led them to face lifelong convict labor. Elsewhere in North America, crimes were also used as a means to extract unpaid labor from Natives originally captured and put to work under other terms.[67]

Such dramatic acts were probably atypical, however. Most Apaches demonstrated what Vincent Brown has termed a "politics of survival." If some Apaches sought to escape or exact revenge, others focused on building relationships that might provide them with some means of protection and support in a world in which their masters had inordinate power, even in settings where the Apaches were supposedly free or even paid a wage. Balderrama's household illustrates as much. At the most basic level, the women described concern for each other, such as small acts of affection or kindness when they were sick. If their own ability to travel was restricted, in part because they were women, their masters may have allowed their godparents to look in on them. When travel was allowed, it involved trips together to Mass or confession, which they also sometimes used as opportunities to escape, hence their master's concern for security. The aim of escape might be to return to a homeland hundreds of miles to the north or simply to find sanctuary in a friend or relative's house, a reprieve from life in their master's home, as had been true for the servants and slaves in Santa Fe discussed in Chapter 1.[68]

These kinds of everyday activities generated few of the descriptive records created by suicides, homicides, or thefts. Yet the social world of Apaches in Parral is not entirely elusive. Archival records make clear some of the ways in which Natives responded to the dilemma of their displacement—their dislocation from their community of birth and the network of support it represented. Baptismal records indicate godparents and co-parents (*compadres*), marriage records indicate unions celebrated between Apaches and others in front of witnesses, and even death records reference surviving spouses. In fact, approximately one in five Apaches is described as married in burial records, and many more likely had relationships unsanctioned by the church. Such relationships not only helped make life bearable emotionally but also could literally mean the difference between survival and death in a context in which food was not always abundant and sickness threatened. Reproductive relationships also helped ensure that an Apache community endured for years to come, even when shipments of new arrivals were temporarily halted in the 1680s.[69]

In his seminal study of New Mexico, James Brooks describes the important role that godparenting and co-parenting played in creating kinship ties between captives and captors. In the Catholic tradition, the selection of a godparent had two implications. First, a godmother or godfather made commitments to look after their godchild, provide moral guidance, and ensure their religious instruction. At the same time, a godparent also created a relationship of *compadrazgo*, or co-parenting, between biological parents and godparents, who through their care for the child in question also cemented relationships of mutual aid and obligation with each other. Brooks finds that masters or their relatives often served as godparents for their Indian captives, and the resulting bonds of affection and kinship could undermine the fixity of Indian slavery as an institution. Just as occurred in many Indigenous societies, slave status might be gradually shed as captives became kin.[70]

While masters in Parral undoubtedly fathered children birthed by Apache women, kinship ties acknowledged through or created by godparenthood appear to have been less common than in New Mexico, at least in the seventeenth century. Only about 10 percent of godparents appearing in entries related to Indians originally from New Mexico are described as the masters of the servants in question or their relatives. More than half of all godparents are described as black, mulatto, Indian, or mestizo servants or slaves. Because priests in the Parral district did not reliably include racial or ethnic designations for godparents, data is missing for the remaining one in three godparents, though some of these are also described as "servants," and thus we should not assume that they were necessarily "Spanish" or of higher status than their godchild.[71]

What does it mean that so many godparents were servants and slaves? Rather than linking master and servant, godparent and co-parenting traditions interlinked a community of servants and slaves in Parral, whether on small estates like Balderrama's, on large haciendas, or at mining enterprises. Newly arrived Apaches probably did not choose their own godparents, but socially sanctioned ties between Apaches and other servants and slaves, including other Indians and enslaved Africans, helped shape the creation of "chosen" families in Parral subsequently, forging networks of kinship and mutual support that helped individuals get by in a new, foreign setting.[72]

Marriages are particularly illustrative of the relationships Apaches drew upon to adapt to life in Parral, especially given that they are more likely to reflect the choice of the parties involved. The historian Chantal Cramaussel has argued that marriages may have been a tool of coercion: by fronting the cost, which was around nine pesos, masters further put their workers, whether paid or unpaid, into their debt. Indeed, as we will see in Chapter 3, masters sometimes advanced wedding costs to Apaches in exchange for their

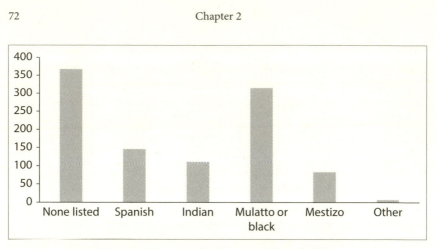

Figure 6. Ethnicity of godparents of "Apaches" or
"Indians from New Mexico" in Parral, 1640–1700.

labor. From the master's perspective, marriages may also have been seen as
a means of discouraging escape. Allowing enslaved Africans or Natives to
form families made them less likely to risk abandoning these ties to head
back north.[73] Yet these social connections were not solely directed by masters
nor were they only tools of control. As Rachel Sarah O'Toole has observed
in the case of colonial Peru, kinship might be best viewed as a verb rather
than a noun, a reflection of action and decision-making rather than a simple
description of biological reality. That Apache and other Native captives from
New Mexico were most likely to marry each other, and their next mostly
likely marriage partner was black or mulatto, reveals how Apaches adapted to
life in diaspora in part by connecting with other exploited peoples. For black
and mulatto partners, such relationships also perhaps provided additional
security. By marrying an Apache, a Native person, one could hope that one's
children might be recognized as free persons based on Indigenous ancestry,
rather than as slaves.[74]

    While I wish marriage records were even more descriptive, they at least
provide momentary glimpses of a social world created for survival in Parral.
Such was the case when Luis, a black slave, married an Apache slave named
Luiza with their enslaved African godparents and other witnesses present in
December 1659; or when Joan de Aguierra, a mulatto slave, married María,
an Apache servant, with two Indian godparents witnessing, in May 1676; or
when an Apache Indian widow named Thomasa de la Cruz married Phelipe
del Santiago, an Apache Indian servant of the local parish, with many people
present in September 1675. Catholic Church records, of course, only go so

far. As the historian James Sweet has argued in the case of the African diaspora, we should be attuned to the existence of other relationships that may not have received official sanction.[75]

Sometimes marriages, like baptisms, occurred immediately before death, opening a window onto the particular concerns of the powerful in this Catholic community—and also onto the lives of the virtually powerless. During 1668, an Indian woman from New Mexico named Francisca de la Cruz had become pregnant. The father was Sebastián de Nungaras, a mulatto mineworker in town. By December, the pregnancy had ended in the worst way possible: near full term, the baby had perished in the womb, and the mother was near death as well. With their masters present, Francisca and Sebastián were married, perhaps to absolve, or at least mitigate, their illicit relationship before Francisca died. What had the nature of their relationship been, however? Had they been a couple for long? Had they simply not been able to afford the costs of Catholic marriage? Or had the relationship been short-lived, and the marriage on Francisca's deathbed a concern of their masters and not their own? Unfortunately, the priest's terse burial record entry does not provide any further commentary that might answer such questions.[76]

Balderrama's household reflects well the broader social ties that linked the Apache and African diasporas in Parral, as well as the joys and sorrows of community life. In May 1676, two of his Apache servants—Miguel de la Cruz and Antonia Josefa—married each other. Two free mulattos served as witnesses. Soon Antonia became pregnant and gave birth to a son, named Simón, the following year. By October of that year, the infant's health worsened, and he was buried on the thirty-first of that month. The couple soon had another child, Joan, who was christened in November 1679. His godparents, who promised to look after his well-being, were two Apache servants of the priest: Miguel and Joana de la Cruz.

Past historians have examined such evidence through the lens of "Hispanicization," arguing that Apache captives gradually "assimilated" into colonial Spanish society and "became Catholics." Apache cultures had their own traditions of sponsorship at coming-of-age events and marriages, however, that would not simply have been cast aside by all upon their coming to Parral. The frequent arrival of newly captured Natives from New Mexico throughout this period would have also provided a further reminder of past traditions and language. As the population of displaced Natives in Parral grew, they were not simply "deracinated" and Hispanicized, but were increasingly a diasporic community in which what it meant to become "Apache" reflected the interplay of previous knowledge and interaction with neighbors, including the large population of African descent with which Apaches married, made friends, escaped, attended Mass, or looted the masters' homes.[77]

From the Apache War for Independence to the Great Southwestern Revolt

Let us take Spaniards at their word for a moment and accept that by the 1670s, most Apaches in the community were not slaves. Let us extrapolate from people like Felipe Catalán that they were not alone on their estates in paying Apache laborers wages. Let us assume that they mourned together the men, women, and children who did not survive for long. Whatever shifts occurred in Spanish treatment of Apache captives, whatever happiness Apaches found in their lives and social interactions with each other and others in Parral, this was no consolation to the communities from which these people had been uprooted in the first place. Apache groups demonstrated as much in their repeated attacks beginning in the late 1660s on Spanish ranches and wagon trains and on the Pueblo communities that had served as Spanish allies in captive-taking expeditions. The decision of Apaches to pursue war had strained New Mexico society, but it did not cause the Spanish and Puebloans to turn away from retaliation or captive taking.[78]

The people most affected by the Apache campaigns were not Spaniards but Puebloans: more than 300 Puebloans were killed in them in the first half of 1669 alone. This was not illogical, given that virtually all "Spanish" slaving expeditions relied upon hundreds of Pueblo Indian allies. In their efforts against Spanish communities, it was the technologies that had led their people into exile that were the most targeted: wagon trains and horses in particular. As one Apache leader explained, the horse was "the principal lever of warfare against them," and they hoped that by targeting Spanish and Puebloan herds they could be "left in freedom, like their ancestors, in ancient times."[79]

The Apache strategies of war did not produce "freedom," however, at least not in the late 1660s and 1670s. Although they took large numbers of horses and other livestock—straining New Mexico's economy and the ranchers' livelihood—Spaniards replaced their losses by transporting captives they took in reprisal campaigns to sell at ranches in Nueva Vizcaya to exchange for more horses and livestock. The Apache war for independence had not succeeded in ending the capture and exile of their kin but in some ways had fueled it, through a cycle of violence and loss that had affected all groups in New Mexico and surrounding Native societies.[80]

Pueblo Indian communities, meanwhile, faced their own challenges. Pueblo groups had multiple grievances that ultimately made a pan-Indian rebellion against the Spanish possible: labor exploitation, Spanish crackdowns on religious practices, the sentencing of those alleged of witchcraft to terms of temporary slavery, Apache and Navajo attacks, and cycles of drought and famine. All these factors helped fuel anti-Spanish sentiment and generated a climate in which a nativist message centering on a return to the old ways as a means of restoring prosperity gained adherents.[81]

By the late 1670s, Apaches likely sensed an opportunity as well. The Spanish export of their kin as captives may have in part been designed to dissuade them from war and continued attacks (and to secure captives from repatriation). As captives were shipped into New Spain year after year, however, Apache communities looked for a new approach. While old alliances with Pueblo communities had broken, they had not broken beyond repair. When Pueblo groups approached Apaches for aid, some proved willing to set aside current animosities and unite at least temporarily in the cause of freeing themselves from Spanish oppression.[82]

The events of August 1680 are legendary. Pueblo leaders circulated knotted cords that they untied day after day as a counting aid to ensure their uprising was coordinated. At the height of their siege, nearly two thousand Indians surrounded Santa Fe. By late September 1680, the Natives had eliminated Spaniards from New Mexico, killed over four hundred of its twenty-five hundred Hispanic residents, and destroyed nearly every Spanish building. Fleeing New Mexicans marveled at how the Pueblos had broken up and burned images of Christ, the Virgin Mary, and "everything pertaining to Christianity."[83]

Less commonly discussed is the Apache role in the revolt, which shocked Spanish observers. Less than a year after the revolt, as Spaniards were still struggling to understand what had happened, Fray Francisco de Ayeta wrote about the assumptions that had led him and others to falsely believe their reentry into New Mexico would be easy. First and foremost, they believed that Apaches would destroy Puebloans in their absence and that the survivors would welcome them back to protect them, "because of [the Apache] being both braver and incomparably more numerous." What they had actually found was Pueblo and Apache communities living at peace, as they often had in old times. The Apache and Pueblo groups had not forgotten earlier modes of interaction, despite the animosities fueled by the slave trade.[84]

Particular Apache groups renewed alliances with and aided Puebloans in the events of 1680 partly in the hopes of ending their victimization in the slave trade and recovering kin. This motivation is made clear by testimony taken by the Spanish in the hopes of understanding the causes of the rebellion, which notes the role that Spanish slaving played in explaining Apache-Pueblo cooperation in particular. One of the first Spaniards whom the rebellious Indians complained about was Francisco Javier, the secretary of government and war in New Mexico. As they noted, he had guaranteed safe conduct to a band of Plains Apaches at Pecos, only to capture them and distribute them among his friends. Echoing their past responses to such Spanish duplicity toward their allies, residents of Pecos Pueblo had responded with outrage. As they explained, Francis Javier was "the reason they [Pecos Pueblo] had risen."[85]

Among the most striking references in the Spanish investigations is the testimony of one Pueblo Indian who parlayed with the Spanish governor Antonio Otermín after the revolt. The Puebloan laid out the terms for peace, if the Spaniards were willing to accept them. Among these terms was included a demand that "all the Apache men and women whom the Spaniards had captured in war be turned over to them, inasmuch as some Apache who were among them were asking for them." Just like the Puebloans, Apaches sought a return to the "old ways," when they had benefited from relations of mutual aid with individual Puebloans and captive taking was small scale. Spanish slaving should be seen as a key cause of the Apache and Navajo war for independence that predated the Pueblo Revolt, initially contributed to Pueblo destitution, and ultimately led to their cooperation with Pueblo rebels in the most successful uprising in North American history. For more than a decade, Spanish New Mexicans would be refugees in El Paso and Nueva Vizcaya.[86]

*   *   *

The Pueblo (and Apache) Revolt disrupted trade relations between New Mexico and New Spain and ended the transport of Apache captives to Parral for a decade. Despite Apache requests, the Spanish made no effort to return their men and women to them in order to make peace, though a number had escaped on their own, fleeing back to their people amid the rebellion or being taken captive by new Native captors.[87] In the Parral district, their presence nonetheless endured, primarily because of the relationships Apaches had forged in the years before with their fellow servants and slaves and with each other. Most Apaches baptized in the district after 1680 were now described as the children of existing residents, indicating that the flow of newcomers had halted. Reflecting the increased number of Apaches who had married, some were described as legitimate births, often to Apache families or Apache-black families, rather than to women with no father named. Such was the case for a girl named Joana baptized in November 1681, the legitimate daughter of an enslaved African named Agustín de la Cruz and his Apache wife, Phelipa de Jesus. Her godfather was an Apache man named Phelipe de la Rocha. The same was true for a boy named Juan, baptized in July 1684, the legitimate son of an Apache couple named Juan and Juana de la Cruz. His godparents were an Apache couple named Juan Catalán and Isabel de Amaia.[88]

After the Pueblo Revolt ignited broader Indian rebellions across Northern New Spain, the Spaniards tended to forget past claims that slavery led to Indian revolts. The anti-slavery sentiment embodied by repeated emancipation decrees appears to have waned, though it had never been universal locally. In 1688, for example, the governor of Nueva Vizcaya suggested than any Indian rebels captured be sentenced to ten years of enslavement. He knew that this was against royal decrees but argued that it was "necessary" and just given the acts Indians had been involved in. The Spanish Crown concurred, authorizing more than four hundred Native rebels to be sentenced to ten-year terms of unpaid labor. One historian has argued that this should be viewed as entirely distinct from slavery, given that such Indians "could absolutely not be sold on the slave market, or taken out of New Mexico," nor were they the legal property of their masters. Yet baptismal records suggest this view lends too much weight to legal formalities, as hundreds of Apaches ended up in Nueva Vizcaya, Sonora, and elsewhere in the coming decades. Amid much continuity, the eighteenth century would also bring changes in the Apache experiences of enslavement and diaspora, as newly powerful Indigenous captors carried Apaches in new directions and as new colonial settlements in New France proved willing buyers for Apache slaves.[89]

Did Nicolás Balderrama discuss the shock of the Pueblo Revolt with his wife María or his children? Did they, like others, rightfully fear that local Indigenous groups might join together and threaten the "total loss" of Nueva Vizcaya? I can say only that Balderrama lived through these tumultuous times. While I have not located a death record for Nicolás Balderrama, in 1682 his wife gave birth to the last of their children, Chatarina. María must have been substantially younger than her husband, because he was now sixty-seven years old.[90]

As their master aged, Apaches in his household carried on as well, reflecting broader trends within the community at large. Undoubtedly, they would have responded differently to the news flooding into Parral of the loss of

Spanish New Mexico. Whatever their awareness of current events, the Apache family of Miguel and Josefa had their own joys and challenges to mark and mourn. They christened their third son, Gregorio, in May 1683 but had already buried him by November. Two years later, the couple had yet another son, Joseph, whose godparents at his christening included a prominent Parral resident. This was probably a good day, a happy moment in lives where death had stalked.[91]

CHAPTER 3

"Some Place to Live in Safety"

Apaches were probably not surprised to see Diego de Vargas lead an expedition north into Pueblo country in 1692. The Spanish had made entrées into New Mexico several times since their removal in 1680, and Natives probably anticipated that they would come back again. Some Apaches had encountered Vargas and his men while on trading expeditions, whereas others heard the news secondhand from Pueblo allies. Their reactions undoubtedly differed from that of the viceroy of New Spain. In Mexico City, bells were rung to commemorate the restoration of "an entire realm . . . without wasting a single ounce of powder . . . or costing the Royal treasury a single [coin]." The ease with which Vargas had supposedly brought more than twenty pueblos back under Spanish rule suggests that some of them had simply placated the Spanish, pledging their obedience while planning their next moves. When Vargas returned with eight hundred colonists, priests, and soldiers the following year, they were met with widespread resistance. Efforts to subdue the Pueblos continued into 1696, spending plenty of powder and coins.[1]

For Plains Apache groups in particular, the return of the Spanish was neither an event to celebrate nor necessarily one to mourn. The slave trade that had swept many Apaches into colonial New Mexico, the mining districts of New Spain, and even to Mexico City itself during the seventeenth century had to some extent spared groups with access to the animal bounty of the plains. While the Tewas at Santa Fe explained correctly to Vargas that Spaniards had in the past "offered peace to the [Plains] Apache and then hunted them down and killed them," such actions had met with protests from Pueblos in northern New Mexico, where relations with Plains Apache groups were strongest. Another way in which Plains Apache communities had shielded themselves from Spanish-directed violence and enslavement was by becoming slave suppliers themselves. The Spanish governors' retinues of Indian slaves illustrated as much. Recall Doña Teresa's "Quivira" women, who were probably Wichita or Pawnee people originally captured and sold into New Mexico by Plains Apache traders. In the Southwest—as in some other regions of North America—slaving could be a powerful tool in relations with Europeans, an "anticolonial" measure to maintain your own people's territory and sovereignty at your neighbors' expense.[2]

The Spanish represented but one group in a larger geopolitical landscape that Plains Apache communities navigated as the seventeenth century came to a close. Looking north and east, they saw old enemies like the Pawnee emboldened and strengthened by trade with a new group of "Spaniards" journeying into the plains—the French. Looking west, they witnessed cooperation between Utes and other new migrants into the region, the Comanche, who had acquired horses and quickly demonstrated an interest in Apache lands. While the Spanish and French had distinct geopolitical interests, the weapons, tools, and horses they supplied in exchange for slaves and hides nonetheless helped tip the scales of intertribal politics in the same direction. During the first half of the eighteenth century, Comanches, Utes, and Pawnees "took possession of" a significant portion of Plains Apache lands by killing or enslaving hundreds of them and turned the survivors into refugees in search of "some place to live in safety," as one Apache leader lamented.[3]

Recent histories examining this process have centered on the Comanche, explaining Plains Apache displacement as one component of the Comanche rise as they migrated south from what is now Wyoming, became skilled horsemen, tapped into trading networks, and eventually took control of much of the southern Great Plains. In the competition for river valleys—key watering sites for Comanche horse herds and Apache crops—Comanche groups gained the upper hand by the late 1700s, yet a focus on the Plains Apache side of the story is worthy on its own terms. It illustrates the existential threat that the intersection of colonial labor demands with intertribal politics could pose, as hundreds of Apache people scattered—and were scattered—across the continent during the eighteenth century.

Plains Apache history also illustrates links between Apaches in diaspora and their kin and the communities left behind. In the eighteenth century, Apaches responded to the existential problems caused by displacement that other Apache people had faced before and would face again. Where can our families live in safety? With whom should we engage to help maintain our livelihood and ensure our people's future? How can we avoid losing so many of our kin to bondage among strangers? Some Plains Apache groups drew upon long-standing relationships with Pueblo allies and on a new alliance with the Spanish empire while migrating closer to New Mexico settlements, eventually coalescing into two Jicarilla bands: the Sait Ndé (sand people) and Gulgahén (people of the plains). They thrived as people who linked the colonial and indigenous worlds, serving as military scouts and guides for the Spanish while also maintaining trading relations with independent Apache bands.[4] Others chose a different path. They traveled south and east, trading with strangers, welcoming refugees from Spanish missions, and taking and incorporating captives of their own. These people with diverse origins eventually came to be known by outsiders as Lipan Apaches and to themselves as Túédine Ndé (no water people) and Kúnetsaa Ndé (big water people). They occupied central Texas and the lower Rio Grande valley at the very moment the Spanish were constructing forts and missions in the area to counter French expansion. After Lipans spent decades raiding and wrangling over captives around San Antonio, pressure from the Comanche and their allies—including the capture and sale of Lipans into colonial societies—ultimately led them to choose a wary alliance with the Spanish around 1750. For both Jicarillas and Lipans, captivity and displacement in the first half of the eighteenth century were key motivations for their coalescence in lands where their descendants continue to live today.[5]

As their kin responded to their loss through migration, war, and diplomacy, Apache slaves in diaspora faced circumstances that were reminiscent of those of past generations of Apaches. New Mexico and Northern New Spain remained the principal destinations to which they were carried, and their status continued to be conceptualized as temporal slavery for the purposes of Christianization and incorporation. For many, the gulf between such rhetoric and reality remained. Yet important changes in the Apache diaspora also emerged during the eighteenth century. In the aftermath of the Indian rebellions of the late seventeenth century, formal crackdowns on Indian slavery waned in the Spanish empire. Residents and officials spoke of a general "toleration" for Indian slavery as they sought legal remedies for botched slave sales, the recovery of runaways, or slave kidnappings. The persistent arrival of a diversity of Indian slaves into colonial communities fueled the rise of new identities within laboring communities, such as in New Mexico with the emergence of self-identifying Genízaros. Elsewhere such traffic ensured that Apache continued to be the most common category of ascription and self-identification for Indian slaves from the Southwest in diaspora. Finally, new destinations to which captors carried Apaches during the eighteenth century mapped the increasingly transcontinental and transoceanic links of trade and travel that entangled Native and colonial societies. It was possible for kin originally captured from the same Plains Apache community to be purchased

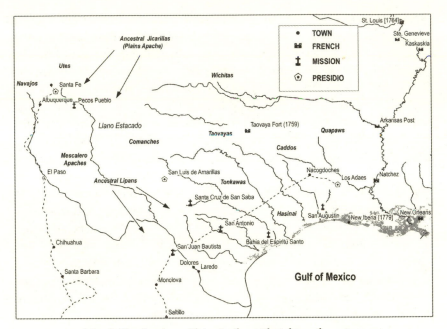

Map 2. The Southern Plains in the mid-eighteenth century.

by a French merchant bound for the Caribbean or a Ute merchant bound for the Great Basin. If this is a story of existential challenges—for both those carried into bondage and their kin left behind—it is also a story of survival, as Apaches in bondage and in freedom made new homes for themselves in new places.[6]

The Roots of the Plains Apache Diaspora to New Mexico

In order to understand the diasporas of Plains Apache groups in the first half of the eighteenth century, we must first consider their world in the aftermath of the Pueblo Revolt of 1680. We start with the ancestors of the Jicarilla, who lived in the grasslands north and east of New Mexico. For seven or eight months of the year, this is a brown sea, occasionally blanketed in white by snows that melt quickly beneath the piercing sun and vast blue sky. Summer is the exceptional season, when heat fuels billowing black clouds, crackling thunder, and pouring rains that turn brown into green. Today this landscape is best known as eastern Colorado, western Kansas, and the Texas Panhandle, but at the beginning of the eighteenth century it was a populated heartland of

Apache people, including the forebears of today's Jicarilla. They built homes in the river valleys, where they could irrigate their corn, beans, and squash and not have to depend on summer rains alone. They planted their crops in the spring, spent the early summer out on the plains hunting bison and other game, returned to harvest crops in the late summer and fall, and then retreated west to seasonal settlements closer to the mountains for the winter. Around 1700 their population likely numbered between five and ten thousand.[7]

Life centered around a local group whose *nantan* was responsible for negotiating relations with neighboring Apache villages and with strangers beyond their country. These local groups varied in density. Some were characterized by concentrated settlements of as many as thirty households. Others were more dispersed, with a few houses of an extended family of twenty to forty people joining together to work fields near a river or stream, separated by four or more miles from the next family group. Women farmed, raised children, produced pottery and baskets, and served as herders and sentinels on trading or raiding expeditions. Men hunted, traded, and protected the people in war. Together they met shared threats in cooperation with other neighboring local groups. Such cooperation was built upon the kinship networks that interlinked Plains Apache communities, facilitating a political system that resembled a fluid confederacy. Spanish observers suggested that leadership followed relatively few patrilineal lines, given that they described chiefs as "brothers." Since men moved into their wives' villages upon marriage, men from the same family were distributed among and led a variety of local groups, helping to bind them together through the expectations of mutual aid that kinship relations fostered.[8]

The appearance of Apache villages illustrated the influence of centuries of interaction with neighboring peoples, especially with the Northern Pueblos of New Mexico. As one Spanish governor explained it, "The Pecos buy from [the Apaches] buffalo meat, lard, grease, buckskins, buffalo hides . . . [and] children . . . whom they capture from the enemies with whom they wage war."[9] In exchange, Apache traders received horses they could use for travel and transport, as well as metal tools and jewelry. In fact, Spaniards who traveled into Plains Apache villages on the plains were struck by the crosses, medals, and rosaries they wore. They explained that they wore them because "for many years they traded and had commerce with the Spaniards and they knew that because they wore [them] they were very valiant."[10] Plains Apache housing also demonstrated varied cultural roots, including a mixture of brush shelters, tipis, wood houses smeared with mud, and adobe homes, which bordered the rivers that watered their fields.[11]

The presence of adobe structures provided but one hint of the long-standing relationship between Plains Apache and Pueblo groups that was not simply confined to trade. Apaches sometimes spent time in Pueblo communities, especially in the winter, and Puebloans had repeatedly sought refuge, especially from Pecos and Picurís, in Apache lands during the seventeenth century. Perhaps it was during such visits that they had built adobe structures or taught Apaches how to build them in exchange for the shelter they provided. Whether through temporary shared residence or simply via annual trade and exchange, such interactions served each group's interests, given the distinct resources and geopolitical dynamics of their respective homelands. It is also likely that a degree of intermarriage, and thus kinship obligations, had developed over time as a result.[12]

It was just such cooperation between Pueblo and Plains Apache groups that helped bring renewed Spanish attention to the plains in the 1690s and early 1700s, revealing in the process Apache concerns about changes in the world around them. Pueblo communities had called upon Apache allies for aid during the Pueblo Revolt and again during Vargas's reconquest. Pueblo resistance was strongest in the northern pueblos, and the Spaniards struggled to suppress a new revolt that broke out in June 1696. After months of fighting, Pueblo forces at Jémez, Taos, and Pecos had escaped to find refuge among Apache allies. In October, a Plains Apache trading party from El Cuartelejo, in present-day Kansas, helped a large part of refugees from Santa Clara, Tano, and Picurís pueblos flee with them to the plains. When Vargas gave chase, he managed to recover only a portion of the group, almost all of them "Apaches," whom he divided up among his soldiers as slaves.[13]

The experiences of these Apaches presaged those of many of their kin who would also be captured and taken into colonial societies to labor in the coming years. In the meantime, across the plains homeland of Apaches, Pueblo people farmed, helped construct new homes, and contributed to the families that sheltered them. By 1706, some of them had already returned south to New Mexico, but dozens of people from Picurís remained behind at El Cuartelejo. Unable to imagine that baptized Christians could want to live voluntarily among "heathens," Spanish observers interpreted the Pueblo people's actions accordingly. They envisioned that after "fleeing into the asylum of barbarity," they must have been betrayed by their friends and were "now suffering a cruel bondage." Word from a Picurís emissary requesting that the Spanish "send several squadrons of soldiers to take them away and restore them to their old pueblo" seemed to confirm this interpretation.[14]

The fact that Apache leaders would allow such a message to be delivered suggests that they were cooperating with the Picurís in a diplomatic overture to the Spanish that they hoped would benefit all. Apache lands on the plains had become less safe in recent years as Comanches and Utes allied with each other and attacked Apache villages. For the Picurís, Apache country may no longer have seemed the safe haven that it had once been, and appeals to Spanish aid and hints at exploitation were likely designed to grant them amnesty to return home. For Plains Apache leaders, meanwhile, a formal alliance with the Spanish had gained appeal, and they hoped that the release of Picurís held as "captives" could be leveraged for Spanish military aid.[15]

For the Spanish, the Picurís' plight represented only a part of their interest in journeying onto the plains, however. Recent Apache reports of "white and blond men" near their lands had struck a nerve, given news of the French explorations of the Gulf of Mexico and efforts to establish a colony on the coast of Texas. The French invaders who brought Native and Spanish interests into alignment were agents of the broader French expansion in North America ushered in by King Louis XIV. The French missions in the Great Lakes that had been established beginning in the 1660s had been followed by new forts after 1679. Such posts provided a base for trading parties to travel west onto the Great Plains, as well as for further exploration down the Mississippi River valley.[16]

The French monarch had his eye not only on areas of the continent unpopulated by other Europeans but also on the possibility of conquering Spanish domains. One of the first to suggest to him a concrete plan to do so was the turncoat former governor of New Mexico, Diego de Peñalosa. He had fled to France after his troubles with the Inquisition for sexual misdeeds and Indian slave trading, among other charges. Beginning in 1678, he repeatedly offered to assist the French in taking over parts of the Spanish empire, based on his expertise and knowledge of New Spain and its frontiers. Ultimately, King Louis and his advisers decided to turn to one of their own, sending Rene Robert Cavelier, Sieur de La Salle, on a long journey from Canada to find a harbor on the Gulf Coast and research a route for invading New Spain. In 1682, La Salle explored the mouth of the Mississippi, claiming it for France as "Louisiana." Drawing upon this success, he returned to France to report that the Mississippi delta virtually bordered New Spain and could thus serve as a launching post for an invasion of its rich mines. Moreover, La Salle believed the French could be aided by an army of fifteen thousand Indians, who would be mobilized by their "deadly hatred for the Spaniards because they enslave them."[17]

La Salle may have been right about Indian slavery, but he was strikingly wrong about geography. The nearest mines to the mouth of the Mississippi were in fact more than a thousand miles away, and his efforts to form a colony on the Gulf Coast ultimately proved so disastrous that the geographic error did not matter much. Landing midway between modern Houston and Corpus Christi at Matagorda Bay in February 1685, the 180 colonists came ill-prepared for the challenges they faced. Half of them died within the first six months before La Salle led a desperate rescue party back east in search of aid. La Salle was in the end killed by one of his own men, and by the time a Spanish expedition located his failed colony, only a few French children living among the Karankawa Indians were left to tell about what had happened there.[18]

The expansionary ambition La Salle's odyssey represented helped spark Spanish settlement in Texas; it also undoubtedly lingered on the mind of the governor of New Mexico when he ordered Juan de Ulibarrí to lead a 1706 expedition to liberate the Picurís from bondage. The expedition even included a survivor of the La Salle colony, Jean L'Archeveque, indicating that they believed they might run into Frenchmen along their journey. The expedition's aims were multiple: to bring the Picurís back into the fold, to investigate rumors of French incursions into the region, and to establish good relations with the Plains Apache groups who might help serve as a buffer between New Mexico and any French advances.[19]

The diary of the expedition is also revealing of the Apache past, present, and future on the plains. A week into their journey, the party of forty Spanish soldiers and militiamen and one hundred Pueblo Indian auxiliaries overtook an Apache family near a stream in present-day southern Colorado. A man reported through an interpreter that they were going to join other villages in the area, "in order to defend themselves together from the Utes and Comanches, who were coming to attack them." The next day, near present-day Pueblo, Colorado, they came across a woman and girl who were gathering wild cherries on the Arkansas River. They repeated the same news of an impending Comanche attack.[20]

It is only with the benefit of hindsight that such rumors seem prescient. Ulibarrí's expedition painted a portrait of an Apache homeland not yet turned into a contested borderland. Women and children traveled out to gather fruits, and families traveled alone, unarmed. This was a world in which people clearly still felt a degree of security. Yet the leaders of the Apache villages spread across the watersheds of the plains were worried enough about the future to see a benefit in solidifying an alliance with the Spanish. Comanche and Ute attacks, Pawnee raids, reports of Frenchmen trading guns to their enemies—all of these made it clear that they needed a counterweight to the alliances that were already benefiting their enemies.[21]

These aims became clear to all parties when Ulibarrí and his men reached their primary destination, the Apache villages of El Cuartelejo. He reported that they were greeted with hospitality, as people approached them with "bison meat and roasting ears of Indian corn, rejoicing, showing pleasure upon seeing us in their country." They were soon greeted by several Picurís as well before talk began of the mutual desire for "peace and good relations." Tellingly, the Apache leaders were quick to report news that they knew would be of particular interest to the Spanish. They had recently killed a white man and woman "whom they called French" and had kept a gun and other booty that they would show the Spanish to prove it.[22]

The next day the alliance was formalized. Spanish officers and an Apache nantan ascended a hill where Apaches had set up a cross. After the Spanish and their Pueblo auxiliaries worshipped it, they continued into the village where many of the rest of the Picurís emerged from houses. The Spanish proceeded to enact their conventional ceremony of possession by renaming the Apache villages and declaring the whole province to be "pacified." Apache leaders, meanwhile, articulated their own hopes for their new allies. While the Picurís were being gathered, the leaders asked whether the Spanish would "go with them to attack their enemies, the Pawnee Indians."[23] Ulibarrí hesitated, noting that he did not believe his horses had the strength for a longer journey, but he promised that the Spanish would return to aid them against their enemies in the near future. For their part, the Apache leaders allowed all of the Picurís to leave with the Spanish, only resisting the release of five Tano or Tigua slaves that they distinguished from the Picurís by saying that they had purchased them from other Indians. Ultimately Ulibarrí agreed to pay thirteen horses for their release.[24]

As Ulibarrí and his men journeyed back to Santa Fe from El Cuartelejo, both they and the Apache groups they had visited viewed this expedition as a decided success. Spaniards returned south with the Picurís whom the Apache had "liberated" in exchange for gifts and promises of military aid against their enemies. If Apaches likely viewed this as an alliance between equals, Ulibarrí imagined that prayer and ceremony had brought a new province of Indians under Spanish vassalage—"the fertile agricultural plains of San Luis." The Picurís, meanwhile, had managed to secure safe passage back to their village without Spanish punishment, despite having spent as much as a decade living as "apostates" among Apaches.[25]

Good relations between the Picurís, Plains Apaches, and Spaniards initially appeared promising for all. Thirty Plains Apache men even joined a

1715 expedition to retaliate against Mescalero Apaches for recent livestock raids. While the month-long expedition proved unsuccessful, it marked Apache men's participation in Spanish campaigns that would continue in the decades to come. With the benefit of hindsight, however, Apache visions of a prosperous future in their homelands with the ability to call on Spanish and Pueblo allies were thwarted as much by Spanish weakness as by the strength of their adversaries. The Spanish never followed through on their promises of aiding them against the Pawnee or other enemies. A later plan to construct a presidio in Apache lands on the plains likewise never came to fruition.[26]

The Comanche and Ute attacks rumored during Ulibarrí's journey in 1706 soon arrived and kept coming. When a new Spanish expedition led by Governor Don Antonio Valverde traveled back into Plains Apache homelands on the plains in the fall of 1719, they were greeted kindly, like Ulibarrí. This time, however, the first people he encountered on the road immediately explained that they faced a dire situation because "their enemies, the Comanches, were persecuting and killing their kinsmen and others of their nation." While Governor Valverde still noted fields of maize, beans, and squash—and described the ditches and canals that they used to irrigate them—he encountered suffering and fear everywhere in lieu of the bucolic agricultural scenes described by Ulibarrí. Days into the journey, the Apache nantan Carlana met up with the Spanish expedition and explained that he had come fleeing from his country in the mountains. He described how he had led his people into "a land of Apaches whom Chief Flaco governed, because of the continual war that the Ute and Comanche enemy made upon them." At La Jicarilla, an Apache nantan had noted similarly that the Comanche, with their Ute allies, had recently attacked one of their settlements, killing sixty and taking sixty-four women and children as captives. "Since that had happened they were sad and filled with misgiving and fear that the enemy might return and finish them entirely," he explained. Governor Valverde tried to console them by promising a campaign against the Comanche to "punish this nation which had caused such great damage to all of them," news they received "with much exalting." Carlana and other Apache men joined with the Spanish in a campaign, but they were in the end unable to track down any Comanches.[27]

It was no coincidence that the Comanche emergence followed relatively soon after the end of the Pueblo rebellions. Native groups had widely circulated the horses that the Spaniards had abandoned during the Pueblo Revolt, and the *kumantsi*—as the Utes referred to people who "wanted to fight all the time"—had soon found distinct advantages in equestrianism. Because a horse could carry four times as much as a large dog and cover twice the distance in a day's travel, the Comanche were able to transport more trade items and hunt for prey over a much wider range than before. As Pekka Hämäläinen has explained, "Their reach of trade was multiplied, as was their ability to wage war, plunder, and defend themselves." For some, including Utes, Comanches would become useful military allies; for others, especially Apache agriculturalists in plains river valleys, they would be a formidable, and ultimately insurmountable, enemy.[28]

As Comanches overran Apache villages, they transported captives of war to sell in New Mexico, while also selling them into Native trading networks that destined them for sale in French settlements deep in the interior. The value of Apache slaves acquired during the early 1700s fueled Comanche expansion further by providing access to horses and guns that helped them displace Plains Apache groups and become key players in plains trading networks. The slave trade and Comanche power went hand in hand, as Comanches offered up Apache slaves to Spanish and French buyers, receiving the horses and guns that gave them additional advantages over their Apache competitors. Indirectly, colonialism made possible the Comanche ascendance by providing both the technologies key to their mobility and martial prowess and also the Spanish and French who would willingly purchase the human spoils of the Comanche wars against Apache groups.[29]

Comanches were not the only neighbors threatening Plains Apache villages, however. The Valverde expedition encountered refugees from Apache villages further out on the plains who reported that attacks by Pawnees and Wichitas, facilitated by French supplies of guns, powder, and shot, had enabled them to "have seized their lands, and taken possession of them and held them from that time on." Drawing upon the kinship networks that interlaced the world in which they lived, they had banded together with neighboring villages, as Chief Carlana explained his people had done. In the end, however, a sense of foreboding remained. The words of an Apache nantan Valverde had encountered earlier in his expedition lingered: "They no longer knew where to go to live in safety."[30]

The Plains Apache Diaspora to Texas

Some Plains Apaches thought they had already found safety elsewhere. They had drawn upon the mobility and hauling capacity of horses and mules to travel down the Rio Grande and east into the hill country of what is now Texas beginning in the 1680s and 1690s. They sensed opportunity in trade with local Native groups, including the Cibolo and Jumano villages at La Junta, where the Conchos River, which flowed past Spanish missions, meets the Rio Grande. By the early 1700s, they were key players in a regional economy centering on the exchange of horses and mules rustled from Northern New Spain for hides, foodstuffs, tools, and clothing from Native trading partners.[31]

Trade between these Apache bands and local Native groups was reported in 1715 during Spanish expeditions to La Junta, where they observed ten towns of Cibolo and Jumano Indians with a population of more than fourteen hundred. They also noted "a friendly Apache band living just north of the Cibolo/Jumano village, and a visiting Apache had agreed to bring his people to meet the Spanish missionaries."[32] The seasonal presence of Apache traders at La Junta continued in the coming decades. When friars returned after being cast out in a 1725 rebellion, they noted that La Junta was "a passage and exit for many nations of Zibolos and Apaches." One friar worried that these Apaches were preventing "many souls [from being] won to God."[33]

The Spanish learned more about these Apaches' seasonal migrations from a former captive, whom Apaches had seized in what is now the Texas Hill Country in 1724. He explained that he was a Christian Indian from the missions of the Conchos River who had been taken captive by Toboso Indians, who then sold him at La Junta to an Apache headman whose people commonly visited to trade. From La Junta, he had been taken by his Apache captors to their buffalo hunting grounds along the Colorado River. The travels that this captive experienced reflected the broader pattern of life for bands of Apaches on the southern plains who were described by the Spanish as the Ypandes, Pelones, Ysandis, and Chentis, all of whom would generally be referred to by outsiders as Lipan Apaches after the mid-1700s. They made their camps for part of the year near the Colorado or Pecos Rivers in present-day Texas, from which they hunted buffalo and fattened their horse herds. Beginning in the summer, they traveled to agricultural villages and mission communities along the Rio Grande to trade. From there they might travel south into Nueva Vizcaya and Coahuila to pursue Spanish livestock or to harvest crops they planted in sheltered mountain valleys.[34]

The fact that observers sometimes distinguished between Lipans and "legitimate" Apaches—Natagés or Mescaleros—indicates that they had varied origins. Some members of ancestral Lipan bands had roots in captivity. Others were refugees from Spanish missions in Coahuila who joined with Lipan groups through alliance or intermarriage. As Gary Clayton Anderson notes, the incorporation of Natives from the Coahuila and Texas mission frontiers provided Apaches on the southern plains with "access to new geographic knowledge and some understanding of the ranching industry of the Rio Grande valley." By the mid-1700s, the total population of Lipans was probably around five thousand, similar to their northern relatives, the ancestral Jicarillas.[35]

Later Spanish expeditions further clarified the connections between mission Indians and bands of Lipan Apaches along the lower Rio Grande and the appeal of such connections for both. The governor of Coahuila, Don Pedro de Rábago y Therán, journeyed north to La Junta in 1747 to investigate repeated reports from area landholders about livestock thefts. Soon after beginning their march, the expedition encountered "many signs of enemy camps, including thirty-five lights." Though this enemy went unnamed, they came across a dead mule "with the brand of a Monclova citizen," suggesting that individuals in the nearby camps were responsible for the recent raids in Coahuila. This was but the first hint of the Native trading economy that was built in part on rustling Coahuila residents' free-roaming cattle. As they continued the march, they came across more tracks of "the enemy," as well as stray horses with the brands of Coahuila residents.[36] Though Coahuila residents blamed a generic "enemy" for rustling their livestock, the ensuing days in the La Junta missions suggested that both Apache traders and mission Indians were involved in this commerce, but it was unclear who the primary supplier was. Rábago and his men passed through missions with no missionaries but numerous mules, horses, and mares "with different brands of Saltillo, Nuevo Leon, Santa Rosa, Rio Grande, and Monclova." Some members of the expedition wanted to reclaim them, but Rábago ordered them to let them be, since they appeared too lean to survive the journey back to Coahuila anyway.[37]

Captives also circulated between Apaches and the La Junta missions, as in years past. At San Francisco de la Junta, for example, the expedition found two Indian captives that Apache merchants had sold "when they came into trade with the mission towns." These captives were originally from the missions of San Bernardo and San Juan Baptista, more than three hundred miles downriver. Rábago took it upon himself to explain to the Indians that they could not sell these women, but the masters proved unwilling to part with them until they were compensated for their losses. "What little fear of God they have," Rábago summarized in his diary, echoing the sentiments of the lone friar who served these communities.[38]

The Apache trading network was not limited to the missions at La Junta. Returning south of the Rio Grande along the Conchos River, the expedition found missions there similarly engaged in trade. At the mission of San Juan, for example, they observed the nations of the Conexos, Cacalotes, Mesquittes, and others living in distinct settlements along the banks of the river, divided by a league or two. As their ministers explained, "They heard Mass, when it suits them, they pray, when they want to," but most of the time, "they went around on horseback, trading with the Apaches." Rábago understood from what he observed and heard that these mission communities "were lost." Such concerns about Spanish subjects' loyalties would prove increasingly influential in Spanish-Apache relations in the coming decades.[39]

Royal officials had commissioned the La Junta expedition to search for a new site for a presidio that would guard against potential Apache invasions. Along the way, the expedition had discovered an Apache-Mission Indian trade that signaled to the Spanish governor that these Indian subjects had "little fear of God" and they had lost their way. The Conexos, Cacalotes, and other groups' decisions to trade with Apache groups illustrate that they saw matters quite differently. They farmed and traded the produce to Apache merchants; they bought slaves and sold horses and mules and went to Mass when they wanted. At the moment, they saw no contradiction in having a Spanish friar living among them while receiving visits from other Natives.[40]

The expansion of Spanish settlements north into Texas, which was fueled by La Salle's failed French colony, provided Apaches on the southern plains with another potential market for their meat and hides, as well as a new source for horses and mules. Lipan expeditions visited San Antonio virtually from its origin in 1718. While they periodically offered hides and meat for sale, they did not hesitate to steal the mission's horse herds even if it meant killing a few Spaniards in the process. The idea of Apaches as raiders soon became so engrained in Spaniards' thinking that they blamed them for any attack in the area, regardless of whether anyone had witnessed the perpetrators, much as the Spaniards' countrymen did in Coahuila, Nueva Vizcaya, and Sonora. Men's frustration about their inability to prevent attacks or protect the settlement led to anger and hyperbole, as some claimed Apaches were engaged in a "war of extermination."[41]

Yet amid raids and reprisals, peaceful exchanges were nonetheless possible, especially in the spring after buffalo hunts. Fairly typical was a Lipan trading party that greeted the Spanish governor with "20 cargos of meat, buffalo and gamuzas [leather clothing]" in March 1734. They reported that this offering was "to cover" two Spaniards they had killed in a raid at San Antonio the year before. Anderson notes that past violence sometimes facilitated exchange, because "frequently the two sides gave each other 'gifts' to cover damages, the Apaches asking for the return of captives taken in Spanish raids while the Spaniards requested the return of stock [taken in Apache raids]."[42]

If stolen property and soldiers' inability to sufficiently protect it were at the heart of Spanish concerns, Lipans worried most about the Spanish penchant for capturing women and children and putting them to work in their homes. Because the Spaniards had a difficult time distinguishing between Apache groups, or simply did not care to do so, they sometimes attacked a group that had little or nothing to do with a recent livestock raid. Such had been the case in 1722, when the Spanish attacked a Lipan band and captured twenty women and children as well as 120 horses. Repeated efforts by the Lipans to barter for their kin's return had failed. They even offered up four men in exchange for the women and children the Spanish had taken hostage, but the Spanish commander at San Antonio refused them. In response, the Lipan delegation gathered their things and prepared to depart, but not before, as Spanish testimony later revealed, "the chief took the hand of one of the little girls held captive, turned with her to face [the Spanish commander] and gestured as if to say, 'This is what you want, not peace.'"[43]

Lipan engagement with San Antonio as a part of their broader trading network often proved a devil's bargain. It not only risked the loss of kin but also one's own punishment for alleged "crimes" that might have been committed by someone else. One leader and his family discovered as much in 1737 and 1738. After approaching the Spanish to trade, Cabellos Colorados and his family were apprehended and charge with "infidelity" for allegedly having raided the presidio's herds. Before the Pueblo Revolt, the idea that the "entire" Apache nation had always been at war with the Spanish Crown served as general cover for capturing and enslaving families from any Apache or Navajo group regardless of their history of interaction with Spaniards. At first glance, Cabellos Colorados's experiences echo that past history. While in this case court proceedings, rather than a general "sentence of death," provided cover for Spaniards to be able to believe that their actions were based on law and justice, in practice the family's guilt was predetermined by San Antonio residents' circumstantial reasoning and prejudices. They live closest to San Antonio, so they must have committed the raid, some argued in testimony to the governor. No raids have been committed since they were in captivity, pointed out others. Besides, to many residents of San Antonio all Apaches were basically "enemies of humanity."[44]

In the end, the Spanish decisions about Cabellos Colorados presaged a policy that would become the norm later in the century in dealings with other Apache groups. Rather than pressing them into slavery in San Antonio, the Spaniards banished the family to the royal jail in Mexico City, drawing upon 1729 military regulations that had authorized the deportation of Indian prisoners to Mexico City for the viceroy to decide their fate. As the official order stated, "Thirteen Indian men and women prisoners in the said presidio, [shall be taken] tied to each other, from jurisdiction to jurisdiction, to the prison of

the capital in Mexico. . . . The two-year-old daughter of chief Cabellos Colorados, María Guadalupe, shall be treated in the same manner." Cabellos Colorados and his family ultimately traveled 102 days on foot, with the men shackled
in leg irons, before reaching Mexico City. Within six months, only five of the
fourteen originally sent south remained alive. As Juliana Barr notes, "Whether
any of [these five] survived is unknown; the last records say only that prison
officials sent two men to a hospital, while two women, although very ill, went
into servitude in prominent Spaniards' private homes."[45]

The fates of the displaced and the decision-making of their kin who
remained in Texas intertwined. At the heart of this episode of diaspora was
the aim of punishment itself, not the acquisition of Native labor. Their march
in irons was a spectacle with both Native and Spanish audiences in mind. For
the Spanish, it was a demonstration of power and mastery in the face of their
all-too-apparent weaknesses. It was a performance of justice in which legal
ceremony—testimony collected under oath and transcribed by a notary—
juxtaposed their supposed civility with Apaches' supposed barbarism. Forgotten in the process was the ultimate outcome: the suffering and death of the
majority of a family, including children with no say in the matter for which
they were being punished. For Lipan groups surrounding San Antonio,
meanwhile, the brutal disposition of these captives was intended to dissuade
them from future raids or attacks, an aim that Spaniards believed was worth
the significant cost the whole affair incurred for the royal treasury.[46]

In another context, the deportation of Cabellos Colorados and his family
might have broken Lipan Apache relations with the Spanish for good. Violent
reprisals filled the coming months, such as when more than three hundred
Apache men attacked San Antonio at night in 1745, killing nine and carrying off countless horses. Yet a shared threat for both groups—the continued
Comanche advance through the plains to the north—ultimately led each to
debate whether setting aside years of bloodshed, lost property, and lost loved
ones might be in their best interest.[47]

Scattered to Distant Parts

Plains Apache groups such as the Lipan and Jicarilla weighed their futures
as hundreds of their kin labored in exile. While numbers do not capture
the human drama of displacement and enslavement, they do help signal the
depth of the challenge these groups faced as they weighed decisions about
diplomacy, migration, and war. Between 1700 and 1760, more than eight

hundred Indians identified as Apache appear in the baptismal records of New Mexico, the largest number of any ethnic descriptor. Many of these Natives were captives sold by the Comanche.[48] Approximately five hundred "adult" baptisms in Chihuahua City between 1725 and 1755 consisted of many Apaches as well, including at least some Plains Apache people originally captured by Comanches or Utes and exported to Chihuahua for sale.[49] Dozens of captives baptized at other presidios, missions, and towns in Nueva Vizcaya and Sonora comprised many Apaches as well, including captives acquired in military campaigns locally—probably from Southern and Western Apache groups—as well as some Plains Apaches transported through the merchant networks that tied New Mexico to the Nueva Vizcaya and Sonora frontiers.[50] Several hundred more Plains Apache captives were circulated east, especially by the Pawnee and Wichita, appearing in places like Natchitoches (Louisiana) and Montreal. "Apaches" represented one-quarter of those with specified origins appearing in New France's records in the 1730s and continued to represent a noticeable presence in the decades to come. Many others remained uncounted, having lived out their lives in Pawnee, Wichita, or Comanche camps or having been transported into colonial societies without receiving the Catholic sacraments before death.[51]

During this period, Apache people who survived forced journeys into diaspora faced similar challenges to those their ancestors had faced in the prior century: labor in strange places not of their own choosing and the need to form relationships that might aid them in some way to survive the difficulties of life. Although "Apache" continued to be a principle means by which masters understood the servants or slaves they were acquiring, it was also a category that came to be meaningful for displaced Natives in colonial societies. New developments in the eighteenth century also distinguished Apaches' experiences in diaspora to some extent from those of past generations: the flow of Native captives with diverse origins to the same places led in some settings to the rise of new categories of identity; a decline in concern about the illegality of Indian slavery by Spanish officials made the circulation of Native slaves to a variety of sites easier; new destinations, meanwhile, separated Apaches further than ever from home.[52]

New identities rooted in the shared experience of the exploitation of diverse Native people were most evident in New Mexico, the most common initial destination for a captive taken in a Comanche attack on an Apache village on the plains. While in the past Plains Apache groups had been slave suppliers, Comanches had largely supplanted them in the trade by 1750. As one observer described a typical trading fair, at least fifty and sometimes two hundred tents of Comanches came together, a multitude so great "it is impossible to enumerate them." The civil officials and residents of New Mexico prepared to join the fair by gathering as many horses as they could and as much ironware as possible: "axes, hoes, wedges, picks, bridles, machetes, daggers, and knives." In exchange, the Comanches offered deer and buffalo hides and "men and women, small and large, a great multitude of both sexes." Because of the continued demand for domestic service in Spanish settlements, women brought a higher price than men—usually two horses. Apache slaves represented a key source of wealth that Comanches used to increase their horse herds and supply of weaponry and useful tools.[53]

The persistent arrival of slaves purchased from the Comanche or their allies also contributed to the growth of a new category of identity within New Mexico society: Genízaro, whose very name reflected the distinct role some played as soldiers, or janissaries, in defending the kingdom against neighboring Indian groups, including the Apache and Navajo. The complexities of the Genízaros' origins and status also illustrate the continued fluidity of Indian slavery in New Mexico, owing in part to the idea that it was a "temporal" institution for the incorporation and conversion of heathen Indians but probably also to the readily available supply that may have lessened masters' concerns about policing the boundaries of slavery and servitude.[54]

Drawing on diverse cultural traditions, the Genízaro identity emerged out of a common experience of displacement, exploitation, and liberation. A 1733 petition from more than one hundred families for permission to resettle in an abandoned pueblo is telling about the roots of Genízaro identity and the origins of those who claimed it. The male heads of household indicated they were originally from Apache, Pawnee, Jumano, Kiowa, Crow, and Ute heritage. While their origins were in slavery, they distinguished themselves in their petition from those who were still "residing as children in Spanish homes and bound to service." They further noted that they would serve the kingdom from their new pueblo "as guardians and scouts along the Apache frontier." Although the governor denied their petition, indicating that they should settle in existing towns, similar requests in the future were met with grants of land, thereby facilitating the persistence of a Genízaro identity into the future.[55]

If the treatment of Indian servants and slaves in New Mexico remained a cause for controversy and sometimes a vehicle to liberty, the circulation and sale of Natives did not. While Indian slavery remained patently illegal, including the "rescue" of Indian slaves from other Indians, slave trading in the eighteenth century posed less of a legal risk than it sometimes had in the seventeenth century. In part, it was because of the degree to which Spaniards had come to emphasize slavery as an institution for incorporating Indigenous children. In the 1733 land petition, for example, Genízaros distinguished themselves from "the children" in bondage in Spanish homes. The words of a New Mexico governor regarding the export of Native children from his jurisdiction are similarly telling. In September 1714, Don Juan Flores Mogollón noted that his subjects were purchasing Apache children, who were being taken to "distant places to sell" without first receiving baptism. Governor Flores Mogollón had grown concerned that they sometimes died on the way to their destinations, especially given that Christianization was the reason the king "tolerates this traffic." The governor offered his observations of the trans-Atlantic slave trade as a model for priests in New Mexico to follow: "Do to [Apaches] as is practiced and I have seen done in the seaports with the loads of blacks," he mandated, explaining that in the port cities of the Caribbean he had seen priests board vessels to baptize African slaves before they disembarked them for sale. In the coming days, public criers made his order heard throughout the kingdom.[56]

If the governor's order is useful in illustrating official toleration of the slave trafficking that characterized this era, it also reminds us of the continued importance of a category that—like Genízaro—was rooted originally in captivity and exploitation: Apache. Though it is not usually discussed in the same vein, for hundreds of Native people of varied origins in the eighteenth century the category "Apache" took on new meaning for them because of their displacement from kin, sale, and forced labor in diaspora. As had been true for many of their ancestors, the name "Apache" was one ascribed to them by masters who understood it to mean they were exploitable persons because of their resistance to colonial rule. And as had been true for so many of their ancestors, Northern New Spain remained a key site to which they were transported.[57]

It is difficult to determine the precise origins of people described as Apaches and carried from New Mexico to other provinces in New Spain. In Sonora, the majority of Apache servants and slaves appearing in archival records in the eighteenth century were probably from the Southern (or Chiricahua) and Western Apache groups, having been acquired by their Tohono and Akimel O'odham enemies and sold to Spanish settlements. Given merchant trading networks, however, at least some Plains Apache captives may have also been carried there, interacting with distant relatives from other Apache groups in diaspora.[58]

In Sonora, as in New Mexico, the persistent arrival of Native captives of diverse origins, including from Apache groups, influenced the use of new categories of identity that reflected slave status. The most common term ascribed to Native servants and slaves in Sonora was "Nixora," a Yuman word for "captive." As one observer explained, Sonora residents purchased these Nixoras when they were young children, baptized them, raised them, and "are served by them, under subjection, until they marry or pass ten years of service." Yet Apache was also a common category of identity, one associated with independent Apache groups to be sure, but also with Natives transported into colonial society to be exploited, and like Nixoras, put to work.[59]

The story of one such Apache woman, María Antonia Yslas, is illustrative of a typical life trajectory. Captured as an infant and transported to Sonora, she said that she did not know her parents but had grown up as an Apache serving in the home of Doña Ana Yslas, a resident of Horcasitas, Sonora. By 1796, she was about twenty years old and still worked as Doña Ana's cook.[60]

Like so many Native servants and slaves, her life entered the archival record because of an unusual event, which lends idiosyncratic, human detail to what was otherwise a quite typical life. In February 1796, María went to confess before a visiting priest and missionary, Francisco Cobas. However it began, their conversation in the confessional booth quickly turned from the sacred to the worldly. The priest reportedly asked her if she would sleep with him that night, wondering, "Who would be hotter in bed, you or me?" "You," she had replied, continuing the flirtation. While she claimed she had not ultimately acted on her feelings—in part because she was afraid her mistress would find out and beat her—the guilt of the interaction had lingered. In January 1798, she decided to denounce the priest for solicitation, which ultimately led to an investigation by the Inquisition in Mexico City.[61]

Evidence from neighboring Nueva Vizcaya suggests that its residents shared a similar conceptualization of Indian slavery as temporary that was rooted in the incorporation of Indian children and associated with particular categories, especially Apache. The population in Nueva Vizcaya had expanded significantly in the decades since the Great Southwestern Revolt, fueled by new mining strikes that had led the city of Chihuahua to supplant Parral as the major settlement by the 1720s. Civil suits in the archives there provide insight into the experience of Native servants and slaves during this period and also into the general acceptance of Indian slavery by area residents and officials. In fact, residents proved able to avail themselves of the courts to wrangle with each other over such matters as botched slave sales, kidnappings, and runaways. When a fifteen-year-old Apache woman named Francisca went missing in September 1724, for example, her master did not hesitate to appeal to a magistrate in Chihuahua for help in her return. In providing context for the case, the magistrate explained that Francisca was a slave "until the age of competence," as was the "common custom." No one voiced concern that Francisca was in fact enslaved illegally, and the case itself was eventually filed away among other instances of "thefts of slaves" in the archives.[62]

The details of Francisca's story reflect the experience of other Native people turned Apache slaves whose lives did not make it into the archival record: lives characterized by relative powerlessness and vulnerability. After leaving her master's house one evening, she had traveled to the home of a couple that she must have thought would assist her. Instead, they had locked her in a tower on their estate and later in their kitchen. Eventually, they sent a servant to take her to their nephew's house, who was an overseer at a charcoal factory. Their ultimate aim in doing so remains opaque in the documentary record. By this time, however, her master was onto her trail, and it was when he caught wind of her location that he appeared before a magistrate demanding that the man "return to him his Apache Indian slave," which he eventually did.[63]

Without concern about putting themselves at any legal risk, other masters similarly complained about slaves escaping or being lured into the service of someone else. In 1737, Ignazio Paes de Guzmán, a resident of Chihuahua City, explained that he had purchased an Apache woman named Rita for one hundred pesos from Don Santiago Barrio de la Bandera. She had soon fled, Guzmán insisted, perhaps even at the seller's urging. She was now serving in another man's house, and Guzmán believed the slave trader might have resold her a second time. Guzmán wanted the Indian woman, or his hundred pesos, returned. While no final resolution to the case is extant, it is nonetheless striking that no one voiced concern about Rita's illegal enslavement or the merchant's slave trading, only about his apparent double-dealing.[64]

The means by which residents of Northern New Spain acquired their Apache slaves in the eighteenth century is illustrated by other extant suits involving cases of botched slave purchases that buyers did not hesitate to bring to the attention of authorities. At some point during 1729, for example, Gaspar Macías had contracted with Félix Sánchez, a soldier from New Mexico, to bring him an Apache boy and girl. He had paid in advance with a new upholstered chair and two good horses. Macías learned the hard way about paying for services before they are rendered. Months passed and he still had not seen his Apache slaves. He was later brought an Apache boy, but still no girl. Finally, in October 1730 he filed suit against Sánchez, demanding that he either pay him back for the undelivered slave or provide her to him.[65]

That the court found in Macías's favor, with no discussion of the illegality of Indian slavery, corroborates other records that illustrate the degree to which the anti-slavery sentiment that had been evident in Northern New Spain in decades past—to the extent that it influenced life for Apaches in the Parral mining district—had declined.[66]

Sometimes it was Apaches themselves, rather than failed transactions, that frustrated Nueva Vizcaya residents to the point that they sought legal remedies. In 1733, an Apache servant named Antonio de Therán was sued by his master, Joseph Pérez de Therán, who alleged that he had advanced Antonio more than 170 pesos for his wedding costs, including food and dress. They had made an agreement that Antonio would pay the money back via his labor. Within weeks, however, he had left his master's service and joined the household where his wife was a servant. Joseph wanted Antonio to either come back to work for him or repay him the wedding costs. In his subsequent testimony, Antonio did not deny any of his former master's claims. He first explained that it was his wife's idea, and her master had offered to pay their wedding costs. He then alluded to some other motivation, however, by explaining that he was serving his new master "against his wishes," for reasons he could not explain. The case was settled in the end by Joseph helping to arrange for Antonio to enter into the service of a third master, apparently resolving the concerns of both Antonio and his wife.[67]

In comparison to some other masters, Joseph Pérez de Therán seems to have had genuine affection for the Apache boy who had grown up working for him in his home. Antonio noted that his master even "viewed him as his son." Joseph also appears to have taken seriously a principle of Indian slavery in the region that other masters did not: by the time Antonio reached adulthood, he was no longer a slave but instead a servant earning pay. Yet the episode illustrates the power relations at the heart of their relationship, which remained tilted in the master's favor. By advancing wedding costs to Antonio, Joseph sought to keep him in his service. If he truly viewed him as a son, why did he not simply pay for the wedding outright? Antonio's choice of phrasing in describing their relationship lingers: he noted that Joseph claimed him as a son. He did not say that he claimed his master as his father.[68]

One Indian woman who ran away in 1758 illustrates that the lure of family led others to flee north toward their original homeland rather than simply change employers. In August, an Apache Indian woman was apprehended near the presidio of El Paso. The commander of the fort noted that interrogating her had been difficult given that she was "mui bozal," that is, "very untamed" (or not very Hispanicized). He had managed to understand that her name was María and she had been trafficked from New Mexico to the Chihuahua mining district, where she had been purchased by an "old man" to work on his hacienda. She had eventually escaped and made her way several hundred miles back north before her recapture. While local officials sought to determine who her master was—evidently with plans to return her to him—they had temporarily placed her in the home of a local resident, Domingo Apodaca. Several months later, in October 1758, Domingo and his wife awoke and seeking out María, had discovered that she had hung herself in her room. The official inquiry that followed the report of her death searched for evidence of mistreatment or malice on María's body, but finding none, ordered her burial and no further investigations into the matter.[69]

María's escape and suicide generated concern about her treatment but not about her enslavement. Authorities abetted regional customs of slavery by seeking to track down her owners and by keeping her in captivity in the meantime. Without María's testimony, we may never know her precise motivations for escape or what she hoped to achieve by journeying north. Undoubtedly her recapture and renewed exploitation were not what she had in mind, if her own actions that autumn day when she was found dead in her room are any indication.[70]

The escapes of Apaches like María also occurred in neighboring provinces, eventually reaching the attention of the viceroy of New Spain. In 1751, Juan Francisco de Güemes, the Count of Revillagigedo, issued a fascinating order banning the "distribution, sale, or ransom" of Apaches older than seven years of age in the provinces of Sinaloa and Sonora. Any violation of this decree risked a two-hundred-peso fine. Lest this appear to be an anti-slavery measure, it's important to note that Güemes merely indicated that Apaches older than seven should be carried farther south, to "Zacatecas, Guadalajara, and other places en route to this court." He explained that his action was a response to correspondence with local officials regarding their investigations into a surge in Apache raids in the last few years. They had come to believe that escaped Apache slaves were a key explanatory factor. These "apostate fugitives" had returned to their Apache homelands with firsthand knowledge of the landscape of Spanish settlements and the routines of residents. After reuniting with kin, they guided them back south to plunder their former masters.[71]

This order presages concerns that would ultimate lead Spanish officials to argue that all Apache captives, regardless of age, be shipped to Mexico City and beyond to be kept secure. Fears of escapes and collusion between Spanish subjects, including servants and slaves, and independent Indians helped spark a war to gain control over Apache groups and helped lead to new strategies for dealing with captives taken in war. Yet the order also illustrates that the basic idea that Native captives could be moved long distances and exploited in this period was explicitly sanctioned even by the viceroy himself.[72]

New identities, a new official acceptance of Native bondage, and also new destinations influenced life for displaced Apache people in the eighteenth century. Restrictions on trade in New Mexico—in particular New Mexicans' reticence to provide Comanches with guns—helped lead them to seek other trading partners to the east. The sheer numbers of Apache baptisms in New Mexico and provinces to the south in Northern New Spain suggest that the majority of Apache captives taken by Comanche groups were transported there, but dozens more were circulated into Native trading networks that carried them east into New France, including Louisiana and Canada.[73]

The development of this slave trade altered older ways of dealing with war captives among some Plains Indian groups. Wichitas, for example, had traditionally killed enemy captives in ritual fashion. But by the 1710s, French demand for Apache captives was beginning to signal a change. When the French trader Bénard de la Harpe visited a Wichita village on the Canadian River in present-day Oklahoma, for example, he was given an eight-year-old Apache boy as part of ceremonial speeches and gift giving. But a Wichita chief also explained that if he had arrived a month earlier, he "could have given (or sold) him seventeen more Apaches, but alas, they had been killed in a public festival." Eventually, Wichita groups would hold on to more of their captives, if the supply of Apaches arriving into New France provides any indication.[74]

The French harbored no particular animus toward Plains Apache groups, and they attempted to trade with them as well in the 1720s. In the process, however, they revealed what Plains Apache leaders had already suggested to Spanish visitors: the burgeoning Native-French trade network was fueled in part by the circulation of Apache slaves. In 1724, for example, Étienne de Bourgmont sent a young woman and teenage boy he had purchased back to a Plains Apache village. His goal was to forge new trade relations with Apache leaders, hoping the gesture of returning their kinsmen would be met by reciprocal goodwill. He traveled to their camps three months later, laying out for them an array of trade goods that they might receive from the French: rifles, sabers, pickaxes, gunpowder, bullets, red cloth, blue cloth, mirrors, knives, beads, brass wire, and much more. Before more than two hundred men and a large group of women and children as an audience, the Apache leader highlighted what had been an impediment to such trade in the past. Although he was open to it, he explained that they would have to "return to us our women and children whom they have taken from us and who are slaves in their country."[75]

The French did not heed this Apache leader's request, as indicated by dozens of baptisms of Apaches in Detroit, Montreal, and Natchitoches in subsequent decades, including some brought back to Canada by members of Bourgmont's expedition, including by Bourgmont himself. As the historian Brett Rushforth has explained, Louisiana was the most logical and proximate destination, but the legality of Indian slavery in Canada and its more dubious status in Louisiana ensured that slave traders funneled more of their captives in directions where they could glean the highest prices. One Louisiana governor summarized the controversies surrounding Indian slavery in his jurisdiction when he noted that the traffic in Indian slaves was "contrary to the welfare of this country." He explained that the slave trade fueled unrest among neighboring Native populations, who presumably acquired slaves through attacks against each other. Even more important, however, Governor Etienne Perier complained that Indian slaves often deserted their masters and "being mixed with our negroes may induce them to desert with them." Governor Perier would not be the last imperial official to fear Apache-black collusion.[76]

This is not to say that no Apaches ended up in Louisiana. The area was a destination for Lipan captives taken from central Texas in particular, and captivity at the hands of Comanches was a concern they weighed in their decision-making around interactions with the Spanish. At the frontier settlement of Natchitoches, Apache slaves were a noticeable presence. As in other regions, their arrival over time, even if in relatively small numbers, facilitated the persistence of cultural identity.[77]

After the Spanish takeover of Louisiana in 1763 at the close of the Seven Years War, Spanish attention to French practices of slavery provided greater insight into the Comanche circulation of Apaches to the Louisiana frontier. After all, discussions of captivity and slavery have long served as means for groups to distinguish insiders from outsiders and to condemn enemies for their allegedly more severe, inhumane, or transgressive practices. Discussing (and decrying) Indian enslavement was a way for the new Spanish administrators of Louisiana, for example, to critique and distance themselves from the French, even as, in reality, the Spaniards also bought and held Indian slaves.[78]

Correspondence flooded in to the viceroy of New Spain in the 1770s regarding an "infamous traffic of the flesh" that characterized trade on the Louisiana frontier and revealed alleged Spanish superiority to the French.

Fray Miguel de Silva described to the viceroy in Mexico City, for example, how in the village of Cadodachos he had met Monsieur Alexi, a French carpenter. He was "so unchristian" that he had a son who was fifteen that he had not yet baptized. "Even worse than this," Silva noted, Alexi had five captive Indian women, "of various nations," in his house. On his way back to the Texas missions, Silva noted that a Frenchman who had put him up for the night had "retired in [his] sight with an Apachi Indian woman." Silva explained that she was pregnant and so near to term that he "prayed to God our Lord that she might be delivered that night in order that I might save the child."[79]

Perhaps it was because the men involved were French—and because Spanish officials were interested in asserting their control over foreign populations—that the Spaniards forbade the trade in horses, mules, and slaves from Indian nations. After all, officials had demonstrated little concern about Indian slavery elsewhere in jurisdictions they had long controlled, such as Northern New Spain. Men's legal actions in relation to their female slaves, meanwhile, provided further evidence of the Apache presence in the region. Francois Morvant, for example, had declared his ownership of a twenty-five-year-old Apache woman named Marie Anne as well as their twelve-year-old son in 1770. Several years later, Marie Anne had been enumerated in census record as Morvant's wife, "Ana Maria, of Apache nationality," suggesting that he may have married her to ensure that her presence in his household would be secure from Spanish meddling. Pierre Raimond acted similarly in marrying Francoise, another Apache woman, following her manumission. The fact that other men simply emancipated their slave women in response to Spanish policy changes suggests that Raimond and Morvant's actions may have reflected more than just practical concerns of ownership and also indicated relations of affection. In comparison, Jacque Ridde freed his eighteen-year-old Apache slave girl, Angélique, after "she pledged to remain in his service."[80]

If the archival record provides little insight into how these women understood their circumstances, the long-term significance of their presence in the region is signaled by an 1806 Anglo-American report after the U.S. takeover of Louisiana by John Sibley, the Indian agent of the region. He described the "still-prevalent Apache women who had been brought to Natchitoches, and sold amongst the French inhabitants, at forty or fifty dollars a head." They had become "servants in good families, and taught spinning, sewing . . . as well as managing household affairs." By marrying Frenchmen, they had become "respectable, and well-behaved women; and have now grown up, decent families of children, have a language peculiar to themselves, and are understood by signs by all others."[81]

As elsewhere in colonial North America, the descendants of Apache captives transported to Louisiana continued to be recognized as a distinct Apache group over time. Observers' descriptions of their unique language provide a tantalizing hint at the processes of cultural change and adaptation in diaspora. Descendants of Apache servants and slaves would continue to play a role in the distinctive cultural makeup of Louisiana communities going forward. People who counted Spaniards, Frenchmen, and varied Native refugees, including Lipan slaves, among their ancestors had coalesced in western Louisiana by the early nineteenth century. Today their descendants continue to live there as the state-recognized Choctaw Apache community of Ebarb.[82]

Owing in part to concerns about Indian slavery in Louisiana, many Apache slaves were carried farther north. French colonists drew upon the example of African slavery in the Caribbean in their acquisition of and treatment of Indians slaves in towns in New France like Detroit, Montreal, and Quebec. French participation in Indian slavery reflected twin motivations: most obviously potential masters' desire for slave labor but also the interests of Native groups like the Ottawa, Huron, and Ojibwe in supplying slaves as a means of forging and maintaining alliances with the French. Although French officials initially rejected captives as a legitimate token of friendship and goodwill, by 1709 they had legalized Indian slavery in New France to resolve confusion over captives' legal status and to ensure the Indian alliance system's stability and longevity.[83]

For Native captives transported into Canada after 1709, the formal legality of Indian slavery influenced their experiences, especially by supporting slave prices that made it worth the long journey and significant risks involved for the slave suppliers to transport them across the continent. In contrast to the circumstances of kin transported to New Mexico or New Spain, Apache slaves' escape and return was even more difficult, and their potential to shed slave status and be recognized as free persons within colonial society was more formally restricted. In Canada, Indian slavery more closely resembled black chattel slavery, with no theoretical end to enslavement other than death. In both colonial contexts, however, the intersection of labor demands with the interests of Native suppliers such as the Comanche, Pawnee, and Huron was central to the trade. In fact, colonial officials often justified Indian slavery, whether officially legal or not, based on geopolitical circumstances and the risks of offending powerful Native neighbors. For both the Spanish and French, Catholic concerns about the need to rescue Native captives from their "heathen," and supposedly more violent and cruel captors, also played an important role.[84]

Like his Spanish imperial rival in New Mexico, Governor Beauharnois of Quebec also drew upon his past observations of African American slavery to make sense of the Indian slaves in his midst. "Apaches, who are sold to voyageurs by our Indian allies . . . are brought to Montreal," he wrote to a colleague, "where they are considered as slaves . . . in the same manner as is practiced in the Americas for the Negros." In fact, Governor Beauharnois was not only an observer of Indian slavery but also a participant. He employed two Apache teenagers in his retinue of personal assistants, which included more than twenty other Indian slaves.[85]

To be carried to Canada and sold as a slave also meant that one might be transported by a master elsewhere in the French imperial world, as one Apache's life story reveals. Étienne de Veniard, Sieur de Bourgmont, who had journeyed into Apache country to seek a new trading partner, acquired one woman during his journey whom he took with him back to Canada. Marie Angelique was not the first, nor last, Native woman to stare out into the ocean and wonder what her future held when her master departed with her for France in 1725. As with so many other displaced Natives, fragmentary glimpses provided by parish records are all we know of her life trajectory. In 1728, a priest baptized her in the town of Cerisy, where her master had retired, describing her as his slave. Four years later, an entry records her marriage to a French man and the birth of a son. Presumably this marriage and her master's death meant her liberation from slavery—but not her return to the distant village on the plains across the world where she had been born.[86]

Loss and Coalescence

Apache communities were not ignorant of the fates of their kin sent away; the latter sometimes managed to return to share their experiences. At El Cuartelejo, for example, Apache leaders reported that they had learned about French men arming their enemies "by some women of their tribe who were made captives among the French on the occasions when they had war, but who had fled and returned." The loss—and occasional return—of kin influenced community decision-making as they weighed where they might live safely and with whom they should ally to improve their circumstances.[87]

In the years after a Spanish expedition to Apache villages on the plains revealed a Comanche-led conquest in progress, Apache leaders weighed the best means to find security and avoid being "finished entirely," as some had reportedly feared. In November 1723, Carlana and other leaders visited Santa Fe, offering to settle in the area, receive baptism, and pledge obedience to the Spanish Crown. After conferring with a council of war, Governor Bustamante accepted their offer, furnishing them with farm tools and seed to work land of their choosing near the Pecos and Taos pueblos. A number of Plains Apache groups would join them in New Mexico in the coming years. In 1752, Governor Vélez Cachupín described three hundred families of Carlanas, Palomas, and Cuartelejos living "neighborly" in the vicinity of Pecos.[88]

The depth of these groups' engagement with Spaniards was new, but their migration closer to Spanish settlements and Pueblo communities echoed a long history of traveling for trade and occasionally spending time near or among Pueblo allies. If in the aftermath of the Pueblo revolt, some Pueblo people had traveled north to live among Plains Apaches, Apaches now did the reverse. Governor Codallos wrote in 1748 about their presence northeast of New Mexico in the past tense, noting that "in times past, the Indians of the Jicarilla nation . . . were numerous and had houses, palisaded huts, and other shelters. Thence the pagan Comanches despoiled them, killing most of them." Now it was Comanches who camped along the Napestle (Arkansas) River, grazing their horse herds and launching expeditions that might travel two hundred leagues. Yet the governor highlighted the presence of survivors in his midst, as well, who had "established and maintained themselves in place nearby in the pueblos of Taos and Pecos, with their families."[89] Spaniards routinely called upon them to serve them in military campaigns, lauding their service as key to enlarging presidio and militia troops as scouts and guides and commending their vast knowledge of the land.[90]

Migration to the vicinity of Spanish and Pueblo settlements had a number of advantages, not the least of which was mutual defense. While the Jicarilla bands had given up much of their plains homelands, they retained access to mountain sites that had been a part of their ancestral territory, such as the Sangre de Cristo Mountains, and still were able to make trips out onto the New Mexico plains to hunt buffalo. Alliance with the Spanish did not preclude them from trading with neighboring Apache groups either, to whom they offered foodstuff, hides, and tools in exchange for livestock. While Spanish governors complained about this practice, they also were powerless to stop it entirely. As Governor Vélez Cachupín noted in 1754, he had discouraged Jicarillas "in every way possible" from associating with Mescalero bands, yet he lamented that it was impossible to prevent. "One wants horses, which they lack," he explained, "and the other, skins for shelter." In the end, it was best to keep them "sympathetic and linked to [Spanish] interests" and turn a blind eye to their role as purchasers in livestock rustling networks targeting Spanish ranches in Northern New Spain.[91]

The Jicarilla-Spanish alliance in New Mexico endured because the Spanish were powerful enough there to provide some measure of protection as valuable allies, and because they were flexible enough to tolerate allied Apaches' interactions with independent groups that rustled Spanish livestock. Indeed, while some Plains Apache communities had pledged obedience to the Spanish crown or received baptism, they remained strikingly independent in community decision-making. The niche role that Jicarillas played in northern New Mexico continued in the coming decades. Governor Pedro Fermín de Mendinueta noted this dynamic in his observations in the early 1770s, explaining how "it has not been possible to reduce some Apaches called Jicarillas who, despoiled of their lands by the Comanches, have been living for many years in this region in huts of their own making near the Pueblos of Pecos and Taos." Gradually, the previous group and band divisions that marked identities in Apaches' old Plains homelands faded, as they coalesced in their new territories as bands known to the Spanish as the Olleros and Llaneros and to themselves as Sait Ndé (sand people) and Gulgahén (people of the plains). Through diaspora and engagement with allies old and new, they prospered in lands where some of their descendants continue to live today.[92]

Like their distant relatives in northern New Mexico, Lipan Apaches' receptiveness to an alliance with Spaniards in central Texas was also fueled by concerns about Native enemies and the loss of kin to captivity and slavery; however, the strength of this alliance proved much more fleeting. Both groups had grown weary of violence by the late 1740s, a time when Apache bands on the southern plains were suffering repeated attacks from Comanches and their Wichita, Caddo, and Tonkawa allies. The combined force of these groups, which Spaniards had begun to identify as Norteños (northerners), increasingly concerned Spaniards as well, because they feared an enemy with more power than the Lipans was looming. After a 1749 ceremony at San Antonio in which Spaniards and Lipans symbolically set aside their enmity by burying a horse, hatchet, lance, and six arrows, they announced the promise to view one another as "brothers" going forward. One Native family even decided to reside at the Valero mission, perhaps because of captive relatives there or in adjacent San Antonio.[93]

The Lipan-Spanish alliance did not endure, however, owing to both groups' relative weakness in the face of Norteño attacks. A mission at San

Sabá designed specifically to serve Lipans was built in 1757 but was destroyed by Comanches and their allies the following year. Subsequent missions to the south along the Nueces River were built in the early 1760s, at the request of Lipan leaders who "assured the missionaries that they represented the wishes of ten other chiefs and their people, and that once they had become settled in the missions, allied Apache bands . . . who were related to them via intermarriage . . . would congregate there as well."[94]

The supposed ties of brotherhood forged in 1749 had unraveled within fifteen years as neither the Natives nor Spaniards proved able to protect mission settlements. Lipans found shelter by abandoning them and retreating south. As Juliana Barr notes, "The defeats warned Apaches that Spanish forces were two few and too weak to aid in the defense of their lands." For their part, Spaniards interpreted Lipan flight as a sign of their perhaps inherently "fickle" and "faithless" character. Increasingly awed by Norteño power, the Spaniards began weighing the possibility of switching allies and openly discussed the idea of crushing independent Ndé groups by joining with their long-standing Comanche enemies.[95]

Chased out of central Texas by Native enemies, Lipan groups migrated south, camping along the Rio Grande and venturing into Coahuila, much to the lament of area ranchers. One Lipan woman later explained her memory of these years to the anthropologist Morris Opler. She explained that they had liked the country around San Antonio when they had found it, and they had made it home. Then they had to move, and liking what they found in Coahuila, they had "made that their country."[96]

*   *   *

By the 1770s, Apaches appeared to some outside observers to be nearly vanquished. In a legend explaining a new Spanish imperial map in 1778, the cartographer Bernardo de Miera y Pacheco noted: "[Comanches] have made themselves the lords of all the buffalo country, seizing it from the Apache nation, which formerly was the most widespread of all known [Native nations] in America. They have destroyed many of them [Apaches], and those which remain they have pushed to the frontiers of our King's provinces." In distilling a complicated and painful history into a sentence, Miera y Pacheco oversimplified. Left out of his gloss were the many Apache captives taken beyond the "frontiers of our King's provinces" to labor in colonial society, lost kin who played a key role in the decision-making of communities left behind. Left out were groups, like the Jicarilla, who played an important role in defending their own communities and Spaniards and Puebloans against Comanche raids. Yet his basic description of both destruction and survival was apt. As Apache groups sought to navigate life on the "frontiers of [Spanish] provinces," Spaniards increasingly feared that their frontiers were receding rather than advancing, and they began debating new strategies for finally taking control over "the Apache nation"—or eliminating it entirely.[97]

PART II

Apaches, Empires, and Nations

Even if they are sent to workshops in the capital, the Apache are so warlike, the men as well as the women, they can easily return to their homelands. . . . Only by transporting them to windward islands in small groups, will we ever see these frontiers free of these enemies.

—Colonel Hugo O'Connor, Chihuahua, 1776

In my talks with the Indians they showed no resentment of the way they had been treated in the past; only wonderment at the why of it. Why had they been shifted from reservation to reservation; told to farm and had their crops destroyed; assured that the Government would ration them, then left to half starve; herded in the hot, malarial river bottoms of the Gila and San Carlos, when they were mountain people? These and other questions I could not answer.

—Lieutenant Britton Davis,
in *The Truth About Geronimo*, 1929

I want to have all our children together where I can see them.

—Chihuahua (Chokonen Apache),
Mt. Vernon Barracks, Alabama, 1894

CHAPTER 4

Family, Household, *Gotah*

In the spring of 1791, three Southern Apache men accompanied Spanish soldiers and a coffle of Native prisoners of war on a thousand-mile journey
to Mexico City. For months prior, Apaches had been asking the Spanish to
return relatives who had been exiled to central New Spain and the Caribbean in recent years. Spanish officials believed that the requests of three
particular leaders—El Compá, Tetsegoslán, and Yagonjli—could not go
unheeded, given that they had negotiated peace with the Spanish and were
aiding them in ongoing military campaigns. The offer to arrange a trip for
three of their representatives to search for kin in New Spain's capital came
with one important condition, however. Any relatives they found who had
already received Christian baptism would not be allowed to return with
them. "It would not be fair," the Spanish commandant general explained,
"for a Christian person on the right path to return among [Apaches] and be
corrupted." After a seventy-three-day journey south to Mexico City, the men
spent another four weeks lodged at a boardinghouse at night while searching for their relatives in Spanish households by day. They ultimately located
only one of them: a fifteen- or sixteen-year-old youth who had already been
baptized. Any disappointment the men felt at this turn of events is not
revealed by the archival record. What I do know is that before they returned
home, the men petitioned the Spanish viceroy with one further request: for
each to be granted a woman from among the coffle of captives they had
accompanied south "to live in their union." This request was granted, and by
June they were on their way home.[1]

This episode throws us into the disorienting fog of war. Coffles of war
captives travel south from the North American West in months-long journeys. Relatives left behind weigh options, negotiating with former enemies
in the hopes of reuniting families and keeping them safe. An exiled youth is
greeted by kin in diaspora but not reunited with them; women captured in

war by the Spanish are granted as wives to them instead. Left unnamed in the archival record, the women's views on their situation and return north are also left unmentioned. Questions arise: When and how had this war begun? Why were Apache captives being shipped so far from home by soldiers? Why were they being placed in Spanish homes? And why, after the effort and cost of doing so, would the Spanish be open to the possibility of returning some of them, as long as they had not been baptized?

This story, and the questions it prompts, serve to introduce a new era of diaspora in Apache history. The slave trade had played an important role in Apaches' lives in the seventeenth and eighteenth centuries, influencing relations with neighboring groups, strategies of diplomacy, trade, and warfare, and the loss of significant numbers of kin to bondage and new lives of labor in proximate and distant lands. But for the Southern and Mescalero Apache groups in particular, imperial aims in the second half of the eighteenth century supplanted market demands and profit motives as the reason behind captivity and forced migrations. This change was especially due to their residence and mobility between imperial population centers in New Spain and the vast lands of the North American West, which, Spaniards increasingly recognized, remained for all practical purposes under Native control. New Spanish efforts to finally subjugate the mobile Apache groups on their northern frontier emerged as a creative response to their own relative weakness and to new political and economic initiatives that made gaining control over frontier zones seem newly urgent. Because the Spanish army regiments and militias were limited in numbers, they relied significantly on Native allies and a divide-and-conquer military strategy that by necessity entailed understanding the relationships between Apache groups in order to locate them, kill or capture them, and seek to pit them against each other.[2]

If the Indian slave trade had been fueled by the generalization that all Apaches are enslaveable, the Spanish officials' imperial drive to subjugate and "take charge of the governance" of Apache groups in the eighteenth century required understanding particulars: Who is allied with us and who is not? Who is related to whom? In fact, both the roots of war between Spanish and Apache groups and the strategies they employed to wage it can be traced to the central concern of Southern Apache emissaries in the summer of 1791: family. The very term "family" is multilayered in its connotations, and its meaning is historically and culturally contingent. When I speak of my "family," I may be speaking of a spouse and children with whom I live, or of other relatives with whom my ties and obligations are more distant: parents, siblings, cousins, aunts, and uncles. I may mean an economic, biological, or

legal unit, but family may also be based on more-abstract ties alone: the chosen family of friends, the spiritual family of a church, the political family of
an empire or nation.[3]

The Apache emissaries' appeal is illustrative of their views on such
matters. Their sense of their own humanity was centrally linked to kinship, "shik'íí" (my relatives), the relationships based on lineage, marriage,
and adoption that defined their obligations, loyalties, and sense of belonging as people in the world. The links between extended family households
that together formed a *gotah*, a family cluster or local group, were central to
Apache people's subsistence and distinguished them from others to whom
the same moral constraints and ideas about reciprocity did not apply. Ultimately, the emissaries sought the return of their relatives not simply because
of a biological connection or their affection for them, but also because they
were their central source of power. Without sufficient kin, Apache groups
would be unable to mobilize raiding or war parties, or gather enough food,
or even birth enough children to ensure a future. This helps to explain why
when the emissaries were unable to bring home the relatives they originally
sought, they innovated, requesting three captives to return north with them
instead, to be incorporated as kin in their place.[4]

The family in its various senses—biological, ideological, political, economic—mattered deeply to Spanish-Apache relations during a war that escalated in the 1770s and continued for more than two decades. The Spanish
targeted the families of Southern and Mescalero Apache groups in military
campaigns during this period in the interests of finally achieving what had
long eluded them: not only control of what they called Apacheria, the lands
across southwestern North America controlled by various Apache groups, but
also control of their own "family," the diverse subjects within colonial society
whose affinities and affiliations sometimes stretched outside it. Closer relations
between the Apache and Spanish spheres over the course of the eighteenth century produced within each group greater familiarity with and knowledge of the
other. Interactions had been rooted in collaboration and cooperation more than
in violence, particularly between Apaches and missionized Native groups such
as the Tarahumara. Southern and Mescalero Apaches drew upon traditional
strategies for incorporating outsiders, including intermarriage, co-residence,
and the adoption and incorporation of captives or refugees from Spanish
colonial society. Amid new imperial efforts to reform the administration of
frontier regions, improve security, and extract greater revenue—the Bourbon
Reforms—Spanish concerns about contacts between Apaches and Spanish-
affiliated communities in Northern New Spain escalated, however. New

investigations revealed what other local officials and residents had sometimes noted in the past. Livestock rustling and homicides usually blamed on Apaches were in fact being conducted by people of a variety of ethnicities: Natives, mestizos, mulattos, and even Spaniards. Unless such cooperation and mutual affinity was addressed, security would never improve, given that "the thief would still remain within the house," as one official evocatively commented.[5]

After war began, the family, household, and gotah continued to be central to each side's methods. Spanish campaigns began attacking the clusters of extended families that composed local groups closest to their own lands, those of the Southern and Mescalero Apache groups. Capturing the relatives of key Apache leaders, as they had done with El Compá, Tetsegoslán, and Yagonjli, was one key strategy in a broader effort to link violence, captivity, and forced migration with offers of peace, gifts, and rations to incentivize them to lay down their arms, settle near Spanish military forts, and agree to aid the Spanish in campaigns against other Apache local groups and bands. Facing the threat of displacement, some Apache leaders proved willing to prioritize the security of their own extended families over that of other, more distant relations, aiding the Spanish in their campaigns to kill, capture, and exile other Apaches. Ultimately, these efforts helped lead to the death or diaspora of a third or more of the Southern and Mescalero Apache populations in a few decades time, while many survivors agreed to live at peace near Spanish military forts under the watchful eye of soldiers who would provide them with regular rations as *Apaches de paz* (peaceful Apaches).[6] For surviving families, difficult political choices prevented them from losing more kin and sometimes enabled them to secure the return of their previously captured relatives. Yet hundreds of captives were not kept safe or returned and instead endured exile in distant Spanish households, which Spanish officials and residents envisioned as key sites through which "heathen" Indians outsiders could be transformed into Christian Indian vassals, members of the imperial "family." The struggle of empires and nations to wrest control of, displace, or confine Southern Apache families and the local groups and bands that interlinked them was at the heart of an Apache diaspora in this period and in the decades to come.[7]

Kinship Knowledge and the Roots of War

Spanish and Apache understandings and practices of family and kinship provide a key to understanding the roots of war between them in the late eighteenth century. Spanish approaches to Southern Apache people in the late

1700s, like Apaches' approaches to Spaniards, reflected a level of familiarity built over time that helps to explain each group's turn to violence. Spaniards, for example, had first encountered Apache groups in the sixteenth century. Seventeenth-century accounts of New Mexico describe the vast territories controlled by Apache people, noting that the kingdom was surrounded by the "Apache nation." Few if any seventeenth-century Spaniards parsed the divisions among Apache groups or demonstrated much of an interest in the nature of their belief systems or ways of life, although there were exceptions, such as the Spanish captain we met in Chapter 1, who faced an Inquisition trial over his bigamous marriage to an Apache woman and the child he had left among her people. The interest of New Mexico residents in slave labor, for use within the kingdom and for export beyond it, lent weight to an expansive understanding of "Apache" people. Labeling diverse groups that understood themselves as distinct facilitated the capture and acquisition of slaves under the justification that their nation had collectively resisted Spanish rule, whatever the actual history of interethnic relations. While the Spanish foothold in New Mexico was in fact tenuous, as the Pueblo Revolt of 1680 illustrated, the idea that an Apache "nation" had waged incessant war against either the Spanish or Pueblo Indian peoples was pure fiction. Both before and after the arrival of the Spanish, Apache groups' relations with outsiders were varied and often characterized by mutual aid. Even violence—including raiding for livestock, foodstuffs, and captives—could be assimilated into productive exchange relations, as the ransom of captured kin offered new opportunities for the exchange of needed resources.[8]

The Apache-Spanish borderlands shifted south in the eighteenth century. While historical actors and some historians describe Apaches as migrating into or invading New Spain from the north during this period, it was as much the northward movement of Spanish colonial society as Apache migrations that led to new zones of interaction. The Bolsón de Mapimí, a dry basin straddling Nueva Vizcaya and Coahuila, emerged as a key site for such interactions. Offensive wars and deportation campaigns against the allied bands of Indigenous groups that had previously inhabited the basin coincided with new mining strikes that led to the establishment of El Real de Minas de San Francisco de Cuella in 1709, which grew into the newly named villa of San Felipe el Real de Chihuahua by 1718. This burgeoning settlement fueled the opening of new ranching and farming lands to supply it.[9]

As Spanish settlements in New Spain spread north and grew in population, some Apaches sensed opportunities and traveled south on raiding and trading expeditions in greater numbers. As in the past in New Mexico, the

Apache presence in Northern New Spain in the eighteenth century generated complex reactions within Spanish colonial society, as fear and misun-
derstanding mingled with perceived opportunities. The lack of a uniform
reaction or approach to the Apache people was in part a reflection of the
diverse interests of the residents of the region during this period. While some
Spanish landowners feared Apache raids, many mission Indian communities saw more benefit than risk in having Apache trading partners. Though
faint in concrete details, investigations by the Spanish authorities in Sonora
and Nueva Vizcaya during the mid-1700s suggest that Native slaves also
sometimes took advantage of the presence of independent Apaches to escape
during raids and return to their natal communities or simply to gain their
liberty and live in maroon communities. This history helped spark a 1751
order from the viceroy mandating that Apache captives be transported further south for distribution, sale, or confinement.[10]

Layered concerns about the loyalties of Spanish subjects and about the
potential expansion of powerful neighbors, Native and European alike, provided incentives for the Spanish to better understand Apache communities
on their northern frontier. Apache groups shared an ancestral language
and many cultural practices and traditions, and they recognized degrees of
kinship with neighboring Apache bands, especially through intermarriage.
Temporary alliances or agreements in the interests of mutual protection or
economic pursuits were not uncommon, particularly when shared relatives
could be identified, even if there was no pan-Apache political structure or
recognition of a collective tribal identity. But the arrival of the Spanish and
resulting changes in regional geopolitics, including the territorial gains and
expanding trading networks of mounted and armed Utes and Comanches,
played a role in both the coalescence and divergence of Apache groups and
identities over time, as the story of Jicarilla and Lipan Apaches charted in
Chapter 3 reveals.[11]

By the late eighteenth century, the Spanish understood Apache kinship
relations to a degree they had not before. Spanish military officers spent
careers in the vicinity of Apache groups, learned their names and even their
language, got to know specific Apache headmen and their families, gained
fluency in Apache politics, and could explain the varied Apache groups that
"govern[ed] themselves independently of one another."[12] They learned about
and named important distinctions between Apache tribal groups. For Southern Apache groups, the Spanish noted that they were divided into bands that
occupied particular terrain: Mimbreños, Gileños, Chiricahuis. Apaches were
familiar with such Spanish terms, which referred to "the people living along

the Mimbres River" or to "the people living in the Chiricahua Mountains." Their own names for band divisions are difficult to recover conclusively from the eighteenth century but almost certainly included the bands that they reported later in the nineteenth century: Chokonen, Chihene, Nednhi, and Bedonkohe—names that also evoked geography or key lifeways: "juniper people," "red paint people."[13]

What some Spaniards had come to understand is that even these bands were not necessarily unitary in interests and loyalty. The "vast" Apache nation described by outsiders in the seventeenth century was in fact no unitary polity at all. As among their distant Plains Apache relatives, the building block of broader political divisions among Southern Apaches was the local group, or gotah, which the Spanish called *rancherias*, or "little settlements." The local group was a cluster of families related by descent, marriage, or adoption that served as the basic subsistence unit of society and also as the primary means through which the Southern Apache people understood their sense of belonging and their obligations as human beings. Traditionally, while Southern Apaches traced their descent through both their mother's and father's lines, they practiced matrilocal residence: a man would join the family camp of the woman he married. While her family would have the largest claim on his labor, he would retain ties to his family of birth as well. The web of kin relations connecting each local group with others helped provide for the needs of the people and also generated broader connections within and between Southern Apache bands. Members of one local group would join with others in raiding, trading, hunting, and horticulture, linking together and providing strength to the larger band. At the same time, in times of utmost need, Southern Apaches reserved their primary loyalty for their local group, to ensure the survival of extended families. The Spanish paid particular attention to the power of the Apache headman who led such families, whom they called a *capitán* and Apaches called the *nantan*, the leader or spokesman. The power of persuasion of a nantan was usually limited to their own network of kin or local group and based on continued success in hunting, raiding, and war.[14]

By learning about Southern Apache headmen, their places of residence, and family relations, the Spanish gained in their ability to either negotiate with or wage war against Apaches by the late eighteenth century. Southern Apache understandings of Spaniards also changed over time. During the seventeenth century, Apaches engaged with Spanish newcomers much as they had with other Native groups in the past: through trade or raids to acquire resources; diplomacy; and experimentation with new belief systems and technologies. Spanish and Pueblo raids for captives had also taught the

Southern Apaches about the invaders' particular interests in exploiting labor on farms, ranches, and factories and in the Palace of the Governors. Written records make it hard to be sure the precise degree to which Apaches came to understand the kinship ties or political links between communities affiliated with the Spanish monarch or the relationship between Spanish subjects and their distant king. Their actions that are recorded, however, suggest that by the eighteenth century they understood the fragmented nature of Spanish governance and the reality that not all Spanish subjects behaved in the same way or had the same interests or loyalties.[15]

A greater degree of proximity and interaction in the eighteenth century helped various Apache groups build a greater understanding of the families, resources, and politics of Spanish-affiliated communities. The rise of the Comanche trading empire during the eighteenth century, for example, had pushed Jicarilla groups out of present-day Colorado and into northern New Mexico, where they thrived in the spaces between the Hispanic and Puebloan Indian communities. Seasonal migrations of Mescalero Apaches increasingly brought them closer to the Rio Grande and its mission Indian settlements, meanwhile, as their buffalo hunts on the southern plains made them vulnerable to attacks from Comanche enemies. To the east, Lipan Apaches had also faced war with the Comanche and had similarly migrated toward the Rio Grande and the Spanish settlements of Northern New Spain. Meanwhile, migration had been less important as a strategy for the Western Apache groups of present-day Arizona, whose homelands were less disturbed by either the Spanish or newly powerful Native foes.[16]

For Southern Apache groups, it is as much the migrations of Spaniards into their homelands as their own mobility that explains a new degree of interaction between them over the course of the eighteenth century. The Spanish formed new presidios, towns, and ranches in the provinces of Northern New Spain after large-scale Indian rebellions during the late seventeenth century, such as the Pueblo and Tarahumara Revolts. The presidios bordering Apache territories in Sonora, Nueva Vizcaya, New Mexico, Coahuila, and Texas housed Spanish military regiments that were supposed to guard the frontier and make it safe for Spanish settlement and new mining and ranching enterprises. Often, however, the presidios served as sites of trade between Spanish-affiliated and Native populations almost as much as they did launching points for war. The same was true for the missions of the Rio Grande, where friars in the mid-1700s had complained that all their neophytes did was "go around on horseback trading with Apaches."[17]

Kinship relations facilitated such trade. Through raiding and the acquisition of captives, Southern Apache groups sometimes incorporated members of Spanish-affiliated communities into their local groups. Spanish towns, presidios, and missions likewise incorporated Apaches through occasional campaigns against Southern Apache bands. When Apache emissaries spoke about the Spaniards "long married among us" in their diplomatic entrees to Spanish officials, they revealed connections between Apache and Spanish groups that help clarify the ability of Apaches to conduct trade "among their relatives" living in towns like El Paso in the 1760s. Concerns about this trade led the captain of the adjacent Presidio del Norte in 1762 to order that no residents, whether Spanish, Indian, or "de color quebrado" (of broken color), could trade with Apaches in seeds, firearms, or livestock. He explained his fear that residents, in seeking their own personal gain, would bring danger to themselves by inviting Apaches into their homes to trade. Yet in his effort to control this trade, he did not restrict dealing with Apaches altogether but instead ordered that it be carried out "in the light of day" in the town plaza.[18]

Kinship relations also help elucidate how and why members of Spanish-affiliated communities, including Indians, mestizos, and mulattos, could join with Southern Apaches in supplying a regional trade in contraband livestock during this period. Apaches' knowledge of the various interests of people affiliated with the Spanish helped make this raiding and trading economy work. They recognized that the nature of Spanish jurisdictions meant that militias or garrisons guarding New Mexican settlements would be unlikely to follow Apache raiding parties into Nueva Vizcaya or Sonora, nor would troops in those locations typically follow them into New Mexico. Spanish communities in one province often proved willing to buy the booty of raids from elsewhere. In a sense, the Southern Apaches, like other Apache groups, learned that the "Spanish," which also comprised mission Indians, mestizos, and mulattos, were not so different from them; like Apaches, they cared more about their own families and local communities than their connections to any broader ethnic, political, or religious affiliation.[19]

Tellingly, Spanish officials governing those communities were often as concerned about the "infidelity" of their subjects as they were about the threat of Apache people as enemies. Some friars, local magistrates, and governors believed that missionized Indians and migrant workers contributed as much, if not more, to the lack of security in the northern provinces of New Spain than did Apaches. In the 1750s and 1760s, friars, governors, and even presidio captains had reported that Sumas, Tarahumaras, and others were raiding

as "thieves from inside the house." While they often blamed Apaches for having "perverted" these Christians Indians, they also reported on observing
a much larger trading economy along the Rio Grande that illustrated that
mission Indians needed little convincing to join with Apaches when it was
mutually beneficial. If some local officials wanted to end the loss of livestock,
they found themselves facing legal constraints, such as the lack of witnesses,
and what they described as "the delicate matter" of punishing Indians living
in missions and risking their desertion.[20]

A particularly thorough investigation into alleged collusion between
Apaches and Tarahumaras in 1773 helps illustrate the intersection of Apache-
Spanish relations with concerns about the imperial "family" and its loyalties. In March 1773, a magistrate in Chihuahua began an inquiry into recent
reports of livestock rustling, kidnappings, and homicides in the interests of
ascertaining the perpetrators. While such actions were usually blamed on
generic "enemy Indians" or "Apaches," the testimony he gathered from several
hundred Tarahumara Indian witnesses suggested that the situation was more
complex. Some of the large groups of men and women involved in livestock
rustling and homicides were actually interethnic in composition, including
mission Indians such as the Tarahumara, mestizos, and mulattos. These raiding bands traded livestock, weapons, foodstuffs, and hides with Southern and
Mescalero Apache associates who were tied into broader Native trading networks. Pedro Queipo de Llano explained the implications of his findings in a
1773 report to his superiors: "Our forces will make little progress even if we
finish with the whole Apacheria, because the thief will still be in the house.
After all, Apaches haven't taken even one horse or mule that wasn't turned
into them by Tarahumaras." This would not be the first time that fears of clandestine relations between subjects and enemies proved influential. Another
investigation ten years later resulted in the apprehension of nearly a thousand
Tarahumara men and women, including some of the same individuals implicated in the earlier episode. This time, witnesses explained how for the past
twenty years they had been dealing with Apaches, who had come to stay with
them in their houses "with the same security as in their own [camps]."[21]

It is impossible to determine definitively how many of the damaging raids
that Nueva Vizcaya, Sonora, and neighboring provinces experienced during
this period were committed by Apaches versus mission Indians or "Spanish"
criminals. Descriptions of Apache camps attacked by the Spanish army do
indicate that at least some of the interethnic trade relations described by witnesses in the investigations into Tarahumara-Apache collusion were occur-
ring. Moreover, the devastation described in some alleged Apache attacks,

including the indiscriminate destruction of property, fits with Apache practices of warfare, which emphasized retaliatory destruction over the apprehension of enemy property. In fact, by the early 1770s, sustained campaigns into Apache lands, including the capture of a growing number of Southern and Mescalero Apache prisoners destined for Chihuahua jails, gave plenty of motivation for Apaches to pursue war.[22]

Queipo de Llano's investigation ultimately reflects a broader tension of the period. Even as Spanish officials gathered knowledge of distinct Apache groups and their places of residence and realized the groups were politically independent of each other, the perceived cultural similarities between Apache groups led the officials to continue to speak of a "whole Apacheria" threatening New Spain. On the one hand, the knowledge Spaniards had gained of Apache groups—and their own subjects' conflicted loyalties—might have assuaged concerns about the threat those groups posed to New Spain and its interests. On the other hand, while specific knowledge of Apache kinship relations would serve the Spaniards well in war, the ways in which they conflated kinship knowledge with broader categories, such as "barbarian Indian" or "heathen," were key sparks for war in the first place.[23]

Spanish investigations into clandestine relations between their subjects and the Southern and Mescalero Apaches coincided with new imperial attention to the northern domains of the Spanish empire. In the 1760s, for example, the Spanish Crown commissioned an important expedition to explore the northern frontier and prepare new military regulations and policy recommendations. The Marqués de Rubí's mission embodied the broader hopes of King Carlos III and his officials that professional management, economic reform, and a streamlined bureaucracy might produce greater royal control over Spain's American kingdoms and generate a greater stream of revenue to the treasury. Questions about the vulnerability of Northern New Spain to a land attack from imperial competitors to the north and east, particularly due to the degree of Native control of these territories, were of particular interest.[24]

The expedition's engineer, Nicolás LaFora, prepared the official diary of the expedition, which illustrates how imperial efforts to better understand Apache groups and the relations between them drew upon and conflated kinship with other means of categorizing human difference in significant ways. In the ways in which he interpreted current affairs, LaFora was clearly influenced by ideas about Indian barbarism. He described and mapped with scientific precision the geographic points of entry of the "indios bárbaros" and their frequent attacks, despite evidence that cattle rustling and raiding were interethnic endeavors. Attributing such attacks solely to "Apaches," he drew upon vivid descriptions of their violence against Spanish communities as evidence of Apaches' "inherent nature and character." For LaFora, history proved that Apaches were inconvertible barbarians.[25]

Or maybe not. Even as he echoed many of his contemporaries in describing Apache barbarism—their allegedly unending "murders and robberies"— he suggested that their behavior might be changeable. He blamed Spanish regiments for laziness in their failure to correct the situation, lobbying for a new "continuous offensive war" against Apaches in "their own homes." Only by targeting Apache families, LaFora believed, could the Spanish ever succeed in "correcting them, vanquishing them, or even annihilating them." Taking Apache women and children captive would be an important strategy in decreasing their population: "Their numbers would be diminished even though few [men] were killed or captured." Breaking apart Apache families, in other words, was key to ending their independent political existence.[26]

LaFora's rhetoric is indicative of the ways in which other Spaniards conflated socio-racial, cultural, and religious categories with ideas about family, kinship, and behavior during this period. On the one hand, Spaniards sometime suggested that the character of all Apaches was so ingrained that they would never embrace Spanish rule or Christianity. In doing so, thinkers like LaFora sometimes advocated policies with genocidal consequences in mind: annihilation, or at least significantly diminishing Apache populations. On the other hand, different ideas worked against any fixed racialization of Apache or other Native people, especially the still prevalent idea that *naturaleza*—a person's native habitat—went hand and hand with character and behavior. In this analysis, the Apache character was fueled by improper kinship relations, their mobile lifeways in a hostile mountain and desert environment, and their heathenism. Displaced from their families and "habitat," Apache people might be transformed, as long as they were embedded in new kinship structures, especially Spanish households and hierarchal relations of dependence. While conceptualized as something other than annihilation, the violence and forced migrations involved in producing such forced acculturation nonetheless often proved genocidal in practice.[27]

In summary, Spaniards like Lafora could simultaneously ignore evidence of kinship relations between and across Apache and Spanish communities in making the case for war while evidencing a keen sense of Apache kinship relationships when such knowledge was useful in wartime. One advisor to the viceroy in Mexico City, for example, referenced evident "confusions of friendship and kinship" even as he argued that Apaches' "perverse customs and inclinations" alone warranted Spanish efforts to "take charge of their governance." If war had not been inevitable as Spaniards and Apaches increasingly interacted and gained knowledge of each other over the course of the eighteenth century, by the 1770s its logic became self-perpetuating. New military regulations adopted by King Carlos III in 1772 incorporated ideas from the Rubi expedition and LaFora's report. While Spanish policy since the late sixteenth century had stressed the formation of peace agreements with enemy Indians—in fact, Indians who asked for peace had to be granted it—the regulations of 1772 deviated from past precedent by authorizing an offensive war against non-Christian Indians. As Spanish regiments sought to punish Apaches for a clandestine economy and violence that was in fact interethnic in nature, Apaches responded with their own attacks.[28]

The "discovery" that Tarahumaras, mulattos, and perhaps even Spaniards may have committed raids and homicides that were attributed to Apaches did not change the course of the ongoing military campaigns against Apaches in the 1770s and 1780s. The very fact that officials ultimately disbanded their inquiries suggests they feared that these investigations might ignite Tarahumara rebellions that could prove costlier than war against Apaches. Maintaining (or consolidating) the Spanish regime in Northern New Spain took precedence over reforming or punishing members of its own imperial family, although hundreds of Tarahumaras nevertheless did face torture and long-term incarceration during the investigations. Official reports drew indiscriminately upon histories of raiding to justify further military action against Apaches. Voluminous and detailed local reports describing raids suffered over time at the instigation of a vague enemy were compiled in a Chihuahua archive and then simplified into clear-cut statistics attributing all the damages to Apaches. In war councils in the 1770s, military officers contended that war had begun in 1748, and that in the years since, Apaches alone had committed more than four thousand murders, stolen thousands of livestock, and caused more than 11 million pesos in losses to the regional economy, statistics that historians have supported.[29]

Broad socio-racial, cultural, and religious categorizations helped lay the groundwork for a war in which a more nuanced understanding of families and kinship relations would be a key tactic. While the Spanish continued to experiment with different strategies of war and debated the proper fate of Native war captives in the coming years, LaFora's basic idea of targeting Apache families remained key. Military campaigns in the 1770s and 1780s pursued Apaches in their own camps, killed or captured men, women, and children, and exiled captives to central New Spain by the hundreds. When Apaches proved able to escape and return north to their homelands, the

Spanish innovated, ordering that all war captives, no matter their age, be sent to Cuba. One Spanish military officer, Hugo O'Connor, had warned as much in the 1770s, when he argued that only by breaking Apaches up into small groups and "sending them to windward islands" could the frontiers of New Spain ever be made secure for Spanish families.[30]

Family and kinship networks were not just targets of Spanish colonialism but also its tools. While not all of the more than two thousand Apache captives ultimately exiled during this period survived the journey, incarceration in jails or forced incorporation into Spanish households as laborers waited for those who did. Apaches arriving in New Spain and the Caribbean were greeted by petitions from area residents eager to receive an Indian woman or man for their homes. Echoing imperial rhetoric, they promised to "raise them like their own [children]" and educate and Christianize them, all while benefiting from their unpaid labor. Spanish imperial officials and subjects envisioned that Spanish kinship traditions such as godparenthood and the criado system ("raising up" heathen Indians through domestic service) represented key means of reducing the number of independent, "heathen" Apaches in southwestern America and increasing the number of useful, Christian, Indian vassals elsewhere. They characterized all Apache people as "inhuman barbarians" or "indomitable savages" warranting "extermination," even as they then drew upon discourses of kinship, civilization, and religiosity to suggest that Apaches might prove redeemable after all, as long as they were separated from kin and homeland. Yet that separation and the conditions of forced migration would trouble the supposed distinction between redemptive and genocidal aims, as we will explore in greater depth in Chapter 5.[31]

The pressure on Southern Apache groups increased as the Spanish gained new Native allies in the mid-1780s—especially the Comanche and Ute—and combined strategic violence with diplomacy in new ways. The influential general Bernardo de Gálvez issued policy recommendations in 1786 that built on three key principles: offensive military campaigns "to the point of exterminating Apaches if necessary"; building alliances designed to make Natives fight other natives; and providing Indians with gifts and rations in the hopes of purchasing peace, which he believed would be cheaper than the "useless reinforcements of troops."[32] The impact of such efforts is illustrated by the fact that between 1786 and 1789 alone, Spanish forces took as captives at least 665 Apaches and exiled the majority of these people to central New Spain and the Gulf Coast. Spanish military officials also tallied the deaths of 595 Apache men, women, and children in military campaigns during this same period. It should be noted that such statistics did not take into account the significant attacks Southern Apaches also faced from the Comanche, Ute, and Navajo allies of the Spanish.[33]

War always influences families, but the degree to which Spanish officials consciously sought to manipulate Apache kinship relations and loyalties was especially striking in this context. It reflected the increased familiarity Spanish and Apache people had built over time and an increased willingness by the Spanish to use any means necessary to finally subjugate people who had long eluded their control. While families and kinship networks were central to Apache efforts to mobilize war parties, their strategies of war were ultimately quite different than those of the Spanish. Apaches distinguished between raiding and warfare. A raid was taken to acquire horses, mules, or other resources from outsiders—"to search out enemy property." Raiding parties aimed to avoid encounters with the enemy, and rituals associated with raiding were directed toward concealment and thwarting pursuit. In contrast, a moral commitment to retaliate for the loss of kin drove war parties, which aimed to kill the enemy and destroy their camps. Rituals in advance of war parties centered on demonstrating the heroic acts that warriors intended to perform, and once on the warpath, men spoke a special ritual language with its own vocabulary.[34] The incomplete statistics of captives taken and casualties incurred during wartime tallied by Spaniards reveal such differences between the Spanish and Apache methods of war. While Spanish and Apache casualties were roughly equal in numbers (though not proportional to population), the number of captives taken by each deviated strikingly: Spaniards took more than ten times as many captives as Apache groups did during this period. Apaches had little interest in ruling over or assimilating large numbers of Spaniards.[35]

For the Southern and Mescalero Apache groups more than for Spaniards, war led to a significant loss of population through death and displacement. War forced difficult decisions about how to confront a demographic crisis through violence, flight, or diplomacy. In seeking to protect their own families, some Southern Apaches turned against others, helping make possible Spanish military successes and forced migrations. The creativity and adaptability of Apache families during this period also helps to explain why the Spanish did not ultimately succeed in either "exterminating" Apaches entirely or necessarily "taking charge of their governance." The varied means through which both Apaches in southwestern America and those forcibly removed far from home drew upon kinship relations for survival warrants closer attention.[36]

Family and Kinship in Wartime

Families and kinship networks played a central role in the unfolding war between Southern Apache groups and Spaniards, especially in the 1780s and 1790s. The Spanish recognized and manipulated the close links that Apaches drew between kinship and political affiliation at this time to kill or capture them in large numbers and threaten genocide, while Apaches' flexible kinship structures and adaptive family strategies remained their primary source of strength. To be without kin was to be powerless. The Spanish success in capturing, killing, displacing, or reaching peace agreements with Apache groups built off this basic truth. Warfare took aim at Apache kinship systems. After Gálvez's instructions of 1786 had encouraged diplomacy and gift giving in addition to offensive war, presidio regiments increasingly targeted specific Apache leaders in hopes of bringing them into an alliance that might grant the region long-term stability. Commanders sent their regiments on strategic campaigns against these headmen's family camps to capture their immediate relatives. Meanwhile, the viceroy in Mexico City reiterated the long-standing order that presidio commanders deport all Apache war captives out of the region. Through this strategy, officials sought to weaken Apache local groups by displacing men and their families. As coffles of captives wove their way across Northern New Spain, sending Apache people to far flung locales—from Chihuahua to Mexico City to Cuba—army officers used both the threat and practice of exiling Apache kin to get influential Apaches to settle with their extended families near military forts or presidios across the region.[37]

The strategy was two-pronged. First, regiments would selectively target an Apache local group and leverage captive kin to coerce the group's leader into alliance. This nantan would then prove his loyalty and regain his captive kin by asking members of his local group to serve in presidio regiments. As auxiliaries, or scouts, they were valuable in detailing the names of Native headmen, "where their camps and hideouts are, and how many warriors we can expect each headman to be commanding."[38] They would build a reputation for trustworthiness by aiding the Spanish against non-allied Apache groups—through violence, as one military officer wrote, "against their own countrymen." Such service would prove useful to bringing other Apache local groups into a peace agreement in which Apaches would settle their extended families on lands near Spanish military forts and receive regular rations in exchange for their loyalty and aid. Though no knowledgeable military officer thought it would be easy, the long-term imperial vision was for Spanish

governance of Spanish vassals on Spanish lands to replace Apache governance of Apache people in Apache lands.[39]

Southern and Mescalero Apaches had a number of motivations for considering such arrangements, including an ongoing regional drought that had
cut off food and game supplies, and attacks by Native enemies. Particularly
important, however, was the onslaught of Spanish violence in recent years
that broke apart extended family networks and displaced their kin to distant lands. Alliances thus proved attractive for a number of reasons. First,
Apaches hoped to be able to reunite with displaced kin. Second, by pledging
loyalty to the Spanish, they could receive regular rations that would help their
local groups to subsist through seasonal scarcities and extended periods of
drought. Living closer to the Spanish might also provide security from attack
by Native allies of the Spanish, such as the Navajo and Comanche. Finally,
while it offered a number of benefits, alliance with the Spanish did not fundamentally alter familiar ways of life. Military service, for example, provided
Apache men with a means of access to captives and livestock that resembled
the tradition of the raid. They could also continue to hunt and raid while
entrusting the security of their families to the Spanish regiments.[40]

It was in this context that the Southern Apache groups led by El Compá,
Tetsegoslán, and Yagonjli—who later sent emissaries to Mexico in 1791—had
entered into alliances with the Spanish. One of the first Apache groups to
settle near the Spanish presidio of Janos in northern Nueva Vizcaya had been
the local group headed by the Chokonen nantan El Compá. He had settled
first at Bacoachi before leaving again. The Janos regiment subsequently took
his wife captive in 1788, along with several other close kin. To redeem them,
El Compá agreed again to peace and to aid the Spanish in ongoing campaigns. Correspondence between the Janos commander Antonio Cordero
and Chihuahua City in December 1790 provides further evidence of the tactic of taking and threatening to deport captives to leverage Apaches to settle at Spanish presidios. Cordero explained that in a recent raid, troops had
captured the wife, sons, and other relatives of an Apache named Gimiguisen.
Filtering his view on recent events through his own religious lens, Cordero
suggested that this "disgrace" would likely make Gimiguisen think hard about
soliciting peace and seeking forgiveness for his "past sins"—previous strikes
on Janos and neighboring Spanish settlements.[41]

When Apache groups offered an alliance, Spanish officials sealed it by
releasing relatives to them that they otherwise would have exiled. In June of
the following year, Commandant General Pedro de Nava noted that Cordero
did not have to send the prisoners taken in the last military campaign to

Mexico City, "because they are the kin of El Compá." Although he relin-
quished these kin to El Compá, who had requested them, Nava also noted
that he would hold onto the other captives until he received word that "the
five Apache men they belong to have come in good faith to settle at Janos."
He added that if they came to Janos to settle, he would "keep his word" by
returning their kin to them.[42]

The gifting of captives continued between Spanish officers and Apaches
after they had forged alliances as a means of illustrating goodwill and generating reciprocity. In July 1791, Cordero wrote to General Nava in Chihuahua
City to inform him that the two little Indian boys taken captive in a recent
campaign would be given to Tetsegoslán and that he would be told that this
was evidence of Cordero's satisfaction with his service and his "good behavior in recent days." Cordero added that ten Apaches and twenty soldiers had
recently gone out on a campaign that had been particularly successful. They
had captured an Apache man and six Apache women and children. Cordero
noted that "Indio Carlos" warranted special mention for the fervor he had
demonstrated in the early days of the campaign.[43]

The ways Natives and Spanish officers understood warfare, gift giving,
and reciprocity sheds light on the role that ideas about kinship and political
affiliation played in interethnic relations around Spanish presidios like Janos.
For Spanish officers, gift giving was "goodhearted," it reassured them of their
superiority to Natives as they sought to establish control over the Southern
Apache population near Spanish presidios. By asserting that gift exchanges
were between unequal partners, presidio commanders categorized Natives as
their dependents and incorporated them into the Spanish hierarchy. Among
Apaches, gift giving had long operated as the means through which men
established respect, prestige, and authority. For Apache men, the generosity
of a nantan created a debt that they could fulfill in their own time and way.
The relationship between Apaches and their headmen resembled and may
have shaped the interactions between Apaches and presidio commanders. It
also sheds light on why Spanish strategies that combined warfare, gift giving,
and reciprocal labor proved effective.[44]

When a lieutenant in the royal corps of engineers, José Cortés, visited
the Apache-Spanish Borderlands in the 1790s, he described in detail the role
that Apache cooperation played in ensuring Spanish military successes. He
reported that four or six or more Native men went out with the Spanish on
almost every campaign. They guided them through country that the Spanish
"did not know," showing them watering holes and campsites. Commanding
officers knew well, he argued, that "without them they would accomplish

nothing." If Apaches made a positive impression on Cortés through such assistance in war, their actions also surprised and unsettled him. He explained that they died in combat with the greatest loyalty and gallantry but noted that they did so battling "against their kin, against their countrymen. . . . Poor Indians! Let us pity them for a moment." On the one hand, Cortés suggested that Apache loyalties were misplaced: "They should feel more affinity [with other Apaches] than to us." Ultimately, however, Cortés valorized the military service of Apaches as evidence that they were not the "inhuman barbarians" other Spanish observers had described. While he suggested that it was true that Apaches had exercised the "natural inconstancy that is attributed to them," he believed loyalty could replace enmity. Cortés reminded the Spaniards that they were hardly blameless: "Every very charge we make against them would be offset by as many crimes committed by our side."[45]

Cortés overstated the degree to which Apaches would have seen themselves as "fighting their own countrymen." In arguing that "Indians" should feel more affinity to other Indians than to Spaniards, and noting the "natural inconstancy" attributed to them, he conflated categories like "Indian" and "Apache" with expectations about behavior in ways that actually contradicted his own attention to the particularities of Apache divisions and closely related ideas about loyalty to their local groups. Cortés's observations should not be discounted altogether, however, and not just because they reveal ways in which Spaniards conflated ideas about race, religion, and kinship in their approach to Apache groups. Decisions related to diplomacy and warfare were difficult for Apaches themselves. Allying with the Spanish involved painful choices that helped some Apache families at the expense of others. The weight of such decisions emerges in archival fragments: in mentions in Spanish records of Apaches' promises to convince other Apaches to join with the Spanish; in discussions of others' efforts to mobilize further resistance to Spanish rule; in examples of Apaches who "did not worry what other Apaches thought" of them, in contrast to those who presumably did.[46]

If influencing Apache kinship relations (and therefore Apache politics) was a key aim of Spanish colonialism, families and kin networks remained the principal means through which Southern Apache groups challenged Spanish methods and continued to persist as a people through difficult circumstances. While sheer numbers give us some sense of the challenges faced by Apache families like those who petitioned to journey to Mexico in 1791, other records provide further insights into how years of war and forced migration had affected them and how they sought to sustain themselves amid the genocidal threats of this period.

When Southern Apache local groups like those of El Compá made the decision to agree to peace and live near Spanish presidios, they came under the scrutiny of Spanish officials. The Spanish routinely conducted censuses of allied Apaches, whom they called Apaches de paz. The censuses that Spaniards conducted in the early 1790s provide some insight into how years of war had affected Apache families and help to explain the varied and difficult choices they made, choices that both helped support the violence and forced migration of other Apache groups while simultaneously ensuring their own survival. While the censuses were devised by Spaniards and shaped by their patriarchal worldview, they nonetheless demonstrated Spaniards' interest in understanding Apache names, family relations, and local groups and provide insight into some of the strategies Southern Apaches had employed to maintain and recreate families during preceding years.[47]

Particularly descriptive are a series of five censuses conducted around the Janos presidio during 1794. These documents list Southern Apache families who had set up their camps near the military fort and were aiding in campaigns against other Apache bands. Whereas other Spanish censuses during the 1780s and 1790s listed Apache headmen and merely tallied the number of dependents in their camps, these 1794 censuses describe the individual camps or households making up each Apache local group, thus providing a more complete sense of their makeup than numbers alone convey.[48]

Especially striking in the 1794 censuses is the number of families composed of widows, single adults, "orphans," and "additions." Such individuals represented nearly 40 percent of all Apaches listed in the April 1794 and other monthly censuses. Whether captive outsiders acquired by Apaches in raids or Apaches whose families had been captured, killed, or displaced, these individuals either had been incorporated into existing families or had created new family formations within a gotah. Not atypical was the family of Edenechi, which included his two children, his sister, and two teenagers of unknown parentage; the family of Queninmenyo, which included his two wives and two orphans; the mother of El Compá, whose household included sixteen young children, probably either orphans or child captives; and a household composed of ten unnamed widows and their six children. A detail from the October 1794 Apache census shows similar dynamics in the rancheria, or local group, of the nantan Bivora (sometimes spelled "Vivora"), which was camped nearby the presidio. His own household included "three of his own women or wives," two *agregados* (additions), and two children. The broader gotah also included a household of four *zagalejos*, literally "shepherd boys," presumably not related to the rest of the group.[49]

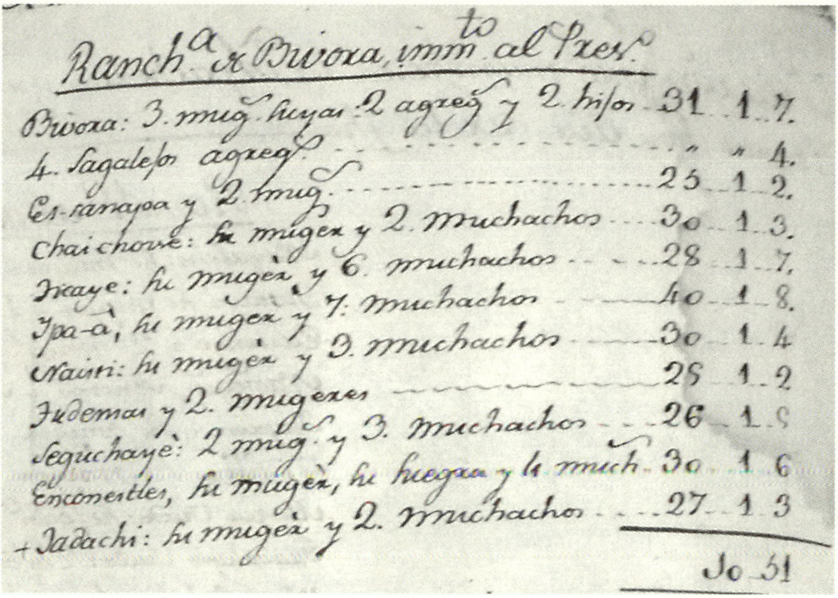
Ranch.a de Bivora, inm.to al Pres.o
Bivora: 3. mug. suyas 2 agreg. y 2. hijos 31 1 7.
4. Sagalesos agreg. " " 4.
Es-sanayoa y 2. mug. 25 1 2.
Chaichowe: su muger y 2. muchachos 30 1 3.
Jxaye: su muger y 6. muchachos 28 1 7.
Ipa-à, su muger y 7. muchachos 40 1 8.
3. muchachos 30 1 4
Naisri: su muger y 28 1 9
Judemas y 2. mugeres
Seguchaye: 2 mug. y 3. muchachos 26 1 5
Enconestles, su muger, su suegra y 4 much. 30 1 6
+Jadachi: su muger y 2. muchachos 27 1 3
So 51

Figure 7. Detail of October 1794 Apaches census at Janos, Nueva Vizcaya. Courtesy of Benson Latin American Collection, Austin, TX.

The close overlap among Southern Apache groups in kinship and political affiliation proved a key source of vulnerability for them during this period. At the same time, flexible notions of family formation among Southern Apaches and Mescaleros through marriage or adoption were also key to their survival and a source of strength amid the broader challenges of these years. The prevalence of orphans and other "agregados" in Apache local groups illustrates this, even as the precise means through which these formations occurred are not generally accessible in the historical record. It is not difficult to imagine how the death or displacement of hundreds of Apaches had created orphans, widows, and refugees. But the process through which people had regrouped and found belonging in families and local groups largely occurred outside the Spanish observers' purview.

The ways in which Apache kinship strategies entered into the Spanish archival records provide an important but only partial portrait. If the journey of three men to Mexico City in search of particular relatives in 1791 may have been unusual in the distance and expense involved, it nonetheless evokes the broader practice of Apaches petitioning for the return of kin throughout this era. The Spanish commandant General Pedro de Nava, for example, complained repeatedly about the frequent visits of Apache emissaries to his office in Chihuahua in the late eighteenth century. It was not just the gifts of food and clothing that these Apaches expected that was proving to be a strain on Nava's patience, but also their repeated requests for relatives that the Spanish had captured and exiled to central New Spain and the Caribbean. "They always ask after relatives who are prisoners among us," he noted in 1795, urging his subordinates across the Southwest to have them make these requests of presidio commanders rather than traveling to Chihuahua, given what he saw as the undue cost of these journeys and the gifts expected of him upon Apaches' arrival.[50]

The importance of Native alliances for the ongoing campaigns against Apache groups is illustrated by the fact that the Spanish agreed to many requests for the return of kin. Sometimes these were relatives still imprisoned near Apache homelands, but on other occasions the Spanish went to great lengths to try and locate relatives who had been exiled as far as Havana, Cuba. In October 1790, for example, they initiated a search for one Apache youth that involved scouting sites where Apaches labored in Mexico City, Veracruz, and Havana. They did not in the end locate him, but in the event that they had found him, Spanish officials had ordered his return north, just as they were open to the idea of the three Apache emissaries returning with their kin from Mexico City in 1791, as long as they were not Christians. A list the Janos presidio commander Antonio Cordero constructed in consultation with the Southern Apache leaders El Compá, Yagonjli, and Tetsegoslán illustrates both their drive to obtain displaced relatives and the Spanish recognition that they needed to act to maintain new alliances. Cordero's list carefully transcribed the pronunciations of eleven displaced people's Apache names—the names of six women, two men, a girl, and two boys.[51]

The granting of war captives who were not necessarily kin was also an important reward for Apache alliances and military service and helps to explain the origins of at least some of the "orphans" and "agregados" in Southern Apache camps. One Apache later described the process though which captive outsiders such as these were adopted into Southern Apache families. He explained that captives acquired in war, especially young boys, were married into the group, and while they might be like servants in the beginning, they would later be viewed as fully Apache. It is unclear whether Apaches preferred young male captives specifically during the late 1700s and early 1800s, especially given that the Spanish language does not distinguish the gender of the plural "orphans" or "agregados" attached to families in Apache camps. But the journey of the emissary Apaches to Mexico City in 1791 and their successful petition to return north with three female captives suggests

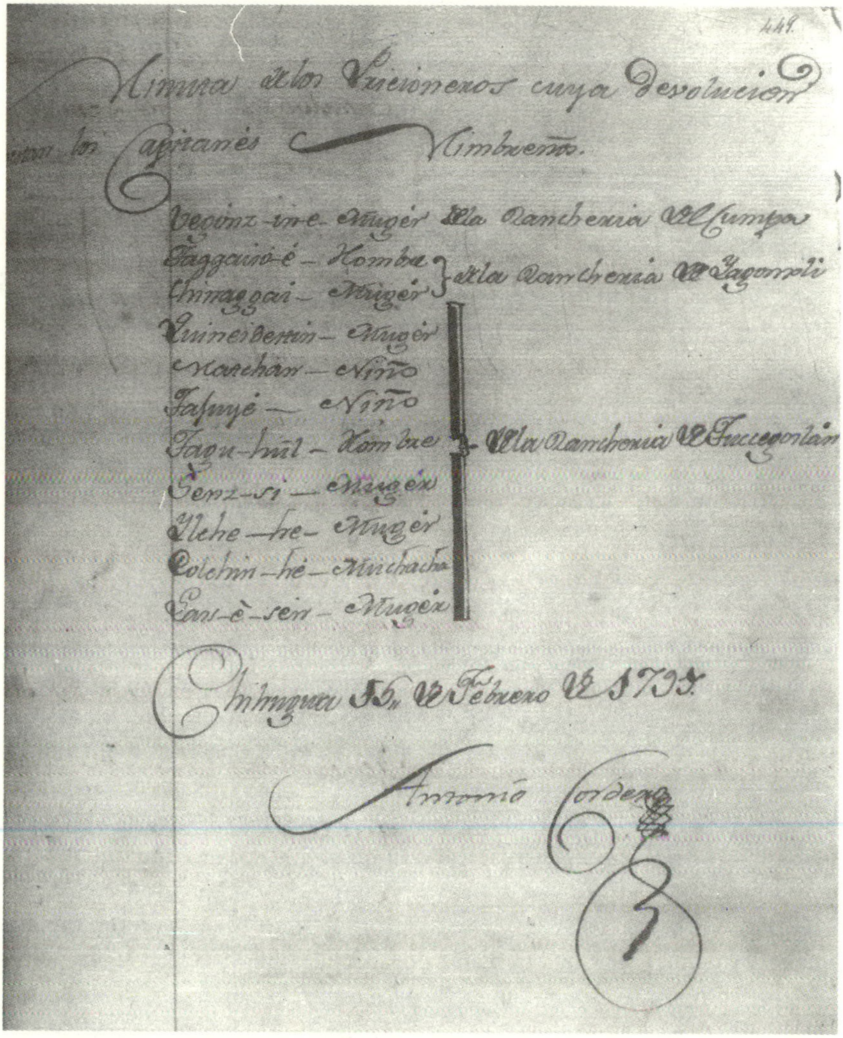

Figure 8. List of prisoners requested by Apaches, 1791. Courtesy of Benson
Latin American Collection, Austin, TX.

that Apaches were flexible in terms of the gender of captives incorporated
during this period of population loss.[52]

The men's petition to the viceroy before leaving Mexico is also sugges-
tive of the ways in which marriage and residence practices may have become
more flexible as a means of surviving this era of war and displacement. In
the reservation era, Southern Apaches described the critical importance of

considering marriage partners carefully. "It was considered essential for a family to be well acquainted in advance," one explained, given the obligations marriage entailed and the role new kinship ties played in the support of the extended family of the wife in particular, whose local group the husband commonly joined. The request of the three Apache emissaries for female captives "to live in their union" suggests that marriage practices were less carefully regulated in the context of population loss in the late eighteenth century, and the tradition of men joining their wife's family may not have been as universal at this time. Three years later, one of the three men, Eustingé, was still living with the woman he had brought back from Mexico.[53]

Other evidence suggests an additional way that Apaches adapted marriage practices to an era of war and diaspora. During times of relative peace, Southern Apaches did not practice polygyny widely—usually only a few of the wealthiest men had the means to support multiple wives. In contrast, in 1794, men with multiple wives were evident in almost all Southern Apache local groups in and around Janos. Of all the men listed as married in the April 1794 census, for example, slightly more than 30 percent are listed as having multiple wives. If anything, Spanish biases may have underestimated the extent of polygyny at this time, because some women are listed separately but immediately beneath their sister and her husband, suggesting the possibility of sororal polygyny that went unrecognized by Spanish census takers. For an Apache man to take in a sister of his wife whose husband had been killed in war or exiled would have fit with customary understandings of his obligations. Such practices may have also represented a response to an imbalanced gender ratio. Spanish censuses should be used with caution in this regard, however, because Apache men who were away from camps hunting, raiding, or on diplomatic excursions were not necessarily counted. At the same time, however, the five monthly censuses between April and October 1794 all reflect a gender imbalance of approximately four adult women for every three adult men, suggesting that Southern Apache groups may have been suffering a deficit of men at this time, which they responded to in part through polygyny.[54]

Whether through aggregation, adoption, or petitioning, Southern Apaches endeavored during an era of population loss, violence, and diaspora to maintain traditional family structures and kinship networks even as they innovated, creating new families and adapting family formations amid the casualties of war and the loss of kin to Spanish forced-migration campaigns. Concerns about families shaped Apache-Spanish relations by motivating some groups to enter into alliance and take up residence near Spanish military forts even as others continued attempts to maintain their political independence beyond the Spanish sphere. If anything, the censuses of Apache groups allied with the Spanish in 1794 probably underestimate the degree to which violence and displacement forced innovation in family structures. After all, it was those groups who remained beyond the Spanish orbit that continued to face the brunt of the military assault from Spaniards and their Apache allies, as well as from other Native groups.[55]

The family strategies of Apaches during this era had paradoxical effects. On the one hand, the Spanish succeeded in manipulating Apache kinship relations because they recognized the close overlap between kinship and political allegiance, even as they often misinterpreted Apache actions and loyalties by also reading them through the filter of their ideas about Indian "barbarism." The willingness of Southern Apache groups to choose the security of their extended families over broader group affiliations and aid the Spanish in locating, attacking, and displacing other Apache groups, facilitated the scale of the casualties and forced migrations of this period. On the other hand, Apaches' flexible family strategies ensured their survival as a people during a time in which their persistence was very much threatened.

The story of two Apache runaways encapsulates the painful choices people made during this period and the real effects they had on kin and neighbors. In April 1796, two Southern Apache men named El Verde and Disoqué managed to return to their homeland after escaping from a coffle of war captives bound for the Caribbean basin. They had traveled at night along the road back north, subsisting on horsemeat and corn gathered from local haciendas until they arrived at the camp of the Chihene Apache headman Vivora, in the mountains southeast of Tucson—the same "Bivora" described in the 1794 censuses as living next to the presidio of Janos. Having allied with the Spanish in recent years, Vivora turned the men in promptly to military officials. "I didn't understand why," El Verde explained, "when we hadn't done any harm." For these runaways, Vivora's decision led them to face exile again, after they had already escaped from central Mexico twice and had walked or rode nearly four thousand miles in a few years' time. If they "didn't understand why" someone they had presumed was on their side would turn them in, Vivora's actions are not so incomprehensible when placed in context. Having witnessed so many Southern Apaches being killed or exiled in recent years, Vivora had likely weighed his choices and decided that the security of his own local group and family mattered more.[56]

Vivora's actions hint at the ways in which Spanish imperial measures intersected with and influenced Apache politics during this period. Leaders like him retained a significant degree of autonomy after allying with the Spanish.

In choosing where to guide Spanish military campaigns and in choosing whether to turn in runaways, they illustrated their continued power not only to a Spanish audience but also to their own followers and other Apache groups. Their decisions were probably shaped by efforts to protect their people from the genocidal threat of Spanish violence and displacement, to be sure, but those decisions could also reflect internal political agendas that were not understood or recorded by Spanish administrators and thus escape mention in the archival record. Alliance with the Spanish brought resources to their people, gifts and rations that leaders could redistribute as symbols of their continued ability to provide and protect. Yet access to Spanish officials and their ability to influence Spanish decision-making was another source of the Apache leaders' power. Evidence suggesting that Apaches tapped into the Spanish system of deportation for their own purposes is not limited to examples of moments in which they turned in escapees from coffles of war captives. Some captives challenged their deportation by arguing that they were in fact Apaches de paz themselves, raising questions about who had turned them in as hostiles. Others indicated that they were actually not even Apaches at all but rather Natives who had served in campaigns against Apaches, suggesting that they had been mistakenly rounded up or that perhaps Apache leaders or interpreters had reported them as belligerent Apaches in retaliation. Such matters remain frustratingly opaque, yet offering such speculations at the very least highlights the limits of the archival record in painting a full picture of the varied ways in which Apache people engaged the existential problems that war and diaspora presented during this period.[57]

*   *   *

Spanish military successes in the late eighteenth century built upon their efforts to learn about, target, and manipulate Apache kinship relations in the interests of ending Apache groups' political independence. While they sometimes discussed annihilating all Apaches, the Spanish were ultimately both unable and unwilling to do so. The failure of Spanish imperialism to take over the governance of Apache families and lands fueled imperial creativity. In lieu of transforming mobile, pagan Indians into Christian farmers in missions in Northern New Spain, exile was envisioned as the first step in a process of transforming and incorporating those they did not kill in war into Spanish society as the servants and dependents of Spanish Christian families. Spanish imperial dreams undergirded by visions of kinship, religion, and socio-racial difference often remained just that, dreams. However imperfectly realized and despite their obviously limited power, the Spanish could nonetheless prove incredibly destructive in the specific contexts in which they were able to link violence with understandings of kinship relations and the relocation of captives through imperial networks of trade and transportation. The many Apaches who did not survive their journeys into diaspora remind us that the distinction between genocidal warfare and forced migration for redemption was much clearer in theory than in practice.[58]

For Southern and Mescalero Apache groups, ideas about family and loyalty that emphasized kinship relations over broader religious, racial, or political categories of identification proved a primary vulnerability, as well as their principle source of power and means of persistence. Apache political economic strategies in the eighteenth century built on the knowledge of the varied loyalties and fragmented political jurisdictions of neighboring Spanish communities. Through much of the century, Apaches found as many friends as they did enemies in their interactions with the Spanish sphere. When Spanish imperial officials and military officers in the 1760s and 1770s drew upon the knowledge they had built of Apache people over time to try to finally end the perceived threat of Apache political independence and mobility, the family and kinship networks emerged as "critical political sites in and of themselves." Apache leaders dealt with the threat of death, displacement, and forced migration by prioritizing their own families in ways that could prove destructive for other Apache people. The conversations Southern and Mescalero Apache families had about such matters largely occurred beyond the reach of Spanish record keepers. The Spanish referenced efforts made by certain leaders to "persuade others" to join in alliance, they described fears of runaways from diaspora fomenting "resistance" to Spanish designs, and they suggested that they would have "achieved nothing" without the help of Apaches in battling other Apaches. Sometimes Spaniards misinterpreted Native actions, conflating their close ties of kinship with broader categories, such as "Apache" or "Indian," that did not reflect Southern Apaches' own sense of belonging and loyalty. Native testimony we do have nonetheless indicates that they did sometimes feel betrayed, wondering why people they thought were their people, their kin, turned them into the Spanish soldiers. These were painful choices.[59]

For Apaches who survived in southwestern America and for the many who faced new lives in diaspora, the family continued to be a central means through which they understood their place in the world as humans and gained some measure of security. Apaches who remained in their home territories or took up residence near Spanish military forts incorporated refugees, went to great lengths to try and recover missing kin, and adopted outsiders into new family formations to sustain their populations amid the demographic crisis of this period. Those displaced from home did not merely accept a life without kin or power either but instead sought to return home against the odds, form new relationships in diaspora, or better their lives in difficult circumstances under the watchful eye of colonial officials.[60]

CHAPTER 5

Island/Prison

They came aboard the *Brújula* and *Polonia* in August 1802, two dozen survivors of a convoy of Apache war captives that had originally numbered more than eighty when it left the northern interior of New Spain. The governor of Cuba, the Marqués de Someruelos, had probably already prepared the announcement of their arrival for the Havana newspaper, informing residents that Indians would be given to "proper persons to instruct them in religion" and that those who wished to "have the advantage of their service [and] contribute to this pious work" should apply to him. Within days, petitions from residents eager to receive an Indian man or woman began to arrive in the governor's office, citing both religious objectives and excitement at the prospect of a free domestic to help with household chores. If we can only speculate about what these Apache captives knew of the fates awaiting them as they neared shore, we do know that to be sent away had become a well-known and feared experience during the last two decades of war in the North American West, as Native men and women were routinely transported to central New Spain and the Caribbean.[1]

Apache Indians who embarked on ships to Cuba at the start of the nineteenth century navigated a world characterized by what one scholar has termed "a spectrum of bondage."[2] Native prisoners of war were not the most common of cargo unloaded in the Havana harbor, but their presence illustrates the far-flung imperial and commercial networks that drew captives of varied origins and statuses into forced labor across North America, the Caribbean, and the Atlantic World. Hundreds of convicts from distant parts of the Spanish empire also made the journey, sometimes in the same ships as Apaches, because courts in Spain, Spanish America, and the Philippines sentenced individuals convicted of serious crimes to servitude in overseas military forts and public works projects. Thousands more enslaved men and women of African descent also arrived in Havana during these years, some born on neighboring islands, others in Africa. Because Cuba was a slave society that also served as an island prison for convicts and prisoners of war, multiple forms of bondage intersected there. Legal and racial distinctions influenced people's life trajectories and perception within the community; being an Indian prisoner of war was not the same thing as being a black slave. Some Apaches, for example, came to understand and exploit Spanish interests in promoting their "instruction in religion" and in distinguishing between their status and that of enslaved Africans. At first, even the best of Spanish intentions probably presented little solace to men and women who had endured an arduous journey into circumstances not of their choosing.[3]

Following the lives of the men and women aboard the *Brújula* and *Polonia* from the roots of their captivity through their arrival in Cuba in 1802 allows us to see in a microcosm the varied experiences of the more than two thousand Southern and Mescalero Apache captives sent into exile during the broader diaspora of the late eighteenth and early nineteenth centuries. The imperial designs sparking this diaspora led to voluminous documentation. Coffles were carefully documented in terms of the age and gender of captives. The expenses of feeding and housing them that were paid to subcontractors on the journey were scrupulously tallied and litigated. Coffle conductors kept journals attesting to every important event in beautiful handwriting indicative of their enlightened educations. After several mass escapes, officials called expert blacksmiths to experiment with and testify about the qualities of different handcuffs used to transport prisoners. They drew upon nascent racial ideas in debating the relative usefulness of different classes of laborers for the public good, while needy municipalities begged for shipments of coffles of convicts—or Native prisoners of war—by the hundreds. All professed the most humanitarian intentions, promising that displaced captives would be well fed and well cared for. Officials even debated the logic, morality, and legality of moving people from cold, dry climates to hot, humid ones.[4]

Yet these rich records also reveal the disconnect between theory and practice, between alleged good treatment and "freedom," between the visions of imperial agents and displaced Apaches' lived experiences. The distinction imperial agents drew between "exterminating" Apaches in warfare and "redeeming" them through transport into Spanish colonial society probably made little sense to the displaced Apaches watching their kin perish. Rampant death—approximately 30 percent of displaced Apaches died on the journey to Mexico City alone—suggests that a supposedly humanitarian policy was in practice a genocidal one. One key factor in Apache mortality was the fact that a significant number of Apaches never labored at all but rather languished in jails and poor houses owing to bureaucratic delays in their transport or potential masters' fears. Such confinement had consequences, which Spanish officials recognized. One explained that deaths could be explained in large part "by the inevitable corruption of a place where many people are confined for some period of time, by the sadness of losing their liberty, and by changes in their diet."[5]

Apaches were not simply passive pawns on a genocidal imperial chessboard, however. Deemed uncontrollable on New Spain's frontiers, they often proved beyond the control of Spanish imperial schemes on their journeys to the Caribbean as well, refusing to march or labor, escaping, and in some cases returning to their homelands to spread news of what had happened to them. This resistance is in part what led Spanish officials to order that all Apaches be taken across the sea to Cuba instead. Even as some residents of the island continued to request Apaches for their homes, the continued escape of Native captives and their collaboration with runaway slaves of African descent eventually led local magistrates and the governor in Havana to demand that no more Apaches be sent to Cuba either. In sum, like exploited people elsewhere in the Americas, displaced Apaches navigated harsh circumstances creatively—through adaptation, resistance, and violence. Their story illuminates the overlapping histories of bondage, deportation, and incarceration that served as strategies of colonial control in North America and the Caribbean at the beginning of the nineteenth century, while also revealing the diverse strategies that captives and slaves employed to make the best of their lives wherever they found themselves.[6]

An Apache Middle Passage

The idea of banishing (or deporting) people deemed deviant or undesirable echoes back into the ancient past and ripples forward to the present. It had precursors in Northern New Spain and in other regions of the Spanish empire as well. It was not unusual for Native people to be moved en masse for various reasons—including as "free persons" under labor draft systems such as *repartimiento*. Spanish vassals who had risen up in rebellion were often transported in groups to more distant places to be auctioned or distributed. This policy of banishment to Mexico and beyond was formalized in 1729 military regulations demanding that military commanders on New Spain's northern frontier send Native prisoners to the viceroy in Mexico City to decide their fates. In part because of local residents' interest in exploiting the captives' labor, this policy was not always followed, although the deportation of the Lipan Apache leader Cabellos Coloradas and his family in 1739 provides one striking illustration of its use. At other times, Spanish administrators discussed plans to deport Native groups to distant places that never came to fruition because they lacked the power to enact them or were overridden by superiors. Such appears to have been the case in the aftermath of the 1751 viceregal order mandating that Apaches be taken further south than Sonora or Sinaloa to be distributed or sold in the interests of regional security. The continued baptisms of Apache servants and slaves in these provinces in ensuing decades suggests that this decree's influence was limited.[7]

In the second half of the eighteenth century, the idea of banishment or "deportation"—of sending recalcitrant groups of people to distant places—gained new purchase. As we have seen, imperial geopolitics and reform policies led to new scrutiny of the spaces "in between": the borderlands where both Spanish and Native polities interacted and asserted political and cultural influence. Concerns about the loyalty of Spanish subjects, including their involvement with Apaches in a borderlands economy of livestock rustling and interethnic trade, helped spark efforts to target Apache families in offensive war and "scare them" into submission through forced removal in coffles to distant lands. Imperial officials hoped that through these means they might finally realize security and sovereignty in frontier zones. Some Apache leaders chose to aid the Spanish in capturing members of other Apache groups, in part to avoid war and captivity at the hands of the Spanish, and perhaps also as a means of prosecuting existing disputes and bettering their own political positions.[8]

This practice also echoed broader trends. One historian has described this period as a "wide-ranging world of imperial experimentation" characterized by creative solutions to the demands of "a vast market for colonial labor." The British, French, and Spanish each pursued their own plans to colonize distant lands with convicts, Acadians, or Canary Islanders or to draw upon the labor of enslaved Africans, smugglers, or Apaches for arduous construction projects, military service, and imperial defense. Sometimes such plans were successful in the sense that the imperial dreams translated fairly well into colonial realities. More often, the schemes of empires did not align with their power to put them into practice.[9]

The Apache diaspora to the Caribbean during this era illustrates just such a rift between theory and practice, vision and reality. The transport of Native war captives from the present-day U.S.-Mexico border region to Cuba was paid for by the royal treasury, orchestrated by soldiers and militiamen, and explained in the interests of the "public good" as a means of securing North American frontiers and incorporating non-Christian Indians into the folds of a Catholic monarchy. Officials imagined that in the Caribbean, where there was an insatiable demand for labor, Apaches and other Natives could surely be put to good use. In addition to more than two thousand Apaches, hundreds more Natives also deemed to be either enemy prisoners or vassals turned rebels faced deportation between approximately 1770 and 1810, especially Seris from Sonora and Coahuiltecan-speaking bands from Nuevo Santander. If Spanish governors and viceroys envisioned the forced removal of Natives to be in the best interests of captors and captives alike, in practice deaths, escapes, and resistance en route consistently frustrated their expectations. A surprising number of captives never labored at all but instead spent months or years confined in prisons and poorhouses waiting transport to their destinations.[10]

This broader history is illustrated in a microcosm by the coerced migration of sixteen Apache men and seven women who boarded the *Polonia* and *Brújula* bound for Havana in the summer of 1802. Their journey had begun months earlier in the rugged mountains of Apache homelands. The captives were drawn from various Southern Apache groups who lived with their extended families in mountain camps they chose for their access to water, security, and food sources. They designed the camps to be temporary so they could abandon them easily if necessary, but they often returned to the same locations at specific times of the year to hunt, harvest plants, or perform ceremonial functions.[11]

Military officials had employed their knowledge of Apache groups to try to turn them against each other and toward an alliance with the Spanish. Promises of gifts and rations and the specter of exile had by the early 1800s led hundreds of Apaches to ally with the Spanish and agree to aid them in their ongoing military campaigns. Throughout 1801, for example, the captain of the Spanish presidio at Janos reported that a number of Chihene Apache leaders were "at peace" in his district and were out on campaigns against other Apaches who remained at war. It was likely with the aid of these Native allies that the Spanish targeted the camps of Apache families who would later compose the cargo of the *Brújula* and *Polonia*.[12]

Though the precise moments of their capture elude the historical record, we know that Spanish and Native warriors usually stormed their enemies' camps at daybreak, seeking to catch them by surprise and capture as many women and children as possible. In the event that the captives were kin of an influential headman, presidio captains might try and leverage them to bring men to the negotiating table. The ability to petition for return of kin was a key motivating factor for some Apaches to negotiate peace agreements at Spanish presidios in the late 1700s and early 1800s.[13]

The captives gathered in the campaigns of the fall and winter of 1801 would not be so lucky, though the Spanish did claim that the success of these campaigns helped lead three Southern Apache leaders—Concha, Chafalote, and Naranjo—to request peace the following summer.[14] Although it was common for entire families to enter into captivity together, military officers sometimes separated young captives from their kin and kept them in the north. On occasion, they gave them to local families as "orphans" to raise. Other times, it was the very Spanish and Native warriors who had captured them who petitioned to receive them, as when the commandant general in Chihuahua City, Pedro de Nava, explained that the little Apache girls that Nicolás Madrid and Mariano Varela had chosen could be left to them and that other soldiers should be given the same opportunity: "to select a little Indian girl, to their satisfaction." The image of soldiers selecting girls for their satisfaction suggests the range of productive and reproductive labor that "adopted" young people might be expected to perform.[15]

Such trafficking of Native children was commonplace and endured well into the twentieth century in the North American West. Indians deemed "orphans," either because their parents had been killed or exiled, might be adopted into Hispanic families and become like kin, just as Hispanic youths were sometimes incorporated into Native communities. Intimacy and exploitation blurred, as the documentary record reveals evidence of Apache boys and girls "sold as slaves for the price of a horse" or used to pay off gambling debts. In this way, the particular case of this group of Apache war captives gathered in 1801 and 1802 evokes a broader characteristic of bondage evident in southwestern America: potential masters coveted children in particular because of the perception that they were more controllable and assimilable into Christian society than adults. The promise of conversion and acculturation served to justify the removal and exploitation of children from their natal communities even as it buttressed the masters' sense of themselves as charitable people who were helping to "raise up" indigenous people from their "barbarism."[16]

In this particular case, officials appear to have endorsed this customary practice, as when soldiers surveyed the captives in the jail at the presidio of Conchos in early February 1802 and reported none under the age of fifteen. Among twenty-one men and sixty-five women, most were young adults or middle-aged. Two ninety-year-old women also awaited the long journey south, including one who later arrived in Havana. In fact, the presence of elderly captives in coffles was not uncommon, indicating how instilling fear as much as concern for frontier security or demand for labor influenced the forced-migration campaigns of this era.[17]

As the captives waited in jail, Sergeant Joseph Antonio Uribe prepared to escort them south. He was a veteran coffle conductor, and his experience and reputation for maintaining good security may help explain why all but three of the Apache captives who departed Chihuahua arrived in Mexico City at the end of March 1802, after a journey of nearly two months. The viceroy of New Spain commended Uribe for his track record of preventing escapes and asked him to report his methods to the troops that he had commissioned to transport the captives on to the coastal port of Veracruz. Uribe explained that he shackled the men two by two on muleback and encircled the group with soldiers whenever they came to a stop. At night, when it was common for them to house the captives in a roadside inn, he posted two guards inside and one at the door, taking care that the guards inside be armed only with clubs. If guards inside carried guns, Uribe explained, Indians might be able to use them to their advantage in an escape attempt. Such attention to security responded to the reality that escapes were frequent and had motivated officials to mandate that all Apache prisoners of war be exiled overseas to Havana rather than remain in New Spain.[18]

Two particularly well-documented mass escapes in recent years may have weighed on Uribe's mind. Just before Christmas 1796, Francisco González approached the town of Xalapa, escorting a coffle of Apache prisoners bound from Mexico City to the Caribbean coast. The mayor reported that González came bearing injuries he had received during a violent escape at a nearby roadside inn. Around midnight, Apache men had sounded the war cry, trampled the guard at the door of their quarters, stolen his gun, and rushed out into the main hall of the inn. The rest of the troop took up arms to prevent the Apaches' escape to the mountains, but the Apache men resisted by lashing out with jagged shards of stone that they had torn from the walls.[19]

Three years later, it was a group of Apache women who had sat silently in the dark inside their quarters en route to Veracruz. Outside the door, the guard wondered why the light had gone out but decided it must be because of strong north winds. In the dark the women were slipping out of their shackles. After a shout—"The Indians are trying to escape!"—the soldiers on night watch all dashed to the men's quarters. Meanwhile, more than fifty women and a little boy escaped into the night. Struggling to secure the Indian men who also had slipped out of their handcuffs, the soldiers gave chase to the fugitive women too late, catching up to only one lone straggler who clung to a tree on the mountainside. As the soldiers surrounded her, she bombarded them with rocks until one of them sliced her wrist with his machete.[20]

Such escapes generated a response. Military officials investigated handcuffs and the quarters of roadside inns and made recommendations about how to improve the security of both, recommendations that had likely come to Uribe's attention. Moreover, at least three convoy conductors were arrested, imprisoned, and court-martialed when escapes did occur. Though two of the three were cleared of wrongdoing, González was found solely responsible for the escape of the Indians in his coffle and sentenced to sixteen months in prison. The impetus to punish González may have emerged from the unusually severe plundering by the Apaches after their 1796 escape. They had stolen dozens of horses and other livestock, set fire to ranches and homes, injured and killed Spaniards on the road north, and had allegedly cannibalized several children. The latter accusation almost surely owed to the hysterical rumors any escape of Apache sparked in central New Spain.[21]

Uribe's emphasis on shackling men but not women on the march in 1802 suggests that the gender stereotypes that had facilitated Apache women's escapes in the past continued to be a vulnerability. In distinguishing in his treatment of captives based on age and gender, he was not unique. In the 1770s, coffles had initially left Indian women in households in Mexico City as *criadas* to be Christianized while being exploited for their labor. But many criadas had little interest in either the salvation or servitude their masters offered. In 1778, the viceroy noted that "having experienced the poor service of the Indian women and the ease with which they escape, there are not currently any households that want to receive them."[22] Despite moments of dissatisfaction, however, the redistribution of Indian women and children in the capital continued. Glimpses of what these Natives' lives were like can be gleaned from the documentary record. In April 1792, three Apache boys escaped from their assignment in the kitchen of the royal palace in Mexico City, stealing a horse and carrying tools and supplies from the kitchen with them. When they were recaptured, they explained that they had escaped because workers in the kitchen constantly teased and bothered them. One man in particular bumped them on the head and told them to go back to where they had come from. Spanish officials were not pleased that the boys had attempted to do just that.[23]

After women and children alike proved able to escape from Mexico City, officials had ordered that all Apache captives, regardless of age, be transported to Veracruz and then on to Havana. This process was not always timely, however. The Apache captives in 1802, like others before them, spent several months in confinement in Mexico City before continuing on to the coast, which helps explain why many of them did not make it all the way to Havana. For a variety of reasons—illness, age, perceived behavior, escape—many Indians never arrived in the Caribbean but instead remained in jails, poor houses, or Catholic parishes or returned to their homelands. In the spring of 1802, Uribe and his men transported their male captives to the royal jail, as was common. They left the female captives at either the poorhouse or the collection house, an institution that focused especially on taking in and "reforming" prostitutes. Wherever captives were lodged, space was at a premium. In places like the collection house, for example, Apache women were usually confined alongside thirty or forty prostitutes. Given that they were cramped in close quarters with strangers, it is unsurprising that house directors complained that Native women not only picked fights with the prostitutes but also quarreled among each other.[24]

If Apache men and women may have felt some physical relief in the temporary end to their march in Mexico City, they faced new psychological challenges in these prisons and poorhouses. After years of diaspora, the return of escapees north had probably given Apaches some sense of what it meant to be sent away. Perhaps they even knew from the stories of runaways that their march would continue to the sea and that they might be embarked on boats leading to some unknown destination.[25] If these and other possibilities occupied their thoughts as the days and weeks passed in confinement in Mexico City, they may have found some comfort in their kin. Because the Spanish targeted extended family camps in their military campaigns, it was common for groups of captives to include mothers and daughters, sisters and brothers. But the presence of family brought new torments when sickness spread through these jails, as it did in the spring of 1802 and on other occasions. Traditionally, Apaches abandoned any place where death occurred, because they believed that ghosts could continue to dwell among the living and do them harm. The inability to respond appropriately to deaths on April 10, May 14, May 16, May 30, and June 11—to flee the prisons where their kin had died from smallpox, cholera, and other illnesses—must have made incarceration all the more terrifying.[26]

Unfamiliar landscapes and uncertain futures beckoned when the captives finally continued their journey from Mexico City to the Gulf Coast in late June 1802. If Natives sometimes rode on muleback from the north to the capital, they always marched on foot on the 250-mile journey from Mexico City to the coast. Soldiers chained Indian men and women two by two, with one shackled to the chain that bound together the whole group.[27] They traveled eight to twelve miles a day (four to six leagues) across rugged terrain. Soldiers described the attitude of Indians on the march as "die first, walk tomorrow." Natives sometimes threw themselves to the ground and refused to march any further. After beating an Apache with a rod, for example, one soldier managed to get him to walk another half mile, until "seeing his resistance, and insistence on throwing himself to the ground," he had to put him on muleback. When three or four other men started throwing themselves to the ground, the conductor explained that he could tell that one of them "did it with such ostentation that I knew his resistance was rooted not in exhaustion, but in furor." In fact, the man inclined his head to the ground as he fell eight or nine times, and any one of these impacts would have cracked his skull "but for the fortune that we were traveling through land with soft, loamy soil."[28]

When the coffle arrived at the coast, Apaches again faced confinement. They were housed in the castle of San Juan de Ulúa, a complex of fortifications, prisons, and a palace originally constructed in the sixteenth century. A modern photograph shows a view over the internal courtyard lined with palm trees toward the picturesque watch tower. Tourists stand and look over the port of Veracruz, a large shipping vessel in the distance. Whatever the displaced Apaches made of the sights, sounds, and smells of their latest prison, they did so not as relaxed sightseers but as captives having already suffered sickness and hunger for months. They were also probably anxious, recognizing that their chances of escape and return north to their homelands were waning.[29]

While no mention is extant of the conditions of these specific captives in 1802 during their time in Veracruz, the prisons of San Juan de Ulúa were notoriously unhealthy. Five years earlier, a group of Apache captives held there had fallen ill with "putrid fevers," possibly malaria. The governor decided that they should continue to their destination because the boat captain had consulted with a doctor who explained that these fevers were not contagious "but result from the change of country, nakedness, and many other causes." Such commentary illustrates how the treatment of Natives on their forced journeys contributed significantly to their premature deaths. Surveying the women in this instance, the boat captain noted that "these Indians are full of miseries because they are virtually naked, and the only clothes they do have are made of wool, which traps their sweats and causes all kinds of illnesses, and especially fevers, as a result."[30]

The Apache captives' diet also contributed to suffering and deaths attributed to scurvy and diarrhea. In addition to smallpox and fevers, doctors

Figure 9. Photograph of San Juan de Ulúa watchtower, Veracruz, Mexico.

noted that scurvy "was an illness to which this nation is especially suscepti-
ble." Apaches were accustomed to a diet that included fruits and vegetables
that they cultivated or gathered. The tortillas, beans, and meat they received
en route and while imprisoned lacked key nutrients that would have prevented scurvy's onset.[31] Though officials mandated that Natives always be
given sufficient provisions, evidence exists that both may have been lacking at
times. One veteran of the convoys explained that, as they traveled south, curious onlookers came from all parts to gawk at the Indians on the march and
the mules carrying the sick. He explained that the Indians would approach
these curious onlookers to beg them for food and water.[32]

At San Juan de Ulúa, Spanish captors also continued efforts to ascribe
new identities to Apaches, even if they could not forcibly alter their captives'
self-understandings. Because soldiers complained that Native names were
virtually impossible to determine—one explained that even those with Christian names might claim to be "Peter today and John tomorrow"—they identified most of them by numbers. In central Mexico and the Caribbean alike,
residents commonly referred to these Indian captives not as Chihene Ndé
or Gila Apaches, or even as Apaches, but as *meco*, which derived from the

word "chichimeco," which had been long applied to allegedly "uncivilized" or "nomadic" Indians. This meant that individual Indians might be referred to as, for example, Meco 3 or Meca 134.[33]

In the case of the captives imprisoned in Veracruz in July 1802, officials also planned a mass baptism to prepare them for shipment to Havana and to give them new Christian names. Some Apaches apparently did see an opportunity for salvation in baptism, but not in the way their captors intended. In the midst of the ceremony, they "fled in all directions," which helps explain why only sixteen men and seven women continued on to Havana.[34]

Becoming Meco in Cuba

As captives boarded the *Brújula* and *Polonia* in early August 1802, they had already lived through months of incarceration and forced migration. No accounts from an Apache perspective of how they viewed their impending transport to Cuba are extant in the historical record. Conversations they may have had about what it would mean to cross the sea are thus unknowable. Their actions, however, suggest the desperation with which some sought to avoid this fate, however they may have understood it. The governor of Veracruz noted, for example that Apaches had "such disregard for life" that they often threw themselves into the water from the castle of San Juan de Ulúa with their chains still attached. He described how their bodies sometimes washed up on shore, even as other times they succeeded in escaping into the countryside. In fact, the belief that such escapees fomented resistance to Spanish rule back on New Spain's northern frontier buttressed the argument that the only way to secure Apache war captives would be to transport them across some expanse of ocean.[35]

The harrowing escapes that Apache men and women carried out in order to return home after arriving on the coast suggest that it was not life they disregarded but rather captivity, incarceration, and bondage. If some took advantage of opportunities to leap into the sea, others faced another forced passage, joining a motley cargo of Native war captives and Hispanic convicts bound for forced labor in the Caribbean, including murderers and thieves sentenced to terms of forced labor overseas by the courts in Mexico City. The ship's captain carried the sentences of these convicts and information about their crimes to report to officials in Havana; for the Indians he carried no such documentation, only a count of the number of men and women on board.[36]

That Havana residents had little specific knowledge of these captives' origins or identities does not mean that they did not have preconceptions about Indians that influenced their reception of them. One official assumed they were criminals, writing to his counterparts in New Spain to ask why information about their individual crimes and sentences had not been forwarded to him. Some of his colleagues had other ideas. Years earlier, when the viceroy of Mexico had first inquired about sending Apaches to Havana, the governor of Cuba responded enthusiastically. Diego José Navarro imagined that after they baptized and catechized them, large numbers of Apaches might form a separate neighborhood in Havana from which they could provide labor useful to the king and their Spanish neighbors. Navarro was not alone in believing that separation from home might help alter the Apache character. One of his successors wrote that "[he] knew about the perversity of these people in their own lands, but [did] not believe them to be ferocious once they leave them." He was convinced that Apaches in Cuba "would not exercise their bloody passions."[37]

If some Spaniards believed that the process of forced migration itself could transform Apaches, others were more skeptical. When the brigantine *General Gálvez* and the packet boat *Oliba-blanca* arrived in March 1784 carrying eighteen Indian women and thirty-three Indian men, Navarro's successor, Governor Unzaga y Amézaga, sent a missive to his counterpart in Veracruz to explain he had received no news about these Indians, where they had come from, or what he should do with them. Moreover, he was deeply concerned about the presence of these "unbelievers" in his jurisdiction, given what he believed to be their "fierce and indomitable" character. Unzaga y Amézaga contrasted his views with those of his predecessor. If Navarro had welcomed the transport of Indians to Cuba because he believed them to be "less corrupt" in their customs than convicts and more likely to work hard, Unzaga y Amezaga disagreed, explaining that far from being hardworking, these Indians' character was "savage." His colleague in Veracruz responded by noting that the viceroy had decided to send Native war captives to Cuba to prevent their escape and return to their country by placing them in "decent homes, where they might be taken care of and educated." Like it or not, he noted, the governor would need to make the most of the situation.[38]

Even as royal officials compared and debated the merits of Indians, convicts, and slaves as laborers, many residents of Cuba proved perfectly happy to employ any laboring body they could get their hands on. When the first shipments of Apaches arrived in Havana in March, May, and August 1784, residents welcomed the captives into their homes and workshops. The governor noted that local citizens "request them enthusiastically," and he distributed the captives within days to individuals requesting them.[39]

Subsequent shipments of Apache captives in the 1780s and 1790s made this process routine. After the newspaper *Papel periódico de la Havana* was founded in 1790, the governor at the time posted an announcement to let local residents know about the impending arrival of "Indios mecos." Subsequent governors may have posted announcements similar to this one, as extant petitions from Havana residents reproduce similar language: "Meca girls . . . will be placed under the care of persons of their sex who are proper persons to instruct them in Religion, [and said] persons may have the advantage of their services. Those who wish to contribute to this pious work should apply to the Governor and Captain General, and they will receive the girls on the condition that they give a receipt for them and assume the obligation to report to the said Superior authority in case the girls die or run away."[40]

Such official rhetoric and Havana residents' views of Natives did not always align. Such was the case for Apaches arriving in August 1802. Extant petitions are often formulaic and usually adhere closely to the tropes of pious charity reflected in advertisements of the arrival of Indians. Others deviate enough to provide more of a sense of how different residents viewed Apaches they received and what they expected from them. In this regard, petitions illustrate that even if Spanish officials claimed Natives were not legally slaves, slavery shaped resident's understandings of them. Since the late 1700s, slavery had been on the rise in Cuba. While neither the sugar nor slave business was yet booming in the same way it would later in the nineteenth century, the island had imported thousands of enslaved Africans both to labor in urban centers like Havana and to work on the growing number of plantations dotting the countryside. The presence of slaves of African descent thus provided a point of comparison through which residents of Cuba sought to make sense of Indian captives.[41]

References to expensive slaves in petitions indicate that many residents viewed Indians equivalently, even if they may also have been motivated by interest in the "pious work" of converting non-Christians. Ana María Gamonales, for example, a widow originally from Cádiz, Spain, explained that she was supported by three sons who as army officers did not make enough for them to be able to purchase slaves to help maintain her household. She thus asked for one of the Indian women who had just arrived, promising to "treat her like a daughter" and noting that "the addition of this girl" to their home would be a "great relief."[42] Lorenzo de Ávila, a sergeant in the infantry regiment, echoed Gamonales's argument in explaining that his wife was ill and to care for their three children they needed the help of a slave. They could afford neither to buy nor to rent one and thus asked for an Indian woman to "assist his wife and care for his three children."[43]

Enslaved Africans were expensive, so the possibility of receiving a free domestic must have tantalized a widow or young military officer. In fact, Havana residents had greeted prior shipments of Indians with petitions making similar comparisons between black slaves and Indians. Six months earlier, Josefa de Castro, the wife of an attorney, had explained that she was sick, had children, and that her husband was absent. She regrettably did not have the means to support a "negra" and thus requested a "meca," who she heard had recently arrived among others. The same was true of Sergeant Major Manuel Cavello, who asked for an Indian woman to serve his daughter Josefa, given that the black slave he had given her "had gone crazy."[44]

One Havana resident slipped from comparing slaves and Indians to calling the Indians slaves. None of the petitioners did so in August 1802, but when a shipment of Apaches had arrived five years earlier, Domingo Correa, a supervisor of public works projects, had explained that "he did not have a slave for the service of his family, because of the small salary he received and the fact that slaves were so expensive." Having received word of the arrival of Indian women, he hoped that the governor of Havana would be willing to "grant him one of said slaves, and he would maintain her and instruct her in the Christian doctrine." Correa had his supervisor write a note testifying to his good conduct, and he was granted an Indian woman for his service.[45]

Comparison to enslaved Africans may not have been the only means through which Havana residents understood the arrival of these Indians, however. One petitioner, María Josefa Martely, for example, explained that she had received word that "conquest Indians" (*indios de conquista*) had arrived from Veracruz. She asked for two females and a male, promising to teach them "and raise them like children with charity." Though conclusions from one petition should not be overdrawn, at least one Havana resident in the summer of 1802 echoed the long-standing custom that war was a legitimate means through which the forced labor of Natives might be acquired.[46]

The interest of Havana residents in acquiring Native domestics opens a window onto the local customs and cultural expectations of potential masters that shaped Apaches' experiences in Cuba upon arrival. Drawing upon the familiar example of elite households with enslaved African women as domestics, middling Havana widows and military officers saw the incorporation of a Native woman or youth as a similar, if perhaps more affordable, symbol of status. An Indian not only provided productive labor, but also served as an illustration of the "charity" and decency of a family in helping to Christianize and educate mecos from a distant land.[47]

A painting from this period helps to illuminate what Havana residents may have understood about the Indians arriving in their midst. It is an example of the famous *casta* genre, in which eighteenth-century artists portrayed the diverse inhabitants of New Spain. Their work usually comprised a series of sixteen paintings, which imagined both racial hierarchy and interracial mixture in quadrants with titles like "From Spaniard and Indian comes Mestizo" or "From Spaniard and black comes Mulatto," and so on. A final quadrant was usually titled "Indios mecos" or "Indios bárbaros," but at least a few examples bear the name "Apache," reflecting the degree to which artists saw all three of these categories as roughly synonymous. Such is the case for Ramón Torres' circa-1780 painting, *E yndios apachis*. Like similar paintings of mecos or bárbaros, his is a representation of primitivism, calling upon cultural tropes evoking Natives' supposed lack of civilization. Scantily clad in colorful skirts, Torres's Apache Indians are placed in an edenic landscape of towering trees, a rushing river, and lush underbrush. An Apache man aims a bow and arrow at a deer in the distance while a woman holding a child looks on, breast exposed. While casting Apaches as stereotypical Indios bárbaros, Torres' work does not evoke fear or danger, in part because it is a family scene. In this respect it is likewise typical of others in the genre, where mothers, fathers, and children are usually pictured together.[48]

When I first saw this painting, the disconnect between the "apachis" on the canvas and actual Apaches living in the North American Southwest is what most struck me—from their dress to the palm trees in the background. While little is known about the artist, it seemed clear to me that he lacked familiarity with Apache history or culture. I would later come to view this image in a slightly different light, particularly as I learned how often Apaches had been displaced to tropical lands, wondering if Torres's vision might have in part been rooted in awareness of that history. Ultimately, however, the painting remains most useful in illustrating historical actors' preconceptions about Native people, the Apaches turned mecos with whom they at first lacked familiarity.[49]

Residents of Cuba may not have held the same ideas about Natives as did artists in the urban centers of New Spain. Their receptiveness to receiving Apaches as mecos into their homes suggest they shared at least some of Torres's sense of their "primitive" rather than "savage" nature, however. The specific fates of Apache Indians aboard the *Brújula* and *Polonia* reflected an

Figure 10. *E yndios apachis* [And Apache Indians], by Ramón Torres, c. 1780,
Dallas Museum of Art. Photograph by author.

interplay between imperial policy and local understandings of race, gender, and slavery. When the ships docked in the Havana harbor on August 2, 1802, the Indians and convicts aboard disembarked at La Cabaña, a fortress complex resembling San Juan de Ulúa that served as both a military base and a prison. Here or in the plaza of Casablanca nearby, Natives' first encounters with Havana residents after their arrival in Cuba were often with enslaved Africans, because it was royal slaves or members of the black artillery company who orchestrated the transport of Native captives. They delivered them to the petitioners who had requested them and returned them to jail at the fortress if they did not suit their masters, as happened on occasion.[50]

Given the urban setting of Havana, most residents who had heard about the arrival of Indians desired domestics, a role commonly fulfilled by women, and it is thus unsurprising that they requested them first. As residents' petitions for Indian women make clear, they intended them to perform the same labor as black slaves would have in their households—caring for children, cleaning, and preparing food. Records also reveal that some captives served in institutional settings rather than individual households, working for the charity house (*casa de beneficencia*), the city hospital, or the tobacco factory. By the end of August, petitioners had asked for all but one of the female captives.[51]

Manuel Cavello, the sergeant major in charge of the plaza of Casablanca (who had also requested an Indian for his daughter), provided more details to Someruelos about the distribution of captives at the end of August 1802. Sending along a carefully crafted chart, he detailed for the governor the new names that subjects had given to the captives they had received: "Meca 1" had become "Maria Dolores"; "Meca 4, "Maria Antonia"; and so on. Three of these women were now living in area households, while three others were serving at the Hospital of San Francisco de Paula.[52]

Cavello also noted that one woman remained in prison because she was "very old." This captive was likely one of the ninety-year-old women noted by officials in Northern New Spain when they had surveyed the coffle before its departure. Her presence reminds us that Spanish raids of Apache camps were primarily intended to fulfill imperial aims—to displace some Apaches in order to scare their kin into submission—not to acquire the most useful or valuable of laborers.[53]

By royal decree, Apache men were to work indefinitely on fortification projects and in shipyards. When the English had captured Havana during the Seven Years War in 1762, the stunning loss of the city had illustrated that it was not adequately defended and had helped initiate the construction of new fortresses at key Spanish coastal cities throughout the Caribbean basin. Reflecting the broader imperial practices of the era, the Spanish drew upon convict labor, rented slaves, and prisoners of war to maintain and expand such sites. In this way, it is striking that they drew upon the labor of the same Apache men deemed too dangerous to be allowed to remain in Northern New Spain to help maintain and expand imperial defenses in another region of the empire.[54]

Such men would have helped with any number of tasks requiring manual labor at the fortress complex. They might have cut and transported lumber needed for the shipyard, composed work gangs for construction projects in and around the port, or formed crews for the pontoons and barges that dredged the harbor. Criminals convicted of the most serious crimes were designated specifically to the arduous task of moving the chain pumps that kept the dry docks from flooding, although it is unclear if any Native captives were ever employed in this function. Across the Caribbean in Veracruz, Native men who had avoided shipment to Cuba performed similar labor: working at limekilns and in shipyards.[55]

In practice, Apache men were sometimes also given to local residents. In August 1802, for example, the ship surgeon aboard the *Brújula* submitted a petition to receive both a man and a woman after the ship docked in the harbor. Don José Muñoz asked for special consideration because he had "assisted them in their journey." Perhaps because the governor had already received a number of petitions, he granted Muñoz only one captive, Meco 3, whom he renamed José María. In the case of this shipment, then, the governor appears to have given residents the opportunity to receive both men and women, though it is striking that by the end of August, Manuel Cavello reported to him that a number of Indian men remained in the plaza of Casablanca "because of their physique or age." This was not the first time that captives' age, gender, bodily appearance, or perceived behavior led Havana residents to pass on the opportunity to incorporate them into their households. Although it is unclear precisely what officials did with the remaining men in this instance, they probably transported them to La Cabaña to work alongside convict laborers maintaining this fortress as they had in the past.[56]

Apache men and women did not in the end form a separate neighborhood, as one governor had once envisioned, but instead dispersed into distinct parts of Havana and beyond: from the plaza and fortifications, to individual homes in the urban center, to quarters on plantations outside the city. The tendency to divide captives along gendered lines shaped distinct life trajectories for women and men. Women's placement in individual households scattered across the city would have made it difficult for them to easily communicate with or reunite with friends or relatives. Women's isolation may have inhibited the appeal of setting off into an unknown urban landscape in search of some alternative to a life of servitude. For women, more than for adult men, familiarity with forms of bondage practiced in the North American Southwest may have played a role in their ability to adapt to their circumstances and the labor their masters expected of them.[57]

If the Apache women's status may not have been entirely foreign to them, this does not mean it was desirable. As with the enslaved with whom people in Cuba compared them, some Apaches probably experienced a range of treatment characterized as much by abuse as by warmth or attachment. As was true in the North American Southwest, intimacy and exploitation could go hand in hand. One man, Juan Manuel del Pilar, wrote with affection about his Indian servant María Vincenta, lamenting in a note to the governor that she had experienced a "violent convulsion of blood" and that he had brought in three doctors and an apothecary to care for her, "sparing no costs to contribute to her cure." In the end she had died and he had buried her outside the Havana cathedral. Submitting similar notes blending affection for Native servants with attention to suffering and death, masters also noted how their parish priests recorded the deaths of Indians in the same ledgers as mulatto and black slaves.[58]

The fact that captives' life events were recorded in the same ledgers as mulattos and blacks also helps to explain the difficulty of tracking Apaches' experiences in Cuba through time. Like enslaved Africans, they may have borne the children of their masters, incorporated Catholicism into their worldviews and spiritual practices, or even married and started families.[59] Children probably had the greatest ability to forge new lives as part of Hispanic society in the Caribbean. In April 1799, a Havana resident forwarded to Governor Someruelos a letter he had received from his brother that hints at just such a possibility. Jacinto de Porras explained that a group of bandits had recently killed a young Indian boy—"un indiecito meco"—in his neighborhood. He noted that the boy had learned shoemaking, played the violin, and had "lived honorably."[60]

For most, however, neither learning Spanish nor "honorable" labor necessarily presented a way out of circumstances not of their choosing. In this sense, it is unsurprising that some Apaches, including some of the men who arrived in the summer of 1802, defied Spanish hopes that "putting the sea between" them and their home would end their resistance to Spanish imperial aims. It was less than two weeks after the arrival of the *Brújula* and *Polonia* that six Indian men escaped from the plaza of Casablanca and fled into the countryside. Their story, like those of others, highlights another means through which Apache men and women navigated diaspora, even upon arrival in Cuba: escape. Native men's escapes and cooperation with runways of African descent occupied the attention of the highest levels of government in Havana and helped fuel demands by Governor Someruelos and others that no more Natives be sent to Cuba. Their concerns were understandable. Amid the Haitian revolution, a slave revolt that began in 1791 on a neighboring island and ultimately upended French colonial rule, the threat posed by Indians banding with slaves understandably raised serious concerns.[61]

The Specter of Escapes and the End
of the Apache Diaspora to Cuba

Though it is unclear precisely when or how six Indian men escaped from the port of Havana in August 1802, we know that they fled south approximately ten leagues toward the mountainous district known as San José de las Lajas, probably in pursuit of food and horses.

Within days, the overseer of a local ranch observed that he was missing an ox, and in searching for it he discovered six saddleless horses tied up on the mountainside. Assuming that bandits must be hiding nearby, he informed the district militia captain, José Gavilán, who formed a party of men to investigate. Before nightfall they discovered six Indios mecos on the top of a cliff. As they tried to capture them, the Indian men resisted "fiercely and barbarously." They were on higher ground and threw so many rocks that by nightfall Gavilán and his men had only managed to capture one of them. They sent him back to Havana the next day, continuing their hunt for the remaining five runaways. After this skirmish with the Indians, Gavilán received an official commission from Governor Someruelos to pursue and apprehend them. If Gavilán lamented the "harm" that the runaways were causing to area farms, the stolen corn and a half-eaten horse he described indicate more than anything the basic means through which the Indians survived on the lam.[62]

It was the discovery of the body of a slave named Pasqual in a corral on a nearby plantation that lent new urgency to Gavilán's pursuit in late August. By following the tracks from Pasqual's body all the way to the abandoned mountain camp of the Indians, Gavilán became convinced that they had committed this homicide. Days later, he located the runaways at last and explained that though he tried "the most humanitarian methods to attract them, they made the cruelest resistance that their barbarity made possible." The fight continued off and on through the next day, until Gavilán reported that he had finally killed or captured all six of the runaways. He wrote proudly to the governor that the planters of the area "could now relax and live in peace, free of the kinds of harm they had been experiencing since the Indians first set foot in these mountains." With a potential monetary reward in mind, he also reminded the governor that he had endangered his own life for the public good, "without fear of sacrificing himself in order to stop in their tracks these enemies of humanity."[63]

While the four surviving runaways awaited trial for the murder of Pasqual in Havana, Gavilán took up a commission to track other Native escapees. Though he probably did not expect it at the time, he would spend the next three years hunting Indians in the Cuban countryside. As for the surviving escapees, they would be tried for the murder of the slave, imprisoned, and shipped overseas again. Gavilán's new commission reflected a hope to finally solve a problem that had vexed residents of the district of Filipinas, sixty leagues west of Havana, for more than five years. In the spring of 1800, for example, a local magistrate in Pinar del Rio, Josef de Aguilar, noted in correspondence with his superiors that a gang of Indians was responsible for a string of murders, homicides, and livestock thefts that had been hindering the prosperity and growth of his jurisdiction in recent years. In a later report, Aguilar detailed with precision the damages allegedly caused by the Indian runaways: twenty-three people killed, including a pregnant woman and her three children; thirteen people injured; eleven houses burned, livestock rustled from ninety-three haciendas; and eighteen haciendas abandoned entirely as a result since 1796.[64]

It was reports like these that had led the governor of Cuba, the Marqués de Someruelos, to lobby against the transport of Apaches to the island beginning in 1799, "unless they were children." He highlighted in particular the "terrible example for African slaves that such barbarian Indians introduced," probably with an eye to the slave-led revolution that was overturning French rule on the neighboring island of Hispaniola. While the Spanish Crown did issue a decree approving the education of Apache children arriving in Cuba, they did not formally agree to shut down the transport of Native prisoners of war to the island, much to Someruelos's chagrin. He continued to plead his case to the royal authorities, however, especially after he became convinced that the "most notorious" runaway community, or *palenque*, on the island— the one reported in the district of Filipinas—was led by two Apache men named El Chico and El Grande.[65]

After Gavilán's success in apprehending Native runaways near Havana in August 1802, Someruelos was hopeful that he was the best man to finally bring under control the broader chaos on the island he believed was being caused by Indians. Though Gavilán later claimed that he was interested only in "the public good," he was probably influenced as well by the bounty on the heads of El Chico and El Grande. Someruelos, the city of Havana, and the Royal Consulate that regulated slave commerce on the island had joined together to offer rewards of three thousand pesos for their apprehension alive, or two thousand pesos dead. This they would pay in addition to any costs that the men who captured them accrued in their efforts.[66]

Gavilán's first task after arriving in the district of Filipinas in western Cuba in October 1802 was to clean up after his predecessors. To supplement local efforts, Someruelos had previously released convicts from Havana-area jails, believing they would be motivated by promises of liberty to kill or apprehend the Indian runaways. From what Gavilán observed, however, they had simply returned to their previous lives of crime: settings fires, stealing, and killing. In fact, these men were probably responsible for at least some of the murders and robberies that local officials had attributed to Indians.[67]

After sending the convicts back to Havana, Gavilán and his men began looking for El Chico, El Grande, and the other members of their group. For weeks they explored the mountains and coasts of the area without sighting Indians or blacks. Before the new year, Gavilán decided to split his men into two groups in the interests of covering as much ground as possible. A few days later, Gavilán's lieutenant, Eugenio Malvar, finally met the Afro-Indian palenque face to face. Malvar described the gang as including the two Indians, El Chico and El Grande, and five other men: two mulattos, one black man, and "two like *guachinangos*" ("red snappers," a term people in Cuba used to describe Natives from New Spain, which was originally drawn from the Nahuatl language).[68]

It was El Grande whom Malvar and his men approached first, as the other members of the palenque kept their distance. Darting for the hills, Malvar ordered that attack dogs be set loose on him, and one dog latched onto the Indian man and pulled him to the ground. Malvar then took matters into his own hands, stabbing El Grande to death with his machete before racing to join his men and provide them assistance against El Chico and the rest of the runaways. As Malvar loaded his pistol, arrows rained down on him from the palenque, striking his left arm as he ran out of bullets and powder. Though Malvar believed he had also injured El Chico, he and his companions managed to escape.[69]

The skirmish had left multiple members of Malvar's party wounded and one dead, but they had succeeded in killing El Grande and made preparation to claim the two-thousand-peso bounty. As proof of their success, they separated the Indian's head from his body and shipped it to the governor in Havana in a vat of brandy. Malvar also presented the statements of eighteen individuals to attest to the alleged crimes committed by the Indians and their companions in recent days. These witnesses reported that the Indians had attacked farms, stealing clothing and furnishings and killing a number of dogs. They had also reportedly severed the hand of the statue of the Virgin Mary at a local parish before urinating in the chapel's holy water.[70]

Other evidence suggests that the threat of Indian runaways was not as clear-cut as some reports made it out to be. Some firsthand accounts of encounters with Indian runaways do not paint them as particularly dangerous. When one party of local men had briefly captured three Indians a few years before Gavilán was commissioned, the Natives had explained through signs that they needed directions to the coast to "find a way to embark" from the island. Conveying a desire for religious instruction, the Indians convinced the men to provide them with food and water before they slipped away again into the hills. While references to seeking some way off the island clearly reflected the unique challenges of forced migration to Cuba, the familiarity of this scene is noteworthy. Runaways were employing cultural knowledge rooted in social interactions in North American borderlands—signing for baptism as a means of obtaining temporary asylum—to navigate life in the Caribbean, and with success.[71]

In other cases, scant firsthand observation of Indians became mixed with racial stereotypes to fuel fears that were outsized compared with the actual threat posed by Apaches and other Natives on the island. Noting a strange absence of black runaways during the 1790s, Magistrate Aguilar in Pinar del Rio had explained to the governor in Havana his theory that this must be because of Indians' propensity for violence: "Indians had killed them all." One creative scheme devised by Someruelos to bring an end to palenques led by Indians was similarly shaped by racialized views. He suggested at one point that the Indians might finally be recaptured if they could be lured onto abandoned farms. Spanish militiamen painted in blackface pretending to be slaves tending livestock would serve as bait. Since Indians would think livestock were tended by "simple" (black) slaves, they would surely attack and the militiamen could pounce and kill or capture these instigators of disorder in the countryside once and for all.[72]

While it is unclear if it was ever carried out, this fascinating plot illustrates the racialized lens through which Someruelos observed the contested lands of his jurisdiction and sought to wrest back control of them: simple black slaves, murderous thieving barbarian Indians, cunning and capable Spaniards. Ultimately, efforts by Gavilán and others to track the Indian palenques in 1802 and subsequent years further illustrate how nebulous much of the evidence mobilized to lobby against the import of Apache and other Native captives had been. Despite expending significant resources, these tracking parties spent long periods of time traveling through the mountains without observing anyone. Even when they came across runaways, observations were sometimes contradictory. Some people, like Malvar, reported seeing precise numbers of Indians and Africans, but others reported seeing blacks or mulattos, guachinangos or Mexicans, or perhaps even "whites" (blancos). That the Indians observed were certainly Apaches is also unclear. As indicated above, Apaches were not the only Natives transported to Cuba from Northern New Spain or elsewhere during the eighteenth century. A significant number of Natives were also forcibly removed from northeastern New Spain in coffles during this same time, especially from Nuevo Santander, and the occasional circulation of Natives from the Yucatan, Central America, and Florida is also documented. It should be further noted that no specific evidence supported the idea that El Chico and El Grande had actually led the palenque that they were a part of—that role simply seems to have been assumed. Some observers reported that the Indians traveled and camped separately from the blacks, raising questions about their degree of collaboration.[73]

None of this is to suggest that runaway communities were merely the figment of people's imaginations. It is likely that El Chico, El Grande, and other runaways were Apaches who had escaped from Havana and its surroundings. While Apaches were not the only Native group to eat horsemeat, descriptions of the "half eaten" horse some runaways had reportedly subsisted on certainly fits with Apache practices in their own homelands. It is even possible that they had managed to communicate with runaway African slaves and masterminded raids on plantations and ranches. Apache men may have found in this Afro-Indian palenque a place in which they could live out a life somewhat like the lives they had lost in being displaced from home, or at the very least, a life that offered an alternative to arduous forced labor. Perhaps they still hoped to return home, as that tantalizing story of Indians seeking "a way to embark" suggests. Whatever the identity and numbers of runaways during this period, it was the Spaniards' shadowy fears of cunning, violent Indians leading slaves in revolt as much as the real dangers they posed that buttressed Governor Someruelos's claims that Apaches were entirely incapable of being kept secure or put to work unless they were children.[74]

There was plenty of evidence to the contrary. In the middle of Gavilán's frantic hunt for El Chico and El Grande, for instance, Apaches continued to labor in Havana residents' households. Others worked in shipyards and on public works projects. If some managed to escape and flee into the countryside, others adapted to the difficult circumstances, navigating their lives as best they could by forging new social ties, by challenging their masters' expectations and demands day after day, or by seeking redress through official legal channels.[75]

The Indians' escapes gained such attention—and provided so much historical documentation—because they fed into racialized fears of a countryside lost to Natives and blacks. The attention Apaches were given by governors and magistrates in Cuba was far outsized compared with their actual threat. As in Northern New Spain, however, fear of Apache Indians and their collusion with other segments of society, however imaginary, had material effects. For some convicts it meant a release from incarceration and a return to crime, which could then be blamed on Indians. For at least two Cuba residents, it meant becoming widows, because their husbands died in the effort to hunt the "wild Indians." One of these women even received three slaves as compensation, entangling the lives of enslaved Africans with the events in the Spanish-Indian

borderlands of Cuba. In one town, the death of a prominent resident, supposedly at the hands of Indians, even became the basis for a folksong that endured
into the early twentieth century.[76]

The idea of a countryside out of control also had implications for displaced Apaches themselves. Of the original six Native men accused of killing
a black slave, the surviving four were put on trial, and officials in Havana
produced dozens of pages of documents as they investigated the case, even
employing an interpreter to collect testimony from them. Unfortunately, only
references to such documents have been located in the archive rather than
the actual trial transcripts. What is known, however, is that after Gavilán captured the four men, he had sent them back to jail in Havana. In their cells,
the men learned of their sentences a year later, in September 1803. While the
court had originally sentenced them to a public execution, officials decided
to commute this sentence for each of the Indian men and replace it with a
ten-year term of forced labor at an overseas presidio.[77]

In a startling turn of events, one of those Native men, Rafael, was ordered
by the court to complete his sentence at the castle of San Juan de Ulúa in
Veracruz, back on the mainland. When officials in Cuba shipped him there,
the governor of Veracruz reminded officials in Havana that by royal decree
Apache Indians were never allowed to return to Mexico, given the risk that
they might escape and make it back home. Rafael did not survive to serve
his full sentence. Shipped multiple times between Veracruz and Havana, he
died awaiting shipment overseas again, this time to Cartagena de Indias in
present-day Colombia.[78]

For many other Apache captives like him, the resistance of Cuba officials to their transport to Havana and the idea that they were uncontrollable
proved influential. Dozens of Apache men and women languished in jails in
Mexico City, some for years, even as jail administrators complained of the
costs of feeding and clothing them. While royal advisors officially denied
Someruelos's demands to stop shipping Apaches to Cuba, few of them appear
to have been transported there after 1804, other than possibly in 1810 and
again in one final shipment in 1816. Some Apache captives were still present
in the royal jail in Mexico City in the 1810s, including a group of Apache men
baptized by the archbishop of New Spain in a public ceremony after months
of catechism. For others, the idea of dangerous Apaches may have contributed to officials ignoring their well-reasoned requests for a release from
bondage. Such was the case for two men named Carlos and Manuel, who
pleaded in 1805 that the viceroy "lift their chains" and allow them some rest
after twenty-two years of labor in Havana and Veracruz. Their only crime, as

far as they saw it, was "having been born among pagans." Their petition was read but left unanswered.[79]

These various journeys—from capture in North American homelands through shipment to Havana, forced labor, escape, incarceration, and death—speak to the complex interplay between imperial aims and local understandings of race, caste, and bondage that influenced displaced Apaches' lives in diaspora during this period. In one sense they were victims of larger processes of colonialism and empire that uprooted many thousands of people like them during the early modern era. Apaches were sometimes put to work, at other times imprisoned long-term, illustrating how deportation and incarceration as much as forced labor were key imperial strategies of controlling populations in this period. Apaches also shaped this history by illustrating that even "putting the sea between" them and their homelands would not prove sufficient to ensure their submission to Spanish designs.[80]

*   *   *

The story of Apaches shipped into exile in 1802 represents one revealing episode during the broader diaspora of the late eighteenth and early nineteenth centuries. Drawing from the ancient tradition of banishing "deviants," as well as from newer ideas and technologies, Spanish imperial agents sought to remake southwestern America by displacing a significant portion of the Apache populations and drawing survivors into an alliance to protect their own kin. Some people profited from this practice: the contractors who supplied food and lodging to Apache prisoners of war and charged high prices; the citizens who received a free Apache to exploit indefinitely. Yet the fact that this forced migration was state-driven and conducted for political reasons also shaped displaced Apaches' experiences from the outset. At an enormous cost, the Spanish Crown transported enemy prisoners of war from one corner of the empire to another, hoping in theory that they might be able to use them to help fortify defenses against other foes. In the process, they linked Apache captives' fates to those of other "undesirables" in the Spanish empire, such as Hispanic convicts. But bureaucratic delays—due to funding problems, manpower shortages, shifting policy ideas, and internal unrest—ultimately led hundreds of Apaches to languish for months, or even years, in jails in New Spain before they ever made it across the sea to Cuba. Incarceration was as central an element of the Apache diaspora of this period as forced labor.[81]

I do not know the ultimate fate of the ninety-year-old Apache woman transported to Havana in 1802 and housed in the plaza in the heart of the city.

Her presence lingers in my mind, however, as an illustration of the disconnect between the lived experience of displacement and the theory of imperial policies. In practice, imperial visions of exiling Apaches who would be free, well-treated persons who simply could never return home went unrealized from the start. Instead, crowds of citizens reportedly gathered to gawk at suffering captives who included babies and the elderly. This policy proved more genocidal than humanitarian. Yet Apaches, like captives and slaves elsewhere, also shaped history through their resistance, adaptation, and escape. In the process, they showed they were more than the pawns of imperial schemes, whether adapting creatively to a new life in diaspora or raiding sugar plantations and stoking fear into the hearts of Caribbean planters.[82]

In the end, the Spanish deportation scheme of the late eighteenth and early nineteenth centuries proved an influential imperial failure. It led to the loss of hundreds of lives. It produced no thriving Apache neighborhoods in Havana. It did not produce the subjugation of all Apache groups that remained in the North American West. Yet the unique horrors of coffles, prisons, and islands did bring a significant percentage of Southern and Mescalero Apache leaders to the negotiating table to protect their relatives. Having tired of years of war and the costs of forced migration, both Spaniards and Apaches proved flexible in negotiating a framework for peace that proved surprisingly enduring.

CHAPTER 6

The Elusive Reservation

In October 1791, the military and civil leader of New Spain's interior provinces, Commandant General Pedro de Nava, issued a remarkable set of instructions to guide the Spanish governance of Apaches "at peace" on New Spain's northern frontier. Running twelve manuscript pages, it represented a handbook of sorts for presidio commanders to consult in their efforts to maintain the goodwill of Southern and Mescalero Apache groups in their vicinity and hopefully lead more Apaches to lay down their arms and agree to live near Spanish regiments as Apaches de paz (peaceful Apaches). Nava's instructions illustrate the flexibility that was at the core of the détente that Apaches and Spaniards negotiated amid the specter of interethnic violence and the Spanish policy of deporting Native war captives to a distant island. Natives who camped near presidios would receive weekly rations of corn, cigarettes, salt, and beef (when it was available). Native leaders would be allowed to administer justice within their own communities, as long as any crimes or disturbances of the peace did not implicate or affect Spaniards. Nava warned against presidio chaplains intervening any time soon in Apaches' spiritual life. He further commented that men should not be expected to farm at first, given his belief they were not accustomed to work or farming. He noted that they could go out for hunts or to visit relatives, and occasional gifts to key Apache leaders were also encouraged to gain their goodwill.[1]

There were some mandates on Apache behavior contained in the regulations. Apaches traveling away from their posts beyond ten leagues (about thirty miles) would be required to solicit a passport. No insults or abuse of troops by Apaches would be tolerated. Women and children should work around the presidios, though they should be paid a fair wage. Apaches should not be allowed to travel to Chihuahua City or beyond to make any diplomatic requests, given the annoyance and costs such trips incurred. Particular care should be taken that no Apache prisoners obtained in military campaigns be given over to Apaches who requested them, but instead they should be shipped away to prevent their return and instill in Apaches a sense of the danger that giving up peace would pose to them.[2]

Even as it reveals a Spanish mindset of governance, the document also invites a reading from Apache perspectives. In detailing what presidio commanders should *not* allow, Nava revealed much about what was actually going on: Apaches were requesting and receiving captives; Apaches were coming and going from posts at will. Their ability to shape the system and its relative lack of constraint on their customary behavior helps to explain why some had agreed to become Apaches de paz in the first place.[3]

Nava's instructions, and the window they open onto Apache-Hispanic relations, introduce a new era in Southern Apache history. The basic framework for interaction devised by Apaches and Spaniards at the close of the eighteenth century—rationing Native families to limit raiding and mobility, mutual military aid, limited efforts to interfere in internal Native affairs or cultural practices—proved remarkably enduring. It served to limit, though not end, warfare and raiding for four decades, thereby aiding in the demographic and economic growth of New Spain while also providing Apaches with resources and military protection to regroup from a devastating war and the loss of kin into the diaspora. Although the system unraveled after Mexico's independence and the Hispanic-Apache borderlands again descended into violence in the 1830s and 1840s, its influence proved long-lasting. In the near term, the demographic recovery facilitated by past peace agreements had increased the capacity of Southern Apaches to raid or make war. In response, Mexican officials, especially in Sonora, supplemented official military campaigns by contracting with mercenary killers and paying bounties for Apache scalps. Apaches decried such tactics and responded by escalating their own attacks, helping to weaken Mexico's capacity to wage war on other nations, including the United States and Comanches, in the process.[4]

After the U.S.-Mexico War ended with the United States laying claim to a significant portion of Apache lands, rations and reservations reemerged as key components of interethnic diplomacy. United States officials, more than their Hispanic predecessors, emphasized bounded reservations as key to constraining Apache power and opening Native lands to citizen settlers, but Natives maintained significant power to shape when, where, and under what terms they would engage with U.S. Americans. It was not until 1872, for example, that Southern Apaches actually resided in any significant number on a U.S. reservation, decades after the United States' supposed conquest of the Southwest. Drawing from their parents and grandparents' experiences with

Spain and Mexico, Apaches played U.S. administrators against each other, traveling from one reservation to another to obtain more favorable rations and supplies, especially during a period when multiple reservations existed for different Southern Apache bands. Apaches used these reservations as safe spaces, to keep women, children, and elders under the protection of soldiers as the men pursued raids to acquire horses and livestock in the United States or Mexico, much to the chagrin of settlers. They sought to negotiate better living conditions, either by requesting permission to move within reservations to new locations; pushing for different lands to be granted to them altogether, sometimes successfully; or leaving the United States entirely to seek a better situation in Mexico.[5]

United States–run reservations reflected the culmination of a century of imperial efforts to fix Apaches in place or eliminate them. On the surface, such measures may seem the antithesis of diaspora: congregating and confining people rather than scattering them. Yet this was not the case in practice, as Apaches eluded imperial aims during much of the nineteenth century by drawing upon practices of mobility, diplomacy, and warfare honed through past experiences of forced diaspora. Even U.S. reservations served more to change Apache patterns of mobility than to constrain them, as Apaches initially created an island patchwork of relatively safe spaces they dominated in a rising sea of white Americans.[6]

The Apaches de Paz Program

Long before U.S. Americans began eyeing the North American West, others had sought to control Natives by settling them in specific places, separating them from non-Indians, and mandating that they farm or labor. Some U.S. Americans even pointed to Spanish missions as a model for their own efforts to control Indians. When prominent New Mexico residents were asked their opinions on Indian affairs in 1865, for example, Governor Henry Connelly noted his admiration for Spanish missions, because he believed that they explained Pueblo Indian lifeways. Thinking about Apaches and Navajos and what should be done with them, Connelly said, "The experiment was tried by the Jesuit fathers; and the situation of the Pueblo Indians shows what can be done." He was not the only U.S. American to admire the Spanish past in the Southwest, even if the Franciscan friars who had actually played a role in New Mexico history might have taken issue with his mistaken praise for Jesuits.[7]

While Apaches had occasionally requested baptism or visits from friars, it was generally only captives transported into lives of bondage within Spanish and French colonial societies who had received sustained instruction in Christianity. The failure of traditional Spanish imperial policies to control mobile Indigenous groups in the North American West helped fuel alternative strategies, especially in the late eighteenth and early nineteenth centuries. Spanish officials negotiated alliances with Native diplomats, paid Native leaders salaries, and instituted a military-run rationing program designed to purchase peace. For their part, Apaches facing military campaigns targeting them in their own camps and witnessing convoys of captives being escorted away to forced labor or incarceration in distant lands had an interest in negotiating an alternative mode of interaction with their neighbors as well. By becoming Apaches de paz, they received beef, corn, cigarettes, clothing, and other supplies regularly between about 1790 and 1830, usually at a specific presidio (military fort) to which they were assigned. Eight such sites existed, at least temporarily, during this period, stretching across the Apache-Spanish borderlands from what is now Tucson, Arizona, to Laredo, Texas. Perhaps as much as half of the population of Southern and Mescalero Apache bands, as well as some Lipan and Western Apaches, engaged with this system at some point or another, though numbers receiving rations ebbed after peaking in the 1790s.[8]

In comparison to the U.S.-run Indian reservations of the late nineteenth century, this earlier imperial program has received less attention. Moreover, those books devoted to the subject have focused more on the rise and fall of the Apaches de paz program than on how it operated in practice. This is in large part due to a frustrating lack of sources that portray in detail the daily life of so-called peaceful Apaches, especially in the early nineteenth century. Documentation for the creation of the program in the 1780s and 1790s is voluminous, but for subsequent years, much of what survives are censuses, ration lists, and expense reports that illuminate how many Apaches were engaging with the system at particular times and places—but not much else. Such records and occasional correspondence between presidio officers and their superiors provide the means by which to understand the patterns of Apache life during this period and the influence of peace agreements on Apache communities.[9]

While a lack of descriptive sources makes it difficult to create as detailed an account of Apache experiences in the Apaches de paz program as those on U.S.-run reservations, it is possible to chart broader patterns that reveal the significance of this system for understanding subsequent Apache interactions with Mexico and the United States. One unusually well-documented Apache

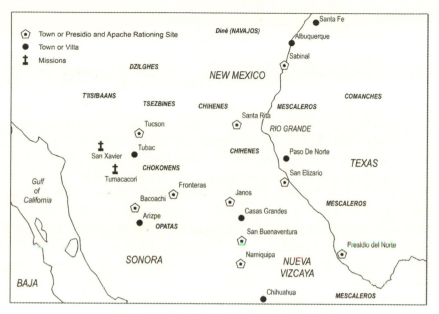

Map 3. Apache-Spanish borderlands c. 1800.

family that participated in the Apaches de paz program from its beginning
to end provides a touchstone from which to consider broader characteristics
of Apache history during this era. The patriarch of this family, El Compá,
was among other Southern Apache leaders who negotiated peace with the
Spanish in the 1780s. He had first agreed to settle at Bacoachi in 1786 but had
subsequently departed. In 1788, El Compá's wife, whom the Spanish knew
as María, had been among a group of Apaches destined to be exiled but who
were returned to Compá in exchange for his renewed promise to maintain
peace and campaign against other Apache groups. By 1790 he was living at
Janos.[10] El Compá was a Chokonen Apache leader who had proven himself
in war and in meeting the needs of his people in order to gain the respect
and reciprocity of his kin. He was thus a key figure in Spanish and Apache
efforts to make the Apaches de paz program a lasting vehicle for enabling
both groups' communities to thrive. Leveraging Native leaders through the
combined threat of violence and the lure of material rewards was central to
growing the Apaches de paz program through the 1790s and maintaining the
population of Apaches engaged with it well into the 1800s.[11]

The material benefits of peace for the Apache leaders are readily apparent in extant Spanish records. Spanish gift giving in the 1780s and 1790s at

the outset of the peace program was especially generous. Cloth and clothing were particularly valuable, and the Spaniards doled out significant quantities of wool, linen, and silk cloth, as well as ready-to-wear pants, shirts, skirts, jackets, and shoes. Additional gifts included muskets, soap, saddles, bridles, chocolate, horses, and more. El Compá and his family regularly received these and other rewards for maintaining peace. Perhaps most strikingly, the Spanish constructed El Compá a Spanish style home within the walls of the Janos presidio. Several other leaders also requested homes, though it is unclear how many of these were actually built or how often Apaches resided in them.[12]

While the numbers of Apaches engaging with this system fluctuated, the weekly presence of Natives and their interaction with Hispanic officials and residents at presidios like Janos remained an enduring fact of life across four decades. The material benefits of peace were significant even for Apaches who were not from prominent families. Every married Apache man was to receive a portion of corn, four packages of cigarettes, a cake of brown sugar, a pinch of salt, and part of a butchered steer. For each additional adult in his family, the man would receive half of this ration, and an additional one fourth of a ration for each child under thirteen. Foreshadowing a dilemma that U.S. officials also faced in administering rations on Apache reservations, Hispanic officials debated whether Apaches should be able to claim rations for relatives in absentia, which was clearly the favored practice of Apaches themselves.[13]

Rations, gift giving, and relative security were at the core of Apache engagement with this peace policy, but some Apaches saw other potential benefits to the program as well. A number of Apache children received baptism at presidios like Janos, including the children of the Apache leaders El Compá, El Güero, Pitaicachi, and Vivora. Commandant General Nava explained such baptisms as reflecting Apache "imitation" of Spanish culture. He disapproved of them given that the children had not received any religious instruction. More than imitation, Apaches probably understood their requests for baptism as a symbol of goodwill and as a means of cementing relationships of reciprocity with Spaniards. Through years of interaction with Hispanic society, Apaches had learned that suggesting interest in baptism was received favorably by a Spanish audience, even if no baptism was actually ever conducted. For El Compá's family in particular, the baptism of his two sons who were christened Juan Diego and Juan José did prove significant, especially for the close relationship with the Hispanic community around Janos that it helped to further. Juan José maintained a connection with one man in particular, Don Mariano Varela, whom he addressed as his godfather, until Juan José's untimely death in the 1830s.[14]

Some Apache leaders also sought a Spanish-style education for their children by requesting that they be enrolled in presidio schools. For Apaches, the potential benefits of their children becoming literate and bilingual were readily apparent, given the value of such skills in diplomacy and trade. Nava had a similar vision, as he had noted in his instructions to presidio commanders that interaction between Apache and Hispanic children should be encouraged to "create a mutual trust." When Apache leaders were told their sons could enroll in the school at Janos, several immediately indicated they would gladly accept the opportunity. Spanish officials saw this as a promising development, instructing the schoolmaster to avoid disciplining the students and driving them away prematurely.[15]

Yet experiments in colonial schooling in the era of the Apaches de paz program appear to have been limited in practice, despite the stated enthusiasm of Apache and Hispanic leaders alike. Only one child, El Compá's son Juan José, is documented to have actually matriculated in the Janos presidio school in 1794. It is likely also Juan José who reportedly received a book of letters as a gift that same year. He was still attending the school in 1804 when he received an award of one peso for his outstanding penmanship.[16]

For Apaches like the Compás, travel was another benefit of making peace with the Spanish. While Spanish regulations theoretically sought to limit Apache mobility, in practice the Apaches de paz program changed but did not end it. Apaches outside the system were in some ways more constrained in their travels than those within it. Spanish military campaigns, which included Apache scouts, were ongoing, and Apache captives continued to be gathered, imprisoned, and shipped into diaspora in central Mexico or the Caribbean. The peace program provided a measure of protection from such campaigns, and although Apaches were ostensibly assigned to a particular presidio or town, in practiced they moved quite freely between them, not only to visit relatives but also to seek more generous gifts or rations from different military commanders.

Juan Diego Compá and his kin's travels serve to illustrate. In the summer of 1795, for example, Juan Diego journeyed with ten other Apaches in a delegation to visit Chihuahua City. The next summer, his kin went to the presidio of San Buenaventura, approximately fifty miles to the south of Janos. Around the same time, Juan Diego traveled to Bacoachi, the town in Sonora to which his father's family had first been assigned after making peace with Spaniards. Later in the fall of 1796, some of Juan Diego's kin were reported to have arrived at Carrizal, a presidio east of Janos, probably visiting family members there. By January 1797, Juan Diego and others from his local group were at the presidio of San Buenaventura again, having months earlier requested land to farm. The next month Juan Diego was back in Chihuahua City with several other Apache leaders. Later in the year, he again resided near Janos and then went away into the mountains to gather mescal and hunt.[17]

Such mobility was indicative of broader patterns of Apache life in the decades to come as well. While descriptive records are sparse for the years after 1800, ration lists indicate both the ongoing engagement of Apaches at sites like Janos and also their continued mobility. In December 1810, for example, Juan Diego is listed at Janos with a local group of forty-three people. A series of ration lists between May and December 1812 shows Juan Diego's group present but varying in size each month between seventeen and forty. Data from 1816 and 1818 are similar, with Juan Diego appearing in every entry and the total of his group ranging from five to sixty-nine. Such fluctuation continues through extant data in the 1820s, similarly suggesting that while Southern Apaches engaged frequently with Hispanic "reservations" like the one at Janos, they were in no sense settled at them.[18]

Apaches outside the peace program, meanwhile, remained at risk of being attacked and exiled at any time during this period. They complained that the dangers of pursuit by Hispanic soldiers and their Native allies had necessitated that they be wary and live in the mountains more than they preferred. As the Chihene Apache leader Mangas Coloradas later recalled of this period, Spanish, and then Mexican, soldiers with Apache scouts had forced Indians not involved in the system to "quit the valley and fertile parts to live in mountains and rugged and unfruitful places."[19]

Such concerns about security were warranted. In the years after 1800, coffles of Apache captives are documented to have departed Northern New Spain or to have arrived in central Mexico in 1801, 1802, 1803, 1806, 1808, and 1816. The perceived threat of violence and deportation was also kept alive by the occasional return of Apaches who escaped from the diaspora and spread news of what had happened to them. One especially concerning instance for Spanish officials was an Apache man named Rafael, reported to be an escapee from Veracruz who returned to the north by 1805 and allegedly killed hundreds of area residents in ensuing years. In contrast, another displaced Apache man named José Antonio Montes sought a nonviolent return to Apache lands in January 1816 with Spanish permission. He appeared in front of the viceroy in Mexico City with two women he claimed to be his wives, requesting he be named "captain" of a group of Apaches de paz in Northern New Spain. After the viceroy gave José Antonio a suit, hat, and fifteen pesos and sent him with his family to Chihuahua to meet with Spanish officials more familiar with Apache affairs, their story took an unexpected turn. The commandant general learned that José Antonio and one of his wives had been captured in war as children and sold in Chihuahua. As was typical of adults, the older woman they traveled with had been carried further into the diaspora, to Veracruz. She had subsequently escaped from her master's home and somehow joined up with the others. Based on this news, the commandant general denied their request, noting that the three Apaches demonstrated a history of "bad habits"—escape from masters, interest in returning to life among pagans, and a bigamous family life—which might only be corrected by an extended period of hard labor in exile. He ordered that they be imprisoned and shipped away in the last Cuba-bound coffle of Apache captives documented to have departed Northern New Spain during the Spanish colonial period in 1816.[20]

The story of this Apache family's fate at the hands of Spanish officials is tantalizing in its details. It suggests the ability of Apaches to connect with each other in diaspora and indicates awareness of Apache politics among those displaced from kin and home. Yet it also reveals how decisions about engaging with Spanish officials had consequences both for Apaches in the diaspora and for those who remained in their homelands.

One consequence of the Apaches de paz program for those involved in it related directly to the title of political leadership that José Antonio Montes requested. On the one hand, such titles were desired because of the special treatment the Spanish lavished on Apaches they recognized as leaders. On the other hand, although some Apache leaders had a broader influence than others, there was not a tradition among Apaches of a centralized leadership structure in which one man was "head chief" of all, and Spanish efforts thus caused controversy. As Apaches warned the Spanish in diplomatic discussions, interest in identifying a hierarchical, centralized leadership structure was not the "Apache way." Despite such feedback, the Spanish nonetheless pursued the idea of naming particular Apaches as "captains" or "principal chiefs" of the Apache nation; for example, El Compá had been named the "principal chief of the Apaches at peace" in August 1791. El Compá's appointment does not appear to have generated widespread backlash among Apaches, in part because he was recognized by them as an influential leader, a *nantan*, and behaved accordingly, distributing resources to his kin and followers. Yet evidence suggests that this was not always the case. For example, in February 1788, a Chokonen nantan named Chiganstege directed a group of his followers to kill another Chokonen man that the Spanish had named "captain," or chief, of a group of Chokonen Apaches de paz at Bacoachi. A few years later, Chihene Apaches attacked a mixed group of Apaches de paz around this same settlement, causing the vast majority of them to flee into the mountains.[21]

Spanish efforts to manage Apache affairs at Janos through specific assigned leaders also proved problematic after El Compá's death at the age of fifty or fifty-one in July 1794. Juan Diego, El Compá's elder son, wanted to be named his father's replacement and reportedly upset other Apaches by spreading rumors that he was going to be selected. That he was not ultimately named principal chief may have reflected the skepticism that some Apaches reported for Apaches who engaged deeply with the Hispanic sphere. This was especially true for his brother, Juan José, who was later granted a title of leadership by the Mexican government, even though he was noted to actually possess limited influence among Apaches. His godfather, Don Mariano Varela, sought to reassure him by explaining that his father "had not worried what other Apaches thought of him," and neither should he. Yet clearly for many Natives, relations with Hispanic officials did generate controversy among fellow Apaches that required delicate negotiation.[22]

Internal tensions among Southern Apache groups escalated as rations and gifts declined. Supply problems were not new, but they became worse during the Mexican independence wars of the 1810s and after an independent Mexican nation emerged in 1821. For Apache men like Juan Diego and Juan José, the ability to distribute generous rations and gifts among the members of their families was a key symbol of their successful leadership and a sign that it was worthwhile to limit raids and aid the Spanish in military campaigns. As Spanish and then Mexican provisioning of Apaches became more erratic, Apaches de paz increasingly joined those outside the system in participating in a raiding-and-trading economy that resembled past patterns of life but was also influenced by new developments. Years of relative peace had emboldened Apache leaders who wondered why constrains on violence and raiding were necessary. Moreover, the increased presence of U.S. American merchants in New Mexico who traveled down the Santa Fe Trail from Missouri beginning in the 1810s provided a new outlet for goods and livestock rustled in northern Mexico. By the late 1820s, even Apaches most closely linked to Hispanic communities like Juan Diego and Juan José were being accused of raiding, especially into Sonora.[23]

As memories of the cost of violence faded, the détente in Hispanic-Native relations began to unravel. As many Apaches de paz tired of the partial constraints on raiding that were necessary to maintain peace, Mexican officials grew more intolerant of mobile Indigenous polities within their claimed territory than their Spanish predecessors had been under the influence of a surge of liberal, nationalist sentiment. The officials were also faced with the complaints of local citizens who lamented that limited resources were being devoted to ration Apaches who also were also raiding their settlements.[24]

The most decisive, immediate cause for the unraveling of the rations for peace policy in the early 1830s was another concern: smallpox. In fact, it was the immediate factor that led Southern Apache families, including those of Juan José and Juan Diego, to leave the vicinity of Janos in 1832. While Apaches had long fled disease outbreaks—or moved to and from presidio sites for other reasons—in this context their decision provided the excuse for Mexican officials to stop issuing rations altogether.[25]

After the Apaches de paz program unraveled, Southern Apache politics remained bifurcated. While the discussions occurred largely beyond the ear of Mexican officials, the actions of Apache leaders suggest that some had decided it was time for Apaches to reassert their autonomy and raid Mexican towns in Sonora, New Mexico, and Chihuahua. They would build their wealth as they acquired livestock and horses in abundance that they could trade elsewhere in the borderlands. Others, like Juan José and Juan Diego, vacillated between participating in raids and seeking to negotiate a renewed peace with the Mexicans in exchange for rations.[26]

Juan José Compá's literacy provides an unusual window onto his personal struggles during this period. A series of letters collected in the Janos archives shows him writing the area resident Don Mariano Varela seeking advice about where to live and how to keep his family safe amid the tensions of the period. After abandoning Janos in 1832, he took his family into the mountains, participated in raids on Sonora, and began to fear for the future. He noted to Varela that other Apaches distrusted him, but neither was he confident about embracing life in Mexican society. "My dear father," Compá wrote in January 1833, "please send me some gunpowder for my defense, because the Apaches aren't going to like the fact I have informed you all [of Apache affairs]." In April, he wrote to Varela again, noting that Apaches de paz had been attacked by Mexicans near El Paso, on the road to Chihuahua, and elsewhere. Varela advised Compá in a reply to "not be a fool. . . . Get yourself to Janos with your wife and kids and no one will do anything to you."[27]

Ultimately, both Juan José's concerns and Varela's advice proved well founded. In 1835, the Sonoran legislature issued a reward of one hundred pesos for the scalp of any Apache male over the age of fourteen. The Sonora governor subsequently contracted with an Anglo-American living in the state named John Johnson to pursue Apaches in exchange for half of the plunder recovered. Juan José and his brother Juan Diego were unaware of this arrangement when they observed Johnson and a party of men under his command lumbering toward their mountain camps in the Animas Mountains of New Mexico in April 1837. Apaches typically traded with Anglo merchants at Santa Rita del Cobre, the copper-mining post founded years earlier in southern New Mexico, and they thus had some reason to be suspicious. Yet the opportunity to pawn off mules they had taken in recent raids in exchange for whiskey, roasted corn, and other goods seemed too good to pass up. After two days characterized by "much friendship," at least according to one observer, Johnson and his men revealed their true intentions. Early on the morning of April 22, 1837, he ordered his men to open fire on the Apaches with whom they had been trading with a swivel gun they had hidden behind their wares. They then chased down and shot as many of the survivors as they could find. More than twenty in the end lay dead, including Juan José and Juan Diego Compá.[28]

The Johnson massacre exemplified a broader shift in patterns of interethnic interaction in the borderlands. Apaches remembered it as the first in "a series of treacherous attacks made upon us by whites or Mexicans." For Americans like John Johnson, it was a sign that money could be made in Mexico by contracting to kill Apaches. Bounties for Apache scalps were eventually enacted not only in Sonora but also in Chihuahua. Many local Mexican residents cheered the news of the deaths of Apaches and the taking of scalps. Some, however, particularly leaders in Mexico City, expressed discomfort, especially with parties of armed Americans operating within the territory of the Mexican Republic. For their part, governors in Sonora or Chihuahua claimed distance from American mercenaries, noting that they sanctioned the ends, not necessarily their means.[29]

A particularly brutal period of violence, characterized by indiscriminate massacres, trophy taking, and bounty hunting, strained the possibility of productive relations between Apaches and Mexicans in the ensuing years. It reflected the bipolar nature of interethnic relations during subsequent decades: truces and moments of cooperation followed by ruthless campaigns of violence. Periko, a Bedonkohe Apache man, captured well the Native perspective on this period and its cycles of violence in a conversation with the anthropologist Morris Opler in the 1930s: "The Mexicans used to take scalps; they started first, before the Indians, and they used to take scalps including the ears and sometimes the whole head. The Indians would make peace with the Mexicans; then the Mexicans would give them liquor and get them drunk and take them in their houses and cut their heads off. Then the war would start again."[30]

Captured in Periko's account are Apache concerns about bodily mutilation and their disdain for treachery as a tactic. His specific critique—of Mexicans attacking Apaches during trade visits—is supported by historical evidence. It also illustrates how temporary peace and trade nonetheless remained possible, especially between particular Mexican towns or families and Apache communities. As is often the case in long-term interethnic conflicts, Apache understandings cast blame on the other group—"they started first"—and branded Mexicans' behavior as savage and cruel. Mangas Coloradas would later explain in a diplomatic entrée with Americans "that people invited my people to a feast—they manifested every shew of kindness towards us. We were lulled into security by their hypocrisy, people drank and got drunk and then the Sonoranians beat out the brains of fifteen of them with clubs. Are we to be the victims of such treachery, and not be revenged?" Geronimo was perhaps most famous in his hatred for and dehumanization of Mexicans. He never forgave them for killing his mother, wife, and children in an attack on their camp in 1858. He later wrote about having lost count of how many Mexicans he had killed, noting that "some of them were not even worth counting." It may in part because such testimony was given to U.S. Americans that Apaches de-emphasized critiques of U.S. tactics and violence. After all, many of the massacres that most concerned Apaches in the 1830s and 1840s had actually been carried out by U.S. citizens, even if they were sanctioned and rewarded for them by the Mexican government.[31]

For their part, Mexican residents and officials cast themselves as victims, arguing that Apaches had begun a war of extermination against them in the early 1830s. Presaging the dehumanization that would also characterize U.S. Americans' descriptions of Apaches in later decades, Mexicans described their Apache enemy as a serpent, a wolf, and other kinds of predator, "who clamps his deadly fangs into us before we see him." The victims were poor Mexican shepherds, woodcutters, washerwomen, even "little children."[32] Echoing past arguments that Natives had threatened the loss of all of New Spain, newspaper editorials sometimes suggested that the very future of Mexico was at stake: "The desperate struggle leaves us powerless and breathless. . . . There is no remedy; meanwhile, the savages trample on our country. We have no other prospect but misery and death because prosperity and progress are impossible for a people who every day lose their fortunes and their lives."[33]

The dehumanization reflected in both Apache and Mexican views of each other fueled, and was fueled by, cycles of violence that took a significant toll on both groups. Yet there were also checks on the degree to which either group truly sought to eliminate the other. For Apaches, reliance on Mexican horse herds limited the extent to which they would go to destroy all Mexican ranches or towns. Mexicans also vacillated between policies intended to kill as many Apaches as possible and negotiation. There were concerns about the legality and morality of scalp bounties, for example, and critiques of the excesses of some of the mercenary killers hired, including whether they were actually presenting Apache scalps.[34]

One of the most important constraints on indiscriminate killing was the taking of captives. It was Apaches rather than Mexicans who most innovated in their captive-taking practices during this period. In the wars of the late eighteenth century, Apaches had taken relatively few prisoners, focusing on taking livestock and killing the enemy. In comparison, Mexican sources indicate that Apaches took a significant number of captives in the 1830s and 1840s. For Apaches, captives were useful for their labor—in tending herds, for example—but they were most valuable as bargaining chips to negotiate truces and to recover kin captured by Mexicans, as was the case in temporary peace treaties in 1835, 1838, and 1842. Apaches may have also drawn upon the presence of Mexican captives to shield them from indiscriminate attack, hoping that Mexican troops would take care in attacking Apache groups known to include Mexicans.[35]

Captive taking and prisoner exchanges followed by brief truces would continue in the following decades and sometimes led to Mexicans briefly providing rations to Southern Apaches. Ultimately, however, peace did not prove enduring and the Apaches de paz program was not restored in a sustained fashion. Ironically, this was in part because of the success of the program in the late eighteenth and early nineteenth centuries from an Apache vantage point: relative peace had allowed them to rebuild their communities from decades of diaspora and increase their capacity to raid or wage war against enemies. While Mexican efforts to control Apache raiding through scalp bounties and the use of mercenary killers in the 1830s and 1840s again threatened Apache communities, they also served to further foment Apache grievances over treacherous massacres.[36]

Another factor also proved central to the lasting deterioration of Apache-Mexican relations: a shift in international boundaries that allowed Mexicans to cast Apaches as someone else's problem to solve. The breakdown of peace between Mexicans, Apaches, and other Natives played a role in the change of borders. By the 1840s, observers described a veritable "desert" created as some Mexican residents abandoned their ranches and farms and fled to safety out of fear of Apache or Comanche raids. While Mexicans warred with powerful Native groups, they became less prepared for the ultimate invasion of the expansionist Anglo-American nation-state to their north. They struggled to muster local support to fend off the U.S. invasion of northern Mexico that began in 1846 and ended with the occupation of Mexico City and the loss of nearly half of Mexican territory.[37]

Between about 1790 and 1830, Spain and then Mexico had administered a rationing program for Apaches at military posts that secured benefits for Hispanic and Native communities alike. This system was rooted in borderlands diplomacy, which was characterized by flexibility and negotiation and a degree of tolerance on the part of Native and Hispanic groups for the self-governance and perceived interests of the other. Although Hispanic officials sometimes discussed this arrangement in spatial terms and sought to limit Apache mobility, in practice the system did not operate as a bounded reservation system. Instead, the rationing program shaped new patterns of Apache mobility as Apaches continued to live in and move through their homelands while also routinely visiting Hispanic towns and forts. After this system unraveled, its basic framework remained influential for momentary truces between Apaches and Mexicans. In the coming years, the Apaches de paz system would also inform Apache diplomats' interactions with the United States.

Imperial Echoes

United States sovereignty in the Southwest remained unrealized vis-à-vis Indigenous nations in the aftermath of the U.S.-Mexico War. The Treaty of Guadalupe Hidalgo that U.S. and Mexican diplomats negotiated in 1848 to end the war indicated as much, even as it also reflected the United States' imperial ambitions. Article XI noted that for practicable purposes "a great part" of the land that was intended to form a part of the United States was "now occupied by savage tribes." These were now deemed to be "under the exclusive control of the Government of the United States," though no representative of any Native group was present at the treaty negotiations. The United States promised to "forcibly restrain" any Indian raids into Mexico, make illegal the purchase of captives or livestock taken by Indians in Mexico, and work to ransom and return any Mexican captives they discovered.[38]

It did not take long for U.S. officials to realize that Article XI was unworkable. Not only could the United States not forcibly restrain mobile Apache Indians, but they struggled to even locate or communicate with them, because early interactions with Southern Apaches in particular largely occurred on their terms in their lands. The first official tasked specifically with handling interactions with them was John Coffee Hays, a former Texas Ranger who was named to be subagent for Southern Apaches in April 1849 and subsequently traveled to the Gila River in New Mexico. As he explained in a subsequent report of his activities, "I sought to have an interview [with the Apaches on the Gila] but I failed in every effort to see them."[39]

Hays would not be the last failed Apache agent, but his experience illustrates just how ambitious U.S. promises of controlling and containing mobile Natives had been. As he explained it, he found Apaches to be "shy and hostile." After substantial efforts to "establish a friendly intercourse with them," he decided to leave Apache lands and return to San Diego. "If I remained long in their country," he explained, "it was at the very great risk of life and I accordingly felt myself forced to abandon as an impossible thing the undertaking of treating with or conciliating these dangerous and refractory Indians."[40] A few years later, when a U.S. delegation sent to survey the border again managed to meet with Southern Apaches, they were more successful in "treating with" and conciliating them. This time, it was the most influential Southern Apache leader of the period, Mangas Coloradas, who was asked to grant the Americans safe passage and prevent his men from taking their animals. He agreed, probably because he as of yet saw little risk in boundary commissioner John Russell Bartlett's project to "run the line between the two countries." Bartlett saw firsthand how little this border meant to Southern Apaches when he traveled to Ures, Sonora, and heard incessant complaints about Apache raids. Even when Mexican officials managed to capture the perpetrators, he noted, it was difficult to hold onto them. "So bold have these Indians become," Bartlett warned, "they visited the capital during my tarry there, and rescued several of their associates who were confined in the state prison."[41]

A wandering party of surveyors was one thing, a gathering stream of gold seekers, soldiers, and settlers quite another. Some simply traveled through Apache lands to the mining camps in California after 1848. Others were lured to stay on the Indian lands—or return from California—by rumors of mineral wealth, such as at the old copper mines in the heart of Chihene Apache territory at Santa Rita del Cobre. In 1851, U.S. Americans occupied the old Mexican fort there and renamed it Fort Webster. Though it was the Americans who had invaded Apache lands, it was the invaders who nonetheless began complaining of "murders after murders, depredations upon depredations, and innumerable other evils." By April 1852, the territorial governor, James C. Calhoun, was lamenting that New Mexico was "in a more critical condition than it has ever been before," noting that he feared a mass Indian uprising. Drawing upon a classic settler discourse of victimhood, Calhoun expressed the pressure from settlers on the government to help negotiate an agreement with Apaches that would bring security to their settlements and property, stating that "if the Government of the United States intends doing anything for our protection for heaven's sake let us know it." For their part, Apaches concerned about the influx of uninvited people into their lands were motivated to negotiate as well. By the summer of 1852, the two parties had reached an agreement that Mangas Coloradas and other southern Apache leaders signed and was ultimately ratified by the U.S. Senate the following year.[42]

At first glance, this 1852 Apache treaty reflected significant concessions on the part of Native leaders. They agreed to cease all hostilities against the United States and its allies, to recognize U.S. jurisdiction and laws, to allow military and trading posts to be established in their territory, and to allow safe passage of American citizens. They promised to cease all "incursions" into the territory of Mexico and refrain from taking captives or livestock. They further indicated that the United States could "at their earliest convenience . . . designate, settle, and adjust their territorial boundaries." In exchange, Apaches obtained little more than vague promises of gifts and other "liberal and humane measures" that the United States saw fit, and only the United States retained the ability to make "amendments and modifications."[43]

Yet what appears to be a quite one-sided agreement on paper makes more sense when contextualized within the *longue durée* of Apache diplomacy. This was not the first time that an imperial power had demanded in its own peculiar language and terminology that Apaches submit to its authority. Under the Apaches de paz program, for example, symbolic submission had coincided with the ability to continue to live among and govern their people as they saw fit. Mangas Coloradas evoked this past history when he explained that his people would not follow certain provisions of the treaty, such as the promise to end travel into Mexico. Even U.S. officials demonstrated sympathy to Apache interests in that regard, noting that Apaches complained of bad faith and treachery on the part of residents of Sonora and Chihuahua, "and if half their statements are true, the Indians would be justified in seeking revenge."[44]

As had been true with Article XI of the Treaty of Guadalupe, much of the 1852 Apache Treaty language was aspirational on the part of U.S. negotiators. For example, while referencing the creation of new territorial boundaries in the future—an implicit reference to a reservation or forced removal of some kind—the treaty also recognized Apaches' possession of their lands in the present. Southern Apaches promised to provide safe passage to Americans through "the territory of the aforesaid Indians": in other words through *their* territory, which the United States recognized remained for practical purposes under their control.[45]

The question of territorial boundaries between peoples remained a live one in the subsequent months and years. The attendance of Southern Apache leaders at diplomatic parleys in 1853, in which the United States pressed them for new concessions, reflected their growing concerns about the interests of their families and their future livelihood. The observations of a new U.S. agent assigned to them that year, Michael Steck, help explain the conditions of life for Apaches at this time. Upon assuming his post at Fort Webster, in south central New Mexico, in late July 1853, Steck noted that "white encroachment on their lands and their long war with Mexico [had] significantly affected their numbers and their ability to make a living." Steck observed the role that violence had played in skewing Apache gender ratios such that many men had "between 2 and 5 wives." The Chihene leader Loco, who would remain important in diplomatic negotiations in the years to come, had three wives, for example, two of whom were widows. Loss of kin to war and captivity was not the only challenge Apaches were facing. Steck observed that "the lack of game in their country made it impossible for them to live without raiding. It is plain as the light of day that they must be rationed or a war of extermination commenced if we wish to prevent these depredations. They must steal or starve."[46]

Steck's philosophy was similar to those of his Hispanic predecessors, and like some of them, he favored rationing to extermination. Yet more than in the case of Spain or Mexico, he strongly advocated for defined reservation borders as a solution to conflict with Apaches. Some Apaches proved amenable to military posts and even reservations in their own homelands in the hopes of ensuring that their lands were not overrun by squatters, miners, and other outsiders. This was in contrast to the late eighteenth and early nineteenth century, when the Hispanic population in Arizona and Southern New Mexico was relatively small. A June 1855 treaty Steck helped negotiate at Fort Thorn between the United States and Southern Apaches illustrates as much, since the Apache leaders present accepted in principal the creation of a reservation of approximately two thousand square miles in southwestern New Mexico, which included the old copper mines of Santa Rita del Cobre. For Americans, peace accords that defined territorial limits meant opening up new lands to white settlement. From the perspective of some Apaches, such accords meant obtaining a degree of protection and assurances that they could live in safety in their own lands.[47]

The ultimate fate of the 1855 Fort Thorn treaty illustrates that neither Apaches nor Americans were yet ready to settle on boundaries between their nations. Mangas Coloradas was most emblematic of Apache concerns because he neither attended negotiations nor ultimately signed the agreement. He instead delayed, claiming that he had wanted to come to the treaty negotiations but was too ill and later noting that it was too hot to travel to Santa Fe in July. If Mangas Coloradas's assent was key for the treaty to actually go into effect, he was not the only leader dragging his feet. American officials involved in the negotiations, including Steck, were unsure that it made sense to grant Apaches a reservation in their own lands. Steck preferred their removal west, down the Gila to an area more remote from white settlements. Remove them farther from the frontier, he wrote to a colleague, and "you throw open for settlements the finest and most desirable portion of New Mexico." Most critically, the U.S. Senate failed to ratify the treaty. Some senators wondered why the United States should expend funds to secure lands they had already fought a war with Mexico over. Others were concerned about mineral wealth in the proposed Apache reservation, including the old copper mines.[48]

Government bureaucracy was not a new concept to Apaches. After all, they had negotiated treaties with Spain and Mexico in past decades. Yet the U.S.-American bureaucracy was more centralized, and local officials possessed less power to make binding decisions on their own. Over time, Apaches would become more familiar with the power of distant officials in Washington and learn to be wary of promises until they were sure those officials had granted their approval. Even then, promised provisions (rations, blankets, clothing) might be slow to arrive and of poor quality. The Chokonen leader Cochise would later explain that he had been "living on promises for 15 years."[49]

With little tangible outcome for all their recent diplomacy in New Mexico, some Apaches traveled to their lands south of the U.S.-Mexico border in hopes of a better deal. Apache-Mexican relations had vacillated between overt violence and what Apaches termed "treaty negotiations," which sometimes resulted in brief periods of respite and rationing. Such was the case after the failed 1855 Fort Thorn Treaty. In the summer of 1856, Chihenes went to Janos, Chihuahua, to begin negotiations there. The border was becoming increasingly meaningful to Apaches as they learned that they could draw upon Mexican and Americans' respect for it to flee mistreatment, seek better arrangements in terms of rations or treaty terms, or acquire property such as livestock and shuffle it to the other side of the international boundary line, where it might be sold on the black market without immediate retribution or reprisals. Mexicans' and Americans' respect for their own borders was qualified as well, but the fact that neither country wanted armed parties of the other's citizens entering their claimed territories served Apache interests by making people think twice about pursuing them across the line, particularly before an international pact in 1882 that allowed cross-border pursuit with notification. Residents of Mexico and the United States alike learned that calm on one side of the line generally meant trouble with Apaches on the other.[50]

Yet Southern Apaches' travels into Chihuahua in 1856 and 1857 illustrate that a better deal with Mexico often proved elusive. When a party of Chihenes visited Janos late in the summer of 1856 to trade and talk peace, thirteen were seized and thrown into prison instead. The Janos military commander, José Baltazar Padilla, released one of them to deliver the message to Mangas Coloradas that they would be held "until certain property stolen by his people was restored to the citizens of Janos." The letter was ultimately delivered to Steck and the governor of New Mexico, David Meriwether, who attempted to intervene on the Chihenes' behalf by noting that the captives held in jail and the perpetrators of the alleged raid "were of different and distinct bands, and one should not be held responsible for the conduct . . . by the other." Padilla ultimately decided not to release the captives until "a permanent peace" could be secured.[51]

The ransom of kin had long been a motivation for temporary treaties between Mexicans and Apaches that briefly revived the rationing programs of the past. Yet these truces usually did not last for long, and each side could prove duplicitous. In this case it is appears likely that Janos officials poisoned the rations they had been giving to the Chihene during the negotiations of preceding months. By the fall of 1857, Steck reported that they had returned north of the border in poor health. "Scarcely a family returned but has their hair cropped short, the badge of mourning for some relative," he noted, adding that they "believe[d] they have been poisoned." He described the Indians symptoms as resembling those of "poisoning by arsenic, probably administered in whiskey as that formed a part of their rations." Disillusioned with the promise of "permanent peace" at Janos, the Chihenes returned to their land in the United States in the hopes of finally formalizing a treaty with the Americans. While Steck hoped this could be done as soon as possible, he knew the bureaucracy well. "You might as well talk Greek to them as try to explain the delays," he noted.[52]

In the meantime, Americans continued to hone their visions for reservations as the means for realizing U.S. imperial dreams in the Southwest. In fact, U.S. officials were quite transparent about why they believed Indians needed to be "colonized" on reservations, as they called the process. Steck argued for reservations from a standpoint of sympathy toward the Apache people. In March 1860 he noted that "if some steps are not taken to set apart a portion of their country as a reserve they will have none worth having left." After a promotion from Apache agent to commissioner of Indians affairs in New Mexico, Steck clashed with other colleagues and settlers who believed "extermination"—genocidal massacres and military campaigns—were a better solution than reserved lands and education.[53]

Presaging conflicts between military and civil administrators in years to come, Steck was particularly at odds with Brigadier General James Carleton. Carleton, a Maine native and U.S.-Mexico War veteran, arrived in the Southwest originally to fight confederates during the U.S. Civil War but subsequently turned to fighting Indians. In the summer of 1862, he commanded a force of eight hundred volunteers known as the California Column, which skirmished with Apaches and wounded Mangas Coloradas in a fight at Apache Pass. Carleton then took command of the New Mexico military department and began what he called a war of extermination against Apache groups and Navajos alike. In January 1863, a party of gold seekers and a unit of Carleton's old California column—now commanded by Brigadier General Joseph Rodman West—orchestrated what Geronimo would later term "perhaps the greatest wrong ever done to the Indians." Luring Mangas Coloradas with a flag of truce, the gold seekers and soldiers took him prisoner and put him under guard. West reportedly left after giving "a strong indication of his wishes." Overnight, the guards shot and killed the Apache leader, claiming that he had attempted to escape. An army surgeon subsequently severed his head and "boiled it in a great black pot," as one Apache later recalled, to prepare it for shipment to a phrenologist in New York for study and display.[54]

This ruthlessness was just what Carleton believed was necessary to scare the surviving Natives into submission, and similar efforts were scaled up in the coming months. Carleton is perhaps best known in Native American history for the spectacular human misery caused by his policy of concentrating Navajo and Mescalero Apache people on a desolate reservation in eastern New Mexico near Fort Sumner. After ordering Kit Carson to wage a scorched-earth campaign through Navajo country in late 1863 and early 1864 in which people, corn, peach trees, and other life was destroyed, he then ordered him to forcibly exile nearly ten thousand Navajos to the new reservation. The military campaign and subsequent Long Walk led to immense losses of property and the death of hundreds along the route and after arrival. Carleton had ordered a similar genocidal campaign against Mescalero Apaches in their homeland in southeastern New Mexico a year before, and approximately five hundred Mescalero survivors had already endured a forced migration to be interned at Fort Sumner.[55]

While Carleton has sometimes been cast as unusually brutal in his approach, he was actually quite representative of U.S. Indian policy. He was an influential proponent of reservations and forced-removal schemes that would be employed with Southern Apaches in subsequent years. Even those who opposed Carleton's worst ideas shared much of his underlying thinking regarding the necessity of Indigenous peoples' dispossession and disappearance. As Carleton explained it, Native people in the West would soon learn "it was their destiny to, as it had been that of their brethren, tribe after tribe, away back toward the rising sun, to give way to the insatiable progress of our race."[56]

Apaches, like other Indigenous peoples, were not content to accept this vision of their destiny. Southern Apaches spent much of the 1860s at war with the United States. The Chokonen Apache leader Cochise gave up on conciliating Americans after he narrowly escaped imprisonment at the hands of Americans in 1861 by cutting his way out of the tent in which he was being held. After the killing and beheading of his father-in-law, Mangas Coloradas, his views of Americans darkened further. War, from an Apache perspective, meant the taking of enemy lives to avenge those they had lost. "We were successful," Cochise later proclaimed to an American official, "and your soldiers were driven away and your people killed and we again possessed our land." The idea that his own children and grandchildren would subsequently live as prisoners of war in Florida, Alabama, and Oklahoma was as yet unthinkable. Apaches continued to envision a future in their homelands, even as the United States claimed the bulk of these lands as the public domain of Arizona and New Mexico.[57]

The Southern Apache Reservation Network

In the late 1860s and early 1870s, U.S.-run reservations for the Apache people finally came to fruition. Hounded by U.S. and Mexican armies and pursued by scalp bounty hunters and citizen mobs in both countries, Southern Apaches became more amenable than ever to some kind of a negotiated peace with the Americans. The tide of white Americans that had withdrawn to some extent during the U.S. Civil War was now flooding back in, and even Cochise was beginning to recognize that his efforts to "drive away" Americans and "again possess [his] land" might be reversed. Stagecoach and rail lines cut their way through Apache lands, carrying white miners, ranchers, and entrepreneurs in greater numbers after the U.S. Civil War ended in 1865 than ever before. In a parley with Americans in March 1869, Cochise reportedly said, "The

Americans are everywhere, and we live in bad places to shun them." At the same time, a new presidential administration under Ulysses S. Grant began debating a shift in Indian policy to a "peace" policy that would center diplomatic negotiations with western tribes in order to create reservations that would be administered by agents appointed by Protestant churches. Apache and U.S. interests appeared to be coming into alignment, though many local settlers resisted anything other than the "total extermination" of Apaches. Such critiques and pressures would threaten Southern Apache reservations in the years to come, but for now, the momentum seemed to be in their favor.[58]

Despite the superior numbers and growing power of Americans surrounding them, Apaches retained significant power to decide where, when, and under what conditions they would engage with U.S.-run reservations. The Chihene leader Loco initiated negotiations in 1869 to finally formalize an Apache reservation in the Chihene homeland. It was probably a recent army campaign that provided the immediate spark for Loco to make overtures for peace at U.S. military forts in central New Mexico in the spring and summer of 1869. This is suggested by the military fort commander's description that members of Loco's band were "still nursing wounds" when they approached Fort Craig that spring and then Fort McRae in the summer.[59]

In May 1869, Loco rode into Fort Craig with a group of between 100 and 150 Chihenes. He asked for food and a safe place to camp, noting that "the Apaches wanted out of the fray and onto a reservation." When the Americans failed to act on his request, Loco decided to approach Fort McRae and its captain with a similar request. The army captain there was more sympathetic to Loco, giving him some food but warning him that he would need approval before setting up any routine rationing program. News of Loco's peace overtures soon gained national attention, reaching Commissioner of Indian Affairs, Ely Parker, that summer. Parker, the first Native American to serve as commissioner, designated Lieutenant Charles Drew as an agent for the Southern Apaches, ordering him in July 1869 to proceed to New Mexico and "endeavor to communicate with the Southern Apache Tribes of Indians." It is striking that two decades after the failures of the first Apache agent, the question of whether a U.S. official would be able even to communicate with Apaches remained a live one.[60]

As the U.S. bureaucratic machinery slowly churned, Loco continued to make his requests and clarify what "being placed on a reservation" meant to him. The vision he laid out through an interpreter in an August conference with Americans near Cuchillo Negro reflected a decades-old framework that Apaches had drawn upon in interactions with Spain and Mexico:

> In speaking on what they wanted, Loco says they want to plant near
> the Cuchillo Negro, where they used to plant before they were driven
> away; also to hunt on the east side of the Mimbres mountains as far
> south as old Fort Thorn, and as far as the mountains east of the Rio
> Grande, known as the Sierra de Caballos [just east of the river], and
> to a distance of 20 miles north of Fort McRae. They want the fort left
> here for their protection. They appear very willing to make peace, and
> I think that with proper care and by treating them honestly and justly,
> the whole of the Apache tribes may be brought in from the warpath.[61]

Loco's vision was similar to that of the Apaches de paz program, as well as of
temporary truces revived in subsequent years with Mexico. First and foremost, he emphasized the need to access Chihene lands that they had long
used to support their people. He spoke of both places and the uses of those
places: planting grounds, hunting and gathering spots. He also demonstrated
flexibility and a willingness to accommodate, as long as Americans provided
rations. In fact, perhaps with an eye to settler violence, he even urged that
Fort McRae be maintained in his lands for his people's protection.[62]

At the center of Loco's proposed reservation was a favorite site of many
Southern Apaches, but especially of Chihenes—called Warm Springs in
English and Ojo Caliente in Spanish. Apaches knew it as Tú sidu-yá—"the
place where the water is hot." It was at a moderate elevation, just under five
thousand feet, and thus possessed relatively mild winters. The springs supplied warm water for winter baths. The river the springs fed cut a gorge that
ran from the base of San Mateo Peak to the Rio Grande. Although accessible
by wagon, an important feature for trade, it was also narrow enough in places
to be well protected, because boulders could be hurled from the ridges onto
unsuspecting intruders below. While Tú sidu-yá was merely one especially
favored site in the broader Chihene and Southern Apache landscape, it was
one that they had been familiar with and occupied for generations. They knew
its climate and plant and animal resources intimately. All told, this knowledge
of the land assured them that their people could thrive there. As one Chihene
man who grew up around Warm Springs later recalled, "That is a good country. . . . It is a healthy place for man and beast. Women nor children get sick
there. Neither do animals. Don't send me any place except there."[63]

It was also a place in which they had allies. During the 1860s, as war
raged with the United States, they had made peace with Cañada Alamosa, a
town primarily inhabited by Mexican Americans founded the decade before
and known today as Monticello. This pattern of interaction with neighbors

had echoes deep into the Apache past, when Apache communities formed relations of reciprocity with Pueblo communities, with Tarahumara bands, or with particular Spanish towns or presidios. Monticello provided an outlet for livestock, meat, and pelts and a source for guns, ammunition, liquor, clothing, and foodstuffs. While Apaches had the power to drive Mexican Americans away from Cañada Alamosa if they had wanted to—as they had other settlements in the past—they instead had decided that coexistence was preferable to independence.[64]

There was clear logic in establishing a reservation where Southern Apaches wanted to be (in their own lands), and initially U.S. officials appeared to act quickly. After a flurry of activity, however, Agent Drew's superiors went silent. He pleaded for provisions, especially blankets for the coming winter, and for news about the reservation. In the meantime, as the U.S. bureaucracy ground to a halt, news of peacefully settled Apaches brought in "a seedy collection of whiskey sellers, bounty hunters, and toughs looking for trouble." Mexicans and Americans reportedly hung around to check Indian livestock brands and claim them as their own. Agent Drew also worried about scalp hunters. He noted that scouting parties from Chihuahua came up who will "pay a premium for Indian scalps. . . . A friendly Indian is worth as much as . . . any other." He was forced to issue an order that any armed party of Mexicans entering the United State would be arrested and disarmed.[65]

After Agent Drew's untimely death in June 1870 after getting lost on a hunting trip, his successors continued to face similar challenges. They struggled to explain to Apaches why the needed blankets had not arrived and why rations were so paltry—because they only had authorization and enough supplies to issue half rations. Agent Orlando Piper worried that Apaches were beginning to question whether the United States would ever formalize the reservation. This was a legitimate concern based on past history.[66]

As bureaucratic delays mounted, Apache agents struggled to keep Southern Apaches calm, fed, and clothed. While a national financial crisis factored into the delays, Americans' continued insistence that Southern Apaches be located somewhere other than in their own lands also played a role. In January 1871, Agent Piper was asked to approach Apaches about the idea of sending them to Fort Stanton, the Mescalero Apache agency. Apaches responded that "this [Warm Springs] is their home and they do not want any other." Agent Piper added that he did not think they could be moved anywhere else willingly and that they had told him that "they would rather have but little food and clothing here; then plenty at Ft. Stanton." Two months later, he reported that the Indians had suffered greatly through the winter because of inadequate blankets to keep them warm. While he had in fact distributed 170 blankets to them, they had sold them, probably to friends in the Mexican American town of Cañada Alamosa, to obtain food.[67]

The arrival of spring and new supplies that enabled the agent to issue full rations improved morale, and by May 1871 some Chokonen and Mescalero Apaches had even joined the Chihenes around the Warm Springs agency. Agent Piper reported that approximately twelve hundred Indians were now drawing rations. This illustrates a dynamic that would continue in future years, as news of improving or deteriorating circumstances at particular U.S. posts or reservations shaped Apache migrations. The number of Apaches at Warm Springs (including Mescaleros and Chokonens) remained constant through the summer. Yet Agent Piper did note that they remained concerned about the fact that "for more than two years" they had been "anxiously waiting for this question of location to be settled." He believed it to be of imminent importance that it be settled once and for all and that "the wish of the Indians be regarded in the location."[68]

Finally, by the summer of 1871, it seemed likely that the formal status of a Southern Apache reservation could be resolved, and the hardships of previous months caused by bureaucratic delay could begin to be forgotten. The Grant administration sent Vincent Colyer as the special agent to New Mexico and Arizona charged with formalizing Native reservations as part of his peace policy. Colyer was a New York–born Quaker who had previously advocated for freedmen in the aftermath of the U.S. Civil War before becoming concerned about Indian affairs. His interest in setting aside reserved lands for Native people on which they could be Christianized and educated generated harsh criticism from many white residents of Arizona and New Mexico who preferred genocidal warfare combined with forced removal. While well-meaning, Colyer's 1871 expedition ultimately illustrated a key problem of U.S. Indian policy and administration that had characterized U.S.-Indian relations in the past and would continue to be influential going forward. Although some army officers, civilian agents, or traders spent significant time around Native people, became familiar with them, and even advocated for their interests, those with the real power were often much less knowledgeable and often driven more by philosophical or bureaucratic concerns.[69]

Such was the case for Colyer. In what must have been a mind-boggling turn of events for Loco and other Chihenes, he decided to select a reservation for Southern Apaches seventy-five miles northwest of Ojo Caliente in the Tularosa Valley, which he deemed better suited to their needs, given its "arable lands, good water and plenty of wood and game." While higher in elevation and colder at approximately seven thousand feet, Colyer and his advisors reasoned that it was better because it was more distant from non-Native settlers. As one put it, Tularosa was "protected from the bad whites and bad Mexicans" and, without evidence, was better for agriculture.[70]

The former argument warrants further attention. Even more than "bad whites," a key concern of U.S. Indian agents were the Mexican American inhabitants of Cañada Alamosa because they believed them to be more loyal to Indians than to Americans based on their long-standing relations with Apaches. One concern raised was the cost of paying for their property, since presumably only Natives could dwell on an Indian reservation and they would have to be bought out. Yet this alone does not explain why Warm Springs was not selected, because the estimated cost of approximately $11,000 to buy out Mexican residents was relatively insignificant and the government would ultimately spend more than $18,000 just to transport the Apaches to Tularosa. Moreover, one observer noted that the Mexican claims to land ownership were not very secure anyway, perhaps a reference to the willingness of the U.S. courts to strike land claims that did not fit the expectations of Anglo-American law.[71]

Decisions about where to locate Apache Indians were inseparable from concerns about interethnic associations, echoing Spanish imperial decisions about the forced removal of Apaches a century earlier. Many white New Mexico residents believed that Mexican-Indian trade was a key spark for livestock raids. As one observer noted, "So long as these people [the Mexicans in Cañada Alamosa] trade with the Indians . . . so long will the Indians be thieves." The commissioner of Indian affairs for the territory of New Mexico, Nathaniel Pope, reported after a visit to Cañada that he was "convinced that the majority of these Indians are wholly under the control of the Mexicans."[72]

Whatever the precise blend of U.S. motivations for the strange selection of Tularosa, Southern Apaches immediately voiced their disdain for the choice and successfully avoided being removed there for almost a year. While Apaches would become famous for resisting confinement to reservations through flight, the story of the Warm Springs and Tularosa reservations illustrates another Apache strategy of resistance that was perhaps more effective, at least temporarily: staying put. In September 1871, after the Tularosa decision had been announced, the Apaches declared at a conference that they would not go to Tularosa, adding that "this is their land[,] here they want to live and be buried with their fathers." A month later, Agent Piper continued to report that "they positively refuse to go" and that they told him he could "take the rations and give them to the bears and wolves."[73] Besides expressing their reasons for wanting to stay at Warm Springs, Apache leaders voiced specific concerns about Tularosa itself. Cochise, for example, explained in March 1872 that his blood "was on fire," but the mountains and waters around Warm Springs "had cooled me." In contrast, Tularosa was, "a long ways off," full of flies that "eat of the eyes of horses," and known for the "bad spirits [that] live there."[74]

As resistance to removal to Tularosa continued, Americans began suggesting that a delegation of Apache leaders be sent to Washington, D.C., to negotiate. Such visits served multiple purposes. U.S. officials hoped that the journey would result in a shift in Apache views on the removal question, including by Cochise, the Apache leader about whom they were most concerned at this time. More broadly, such visits were intended to impress upon Native leaders the weight of the U.S. population, technology, and resources they were up against. Yet Southern Apache leaders proved reluctant in this case, in part based on past experiences. "They have so often been deceived," Agent Piper wrote, "that they are afraid of treachery and decline to go." Among Loco, Victorio, and Cochise, Victorio proved most amenable to the idea of going, but ultimately all three balked, saying that perhaps they could go at some later date. Reflecting his knowledge of the technological innovations of the era, Cochise offered that perhaps he would allow a photograph to be sent in his place.[75]

U.S. officials struggled with the fact that they needed some degree of Apache assent for the removal to be successful. They could temporarily round up several hundred Southern Apaches and forcibly carry them to Tularosa, but maintaining the army presence necessary to force them to remain would be impractical. Moreover, they did not have the power to simply prevent Apaches from leaving. In December 1871, Agent Piper noted that since the Indians had learned of the decision to remove them to the Tularosa Valley, many had left and "gone to the mountains." Finally, in late March 1872, the agent explained to his superiors that Victorio and Loco had agreed to go to Tularosa if some of their people currently at the Mescalero reservation could be returned to them. Piper scheduled the removal for April 15, writing that "I am anxious to get to Tularosa as soon as possible, so that we may be able to do a little farming and gardening."[76]

The coerced migration of Apaches from Warm Springs to Tularosa in the spring of 1872 was the first collective Southern Apache experience of removal at the hands of U.S. Americans, but it would not be the last. After continued delays, approximately 350 Natives finally left their home at Warm Springs for the new Tularosa reservation on May 17. This number represented a mere fraction of the population at the Warm Springs agency during the previous year. An escort of sixteen U.S. Cavalry watched over a caravan of twenty wagons that commenced the approximately one-hundred-mile trek to Tularosa. Fifty or sixty elderly or sick Apaches rode in the wagons, while the rest walked across the mountains or traveled on horseback. Ascending the San Mateo and Black Mountains to elevations of nearly nine thousand feet, they finally descended into the Tularosa Valley, where they found Chiva, a Western Apache ally, waiting for them. By the first of June, there were about four hundred Indians on the reservation, and Piper reported that they were "well satisfied" with their new home. If he was telling the truth, that pleasure did not last.[77]

The forced migration from Warm Springs to Tularosa foreshadowed those of years to come. It also illustrates a key consequence of U.S. decisions to create, dissolve, or move reservations. United States reservations and their management often served more to displace Apaches or initiate new forms of mobility than to confine them in place. In this respect, the reservations echoed Spanish and Mexican efforts to control Apache mobility in the past. Empires and nations could sometimes muster the power to move Apaches collectively, but it was another matter to get them to stay around their intended destinations; for example, while 350 Southern Apaches had made the journey to Tularosa, another 250 had gone to stay in Mescalero Apache lands, while still other families had fled into the mountains or into Mexico. Although Piper noted that "they were very reluctant to sever the ties that bound them to their previous home," it would perhaps have been more accurate to state that they were very reluctant to tie themselves to a place they viewed as unhealthy and undesirable. Soldiers swarmed the mountains to locate refugees and bring them in. For his part, the Chokonen leader Cochise decided against going to Tularosa, eventually heading to his favorite camping spot in the Dragoon Mountains of what is now southeastern Arizona instead, where Americans would look for him in the coming months.[78]

Southern Apache testimony regarding Tularosa was consistent. After a new agent, John Ayers, replaced Piper at the end of October 1872, Ayers noted that the Apaches "hate this place." They pleaded with him and said they would do anything he asked, "if we only move!" Their concerns went beyond the weather or distance from home, as Apache testimony before removal had indicated. As Ayers noted, "They have a superstition that the water kills their children, and that the whole place is haunted by evil spirits." Though Ayers derogatorily termed Apache concerns to be "superstitions," in fact Apaches shared certain ideas with white Americans of the period about the links between health, climate, and landscape. In the case of the Tularosa

Valley, Apaches noted that there was evidence that a past civilization that had lived there had passed away, as still evident by visible ruins and artifacts. The spirits of the dead haunted the land, contaminating it and the waters that ran through it. Their presence was indicated by the ubiquity of owls, the animals that Apaches associated with haunting and sickness. Victorio expressed his understanding that the "world there is getting old," as evidenced by its lack of fruit and other resources and by the thick flies that covered everything during the summer.[79]

Despite universal disdain for Tularosa among Apaches, the two years they spent there also indicate how Natives made the most of difficult circumstances and navigated the idiosyncrasies and cruelties of U.S. Indian policy. Apaches taught U.S. agents two lessons they had also taught their Hispanic predecessors: generous rations were necessary to gather a significant population of Apaches at a particular post, and keeping Apaches from moving from one assigned post to another was a tall order. More often than brute force, Agent Ayers drew upon rations of food and other provisions to get Natives to come to a place they did not want to be and stay there, just as Hispanic predecessors had learned to do decades before. In December 1872, the agent commented that Apaches continuously came to him showing their children and crying, "Tatta Tatta manta camisa" (Father father, blanket, shirt). Ayers noted that more than a decade of war had left Southern Apaches destitute and he needed blankets and calico cloth to be generous to them "until they get confidence in us." When he was able to increase rations and finally received supplies of manta and calico, the population on the reservation gradually increased. Yet the increased population was not of Natives actually assigned to the reservation. As Ayers wrote to Pope, "Most of the new Indians arriving are from the White Mountains and belong to Chiva's band"—in other words, they were Western Apaches. By the end of 1872, there were nearly as many Western Apaches on the reservation as Chihenes, in addition to about fifty Nednis and eighty Bedonkohes.[80]

The situation at Tularosa worsened as a new agent, who was arrogant and incompetent, took over in January 1873. Trained as a dentist, Benjamin Thomas arrived with high hopes in his ability to take control of his Apache charges. In his first (and last) annual report from Tularosa in September, Thomas echoed the views of many Arizona and New Mexico settlers, who talked of Indians being the favored "pets" of the government and reservations as their "winter resorts." Yet Thomas was correct in noting that Apache mobility had continued in spite of U.S. reservation policy, and he assured his superiors that he was making progress in turning the situation around.[81]

The fact that Apaches had faced a coerced migration to Tularosa and some had remained there reflected the growing power of the United States in the Southwest, but life at Tularosa indicated that U.S. control over Southern Apaches remained qualified. Whatever Thomas' ambitions, his reports paint a picture of a reservation completely out of his control and his own efforts as ineffectual, even laughable. Thomas described young Apache men using his interpreter for arrow target practice. He lamented the influence of liquor on the reservation, noting that Apaches explained that they made tiswin from their corn rations and drank it to forget their circumstances. Thomas was not the first nor last agent to suggest that Apaches be given flour instead. Yet the influence of liquor—and the limits of Thomas power—were not restricted to Apaches. In June 1873, drunk soldiers fired on Apaches indiscriminately, killing one woman and leading Apaches to berate the agent for his incompetence and demand retribution. Thomas feared for his own life, noting that Apaches "act ugly and talk ugly about the killing."[82] During July 1873, Thomas sought to arrest one Apache man named Sancho for leaving the reservation and rustling horses. When he could not capture him, he took three other young men prisoner instead and put them in irons, but rather than leading to Sancho being turned into him, as he hoped, this act resulted in many Apaches leaving the reservation. By the end of the month, he was issuing rations to fewer than two hundred Natives. In the end, to ensure that the reservation was not completely abandoned, Thomas was forced to back down and simply release his prisoners.[83]

Other colonial meddling was also frustrated by Apaches. Like his Spanish predecessors seventy years earlier, Thomas hoped to establish a school that would be attended by Native children. With his wife as teacher, he envisioned that the school could be a success, at least "by the standard of wild Indian schools." But within months he admitted that despite the funds expended to build the schoolhouse, it had proven to be a complete failure and no children attended. "There are not any worse Indians in the whole country to bring under the influence of the policy of the Government for civilizing and Christianizing them," he wrote to a superior.[84]

The winter of 1873–1874 proved worse than the last and helped to bring the Tularosa experiment to an end. The thermometer reached ten below zero, at least five Apaches died of starvation, and horses froze to death. Thomas reported that "they want to leave the place, say they will never plant here, want pay for horses that have died." After two years in exile, the government finally decided to allow Chihenes to return to where they had always said they wanted to be: to a formal reservation around Warm Springs. The cost of this misadventure—from the forced removal of Apaches, the lives and property lost, the school buildings built but never used—was many times the $11,000 bureaucrats had claimed to be concerned about paying to purchase Mexican Americans' property at Cañada Alamosa, which had helped lead to their choice of Tularosa in the first place.[85]

Even before Chihenes were finally allowed to return to Warm Springs, some had found safe haven elsewhere. In the same year that several hundred Southern Apaches had faced coerced migration to Tularosa—or chosen to join Mescaleros or seek refuge in the mountains instead—another reservation had been created for Southern Apaches in Arizona. This reservation emerged out of Colyer's failure to contact Cochise, the Chokonen leader who despite his advanced age commanded formidable respect and concern among U.S. Americans. The Grant administration selected General Oliver Howard as a new special agent to observe the reservations previously created and settle ongoing questions about Apache reserves. A West Point-educated veteran of the Civil War, he shared many ideas with Colyer, including an interest in humanitarian activism on behalf of Natives and African Americans. He had served as commissioner of the Freedman's Bureau, the agency created to oversee the nearly four million liberated slaves, and was known as a scrupulous and deeply religious man. Like Colyer, Howard was well meaning and capable in many respects, but also initially ill-informed. For example, he confessed after his delegation had spent some time in the Southwest that "in dealing with matters in Arizona, we have been under error in regarding the Apaches as one people." He only now realized that some of the groups whom white Americans termed "Apaches" spoke "substantially different languages and live hundreds of miles apart." One would hope that the man put in charge of creating Apache reservations would have at least known this much at the outset.[86]

Powerful bureaucrats with limited knowledge of Apache affairs making critical decisions about the latter's future would remain an issue in the years to come, but at least initially, it seemed like Howard might correct Colyer's wrongs and provide a means for Chihenes to return to Warm Springs. Before focusing on contacting Cochise, Howard had traveled first to Tularosa. He stayed there eight days and the Indians had shared with him through an interpreter the same complaints they shared repeatedly over time with their other agents: the cold climate and early frosts, the "past races [that] had been consumed by floods and other causes," which helped to explain to them the "sickness and death amongst the children."[87]

That such a return did not occur for another two years reflected Howard's focus on finding and making peace with Cochise above all else and on Cochise's power to influence decision-making about reservation policy. Americans were sure that if they could get Cochise to agree to a reservation, it would be at Warm Springs; after all, he had been amenable to such a reservation the year before. Before any such talk could begin, however, the U.S. expedition had to find Cochise. They set out from Warm Springs with two Chihene Apache guides, named Ponce and Chie, and Tom Jeffords, a trader who had built trust with Apaches and was well regarded by them. After traveling through Silver City, fending off citizen mobs that wanted to kill Ponce and Chie, they ultimately tracked Cochise to one of his favorite camping sites. Led by their Apache guides, they had scrambled up the bed of a narrow stream through a pass into a valley deep in the Dragoon Mountains.[88]

The valley was about forty or fifty acres in extent and naturally fortified. On each side, cliffs descended three or four hundred feet to the rocks below. A spring provided fresh water, its stream meandering through the center, surrounded by scattered oaks that provided shade from the alpine sun. The expedition had arrived at dusk, and after camping for the night and greeting some of Cochise's people, they anxiously awaited the arrival of Cochise himself. After eating breakfast, they heard a commotion, and a mounted party approached. As Captain Sladen wrote in his journal, "It consisted of a fine looking Indian, who rode up with great dignity followed by a young man and two Indian women. The man was Cochise."[89]

After pleasantries, talks turned to serious matters. Cochise proved willing to settle on a reservation, but not in New Mexico. "Give me Apache Pass," he said through his interpreter, "and I will protect the road to Tucson. I will see that the Indians do no harm." For Jeffords and others equally knowledgeable of Apache affairs this may not have been a surprise, since the Dragoon and Chiricahua Mountains surrounding Apache Pass were the heart of the Cochise's Chokonen homeland. But Howard was surprised and tried to persuade him in favor of Warm Springs. Cochise at least offered to consult with his people but said that he would need time and a truce to do so. Reflecting the military and settler pressure Apaches were under at this time, he noted that his people had separated into small bands—they were essentially refugees in the mountains—"because the soldiers are hunting us all the time and food is scarce." He demanded that Howard himself go and give an order that the troops cease hostilities so that Cochise could send runners to disparate places to tell Apache families to come in so a treaty could be completed.[90]

When Howard returned, negotiations continued on the question of location. The U.S. preference for getting Cochise to agree to a reservation at Warm Springs was twofold. First, to remove them from the area where they had raided for many years. And second, to appease the Chihenes at Tularosa, who had been begging for a reservation at Warm Springs for years. After conferring with advisors and leaders of other local groups, Cochise's view that only Apache Pass would do only hardened. Sladen summarized the discussion when he wrote that "they had a warm attachment to the land they had always lived in, and no persuasion would make them consent to leave that section." It is striking that such rhetoric paralleled the arguments Cochise had made the year before in arguing alongside Loco and Victorio for a reservation around Warm Springs: Cochise had repeatedly stated his hope was to "live and die" at Warm Springs and "not be removed to another reservation." As he explained it, "I like the country and wish to spend the remainder of my life here at peace with all men."[91]

Why had Cochise changed his mind? Three facts help to explain the shift in his point of view. First, the Apache emphasis in diplomacy on having a warm attachment to the "land of their fathers" was not only sincere but also strategic. To convince Americans to grant them a reservation, they found it useful to stress that they would go "nowhere else" even if there were, in fact, sites within their traditional territories to where they might consider going. Second, it had always been Loco and, to a lesser extent, Victorio (both of whom were Chihenes) who had been leading the push for a Warm Springs reservation. That area was in their traditional lands, not in those of Cochise's band. Third, given the present situation within the United States with settlers, soldiers, and untrustworthy bureaucrats, the possibility of obtaining more secure access to Mexico and its resources was a strong factor. When it is also considered that the Chiricahua and Dragoon Mountains were Cochise's favored settlement sites, his push for a reservation there makes sense, even if it had negative consequences for his Chihene compatriots who had been hoping for a return to Warm Springs that Cochise could have helped orchestrate.[92]

While Cochise eventually decided to negotiate a reservation specifically for Chokonens—the Chiricahua reservation—rather than push for Warm Springs, he did not do so without pointing out the injustice of what was being asked of him. "Why shut me up on a reservation?" Howard remembered him saying. "We will make peace. We will keep it faithfully," he said through his interpreter. "But let us go around free as Americans do. Let us go wherever we please." Even as Cochise was amenable to having his people's land recognized, he made clear the colonial distinction that Americans were drawing: Americans could have land and move through the land of others as they pleased. Apaches could have land, but they were supposed to stay on it and only it. Cochise—or his interpreter's—favorite analogy was that of a corral.

In a variation of a talk he had with Americans on multiple occasions, Cochise explained that Apaches did not want to be shut up in a corral but rather desired to run around like coyotes. Howard responded that "all this country did not properly belong to the Indians; that all God's children had an interest in it, and therefore to keep the peace we must [create boundaries]."[93]

Cochise's concerns illustrate a key difference between past Apache diplomacy with Hispanic officials and their interactions in this period with those of the United States. Neither Spain nor Mexico had sought so intently to confine Apaches in "corrals" as a necessary component of a peace agreement. Yet while Cochise voiced his concerns with U.S. policies, he also selected as a reservation a location that minimized the degree to which it was actually confining. The borders of the reservation encompassed the southeastern swath of Arizona, including the Chiricahua and Dragoon ranges and the valleys between. Most important, the fifty-five-mile southern boundary of the reservation was formed by the U.S.-Mexico border, which in this era had no walls, fences, or patrols. While Cochise promised to stay at peace with Americans and protect the road to Tucson, he also recognized that the corral he had agreed to had only three sides, and even those were porous.[94]

If Chihenes were dissatisfied with Cochise's decision to ask for the Chiricahua reservation—which helped lead some of them to remain at Tularosa for another two years—their discontent does not emerge clearly from the documentary or oral history record. This may be in part because for a time, they held out hope that Howard would fulfill his promise to allow them to return to their Warm Springs reservation. As the months passed and the situation at Tularosa deteriorated, however, the Chiricahua reserve beckoned as a place in a growing network of Apache places that Anglo-Americans defined as "reservations" with the intent to dispossess and control but that Apaches drew upon as they saw fit.[95]

The treaty with Cochise was formalized with fanfare and celebration in October 1872. The agency—which typically housed the Indian agent and from which supplies and rations were dispensed—was set up in a tiny ten-by-twelve-foot shack belonging to a local trader. This was the physical manifestation of American governmental presence within a roughly five-thousand-square-mile reservation. In another diplomatic feat for Cochise and his advisers, the Indian agent assigned to oversee them was Tom Jeffords, the licensed trader at Warm Springs who had helped to orchestrate the negotiations with Cochise in the first place based on his longtime relations and position of respect among Apache people. Those close relations also made him suspect among some Americans, leading them to question his loyalty and honesty.[96]

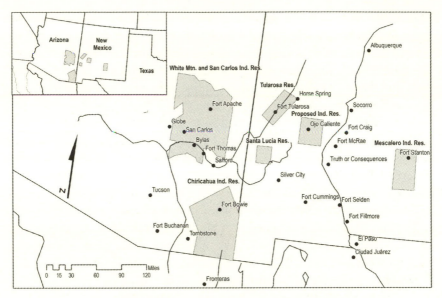

Map 4. Apache Reservation sites in the 1870s.

The creation of such Apache reservations fostered new patterns of mobility, as had been true in the past during peace-for-rations arrangements at the Spanish and Mexican presidios. Historically, Apaches had often traveled widely to visit allies, trade, raid livestock, hunt, gather, and farm, yet the burgeoning U.S. presence had altered the possibilities for travel due to the dangers of soldiers and settler attacks and now channeled movement within and between reservations instead. The Chiricahua reservation added a new southern peg to a network of reservations that Southern Apaches and some Western Apache allies navigated and drew upon for subsistence. The formalization of a peace treaty between Chihene Apaches and Navajos at Fort Wingate in late 1872 helped make the Navajo reservation a site to which Apaches might travel, trade, or seek refuge as well.[97] The eastern peg in the network was the Mescalero reserve around Fort Stanton, New Mexico, which had been negotiated in 1871 and formalized two years later, in May 1873. The north peg was the Navajo nation (1868) and Fort Wingate, New Mexico; in the center were San Carlos (1871) and Tularosa (1872). Even Tularosa, the most despised of the bunch, could gather residents in times when rations were more bountiful or as a zone of refuge while Indians were traveling elsewhere.[98]

While intended for Cochise and the Chokonens, the Chiricahua reservation also temporarily housed other Apaches almost from its beginning. In

September 1873, for example, Jeffords reported to his superior that three to four hundred residents of the reservation technically "belonged" on other reservations. Many of these were refugees from Tularosa, who found Jeffords to be a better agent then their own, supplies to be more plentiful, the weather better, and access to Mexico for raiding or trading to be easy. Families of Chihenes from Tularosa traveled to the new Arizona reservation in such numbers that Jeffords reported in June 1874 his fear that "in a short time we will be overrun with Indians from the north." There were also Nedni and Bedonkohe Apaches, for whom no specific reservation had ever been created, in part because Americans like Howard did not fully understand the divisions and distinctions among Apache bands. Gordo, a Bedonkohe, had complained to U.S. officials of multiple removals—first to Warm Springs and then to Tularosa.[99]

While the new reservation had its own draws, including Jeffords as agent, its immediate proximity to Mexico was a particular pull. Arizona soon saw benefits from peace with Cochise, who lived up to his promise to keep the road safe to Tucson and not raid in Arizona. Yet the reservation employee Frederick Hughes reported that "wails were continually coming up from our Mexican neighbors." The easy travel between Apache reservations and Mexico that the Chiricahua reserve facilitated provided access for Southern Apaches to travel into Mexico to raid, trade, visit old acquaintances, and return to their U.S. reservations with livestock and other goods. Cochise himself had stated during negotiations that he could not prevent his men from traveling into Mexico, which proved true as the months went on. For some Americans, this suggested that the reservation never should have been allowed in the first place and that Agent Jeffords was completely incapable of keeping Apaches under control.[100]

A November 1875 surprise inspection of the reservation was particularly illuminating. At this time, Inspector Edward Kemble provided a vivid description of the status of life on the Chiricahua reservation while opining on all that he thought was wrong with it. His description could easily have been written by a Spanish military officer talking about a previous generation of Apaches de paz. "Upon any pretext of dissatisfaction at their own reservation Apaches leave with or without permission of agent and go to Chiricahua where they are received and rationed," he wrote. It was not just Apache mobility, which ran completely contrary to bureaucratic regulations that said they could not move without permission, that was concerning to the inspector, however. He found the Indians to be "well mounted and well-armed and carry their arms with them at all times and move about their reservation and off it pretty much at will. The agent says they live mostly in camps situated from ½ to 15 miles from the agency." He concluded that "the reservation on which they are living is totally unsuited to their actual needs," recommending their removal north to the Apache reservation at San Carlos.[101]

Jeffords did not deny the inspector's claims but did ask what he was supposed to do with Apaches from elsewhere who kept showing up asking for rations. Indeed, the frequency with which that happened is likely why a formal administrative order had been promulgated in 1872 stating that no Apache assigned to one reservation should be received at another.[102] Jeffords clearly believed this was impractical, particularly when the Indians who came were sometimes destitute and starving because they were fleeing poor conditions on their own reservations. Yet such Apache travel continued even after Tularosa was finally disbanded and Chihenes allowed to return to Warm Springs in 1874. In one of Jeffords's last reports as agent, for example, he noted the coming and going of what he termed "strange" Indians month after month. In September 1875, he rationed 197 Western Apaches who were on the reservation. The next month, over two hundred Indians from other agencies passed through. For allowing such mobility Jeffords had been reprimanded by the inspector, who advised him that "Indians from other reservations should be restrained or returned and not harbored and protected." Yet in practice Jeffords had little power to do so. Not only did he lack the manpower to forcibly restrain or remove hundreds of armed Indians, but to refuse to ration them would have probably risked his own life.[103]

Prior to his death in June 1874, even Cochise had become concerned about the various bands of Apaches traveling to and through his reservation. The frequent presence of Apaches from Warm Springs and their raids into Mexico led him to ask in October 1873 that Jeffords remove all the Chihenes from the reserve. He was concerned about his Chokonens being blamed for their actions. Geronimo, a Bedonkohe, would later note that he and his kin had not been able to get along with Cochise's people and had left to live with Victorio at Warm Springs instead. Disputes between and within Apache bands living on the reservation were not uncommon. In December 1875, for example, Western Apaches killed a Chokonen named Coha on the reservation and were nearly all driven out as a result. These disputes sometimes entangled Jeffords, who faced death threats when he tried to mediate a conflict between family groups in May 1876.[104]

While this reservation was generally a far healthier place than Tularosa or San Carlos, health concerns also challenged Jeffords's management. When smallpox threatened the reservation in February 1876, for example, he managed to get a few Apaches vaccinated. He reported that most, however, had scattered around the reservation in small groups and were unwilling to come in.[105]

Jeffords's limited power to manage reservation affairs was ultimately based more on negotiation than on coercion. Like some of his Spanish imperial predecessors, he recognized that maintaining peace required generosity to generate goodwill and reciprocity, and it meant not meddling excessively in Apache politics. As much as Jeffords faced criticism for it, he learned that peace also meant not seeking to restrain Apache mobility to any great extent, as long as it did not involve significant damage to U.S. settlers' lives or property.

*   *   *

Years of diplomacy and a significant investment of funds had led to the creation of a chain of Apache reservations that by the mid-1870s had brought relative peace to Apache and U.S. communities. The fundamentally discriminatory nature of this system is undeniable. The essence of U.S. approaches to Apache and other Indigenous peoples was their treatment as "wards," childlike dependents of the U.S. government who could be told where and how they must live, in comparison to white citizens, who could move freely. Reservations fragmented the territories and subsistence strategies of groups that were reliant on mobility through different climates and ecosystems to maintain the health and well-being of their people. Yet in practice, Apaches proved able to shape the system to fit their interests better than we might think—by pressing for the right to choose reservations sites, by challenging agents to improve provisions, by leaving one reservation for another, and by continuing to travel into Mexico to raid and trade.[106]

This development paralleled in many respects the arrangements Apaches and Spanish officials had negotiated nearly a century earlier that had endured until the 1830s and remained influential as a framework for peace for years to come. United States officials sometimes wittingly modeled their ideas off their imperial predecessors'. Such was the case when James Carleton envisioned turning his failed reservation of Navajos and Apaches at Bosque Redondo into "what is called in this country a pueblo" with a Spanish-style central plaza. Yet more often than not, Americans believed they were trying something innovative, even as they were in fact echoing their Spanish and Mexican forerunners.[107]

Equally important, if not more significant, in explaining the parallels between Hispanic and U.S. American approaches to peace and reservations are Apaches themselves. After all, it was generations of Apache leaders who represented a constant as Hispanic or U.S. imperial officials came and went. Across the decades, through diplomacy, mobility, and martial strategies of their own, Apaches navigated policies of empires and nations intended to confine or eliminate them. There were ebbs and flows in Apache power and moments of existential crisis. Yet more than three hundred years after the first European expeditions had set foot in Southern Apache lands, Apaches continued to raise their families in many of the same places and to govern their own communities, even as displaced Apaches and their descendants lived out their lives scattered across North America and the Caribbean.

CHAPTER 7

The Displacement of Confinement

As an old man, Sam Kenoi still recalled the rock piles that marked the borders of the Arizona reservation where he had spent his earliest childhood years. He had not understood their significance at the time, but he reasoned that his parents and other "old people" had known why the markers were there. He heard stories about how the army had herded them inside, "naked, starving, [and] sad," but the earliest experiences he remembered firsthand were of a better time, after they had petitioned successfully to move within the reservation from the mosquito-infested lowlands along the Gila River to forested higher country. While they still felt like the reservation belonged to Western Apaches—"it was their land"—they made it home as best they could, planting, tending cattle, and "attending to business."[1]

If Kenoi stressed adaptation, he also noted the problems of reservation life. There were the intertribal tensions, reflected in thefts, fights, and rumor mongering. Worse still were the people who, in his view, lived like "wild animal[s]" rather than settling down like the rest. He explained that sometimes they would leave the reservation and force others to go with them at gun point. For those who remained behind, a sense of foreboding built with the passing days. "Someone would say 'Geronimo is out again,'" Kenoi recalled, and "pretty soon he would raid a settlement here, or kill a person, and the whole tribe would be blamed for it." The fact that Apache scouts from the reservation helped track down those who left caused further trouble, leading "Apache to fight Apache and all sorts of trouble to break out among our people."[2]

Sam Kenoi's recollections introduce a turning point in Southern Apache history in the years after settler pressures and new bureaucratic initiatives led U.S. officials to disband the Chiricahua and Warm Springs reservations in 1876 and 1877. The idea of reservations, as we have seen, had been long in the making. Initially, Apaches had proved able to shape reservations to their own aims, creating a network of relatively secure Apache places amid expanding U.S. settlements with easy access to Mexico. Kenoi's remarks evoke a world in which the idea of confinement at the core of U.S.-run reservations came to matter for Apache people in new ways. Efforts to congregate all Apaches on an Arizona reservation at San Carlos served to separate Southern Apaches further from familiar landscapes and make journeying across reservation borders more difficult and dangerous. White settlers increasingly served as a border patrol of sorts, complaining to reservation agents and petitioning their political representatives whenever an Apache was found off-reservation, even if it was just to gather wild fruits to supplement their meager rations. While not always physically marked, reservation borders served as the dividing line for an Apache man or woman between being viewed as a "ward" of the United States—a childlike Indian to be cared for and provisioned, however inadequately—or a "hostile" to be killed or captured. This is probably why Kenoi's parents knew the significance of the rock piles, even if he had not.[3]

At the same time, the international border between Mexico and the United States was of less significance for Apaches during these years as a symbol of safety or opportunity. It had once served as a conditional line across which Apaches could flee for refuge or to acquire needed resources, but across which U.S. or Mexican troops generally did not follow. In the late 1870s and early 1880s, both Mexico and the United States intensified their campaigns to eliminate independent or refugee Apaches from their territories, including signing a diplomatic agreement in 1882 that allowed cross-border pursuit. While Southern Apache flights from U.S. reservations into Mexico continued, they proved increasingly counterproductive, scattering men, women, and children between U.S. reservations in Arizona and jails, households, or mountain hideouts on both sides of the international border.[4]

Between 1876 and 1886, diaspora itself proved a principal driver of Apache mobility. Apaches fled across the borders of their reservation in response to rumors of new forced migrations or in search of kin lost in Mexico during prior forced removals, flights, and military pursuits. Unfortunately, their efforts were usually unsuccessful, leading to further casualties at the hands of Mexican or American troops and the loss of more kin to captivity. In the end, the inability of either nation-state to fully contain Apache mobility helped spark another misguided imperial solution: exiling Southern Apaches to distant, unfamiliar lands where it was hoped they could finally be brought under control.[5]

The Fall of the Reservation Network

In the peace diplomacy of the late 1860s and early 1870s, Apaches understood that reservations set aside were to be permanent. Interpreters, who were as much diplomats as translators, emphasized as much by explaining that a particular site was where they had always wanted to live or by referring to the fact that they had been promised they could stay there forever. In the broader context of U.S.-Indian relations, false promises and broken treaties are not surprising. A basic tenant of U.S. Indian policy has been the U.S. assertation that only it has the power to change its mind.[6]

The Southern Apache experience exemplifies this larger context even as it also demonstrates unique circumstances of place and time. As in other border regions, Apache mobility and proximity to Mexico brought international relations into play. Settler interest in prospecting and mineral wealth, particularly in Arizona, influenced relations with Indians and risked the longevity of any one reservation's borders. Moreover, the U.S. decision to stop negotiating formal treaties after 1871 and instead create reservations through presidential executive actions made it easier not only to formally set aside Indian reservations but also to change or dissolve them. Settler-citizens soon learned of this change. Realizing that shifts in reservation borders did not require even the semblance of negotiation with the Native people impacted or an act of Congress, they lobbied and petitioned accordingly.[7]

Southern Apaches had suffered through U.S. efforts to force them to Tularosa and then finally witnessed the creation of the Warm Springs and Chiricahua reservations instead. Beginning in 1876, they faced a new U.S. imperial initiative. With pressure from Mexico to manage "American" Indian incursions across the international border, and pressure from settlers to change reservation boundaries or dissolve them entirely, the United States began a policy of concentrating the majority of Apache groups on the White Mountain Apache reservation and its adjacent San Carlos division. John Clum, appointed by President Grant in 1874, served as the civilian agent to enact this policy with the aid of Commander George Crook. The forced removals to San Carlos began first with the dissolution of the Rio Verde reservation and its inhabitants' forced removal, which included Yuman-speaking groups that Arizona settlers called Apaches Mojaves, although they shared little in common with the Athapaskan-speaking Apaches other than whites' vague sense of cultural similarity. Other Natives were forcibly removed within the reservation itself. In June 1875, Coyoteros (White Mountain Western Apaches) were forcibly marched from the higher country around Fort Apache to the low-lands along the Gila. Supposed bureaucratic efficiencies—it would be easier to administer Apaches at fewer agency sites—led to human suffering and masked other motives, especially settler pressures to reduce reservation size and open up more lands to prospecting and ranching. One army officer had captured the imperial logic of the broader U.S. reservation policy concisely in a letter to a U.S. senator in 1865 when he stated that Indians needed to be "exterminated or placed on reservations." Only then could "the country now inhabited by many bands of [Indians] be left open to the enterprise and skill of the miner."[8]

The idea of concentrating Southern Apaches at San Carlos soon gained purchase. The groundwork to dissolve the Chiricahua reservation was by this point already in place: complaints of lax discipline, Indians present on the reserve who did not officially belong to it, and raids into Mexico. In fact, Cochise and the vast majority of Chokonens had kept their promises to keep peace in Arizona, but they had never promised not to travel into Mexico to raid. Bureaucratic concerns and initiatives, international complaints, and settler interests made the future of the Chiricahua reservation increasingly uncertain.[9]

An isolated event on April 7, 1876, provided the immediate rationale for Americans to close the Chiricahua reservation. Two Apache men from Skin-ya's local group, Pionsenay and Gordo (Nay-zar-zee) got drunk on whiskey they had purchased from Americans at the Sulphur Springs Station, a rail stop in the valley of the same name that ran through the heart of the reservation. When the Americans refused to sell them more, they killed them in a drunken brawl and rounded up seven or eight compatriots to flee the reservation and steal stock from two ranches in Arizona along the San Pedro River. They then crossed into Mexico. United States officials might have reacted by asking for Apache leaders' assistance in recovering the stock and apprehending Pionsenay and Gordo. The Americans would eventually apprehend Pionsenay and deliver him to state officials to be tried. However, as was typical of the era, this act also provided justification to punish all residents of the reservation and dissolve it. Within weeks, the commissioner of Indian Affairs had ordered John Clum to proceed to the Chiricahua reservation, where he was to "assume charge of the Chiricahua agency, and remove the Indians to San Carlos."[10]

Clum took the job seriously: he brought with him a regiment of cavalry and ten companies of Indian scouts, and more than five hundred Native volunteers. This force outnumbered the entire Southern Apache popu-lation on the reservation and was clearly intended to dissuade them from any resistance. Faced with these overwhelming numbers, Cochise's son Taza agreed to remove to San Carlos almost immediately. His father had died two summers earlier and had reportedly asked him to promise to keep the peace with Americans, a promise he kept by agreeing to the removal. In the coming days, more Apaches came in, including Pionsenay, badly wounded, with one old man, a boy, and thirty-eight women and children.[11]

Concentration was merely the latest method in the U.S. American pursuit of control over Apache lands and people. As had been the case in the Chihenes' coerced migration from Warm Springs to Tularosa in 1872, Clum succeeded more in a coerced displacement than in a forced removal. Three influential Southern Apache men of the time—Juh (Nedni), Geronimo (Bedonkohe), and Nolgee (Nedni)—had come into meet with Agents Jeffords and Clum but had said they needed twelve days to gather their families. Clum gave them four. After that deadline had passed, he sent scouts to their camps who reported seeing "camp kettles axes, dead horses and dogs, [and] corn . . . strewn about the camp." Commenting specifically on the killing of the dogs, the scouts surmised that the inhabitants of the camp had probably been concerned about being betrayed by barking dogs during the flight into Mexico.[12]

Just as Chihenes had fled the forced removal to Tularosa, many residents of the Chiricahua reservation left or hid rather than go to San Carlos. By one estimate, Clum succeeded in removing less than half of the reservation's population. By July 1876, about 135 Apaches, including Gordo, had reported to the Warm Springs reservation in New Mexico instead. A number of groups, including those of Ju and Geronimo, had fled into Sonora or Chihuahua. About forty, including the families of Nolgee, Piosenay, and Kissnahey, decided to stay put and remain in hiding in the mountains on the former Chiricahua reservation itself.[13]

In the meantime, Clum set off from the Chiricahua reservation to San Carlos with his Indian police force and a little over three hundred Apaches in tow. Among them as a prisoner was Pionsenay, one of the men involved in the drunken episode that had sparked the closure of the reservation. Unfortunately for Clum, Pionsenay escaped after he was turned into Arizona authorities for trial. But neither this incident nor the relatively small number of Apaches he had succeeded in corralling prevented Clum from declaring the removal "a grand success" or announcing that "the terrible shade of Chiricahuas had passed away forever." Arriving at San Carlos on June 18, he would later tell stories to his son about teaching the "entire band" of Chiricahuas "how to make and lay adobes, and [how] they developed into good Apache citizens." In reality, this group represented only a fraction of the larger

Southern Apache population, since it consisted solely of Cochise's sons Taza
and Naiche and related local groups numbering 42 men and 280 women and
children. These Chokonen Apaches would be the first Southern Apaches to
experience life at San Carlos, but they would not be the last, and contrary to
the happy scenes of Apaches laying adobes and beginning to farm that lingered in Clum's memory, circumstances were difficult and deteriorated from
the outset. The Chokonens complained of fights with the Western Apaches
who had helped escort them there in the first place. They complained of life
in the malarial bottomlands of the Gila and San Carlos River valleys, and they
worried about American treachery.[14]

Developments immediately following the return of the Chiricahua reservation to the public domain by executive action illustrate the settler pressures
that threatened all Apache reservation borders during this period. Within
five years, the boomtown of Tombstone, Arizona, had sprouted just outside
the borders of the old reservation and had a population of ten thousand.
Mining activity and the rush of settlers crisscrossed the old reservation as
well, as illustrated by an 1881 map of the area. The Turquoise District, com-
prising the Dragoon Mountains, which included Cochise's favorite camping
spot, was now blanketed with mining claims, as was the California District in
the Chiricahua Mountains. While informational, the "map" also reflects the
boosterism of the era, showing the steaming smokestacks of smelters and the
impressive masonry of the Tombstone stock exchange building.

Almost entirely absent from the map and imagery are the Southern
Apaches upon whose homelands this infrastructure stood and from which
mineral wealth was being extracted. Some of them were even still living in
the mountains in question, although settler and U.S. military actions had
displaced most elsewhere. Yet hints of their dispossession remained: in
directional symbols stylized as feather arrows and in the "Tombstone" logo,
crafted with stereotypical "Indian" geometric iconography. Most explicitly,
the dispossession was memorialized in the creation that year of a new county:
Cochise. Less than five years after the forced removal of Cochise's sons and
their people from the landscape, a mining boomtown now served as the seat
of a newly minted county named for the late Apache leader.[15]

The closure of the Chiricahua reservation in June 1876 also set the stage
for the disbandment of the Warm Springs reservation less than a year later,
in May 1877. Chihene Apaches would long remember the pain with which
they felt the loss of this reservation in their homeland so soon after they had
finally managed to secure it. For some, the blame was clear: Geronimo, who
had gone between the Warm Springs reserve and Mexico after the Chiricahua

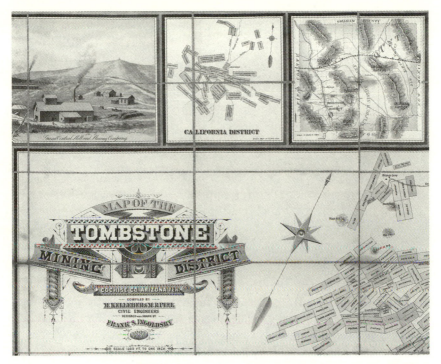

Figure 11. 1881 map of the Tombstone District.

reservation had closed. As Sam Haozous later remembered it, "A peaceful group of the Apaches, called Warm Springs Apaches, was accused of aiding Geronimo . . . and the first thing we know, without no trouble, all the cavalry horses surround us all in that reservation, in that camp. So they told us—they took us out there to Arizona."[16] Haozous stressed the suddenness of the decision to remove Apaches from Warm Springs, the lack of warning, and what he saw as the lack of any justification. He recounted the words he remembered an Apache leader speaking at this time, dramatizing the pain of facing another forced removal. "Why they trying to take us away from here," he remembered him asking, "I don't like to do that. I don't want to get away from there. They took me away from there before but this time, I just can't get away from here."[17]

Clum was again the agent to orchestrate this latest forced removal. If Pionsenay's drunken brawl had served as the immediate justification for the Chiricahua reservation's closure, it was, as Sam Haozous accurately recalled, Geronimo and his compatriots' presence with Mexican livestock that served to facilitate the removal of Chihene Apaches from Warm Springs. Clum traveled from San Carlos to Warm Springs in April 1877 with his Western Apache police force and U.S. Cavalry. Employing the subterfuge of a parley, he managed to surround the Warm Springs and other Southern Apaches present on the reservation, imprison and shackle Geronimo and sixteen other men accused of recent raids, and march the other 450 Apache men, women, and children on foot or in wagon on a nearly month-long journey to San Carlos, where they arrived on May 20, 1877. This was a journey that no one who lived through it forgot about, including Geronimo, who added what he viewed as his own unjust imprisonment to what he later called "the memory of all our past wrongs." But this would be neither the last wrong—nor the last forced removal—that he and other Southern Apaches suffered.[18]

Life Within the Borders of San Carlos

For the next decade, the San Carlos reservation became an important place for Southern Apaches. It encompassed Western Apache homelands, though a diversity of other groups ended up there through U.S. forced-migration practices. Although Southern Apaches had close relations with a few Western Apache groups, they did not consider this landscape to be home and found much of it to be unfamiliar other than at its eastern and southern edges. Like much of the Greater Southwest, the reservation encompassed a variety of climates and ecologies largely defined by elevation. The arid valley of the Gila River at two thousand feet transitioned through scrub, oak, and pinyon growth above four thousand feet to dense ponderosa pine forests beyond six thousand feet. The best lands were already inhabited by Western Apaches, and concerns about "wild" Southern Apaches led agents to assign them lands close to the agency site near the junction of the Gila and San Carlos Rivers.[19]

The conditions of life in the Gila and San Carlos bottomlands were bad. Reservation agents assigned tags to males capable of bearing arms that indicated the band to which they belonged and designated their number within each band. The numbers corresponded to the full name of the individual that was kept in agency records. To be tagged or branded like cattle probably lingered in Apaches' memories, like the warning they received about what it meant to be found without it. They were reminded that "anyone found outside the reservation or without his tag would be considered as hostile and treated accordingly."[20]

While no Apache believed that removal from their own reservations at Chiricahua and Warm Springs had been justified or was desirable, the

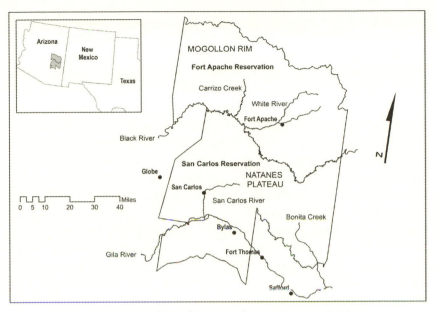

Map 5. San Carlos and Fort Apache reservation, c. 1880.

experience of being marched at gunpoint by U.S. Cavalry and Western Apache police forces down the Gila in the driest time of the year (late spring and early summer, before the monsoon) must have further disheartened them. One observer explained that only those who had made this journey—whether in wagon train, on horseback, or on foot—could appreciate "the heat and dust on the ride."[21]

Upon arrival, the Apache women constructed wickiup homes quickly to beat the summer rains. They used whatever materials they could gather: brush, saplings, discarded agency supplies. They excavated a floor a foot deep and bent boughs or saplings and stuck them into the ground to create a dome. The roof and walls were built from thatched brush, hay, and canvas to help shed the infrequent deluges of the Southwestern monsoon. The last step was to pack the loose dirt dug for the floor back around the base of the structure to solidify the foundation against the driving wind. Visitors who traveled through Southern Apache camps noted the meat, supplies, and spare clothes hanging from the wickiup walls. One described the children running around outside, running and jumping and causing a "clatter" before darting behind a wickiup, frightened at the sight of strangers. Another remembered the adult men and women as saying little but watching everything. "A feeling of restlessness, discontent, fear, and uncertainty for the future possessed the entire people," Lieutenant Britton Davis wrote, adding that "the attitude of all was that of watchful waiting, wondering what was going to turn up next."[22]

Southern Apaches traveled the ten miles to the agency site to converse with U.S. officials and to receive the provisions they relied upon for survival in the desolate and foreign site to which white Americans had decided to remove them. The agency overlooked the Gila River and comprised adobe buildings that formed a hollow square and included the quarters for reservation employees, a guardhouse, the telegraph office, a storehouse, and corrals. At a distance was a larger schoolhouse, which was used primarily for meetings, since reservation agents struggled to recruit any children to attend.[23]

On ration days, when Apaches gathered around the agency, they received one ticket for each person in their family, "no matter whether they be a gray-haired buck or a two-day-old baby." Women and children passed from window to window along the main supply building, receiving sugar, coffee, flour, soap, tobacco, and beef, which they carried in deer skins, in the corner of their waists and skirts, or anywhere they could find room. A later photograph by Katherine Taylor Dodge of the San Carlos agency on issue day gives a sense of the scene, showing Apaches lined up against the adobe wall of the building waiting to receive their rations. Corrupt agents and suppliers helped ensure that rations were skimpier and of a lower quality than those paid for by the government. Contractors quickly learned tricks to maximize their profits, such as having their livestock spend some time drinking Gila River water before they were weighed and slaughtered. As Davis noted, "The contractor was getting paid every week for about 1,500 pounds of beef that he did not deliver." In part because rations were meager, many families consumed them within four days and spent the remainder of the week living on "rabbits, rats, birds, and herbs . . . or went hungry."[24]

During the summer of 1877, immediately after Chihene Apaches were removed from Warm Springs, most Southern Apaches resided together on the same reservation. Census rolls collected in July provided a snapshot of Southern Apache families at this time. While neither of Clum's forced removals had been as "complete" as he believed, these records nonetheless indicate the severe toll that decades of intermittent war with Mexico and the United States, as well as repeated removals and life on inadequately provisioned U.S. reservations, had taken. Most striking is the severe gender imbalance evident among them. Among Chihenes, called Southern Apaches by the Indian agent, adult women outnumbered adult men 2.6 to 1. Though slightly less severe, the Chiricahua (Chokonen, Nedni, and Bedonkohe) gender imbalance was still notable, at 2.2 to 1. In all, Chihene residents of the reservation

Figure 12. Apaches at San Carlos on Issue Day, c. 1899.

numbered 76 men, 201 women, and 176 children, while so-called Chiricahuas numbered 57 men, 124 women, and 103 children.[25]

Despite the challenges of supplies, graft, corruption, and intertribal conflicts, the population of Chokonens and their associates had actually grown
since their arrival at San Carlos. Some who had fled forced removal had
decided to come in and try out life there rather than continuing to live as refugees pursued by citizens and soldiers in the mountains or in Mexico. By the
spring of 1878, they had decided to farm. An inspector who traveled by their
settlements along the Gila River vividly described men, women, and children
at work opening an irrigation ditch in April 1878: "Men women and children
were at work. Many of them with their hands, scraped the dirt into baskets
of their own construction. Others loosened it with sharp sticks while others
emptied the filled baskets on the banks of the ditch as they were handed to
them by their companions."[26]

Such work reflected Apaches' persistent drive to make a future for their
families, despite the fact they were doing so in a place they had not desired
to live and without sufficient tools or aid from the U.S. government that so
frequently stressed the need to turn them into farmers. One hundred or so
Chokonen Apache laborers had by this time dug a trench about eight feet

deep and ten feet wide that stretched for more than a mile. The inspector explained that their work would have cost $15,000 if the Indians had been paid, "three times that much for white labor." Already, they had planted forty acres of barley that was six to eight inches high, and families were preparing to plant corn and other vegetables as well.[27]

From the summer of 1876, when they first arrived at San Carlos, through the spring of 1878, Chokonen Apaches were clearly engaged in more than just "watchful waiting." Uprooted from their own homelands, they nonetheless demonstrated the intention to build a future for their community on the new reservation. In the coming months, however, another problem challenged them: malaria, which was endemic to the river bottomlands where the United States had decided to locate them. It first struck late in the spring of 1878, killing fifty or sixty Chokonens within weeks. Naiche's people suffered especially. His settlement was located near an old army post named Camp Goodwin, just south of the Gila River. This post had been closed in part because of malaria, and only a few years before Southern Apaches had been forcibly removed there the Arizona governor had described the place as a "fever hole."[28]

We now know that malaria is caused by a parasite transmitted through the bites of mosquitos. While this etiology was not understood in the late nineteenth century, the illness was nonetheless linked in white and Native minds with particular places, and it was well known by U.S. officials that the site of Southern Apache camps was prone to it. Apaches associated the lowlands near rivers with the illness, and after it broke out among them, they responded by requesting to move to higher country. Given officials' fears that malaria might cause them to leave the reservation entirely, they were given permission to move about fifteen miles southwest to Black Rock in the Santa Teresa Mountains. This temporary solution would be reversed in the future as reservation agents required Chokonens to move back to the lowlands, where they again suffered from malaria. At least for now, however, this reprieve led Naiche to decide to stay at San Carlos and maintain the peace with Americans that he and his brother Taza had promised their father.[29]

While health, provisions, and intertribal conflicts were most influential in Southern Apache life on the San Carlos reservation during this period, they also felt pressure from white settlers. In some cases, it involved citizen mobs threatening to take matters into their own hands and "exterminate" Apaches. Less violent but still influential land pressure also played a role in reservation life and policy. More than anything, such actions contributed to Natives' sense of instability—to Native fears that however undesirable they might find San Carlos, something worse might be just around the bend. By this time, the

United States already had a long history of changing reservation boundaries or dissolving them entirely.[30]

Almost as soon as San Carlos had been created, whites had begun arguing for it to be made smaller. A settler petition to the president in July 1877 from Globe, Arizona, for example, recommended that he issue an executive order cutting off the western five miles of the reservation. It was signed by seventy-six citizens and noted that this area of the reservation was "valuable only for its rich deposits of minerals." A U.S. Indian inspector confirmed that the west line of reservation "passes over a series of irregular mountain ranges that are supposed to be valuable mineral depositaries." He noted that it was impossible to prevent prospecting without fencing and supported cutting off that portion of the reservation. As he explained it, there was more than enough land elsewhere for Natives, and too much land had a negative effect on Indians because it encouraged them to "roam about." In fact, it was not too much land but rather the restricted borders of reservations like San Carlos that limited Apaches' potential to thrive.[31]

Naiche and his Chokonen band's emphasis on negotiating better circumstances at San Carlos contrasted with the approach of the majority of Chihenes. Only a few months after they had been forcibly removed from Warm Springs in May 1877 by Clum, the majority of them fled. They sought safe haven in Navajo country and tried ultimately to return to their Warm Springs reservation. Southern Apache "breakouts," as whites termed them, sometimes involved the killing of settlers and theft of their property. But in many cases, flight from the reservations was motivated primarily by an effort to return to lands viewed as "home" or to reunite with or recover kin captured during past flights or past skirmishes with Americans or Mexicans. This was true even for the most complicated and controversial (from an Apache perspective) of figures like Victorio, Juh, Chatto, and Geronimo. The lure of kin and home in shaping Apache mobility in this period warrants further attention.[32]

Breakouts and the Scattering of Southern Apache Families

Southern Apaches had good reason to leave San Carlos: it was not their land, it was a corruption-filled and poorly supplied place, the climate in the lowlands was hot and unhealthy, they had previously been promised better areas in their own homelands, and past and present interactions with the United States and Mexico had scattered relatives whom they hoped to recover. There were some individual successes, moments in which Apaches were able to reunite with kin as a result of their desperate flights across borders, but in general, the so-called breakouts proved disastrous for the Southern Apache people in the period between 1877 and 1886. Pressure from white settlers and international cooperation grew to the point that they not only threatened the lives of any Apaches caught off the San Carlos reservation, but also called into question whether Southern Apaches would be allowed to remain on that desolate reservation.[33]

The first mass flight of Southern Apaches from San Carlos occurred only months after the Chihenes' forced removal from Warm Springs to be "concentrated" with other Apaches at San Carlos. Most of those who left in late August and early September 1877 were Chihenes, though Pionsenay and his Chokonen band also fled the reservation. They split from the larger group of Chihenes and headed south into Mexico. Loco, Victorio, and three hundred of their people, meanwhile, headed east into New Mexico and toward the Navajo reservation.

The runaways soon faced pursuit. Before they left, they had rustled horses from Western Apache neighbors during the night and packed large quantities of flour and other provisions they had stored. Once U.S. officials took note of their absence, they sent U.S. Cavalry and volunteers from the San Carlos agency in pursuit. Some Western Apaches pursued Chihenes independently, seeking to recover their stolen horses. Within a week, U.S. troops cornered Chihenes at Ash Creek, taking livestock and thirty women and children as captives. San Carlos Indian police caught up to them as well, killing a dozen Chihenes, recovering a number of horses, and capturing more than a dozen women and children.[34]

Captives taken in these attacks described how they had planned to meet in the mountains east of the San Francisco River but that pursuit had come quickly and had been more severe than they had anticipated, causing "considerable panic and suffering among some of them and they had abandoned much—even some of their children." Their intention, they explained, was never to go to war with the United States; instead, they were "seeking a place of safety." They planned to go to Navajo country first because they feared the troops stationed at Warm Springs, but their eventual goal was to negotiate a return to their old reservation. By late October, continued pursuit by troops and Western Apaches had led more Chihenes to begin surrendering at Fort Wingate in Navajo country and to explain their motives and hopes. By the end the of month, 233 had surrendered and were being provisioned as U.S. prisoners of war.[35]

Captive testimony at Fort Wingate provides a fuller picture of what had motivated Chihenes to leave the reservation in the first place. Victorio and

Loco later reported that more than anything, they had left because of conflict with the Coyoteros (White Mountain Western Apaches). They had tired of the "unfriendliness manifested toward them by the Coyotero Apaches and of the hostility of a part of the Chiricahuas." Other comments suggested that intertribal tensions were not the only factors prompting them to leave. In particular, they explained that the food and water was bad and made their people sick. They repeatedly noted that they wanted to go anywhere other than San Carlos. "These Indians have an invincible objection to returning to San Carlos Agency preferring to go anywhere else," a U.S. officer at Fort Wingate summarized.[36]

By November 1877, the Chihene refugees appeared to have achieved their aim. They were escorted to Warm Springs, where they were allowed to remain until the summer of 1878. United States army officers justified the move as necessary to facilitate the continued surrender of other refugee Apaches and as a preferable alternative to keeping them on the Navajo reservation, where they might unsettle the relatively calm state of affairs there. This period of return to their homeland was probably a time of hope. For a while, it seemed like the costs of flight from San Carlos in lost lives and separation from kin might have been worth it, allowing them to secure their preferred "place of safety." It certainly would not have been the first time that Americans changed their mind about a reservation site. Within weeks of their arrival, military officials at Warm Springs charged with temporarily provisioning the Chihenes began to raise questions about their future. Inspector E. C. Watkins noted, for example, that while Chihenes "told the same old story about this being the homes of their fathers," he believed it preferable to exile them to Indian Territory.[37]

The Chihene perspective was simple and reflected the same argument they had made for nearly ten years: they wanted to be allowed to stay where they were. Yet the forced removal during the prior spring and their subsequent flight from San Carlos had created new challenges. Their temporary agent reported that "it was an almost daily occurrence of one or two coming to me, and begging, in tears, to have either a father mother or children restored to them." In fact, they helped their agents construct a list of 143 relatives with whom they urgently requested to be reunited. From a U.S. vantage point, it made little sense to bring their kin from San Carlos to Warm Springs if they were just going to be taken back to San Carlos again. In asking for their relatives day after day, they probably hoped not only for a reunion but also that the movement of these people from San Carlos would lend further weight to their request for their reservation to be reestablished in New Mexico. While this approach was logical, it ultimately proved to be in vain. Officials at the

Office of Indian Affairs ultimately decided to reunite Apaches with their relatives, but that reunion would take place at "their proper agency," San Carlos.[38]

The military officials who had been provisioning Chihenes at Warm
Springs (and were tired of doing so), disagreed with this decision. They did
not think it made sense to send Chihenes to a place they had fled and obviously continued to disdain.[39] In October 1878, after further delays, the Office
of Indian Affairs ordered that the Chihene refugees be removed to San Carlos
again. In this case, the most important explanation officials provided was
not mineral wealth, international diplomacy, or settler complaints of raids.
It was instead "the high price of beef at that point" and the cost savings of
provisioning them someplace where beef would be cheaper. A shortsighted
bureaucratic rationalization was thus the primary spark for a decision that
significantly impacted Apache futures.[40]

This latest forced migration of Southern Apaches from Warm Springs
was influenced by past precedent from the start. Captain Frank Bennet and
the 9th Cavalry were charged with escorting the Indians to San Carlos. They
brought six wagons for the sick and elderly and were aided by twenty Navajo
Indian scouts. It was perhaps through these scouts that word had already
reached Warm Springs of the impending forced migration. This happened
even though the enlisted men were supposed to be "kept in ignorance of . . .
the purpose or destination of the move." On their arrival, however, Bennet
reported that he learned that "the Indians had known for ten days (or more)
that troops were coming to move them to San Carlos. Nobody knew how
they got their information." During a visit to their camp a mile or so from
the agency, Captain Bennet explained to them that while they had been held
as prisoners of war, it was now time "that they should return to their home."
The fact that they strongly disagreed with the idea that San Carlos was home
immediately became clear. He reported that "they made strong protests
against going." They detailed many of the same complaints they had repeated
in the past: Western Apaches were unfriendly, the water did not agree with
them, their horses and arms had been taken from them.[41]

The protests and tension continued after one Mescalero woman who was
among the group of Chihenes began yelling at the top of her voice that "the
soldiers were coming and going to kill them all, and for all to leave and get out
of the way and save their lives." Many did flee: between sixty and eighty men,
women, and children, including Victorio. Bennet reported to his superiors
that the Apaches who remained with him continued to protest against going
to San Carlos. "Force will be required," he added, noting that if the decision
to remove them was reversed, "they will go anywhere else."[42]

The third forced removal in less than ten years may have been even more disheartening than the last. After marching thirty miles, observers noted that "a great many old women, and young children were very tired some sick and in a very bad condition." A few nights into their journey, there was new commotion when "outside Indians hollered at the ones being marched." By early November, they were nearing Fort Apache when a winter storm rolled in. It rained and snowed for four days, during which time "the Indians suffered terribly." Muddy roads made travel impossible. When they finally arrived at San Carlos on November 25, after a 350-mile journey, only 173 Chihene Apaches were given over to reservation agents.[43]

The rest of the Chihenes had gone elsewhere—some to the mountains, others to Mexico, still others to the Mescalero reservation. Another forced removal had served as much to displace as remove. Throughout 1878, Victorio and members of his band flirted with surrender on various occasions, but as one official rightly explained, "They prefer death to being sent to San Carlos." Ultimately, Victorio succeeded temporarily in negotiating for his people an alternative to forced removal or death. In April 1879, U.S. officials agreed to let him go to the Mescalero reservation instead. As the commissioner of Indian Affairs Ezra Hayt noted, "They affiliate well with the Mescalero Apaches," and indeed, some had already joined them there after eluding the forced removal to San Carlos of the prior fall.[44]

Yet despite this agreement, Victorio and his band delayed. When he finally arrived at Fort Stanton (the Mescalero agency site) in June 1879, Agent James Russell reported that Victorio and his people seemed very wary, afraid that they were being deceived. He noted that they "begged me to be candid with them and that if I intended to send them to San Carlos to tell them so now." Victorio was reassured when Russell promised them he would not send them away, and if they stayed on the Mescalero reservation and were "good Indians," there would be no more trouble. Mescalero was preferable to San Carlos (if not Warm Springs), but there remained the issue of kin who were presently on that Arizona reservation. One of the first requests Victorio and others made to Agent Russell, "in the strongest manner possible," was "to try and get their families here." Russell formally made this request to the commissioner of Indian Affairs in Washington, stating that he believed if this could be accomplished, "it will be the end of all the long and serious trouble with the Warm Springs Indians."[45]

Trouble, particularly for Victorio and his Chihenes, was not over yet. News that a sheriff in Grant County, New Mexico, had issued a warrant for his arrest sent him fleeing from the Mescalero reservation into Mexico in late

August, even as women and children were currently on the way from San Carlos to be reunited with them. On August 25, Russell reported that "Warm Springs Indians have all left this reservation going west, will probably try to intercept those supposed to be on the way from San Carlos." It is unlikely that federal Indian agents would have turned Victorio in to be tried, but he clearly was not taking his chances.[46]

Victorio's decision to flee from the Mescalero reservation out of fear of his own apprehension would have unintended consequences for other Southern Apache men, women, and children. Although most of the Chihenes might have been reunited on the Mescalero reservation in the fall of 1879 and spared further odysseys of forced migration and displacement, their families were further shattered. After months of hiding, flight, skirmishes, and raids, the Chihenes and some of their Mescalero allies were surrounded by a Mexican contingent at Tres Castillos in northeastern Chihuahua in October 1880. General Terrazas and his force killed eighty Apaches and took sixty-eight captives, who faced years of forced labor or imprisonment. Of 145 Chihenes who had left the Mescalero reservation with Victorio, only about half survived, most of them as captives in Mexico. Illustrating the communication links between Apaches off and on reservations, officials at San Carlos described observing Indians mourning Victorio and other Chihenes' deaths.[47]

For his part, General Terrazas reportedly entered Chihuahua triumphantly in the days following his victory. An American journalist present described the scene in an article later reprinted in the *Daily New Mexican* that December. "The whole city turned out," he noted, remembering the cacophony of church bells and bands that preluded the arrival of Terrazas and his men. Amid a procession of excited residents and marching bands came Terrazas and his officers, "looking worn and travel-stained," sedate in comparison to the wild crowd. Following them were Apache prisoners riding mules and ponies, almost all women and children, from infants to the elderly. Next came the bulk of the Mexican soldiers and volunteers, men "bloody and dirty in the extreme." Some of them bore ghastly trophies as evidence of their victory, "a long black line of terrible looking objects" they waved in the air on ten-foot poles, the scalps of the Apaches killed in the fight. The leering crowd reportedly yelled and cried with emotion, "perfectly wild" at the sight.[48]

The Apache prisoners probably had some idea of what awaited them, given the frequency with which Apaches had experienced captivity in Mexico before. The procession led them to the city's prison, where they were dismounted and escorted inside. The next day all the children under the age of thirteen were separated from the adult women and "taken into the best and

wealthiest families in the city." Given that the U.S. journalist expressed surprise at this, he was clearly unaware of the many past generations of Native
children similarly requested by families who promised to civilize and Christianize them while putting them to work. Terrazas reportedly claimed two
Apache captives for himself, a boy and a girl. Their mothers, if they were
among the survivors, were still in prison months later.[49]

The Chihene experience in 1879 and 1880 foreshadowed the results of
similar flights across borders into Mexico in the coming years. Motivated in
part by feared forced migrations or imprisonments, traveling across borders
invariably led not to safety but instead to casualties in confrontations with
Mexican and U.S. troops and the loss of community members to captivity
and incarceration in households and jails. While Apaches were aware of the
risks—and some chose instead to stay on the San Carlos reservation—past
flights and losses helped trigger new ones, as Apaches went to or stayed in
Mexico in the hopes of recovering displaced kin, including those captured at
Tres Castillos and in subsequent campaigns.[50]

By the end of 1880, almost all Southern Apaches had again coalesced on
the San Carlos reservation, including Juh's and Geronimo's bands, which had
come in at the beginning of the year, and survivors of Tres Castillos in October. In all, they numbered around eight hundred, about five hundred fewer
than in 1876, when the United States disbanded the Chiricahua reservation.
The Chokonens and Nednis had each lost about 150 since that time; the Chihenes (after Victorio's defeat), about 120; the Bedonkohes, about 75.[51]

The experience of Naiche's band illustrates the hard choices that Southern
Apaches faced during this period. On the one hand, life off the reservation
meant constant risk of ambushes, hiding in perilous mountain camps, and
cross-border travel into Mexico, where circumstances for Apaches were no
better. On the other, life on the reservation in the Gila lowlands meant U.S.
supervision in an undesirable place where malaria threatened the health of
their people. In 1880, for example, Naiche said he had lost one-third of his
band to sickness since they came to the reservation in 1876. While American
officials were aware of the problem and had given him permission to live in
the higher country away from the agency, Victorio's flight from the Mescalero
reservation had led to new problems. When rumors suggested that Victorio
might be near San Carlos, reservation agents would order Chiricahuas from
the mountains back to the malarial swamps of the Gila River. After only a few
weeks back in the lowland, malaria would again strike. While the United States
had moved Apaches for all kinds of reasons—from international diplomacy
to the high price of beef—they claimed that they were unable to act to help

Southern Apaches afflicted by malaria. As Colonel Eugene Carr noted after he was sent by his commanding officer to observe the situation on the reservation in June 1881: "The subject of sickness and death at San Carlos is a painful one and is apt to be shirked. I suppose it is now impossible to change their location and they must submit to what is in store for them palliated only by such sanitary and medical provision as can be made available and by the gradual acclimation of those who survive." Carr's perspective reflects overarching ideas about Native Americans and their futures that many white Americans of this era shared. When it was convenient for Americans to change the location of Apache reservations, they did so without hesitation. When Apaches were dying by the dozens of malaria, it suddenly became "impossible" to envision moving them. Instead, they needed to "submit to what [was] in store for them," presumably death. If it was the fate of all Native Americans to disappear, Carr suggested, then why should anyone go out of their way to help them now, however "painful" it might be to watch their suffering? Carr likely would have contested the idea that he intended for all Apaches to die, but the genocidal effects of his indifference are readily apparent.[52]

Malaria would eventually become less of a menace as Apaches successfully negotiated with more sympathetic officials to allow them to move to higher country indefinitely. In the meantime, however, the disease represented an underlying source of concern and dissatisfaction that factored into Apaches' decisions to consider fleeing beyond the borders of the reservation. Flights from the reservation in turn proved another significant source of casualties. The next major flight of Southern Apaches off the reservation occurred in 1881, after a messianic religion surged among Western Apaches in particular. The message centered on a prophesized return of dead Apache leaders after which Apaches would eliminate white Americans from their lands. In August, tensions surrounding a Western Apache gathering boiled over into a clash between troops under Colonel Carr and several hundred White Mountain Western Apaches.[53]

In this context, the rumors spread by Western Apaches that American troops were coming to "murder [Apache] women and children" probably seemed plausible. Expounding on these rumors, one Western Apache man named George reportedly said that "the soldiers planned to arrest the Chiricahua chiefs and deport them to a distant place." Other Southern Apaches later testified that Peaches, a Western Apache man who was married to a Chihene woman and lived with her people, claimed that Agent Tiffany had mistreated them and had "threatened to have them removed from San Carlos to a far distant country, so the Chiricahuas broke out."[54]

Rumors of arrests and deportations would play a central role in the two most important mass breakouts of this period: in late September 1881 and in May 1885. For Naiche and his people, who had suffered through years of malaria outbreaks and yet had remained at San Carlos, it was fear of another forced diaspora that proved the last straw: "I was afraid I was going to be taken off somewhere I didn't like; to some place I didn't know. I thought all who were taken away would die." While U.S. officials had no forced-removal planned in 1881 when Naiche left San Carlos, the fact that he and others found the circulating rumors to be believable is not surprising, given how many times U.S. officials had arrested or forcibly moved Southern Apaches in recent years. Moreover, discussions in the local and national press about the forced removal, arrest, or extermination of Apaches were ubiquitous and ongoing. United States' civil and military officials also continued to discuss and debate whether banishment elsewhere was the best long-term solution to the supposed Southern Apache "problem" throughout this period. Rumors of U.S.-American violence or apprehensions were not the only factors that motivated Apaches to leave San Carlos on these occasions or to stay off the reservation. For some Apaches, material interests, anger, and hopelessness played a role. As Geronimo later wrote, "We were reckless with our lives. . . . If we returned to our reservation we would be put in prison and killed; if we stayed in Mexico they would continue to send soldiers to fight us; so we gave no quarter to anyone and asked no favors."[55]

Another important factor that led Apaches to leave San Carlos was concern about previously displaced relatives and efforts to recover them from the diaspora. This influenced the decision of some Apaches to leave the reservation without authorization and also likely played a role in some Apaches' decision to aid the U.S. military as scouts to help bring back their relatives from Mexico. An immediate motivation for some Chihenes to leave San Carlos in the fall of 1881, for example, was the hope of recovering relatives taken the year before at Tres Castillos, including by taking Mexican captives in order to be able to ransom them for their captive kin. Chihenes banded together with Mescalero allies who had also lost kin to captivity in this same campaign. Yet recovering their relatives would prove difficult. In November 1881, they lost another forty people to Mexican troops near Presidio del Norte when Mexicans opened fire on them after feigning interest in negotiating a captive exchange.[56]

Many Southern Apaches would ultimately regret their decisions to leave San Carlos. Naiche later stated that he had "always been sorry that I left for I have suffered a great deal." Of the 375 who left San Carlos at around 10:30

p.m. in the evening of September 30, 1881, about 25 percent died within two years, while others experienced forced labor or incarceration in Chihuahua and Sonora. In part because of their losses in Mexico, Naiche, Geronimo, and Chatto returned to San Carlos in April 1882 to gather reinforcements, whether the latter wanted to come or not. Just before dawn, the Chihene village near San Carlos awoke to a commotion. Those present remembered Geronimo ordering his men to shoot anyone who would not come with him. Sam Kenoi remained disgusted years later by Apaches forcing other Apaches to leave the reservation at gun point, "even women." Most of the Southern Apaches then residing at San Carlos, numbering about three hundred, were forced to go to Mexico, although a small group from Loco's band fled to Fort Wingate and requested to live on the Navajo reservation instead.[57]

Apaches in Mexico suffered repeated military losses in the coming weeks and months, owing to U.S. and Mexican cooperation and combined pursuit, and probably also to Apache difficulties in obtaining supplies and ammunition. Each loss to Mexican forces entailed a loss of life and also a loss of a significant number of kin to captivity. Chief Loco's group of Chihenes faired particularly poorly. Weeks after being coerced off the reservation by other Southern Apaches, nearly 40 percent of his band was killed in a morning ambush by Mexican troops at Alisos Creek, Chihuahua. Led by Colonel Lorenzo García, the group of two hundred men, including federal soldiers and Sonoran volunteers, successfully exploited Apaches' exhaustion and hunger from days of flight from U.S. and Mexican troops alike. Colonel García later came under criticism for the brutality and indiscriminate casualties taken in the fight. Jason Betzinez, who was present that day, recalled Mexicans emerging from their hiding places "shooting down women and children right and left . . . dying on all sides of us." Most of the seventy-eight dead were Chihenes.[58]

After García's ambush at Aliso Creek, U.S. troops and Apache scouts led by Lt. Colonel George Forsyth toured the grisly site. They also managed to see thirty-three Southern Apache women and children taken captive despite Mexican admonishments to the U.S. troops to stay away from them. One observer wrote that their plight "touched the Americans and Indian scouts." He went on to describe the scene: "The women wanted us to give the Mexicans money to ransom them, as they wanted to go back with us. They were afraid to be taken off with the Mexicans as captives. We did not have any money so could not do anything."[59]

The women's fear of captivity in Mexico was probably due to knowledge of past captives' fates. While most Apache captives were not able to return to their people, enough did that they spread knowledge of what life in diaspora entailed and about Mexican practices of bondage. Apaches recounted stories of captives' daring escapes and long journeys back home not only to celebrate Apache valor but also to serve as reminder of the dangers of falling into the hands of the enemy. Among the most often told tales was that of a woman known among Apaches as Id-is-tah-nah but renamed Francesca by her Mexican captors. She had been captured in a raid on Geronimo's camp in 1861 when she was about seventeen. Along with three other Apache women, she had been sold to an agave planter in Sonora, where they had labored for five years until they managed to slip away from a celebration at the local church and flee north toward home. Sleeping by day and traveling by night, they ate the fruit of the prickly pear cactus and other food they managed to gather in the mountains. One night, the girls were attacked by a mountain lion, and Francesca was nearly killed. After nursing her wounds for a month, the group continued their journey, finally reuniting with their people after a harrowing odyssey of captivity, enslavement, and escape. As Geronimo later recalled, "Her face was always disfigured with those scars and she never regained perfect use of her hands." Yet to fellow Apaches those scars, and her story served as symbols of her strength and resilience to overcome the challenges posed by her captivity and separation from her people.[60]

The experience of one of Geronimo's wives, a woman known to outsiders as Mañanita and to Apaches as Taayzslath, paralleled that of Francesca. Her story helps to illustrate the range of captives' experiences in Mexico during this period, as well as the means by which their relatives sometimes were able to learn of their whereabouts. If Francesca's story points to the persistence of long-standing systems of bondage for Native people in Mexico, including its justification as a means to "civilize" and "Christianize," Mañanita's story illustrates other possibilities, including long-term incarceration. After her capture by Mexican troops, she was taken with twenty-two other captives to Chihuahua. As was typical, the eleven children among them were distributed to families in the city, but the adults, including some of the children's mothers, were kept in jail. The obvious pain of this separation generated sympathy among city residents, and Mañanita later remembered that officials had brought the children to visit them in the jail in Chihuahua City every eight days. The children "could not tell us where they were kept or how they were getting along," she explained, "because they were too small to know anything about the city."[61]

As Francesca had two decades prior, Mañanita ultimately appealed to her captors' sympathies to escape and return to her husband in the United States. On one occasion, officials allowed her to stay overnight at the home of the family where her daughter was being kept because the girl was "so low-spirited that she would not eat or drink and did nothing but cry." In the middle of the night, Mañanita escaped and headed north toward Arizona. She lived on what she could find—"herbs, roots, berries"—and her feet and legs swelled so much that she could hardly walk. At last, after forty-four days travel, she located the camp of her husband, Geronimo, on the San Carlos reservation. She subsequently told her story to U.S. military officials and pleaded with them to work to obtain the release of her daughter, sister, nephew, and other kin.[62]

Having fled exile at San Carlos in part because of rumored exiles elsewhere, Apaches now faced the consequence that their flights had served to further separate their people. Prospects for a future in Mexico dimmed over time. A growing international crisis sparked by the Apache flights of 1881 and 1882 had led to an agreement of cooperation signed in July 1882 that allowed Mexican and U.S. troops to enter each other's territory in hot pursuit of "savage Indians" but with certain restrictions, including notification of officials in the other country. This binational effort to end Apache mobility by killing or capturing them had already devastated Southern Apaches when a new U.S. military commander, General George Crook, entered Mexico in pursuit of the final surrender of all Southern Apaches in Mexico in the spring of 1883. Among Crook's controversial tactics was the use of Apache scouts, who he, like many of his Spanish imperial predecessors, believed was essential to successfully tracking Apaches. The reliance on scouts went beyond their fighting or tracking skills, however. When Crook asked for permission to hire Apache scouts, including Southern Apaches, he noted that catching Apaches "must be done through their own people." This was in part because they possessed the ability to negotiate and persuade.[63]

On May 15, 1883, in a critical moment of the campaign, the Apache scouts proved Crook correct in an ambush on a large Chokonen camp in the mountains near Bugatseka, Sonora. This camp included kin of influential men, including of Chihuahua, Naiche, Chatto, and Bonito. It was, in fact, a large settlement, with about thirty wickiups in two clusters. While the casualties inflicted by the scouts were relatively minor, they set flames to the wickiups to destroy the camp. The destruction of what Southern Apaches had believed to be a safe stronghold in the Sierra Madre Mountains was the last straw for many Southern Apaches. It cemented among many the sense that in Mexico they were not safe. However undesirable they found the San Carlos reservation, they at least did not have to constantly fear for their lives there.[64]

Many Southern Apaches decided to surrender to Crook with concerns in mind about reuniting families and keeping them secure. Gordo explained that he "wanted [his] wife and children to live in peace," adding that he was "tired of living in the mountains like a beast. So I want to live on the reservation." As Crook had hoped, the scouts helped with the negotiations. Ultimately, 325 Southern Apaches marched north under Crook's watch, across the U.S.-Mexico border and back to San Carlos. About two hundred others remained in Mexico, including some who had promised to come at some future date, among them Geronimo and Chatto.[65]

Those Apaches who stayed in Mexico later explained that they had two principal concerns that led them to remain there: their relatives who remained in captivity, and the hope that they could rustle some horses to bring back with them to Arizona. Naiche explained, for example, that before leaving Mexico they decided they had "better go to see the Mexicans at Casas Grandes to see if our people who were prisoners were still alive" and make a treaty to get them back. "I'm not as bad as people think I am," Geronimo reportedly stated, "I intend to go where my children and people are [back to San Carlos]," but "we want all our captives . . . they are in Mexico." He added that he had wanted ponies too since he did not have any in Arizona.[66]

Chatto provided a particularly poignant explanation of why he stayed in Mexico rather than joining Crook when he escorted the bulk of Southern Apaches to San Carlos. He noted that he stayed to get horses since he did not have any, but more than anything to try to get his family, who had been captured in a Mexican campaign the prior year. "If you were placed in our position with your relatives in captivity," he said, "I think you would have done the same—try and get them out." Chatto also lamented the toll of violence and flights in recent years, noting that "what there is left is all scattered—one member of each family is about all that is left." After he ultimately joined other Southern Apaches at San Carlos, he continued to plead tirelessly to officials to help him get his family back.[67]

After Crook returned to Arizona with most of the surviving Southern Apaches, the Departments of War and the Interior wrangled over how Southern Apaches should be administered given that they were technically prisoners of war. Tensions over jurisdiction lingered, but an arrangement to coadminister Southern Apaches provided a technical resolution. A military agent would serve to police Southern Apaches and ensure they did not leave the reservation, while the reservation and its supplies and rations would remain under the civilian administration of the Indian bureau.[68]

Crook also faced challenges in terms of public opinion. While never known for their subtlety, the Arizona territorial newspapers raged even more than usual at the prospect that the Apache people they believed to be murderers and thieves would be allowed to return to Arizona and not face punishment for their crimes. Editorials lobbied for the government to hang all the Southern Apache men, though perhaps the women and children could be saved and divvied up among the tribes of Indian Territory. Pressed to defend his own actions, Crook sought to make clear the difficulty of the situation, writing in the *Arizona Citizen*, "No one likes to see these red-handed murderers, as nearly all of them are, go back to the reservation. . . . But what are we going to do? To kill them will not bring back the dead and to punish them will only lead to them leaving the reservation."[69]

Crook faced pressure from the national press as well. In the summer of 1883, a *New York Times* editorial titled "What Will We Do with Them" noted that Crook had recently returned from Mexico with hundreds of Apache captives and that their fates now hung in the balance. The editorialist explained that as American Indians, unruly "wards" of the United States who had run away from their "guardian," the United States government could send them back to their reservation in Southern Arizona. But what would prevent them from simply leaving again? Another alternative would be to declare them foreign belligerents, enemies like the British or Mexican soldiers in past wars, but to many they seemed more like criminals. Like outlaws of the Wild West, they had allegedly committed murders, kidnappings, and robberies, and they could be charged and tried for their crimes. There was limited evidence to put individuals on trial, however, and many Apache raids had taken place in Mexico, beyond the bounds of American jurisdiction. Popular opinion in Arizona suggested yet another possibility—to forgo legal formalities and lynch them—but it seemed "impractical," given their numbers. There were women and children to think about, as well as the problem of what to do with them if their "natural protectors" were executed. In the end, the editorial raised a number of possibilities and concerns but offered no solutions of its own. The author concluded with a call to General Crook to suggest his ideas for how to proceed in this "novel situation."[70]

The situation U.S. officials faced was not in fact novel, but the editorial's framing of the issue—"what will we do with them?"—was unusual in revealing a central premise of U.S. approaches to Apache and other Indigenous people over time. Amid much philosophizing over theoretical possibilities and much haranguing of Crook for his ideas, few stopped to consider that Native people might have solutions of their own in mind. The idea that they might warrant consultation was anathema to a system that centered around the idea that they were at best childlike dependents and at worst "red devils" deserving of hanging.[71]

Apaches had in fact offered and continued to offer a number of proposals about their future during the summer and fall of 1883. Geronimo proposed they be given land around Eagle Creek in eastern Arizona, which was off the reservation but which he believed to be a good spot. "There is plenty of land, plenty of grass, and his people can all live there," he said through an interpreter. "Those Americans who live on Eagle Creek, can't their land be bought from them?" he asked.[72] Chatto asked instead for the old Warm Springs reservation to be reinstated. "He is thinking about the land he had left behind and maybe the Government will give him back his land," said the interpreters he spoke through, adding that "their land used to be from Bowie to Huachuca and down to the Hot Springs."[73]

Such testimony is striking in its challenge to contemporary settler reasoning. Outraged to discover a party of Southern Apaches gathering saguaro fruit with authorization off the reservation in August 1884, white residents of Gila County, Arizona, fired off a joint letter to the civilian reservation agent, Philip Wilcox. They noted that they had been "greatly annoyed and inconvenienced" by the presence of the Apache party and protested "against their being permitted to roam at will beyond the lines of the reservation." White residents served not only as a de facto reservation border patrol but also as armchair architects of U.S. Indian policy. They had lobbied for years for other Apache reservations to be closed and the San Carlos reservation to be reduced in size, usually successfully.[74]

Yet Apaches pushed back against the logic of dispossession. Earlier that year, Geronimo had questioned why settlers could not give up land, and Chatto noted that Apaches "want the mountains back," even adding that "after a while, his people will work the mines the same as the white people." If whites were so concerned about Indians "roaming" off the reservation, Natives had a reasonable answer. Chatto argued that "if the reservation was larger it would be better." To U.S. officials it was unthinkable that Indigenous people might actually have better ideas than they did about how to live at peace with their neighbors and ensure that their communities had what they needed to thrive.[75]

"Getting Along Well" and the Lingering Lure of Mexico

Apaches later remembered the time after Southern Apaches returned from Mexico in 1883 as a good one, one when their families got along well. Key to this was a move from the Gila lowlands to the higher country surrounding

Turkey Creek, near Fort Apache in the spring of the following year. In contrast to the numerous coerced migrations of previous years, the northward march of Apaches out of the dusty Gila valley in June 1884 was a happy one, described in vivid detail by the army officer charged with policing and overseeing Southern Apache affairs, Britton Davis. The 512 Southern Apaches he escorted had over three hundred pack trains and nearly one hundred mules, "to say nothing of the Indians' wagons, personal effects, families, and my two pack trains of supplies." Davis explained that Apaches took the usual government mismanagement in stride when the harnesses they had been provided for their ponies were of the wrong size. By working together to shred old rags and stuff them into the collars, they managed to hitch up the wagons, "whooping and laughing . . . getting as much fun out of the circus as we were."[76]

After a harrowing but successful crossing of the Black River, they arrived without further incident at Turkey Creek. The Apaches' new home was about seventeen miles southeast of Fort Apache in a high valley "with pine trees, clear water, game, and a mild summer climate." Within hours of arrival, three men went out to hunt and returned with a deer. Others set to work building homes scattered among the pines in the valley. They used whatever material they could find: "cotton cloth, old shirts, pieces of blankets."[77]

Life at Turkey Creek represented a reprieve from the hot summers, malaria, and dust of the Gila lowlands. In critiquing life around San Carlos, Kayetena had explained after returning from Mexico that "it is not a healthy place. He would like to go to some place where there is good grass, water, and plenty wood." Turkey Creek seemed like it would fit many of these requirements. Others noted their sense of relief that they finally did not have to worry about pursuit. As the Apache leader Chihuahua explained, they could "rest and did not have to watch all the time."[78]

The move away from the Gila lowlands and the reuniting of Southern Apache people sparked hope for the future. In the coming months, most of the five hundred or so Southern Apaches at Turkey Creek cleared ground and planted corn and barley. Even Geronimo reportedly joined in, as one observer described the family's cooperative effort: "[Geronimo] held the plow in virgin soil until his hands were blistered, while his boy led the mule that was hitched to it, and his squaw urged them on with vigorous applications of a branch of tough scrubby oak." Soon Southern Apaches were joined by some Western Apache allies, and the population of the valley grew to more than 550.[79]

Not all was paradise, however. Farming in the valley was difficult given the high elevation and short growing season. Noting Southern Apaches' evident interest in horses and stock raising, Britton Davis supported encouraging them to be a pastoral people instead of farmers. "We proposed that they be given sheep and a few cows to start with," Davis wrote, "hoping that in time they would become independent, peaceful, and prosperous as the Navaho." He believed that General Crook concurred, but since the administration of Southern Apaches was shared with the civilian Indian agents, they ultimately got the last word. "The Indian bureau at Washington was again in the saddle and farmers they must be," Davis lamented.[80]

It was not just on the question of subsistence strategies that U.S. officials intervened in Apache affairs, creating tension at Turkey Creek even if circumstances were still preferable to San Carlos. They also seized and sold the cattle that Apaches had brought back with them from Mexico, which was a particular grievance of Geronimo, who argued that the United States should not interfere in his relations with Mexico. United States' bureaucratic restrictions on tiswin making, Apaches' favorite corn beer, also caused dissatisfaction, as did interventions in family affairs, including efforts to regulate husbands' treatment of their wives.[81]

During his time overseeing Southern Apaches, Davis's views on them changed. He wrote honestly about initially having shared in the broader white American view: "that ill-defined impression that they were something a little better than animals but not quite human; something to be on your guard against." Based on experience with them over time, however, he said he "began to feel toward them as we would feel toward any other class of people. . . . We began to find them decidedly human." As his understandings of Apache people changed, so too did his sympathy for their historical experiences with the United States. He marveled at the fact that Natives appeared to harbor no resentment at their past treatment, though they did demonstrate "wonderment at the why of it." Why had they been moved from reservation to reservation? Why had they been promised food and then left hungry? Why had they been forced to live in unhealthy hot places? If Davis claimed that he could not answer "these and other questions," he in fact had unwittingly answered them in describing his own shifting views on Apaches' humanity. Other Americans thought little of the weight of their decisions about provisioning, moving, or warring against Apaches because they dehumanized Native peoples generally and Apaches specifically. If they were like "any other class of people" that was one thing, but if they were "little better than animals," that was quite another. As long as most Americans continued to view Apaches as something other than human, the histories of displacement that coursed through their past would continue into their future.[82]

As Apaches settled down in Turkey Creek in the summer and fall of 1884, it seemed possible that this pattern had finally broken—that Americans were done moving Apaches and that Southern Apaches would be able to build lives for themselves on the reservation. Yet concerns about another potential breakout lingered, especially because Apache captives remained in exile in Mexico. In fact, General Crook began lobbying his superiors in July 1884 to resolve this situation, reporting that "their only grievance is the fact that some of their relatives are prisoners, [and] they are constantly urging that steps be taken to track them down." As he saw it, "so long as these prisoners remain in Mexico, just so long will there be danger of the Chiricahuas continuing their forage, and with their return the last danger from this formidable tribe will be past.[83]

Crook was being practical, knowing that any move of Southern Apaches off the reservation would be devastating to his own reputation as the man in charge of Southern Apache policing. Yet he was also fulfilling personal promises he had made to Apaches themselves, including Chatto, who continued to implore the Americans to help him find his family, who had now been held captive in Chihuahua for two years. Crook's request was forwarded to the U.S. Department of State, where the U.S. ambassador to Mexico, P. H. Morgan, sent it along to his Mexican counterpart, José Fernández, in the Mexican Department of Foreign Relations. While Mexicans certainly understood and shared American concerns about any further Apache migration across the international boundary line, they were in no rush to comply, particularly given the lingering memories of Apache raids, loss of livestock, and killing of Mexican citizens. It was not until February 1885 that Mexico formally responded to the U.S. request, and this was only to indicate that President Porfirio Díaz had requested more information, including "reliable data" as to the number, names, and ages of the Apache captives in question, where they were being held, and whether they were "under the protection of the authorities or of Mexican families." In the meantime, the government would also investigate by seeking information from authorities in Chihuahua and Sonora.[84]

During March, Britton Davis worked with Southern Apaches to construct a list of those people Apaches believed were being held captive in Mexico. In the meantime, Mexican officials had finally made a decision regarding the Apache captives' fates: to return minors "whose relatives are on the reservation" and give adults the option of remaining in Mexico. When Crook forwarded to the Department of State the list Davis and Apaches had created of their captive relatives, he indicated his staunch opposition to Mexico's policy, noting that "so long as any of them remain there . . . so long there will be an active, stimulating pretext for those in Arizona to go to their rescue or to secure hostages for them." He added that it was impossible to convince Apaches that any of their relatives would want to stay in Mexico "away from their home and tribal relations."[85]

The list itself reflects the Apache memory of displaced relatives and their last known whereabouts, in some cases many months or even years out of date. Crook feared that "many of those named, especially adult males, are not living." A few escaped captives had been able to provide more current information, however, especially Mañanita, who provided news about the women and children who remained in the city of Chihuahua. In all, Southern Apaches provided specific names and ages for ninety-three captives, including seventy-two women and girls, and twenty-one men and boys. This number represented about 20 percent of the entire surviving Southern Apache population, which helps to explain Apaches' insistent diplomacy on their behalf. The hope that the list would be as helpful as possible to Mexican officials in locating Apaches and facilitating their return is also indicated by a concluding note that provided pronunciation tips for Apache names. "The long sound of 'a,'" it explained, "is represented by "ah" pronounced as in the exclamation—'ah!'; 'A' not followed by 'h' has the sound of 'a' in 'pay', 'hay', etc.'" Whether this pronunciation note was added by Davis or at the insistence of his Apache informants is unknown.[86]

The extent to which this painstaking list was used in Mexico is also unclear, but by the beginning of April the release of Southern Apache captives had begun. A retired U.S. Army officer traveling on the Mexican Central railroad in Chihuahua reported observing in April 1885 thirteen Apache women and children about one hundred miles south of the city of Chihuahua, "trudging slowly back to San Carlos without assistance or escort." He wondered why the United States was not furnishing them with assistance. The office of the War Department in Washington, D.C., responded on April 28 to this news with an order to furnish any Apache women and children entering the United States with supplies and transport. Released captives would continue to trickle north through the coming months, such as when two Indian women were found traveling north across the border near Fort Bowie at the beginning of August, and seven others were provided food around the same time near Warm Springs, New Mexico.[87]

Even as Mexico began to release captives, a minority of Southern Apaches decided to make one final break across the border into Mexico. As in the past, this flight emerged out of long-standing tensions but was immediately sparked by rumors of death, imprisonment, and forced diaspora. In particular, rumors swirled that Davis and the scouts were going to arrest Geronimo and Mangas and that they had authorization to kill both men if they resisted arrest. One Apache man, Periko, added that "the Chiricahuas feared that Crook would punish them as he had Kayetena [by sending them to Alcatraz] and then remove their families out of Arizona."[88]

Such rumors were false, but nonetheless believable to Geronimo and others. After all, U.S. actions in the past supported the idea that Natives might be banished or imprisoned for any pretext. Francesca, the woman who had escaped bondage in Mexico and lived through a mountain lion attack, may have prompted the men to act. She reportedly challenged men's manhood if they were to merely sit around and wait for arrest: "If you are warriors you will take to the warpath and then the Gray Fox [Crook] must catch you before you are punished."[89]

Whatever their beliefs about the rumors, most Apaches proved unwilling to join Geronimo in flight from San Carlos, probably thinking about the costs of past flights. Geronimo initially gathered only fifteen followers. To gain more he decided to turn to subterfuge. The next day he told Chihuahua and Naiche that his cousins had killed Britton Davis and Chatto. Chihuahua feared his kin would be assumed guilty by association and perhaps sent to Alcatraz or someplace worse. This moment—and Geronimo's decision to lie to gain followers—would further fracture Southern Apache communities and cause further "trouble to breakout" among them, as Sam Kenoi and others would later remember. At dusk on May 17, 1885, thirty-four men, eight teenage boys, and ninety-two women and children left the reservation. The majority of Southern Apaches—more than four hundred—remained behind. While smaller than past flights, it would prove incredibly consequential.[90]

Envisioning "Final" Solutions

As Geronimo and his followers raided and then hid in the mountains in Mexico, pressure in the United States for an end to Southern Apache mobility built. Officials called public meetings across Arizona to discuss what should be done about the situation. On the Saturday evening of June 13, 1885, one such meeting in Tucson was reportedly attended "by a large body of earnest and determined people" and called to order at 8 p.m. by the mayor. The Society of Arizona Pioneers had already met and passed resolutions arguing for "the removal of all the hostile Indians from the Territory," and the governor of Arizona had expressed his sympathy, a point that was raised at

this meeting. Yet not all Tucson residents concurred with the Pioneers' resolution. Some argued that *all* Indians should be removed from the territory,
and a resolution was passed declaring the Indian reservation system a failure:
"The policy of colonizing the Indians in the Indian territory is the only policy
which has borne good results, as illustrated by the civilization, happiness,
and prosperity by the Indian tribes permanently located there."[91]

Residents of Tombstone apparently agreed. At their public meeting there
was reportedly broad agreement that "Apache Indians should be removed
from the territory to some region where it will be impossible for them to continue the outbreaks which result in sacrificing the lives and property of our
people." By comparison, a meeting in Yuma, a place little impacted by Apache
affairs, nonetheless proved more extreme in its conclusions. Residents there
signed on to a statement that noted that Indian policy had been guided by
"religious sentimentalists and romantic female emotionalists." The statement
continued: "A tribe of Apache Indians, fattened at the expense of the government, pampered by the truckling policy of the Department of the Interior,
and encouraged through the weakness and incompetency from some cause of
military managements, has left its recuperative winter resort, called by courtesy a reservation, and is now engaged in embellishing a tiswin drunk with
bloody orgies over the dead bodies of our fellow citizens."[92]

The Yuma citizens' proposal to resolve this situation was simple: Apaches
should be pursued in war "until every member thereof is either shot or captured." Even as they called out Southern Apaches as "murderers by instinct,
inhuman by nature, and fiends by choice," they nonetheless still reserved the
possibility that survivors of a genocidal war might be "moved to Indian territory [present-day Oklahoma] or some other safe place." The editors of the Clifton, Arizona, newspaper endorsed a less nuanced policy, meanwhile: "There is
but one place where Apaches should be colonized, and that is a bone yard."[93]

Beneath such dramatic visions and rhetoric, a simple fact remained: the
majority of Southern Apaches were at peace on the reservation or aiding the
United States in efforts to recover those who had fled into Mexico. Yet as
the U.S. Army and the Apache scouts, including Chatto and other Southern
Apaches, pursued those who had left the reservation, officials joined citizens
in debating solutions and destinations. Like Arizona residents had suggested,
Indian Territory, and Fort Sill in particular, was discussed as a possibility,
but an 1879 law prohibited Apaches from being located on Indian Territory,
which had been a political compromise required for the authorization of
funds for reservations in Arizona and New Mexico. Others proposed relocat-
ing them all to the Carlisle Indian Industrial School, in Pennsylvania, or to

Florida, where in recent years Comanche, Cheyenne, and Kiowa prisoners of war had also been sent. This latter proposal received criticism, because some noted that Apaches were "a mountain race accustomed to high altitudes and would, in a short time, most likely die if kept in the lowlands of Florida." Such discussions paralleled the Spanish imperial officials' debates surrounding Apache deportation to the Caribbean a century before.[94]

The final U.S. campaign to recover Geronimo, led first by General Crook and then by General Nelson Miles, has been recounted countless times. It is the stuff of which Western films were later made: bounties were placed on the heads of the so-called renegades, who eluded capture for months in skirmishes with Mexican and American troops. More than fifty Southern Apache men served as scouts in the effort to recover their relatives. Some were motivated out of personal feuds, others out of a genuine interest in reuniting families and bringing this period of turmoil to a close.[95]

The role that family, kin, and community played in Apache decision-making during this period has not received sufficient emphasis. In the weeks after the outbreak began, strikes on Apache camps in Mexico led to the recapture of several dozen women and children, including the extended family of the Chokonen leader Chihuahua. John Gregory Bourke, who would later gain renown as an amateur Indian ethnologist publishing on Apache lifeways, language, and culture, wrote about these women because he believed them to be ideal informants. Housed in a jail at Fort Bowie upon their return, Bourke described them and their potential utility to him: "As there are some 30 odd Chiricahua captive squaws in the guardhouse at this point, it seems to me that I would find them more plastic, more anxious to impart information and with more leisure in which to impart it, than could be reasonably expected of those at San Carlos who had domestic cares to occupy their time."[96]

Echoing experiences of their ancestors, these women faced difficult lives in confinement, rather than the "leisure" that Bourke claimed. Among the jailed prisoners was Francesca. She now worked as a midwife for other Apache women who gave birth in captivity. As Bourke explained, since the prisoners were not allowed knives, Francesca had been forced to improvise, cutting umbilical cords with "the rim of a tin cup." Perhaps Apache women gained some strength from the awareness that their ancestors had faced similar challenges bringing children into the world in captivity.[97]

In negotiating the surrender of Apaches who remained across the international border in Mexico, U.S. military leaders drew upon these jailed captives and also on relatives on the reservation as leverage. During negotiations to surrender in March 1886, Apache men made their concern about relatives clear. "If you don't let me go back to the reservation," Chihuahua said, "I would like you to send my family with me wherever you send me. I have a daughter at Camp Apache, and some others, relations of myself and of my band at San Carlos. Wherever you want to send me I wish you would also send them." Geronimo also thought of relatives from whom he had been separated. "We think of our relations, brothers, brothers-in-law, fathers-in-law, etc. over on the reservation, and from this know we want to live at peace just as they are doing, and to behave as they are behaving," he said.[98]

Although Geronimo ultimately fled back into Mexico, Chihuahua surrendered, probably in part because of his relatives jailed at Fort Bowie. In April he was reunited with Francesca and other captives. They were allowed to erect a temporary camp of wickiups near the fort, while the U.S. prepared to ship them to Florida. The decision to exile them to Fort Marion (adjacent to the town of Saint Augustine) was rooted in past precedent, as Plains Indian prisoners of war had also been shipped there. More than anything, it reflected military commanders' utmost interest in ensuring their security while they pursued the final surrender of the Apaches who remained in Mexico. Chihuahua's group left on the morning of April 7, arriving at Saint Augustine, Florida, a week later.[99]

In the meantime, Geronimo's flight had led Crook to resign from his post. He later argued that his basic methods, such as targeting Apache family relations and using Apache scouts, nonetheless remained critical to Geronimo's final surrender. In employing such tactics, Crook explained that he was drawing from his knowledge of past U.S. wars on Indians. "As in the Seminole, so in the Apache war," Crook later wrote, "surrendered Indians were sent to a distant part of the country." As he saw it, in both cases "love for kindred, wives, and children, were strong incentives which induced the Indians who remained out to surrender." The love of kin Crook referenced in his analysis was most directly involved in U.S. tactics in two ways: first, the decision to exile Chihuahua and his band in advance of the surrender of the others; second, the promise that if the so-called renegades surrendered they would be reunited with their families.[100]

Yet on an individual level there remained a third factor that influenced the ultimate surrender of Southern Apaches to the United States: kin who remained as captives in diaspora in Mexico. Though the motivations of all of the more than fifty Southern Apache men who assisted the U.S. military as scouts were not recorded in the historical record, one of the most influential, Chatto, took every opportunity he could to note that he was assisting the United States and expected that they would aid him in recovering his family from captivity in

Mexico. Chatto had sought their return tirelessly. Although Crook and U.S. diplomats had succeeded in getting some captives released, Chatto's wife and children had not been among them. He had managed only to obtain a photograph of them from the Mexican family in Chihuahua with whom they lived.

In the summer of 1886, Chatto took his argument to Washington, D.C., though he left the photograph behind, explaining that he "weep[ed] if he looked at it." General Miles, Crook's successor, had arranged for this delegation of Southern Apaches to visit Washington, D.C., to discuss the future of their people. In reality, however, U.S. officials had already made up their minds that Southern Apaches would not be allowed to remain on their Arizona reservation. They went forward with the diplomatic visit in the hopes that Apaches might be made more agreeable to their fate, whatever the officials ultimately decided it would be.[101]

In a White House meeting with Secretary of War William Endicott in late July, Chatto asked through an interpreter for three things: to be able to keep his land in Arizona, for his wife and two children in Chihuahua, and for some paper or medal testifying to the good words exchanged between him and the Americans. "He has feelings just like the white people," his interpreter explained, "and for that reason he wants to have his people with him once more." Endicott said he would try to help, and Chatto made one final request: to have a photograph taken of him in Washington sent to his family in Chihuahua so they could remember him. After a brief introduction with President Grover Cleveland, he was given a silver medal to take with him as a token of goodwill.[102]

Chatto still held out hopes of being reunited with his family years after their capture, a hope that had in part motivated his decision to aid Americans in pursuit of the so-called renegades like Geronimo who remained in Mexico. Though it is unclear whether his family ever received a photograph of him, an 1884 portrait by A. F. Randall gives some sense of the man they would have seen in it if they did. Chatto stands next to cacti that make the Arizona setting clear, his scout's rifle in hand.[103]

Neither Chatto's requests for his land nor his family would be fulfilled. As the delegation left Washington and made its way to Carlisle, Pennsylvania, where a group of Apache children had been sent from Arizona the year before, work was already underway to send all Southern Apaches in Arizona somewhere else. Some Arizona residents argued that any Native men surrendering should be tried and hung, a view with which President Cleveland was sympathetic. After Geronimo's surrender was finally obtained in the rugged Sierra Madre mountains in the summer of 1886, however, Cleveland's

Figure 13. Chatto, c. 1884.

vacillation was overridden by General Miles's decision to treat them as prisoners of war rather than criminals. Inquiring as to the feasibility of sending
Apaches to Florida, a response came from the supervisor of Fort Marion. He
could handle seventy-five more prisoners, although he added that the fort
was really quite unsuited to human occupation. Rational views on the suit-
ability of moving Indians one place or another had often gone unheeded, and
such would be the case here.[104]

While U.S. perspectives differed on exactly which Apaches should be
exiled to where and under what terms, by the summer of 1886 the consensus

that Southern Apaches could not possibly remain in the Southwest was nearly universal. Only a few lone sympathetic voices like Crook argued otherwise, highlighting the fact that the majority of Apaches had remained at peace on the reservation or had aided the U.S. in recovering the "renegades" and that it would be unjust to send them away. Yet most Americans were not interested in parsing such distinctions and instead pointed to the persistence of any Southern Apache mobility across reservation or international borders as categorically intolerable to their future prosperity. Mobility sparked by displacement justified yet another displacement.[105]

*   *   *

Sam Kenoi never forgot the rock piles marking the San Carlos reservation he had grown up on as a child, and he also never forgot when he was taken beyond its borders for good. He recalled that Apaches were forcibly removed from the Southwest in three groups. First had been Chihuahua's band, shipped away to Fort Marion that spring. The second group was Geronimo's band, who finally surrendered later that summer and was taken by railcar to San Antonio, where they were imprisoned for several months while the United States debated what to do with them. The final group, of which Sam was a part, was the group of "Faithful Indians that lived at Fort Apache." He remembered that after all the scouts had come home from the long expedition to track and obtain the surrender of Geronimo, they were called together on August 29 and asked to line up. To their surprise, they had their firearms and ammunition taken away from them and "by order of the commander to his soldiers, they herded the scouts into the horse barn and guarded them day and night." The only thing they were offered to sleep on was a horse blanket. They were so closely guarded that even when they needed to urinate "the soldiers went with them." Decades later, Sam Kenoi remained bitter about this injustice: "After these Indians had gone through all these hardships for the good of the people of these two states, they did this to them."[106]

The rest of the people were not yet fully aware of what was going on, however. Soon after the scouts' detention, Western Apaches held a social dance, and Southern Apache women and children and older men attended—"no one was worried." The next thing they knew, the wagons with troops suddenly arrived, ordering the children, women, and old men to leave with them. All they could take was what they had on their backs, "a shawl, a blanket."

CHIRICAHUAS ENTRAINING AT HOLBROOK, ARIZ.

Figure 14. Soldier's drawing of Apaches at Holbrook, 1886.
Courtesy of Arizona Historical Society.

Kenoi thought about what they were leaving behind. The crops were nearly ready to be harvested. They had sheep, goats, mule teams, wagons, harnesses, horses, and fine saddles. Kenoi never forgave Geronimo or the United States for his family's fate. "These people, these Chiricahua Indians, who lived at Fort Apache peacefully, and the scouts who helped the army to run down Geronimo's band were taken to prison for what Geronimo had done." As he recalled, "The shadow of the shameful way they treated these faithful Indians and United States Scouts is still existing. . . . I was eight or nine years old, and I was one of them."[107]

They traveled a hundred miles to reach the nearest railroad station, at Holbrook, Arizona, which was a two- or three-day trip by wagon, "strung out, a long way." The caravan included nearly 100 soldiers and Western Apache scouts, 383 Southern Apaches, 140 horses, and "what one of the officers thought to be thousands of dogs." An unknown soldier's drawing captured the scene. Titled *Chiricahuas Entraining at Holbrook, Arizona*, it shows armed soldiers surrounding a group that consists primarily of women and children. Apache mothers pick up belongings while children run in front of them. It's a scene of motion, chaos.[108]

Images from September 13, when the group was forced to depart from Arizona, remained seared in Sam Kenoi's memory, images that confirm the U.S. soldier's drawing of the scene: "Lots of the children were running out in the brush. They were afraid of the train. The soldiers had to chase them and get them in. I ran away from them; they had to catch me." Kenoi remembered hearing old men and women praying, "Bless us, that we may be blessed where we go." He remembered being filled with fear.[109]

CHAPTER 8

The Barracks and the School

They came on the Southern Railway, disembarking just before midnight at an old Spanish fort made of cement and stone lit by the moonlight. Exhausted from the journey, they fell asleep in tents pitched on the terreplein, the level roof of the fortification. When they woke up the next morning, they looked out on a foreign, Florida landscape that appeared at first glance to be a "limitless field of waving grass" but was in fact a vast ocean.[1]

In the coming days, tourists began to arrive regularly at the old fort, which the original Spanish builders had named Castillo de San Marcos but white Americans had renamed Fort Marion after a revolutionary war hero. They hoped to glimpse the Apaches, who had become infamous across the country from years of sensationalized reporting about reservation breakouts, raids on settlers, and harrowing battles with the U.S. and Mexican armies. Such curiosity had shaped the Apaches' journey as well: at each stop on their forced march east, white Americans had gathered to watch them in a way that made the prisoners feel as if they were "some kind of wild animals."[2] The fort's moat, once intended to guard against an enemy siege, now served to separate the Native prisoners on its grounds from the residents and tourists of adjacent Saint Augustine, which in the late nineteenth century was a popular resort town. Fort Marion itself had served little military function for years, other than as an occasional prison for Native Americans—Seminoles, various Plains tribes, and now Apaches.[3]

The 469 captives present at the fort on the morning of September 20, 1886, had arrived in three separate groups. Months prior, U.S. officials had shipped 75 recently surrendered men, women, and children to Fort Marion to put pressure on their relatives who remained in Mexico to surrender as well, and to set an example for the many Southern Apaches still living peacefully on their Arizona reservation. More recently, thirteen members of the diplomatic delegation that had traveled from Arizona to Washington, D.C.,

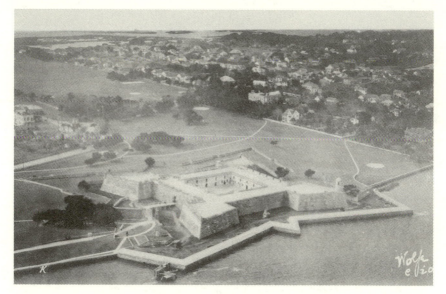

Figure 15. Bird's-eye view of Fort Marion, 1920.

over the summer had arrived. Chatto and other leaders had sensed something was amiss after they had been detained at Fort Leavenworth, Kansas, while on their way back to Fort Apache in late summer. Two days after their arrival on September 18, they were joined by the larger group of 381 Apaches who had been rounded up and shipped east from Arizona.[4]

The relative compliance Apaches demonstrated during their forced migrations was rooted in three key promises U.S. officials had made to them: Apache leaders would not be killed, families would be kept together, and transport east would be temporary until Southern Apaches were granted their own reservation. The Cleveland administration broke promises from the start. They separated Geronimo and fifteen other men deemed dangerous from their families and housed them three hundred miles away at Fort Pickens, another military installation, which was on Santa Rosa Island, off the coast of Pensacola, Florida.[5] In the coming months, meanwhile, U.S. officials separated more than one hundred children from families at Fort Marion and shipped them via steamboat and railroad to the Carlisle Indian School in Pennsylvania and to Hampton Institute in Virginia. Based on age or disability, a few students ended up elsewhere, such as the Philadelphia School for the Blind.[6]

Inadequate rations and illnesses contributed to a striking mortality rate that continued in the following months and years. Approximately half of the prisoners died in the eight years between 1886 and the fall of 1894, as U.S.

officials moved them from forts in Florida to military barracks in Alabama, to boarding schools like Carlisle and Hampton, and then to yet another military installation at Fort Sill, Oklahoma. While Apaches and many U.S. observers highlighted the humid climate of these places as a primary explanation for the deadliness of tuberculosis, malaria, and chronic diarrhea, among other ailments, additional factors probably played an even more important role: malnutrition, depression, tainted water. U.S. officials, like their imperial predecessors, claimed that exiling Apaches to coastal lands represented a humane alternative to killing them in war or execution after criminal trails in Arizona. Yet in practice, the policy of exile proved genocidal, as the U.S. government delayed in responding to health crises the Apache prisoners faced and encouraged the separation of Apache children with the overt goal of preventing the growth of the prisoner population.[7]

Death and suffering were not the only aspects of life that Apaches remembered from this time in their history. They also recalled the strategies they employed to survive genocide and maintain themselves and their broader diasporic community. As Jason Betzinez, one of the prisoners of war, later recalled, "Our women sold beadwork and other handicraft to these sightseers while the men and boys sold souvenir bows and arrows which they made." For his part, Betzinez drew upon his talent for drawing and painting, making "pictures of various wild animals and other scenes from the west," which he sold to visitors to help feed himself and his kin before he was shipped off to Pennsylvania. Soon Apaches began requesting permission to visit the town of Saint Augustine "for the purpose of making little purchases of articles not supplied by the government."[8] Others challenged their captors' treatment more directly. Geronimo complained to the post commander at Fort Pickens about everyone suffering from the "smallness of the ration." The commander agreed to work to increase it.[9]

Such actions during the early days of captivity in Florida illustrate key ways in which Apaches maintained life in diaspora in the months and years to come. The railroad, mail, banks, and newspapers all played a role in the forced exile of hundreds of Apaches to the U.S. Southeast and the removal of their children to distant boarding schools in Pennsylvania and Virginia after their arrival. But Apaches utilized these same technologies to defy U.S. imperial policies. Drawing upon sympathetic citizens and bureaucrats, interpreters, and kin who had become literate, they helped with the publication of newspaper articles and books that spread news of their experiences. As they pressed for new and better living conditions, Apaches also sought any information they could get via letters and reports about children at boarding school or relatives who for one reason or another remained on or had been able to return to reservations in Arizona or New Mexico. They learned to send money, letters, and care packages to each other, drawing upon the sale of Apache-made crafts to curious tourists or on funds received when U.S. officials had auctioned their horses and mules left behind in Arizona. Students who survived boarding school, meanwhile, almost universally returned on the railroad to relatives rather than remaining in white society. Like generations before them, Apaches adapted creatively to life in diaspora and remained linked to kin and community despite displacement.[10]

Another Forced Journey

The story of the exile of Southern Apaches beginning in 1886 is one of broken promises, suffering, and death, yet it is also a story of creativity, reinvention, and persistence. These stories cannot be separated, as the existential challenges that Apaches faced sparked their efforts to remain connected and assert a future for their people despite their limited power as prisoners of war. Their struggle was evident from the moment they disembarked on the forced journey to Florida. The main group of nearly four hundred Apaches left Holbrook, Arizona, in a twelve-car train, with two cars for guards, two for baggage, and eight for the prisoners. While not excessively crowded, U.S. agents had modified the cars to seal the windows in the hopes of preventing escape. Such concerns proved warranted when one Chihene prisoner, Massai, managed to slip out of his car somewhere between New Mexico and Missouri. Sam Kenoi remembered the escape happening in a sandy corner of Colorado; others said it had happened nearer to St. Louis. Whatever the precise location, this story joined other Apache tales of heroic escapes from captivity, ending with his return to Arizona, where he lived out the rest of his life at liberty in the mountains.[11]

Those who experienced the journey remembered the abominable conditions of travel, which one officer described as "simply brutal," highlighting the heat, smell, and lack of fresh air. Apaches remembered being confined to the cars for hours on end, thinking about what they had left behind—livestock, crops, the few kin who had managed to avoid the roundup or had escaped on the way to Holbrook station. They remembered the soldiers standing guard, who sometimes passed through the cars "making motions as if they were going to cut our throats." They remembered eating hardtack rations from barrels when the train stopped to add water to its boilers.[12]

Conditions worsened over time. At St. Louis, soldiers moved them from tourist sleeping cars to older day coaches, where there was no place to lie down as they traveled south through Kentucky and Tennessee. "On that train we slept the best way we could sitting up," Kenoi remembered, adding that "little children were put in that rack where you put packages." By the time they arrived in Jacksonville, Florida, greeted by a rowdy crowd of more than six hundred, a journalist onlooker expressed his view that "a more dirty, disgusting, strong scented mass of humanity [had] never before alighted from a train in Jacksonville." He noted with disgust the "slovenly and scant" manner in which they were dressed, the shocking "amount of filth," and the naked children "clinging to the backs of their mothers." He apparently did not consider that the poor condition of the Native prisoners reflected their white American captors' treatment, rather than any choice of their own.[13]

After arrival at Fort Marion, Apaches learned how inadequate it was to house them. Since the living quarters (casemates) built into the fortification all leaked and were uninhabitable, the group that had arrived first in April had initially camped on a beach nearby, until a new commander had taken charge of the fort and realized they needed better shelter. Large military tents pitched on wood-slat foundations on the fort's grounds by the time the bulk of the prisoners arrived in September were perhaps an improvement over beach camping in the Florida heat and rain, but sanitation and water supply issues remained. Two bathing tubs for 469 people were reportedly in "constant use."[14]

Although the post commander asserted that the first group of prisoners, Chihuahua's band, had generally remained healthy, they had already suffered several deaths by the time they were joined by the rest of the Southern Apaches. With no interpreter present, post officials had assigned them numbers rather than names to facilitate reporting on them. Perhaps they prided themselves on their ingenuity in devising this method, though they were hardly the first to think of it. Spanish soldiers had arrived at the same solution to track Apache prisoners of war a century earlier when they transported them to the eerily similar coastal fortifications. Thus when a child died on July 31, news was forwarded up the chain of command of the death of "a female child, about four years old, the daughter of the Indian Woman No. 22, one of the wives of the fugitive Chief Geronimo."[15] The trains that carried newly arrived Apaches into exile at least included interpreters: Sam Bowman, Concepción, and George Wratten. They would play an important role in helping Apaches press to better their circumstances, by reporting to visitors on the conditions of their captivity, by pressing post commanders to

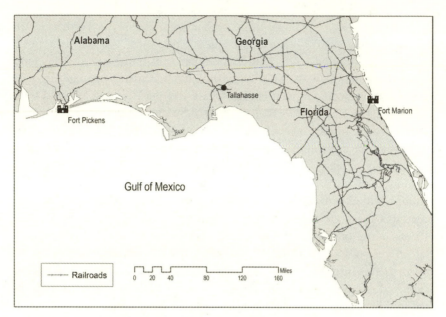

Map 6. Florida with Fort Pickens and Fort Marion.

increase rations, and by facilitating their communication with children away at boarding school and with relatives in Arizona and New Mexico.[16]

Geronimo and his group's journey to Florida roughly paralleled those of the others in terms of experience on the railroad, but it also included several weeks of imprisonment in San Antonio as U.S. officials tried to decide their fates. While in San Antonio, local residents had thrown a "roman holiday," profiting off the sale of photographs and souvenirs as they gawked at the suffering Apache prisoners. While General Miles, like Crook before him, had promised Geronimo and others surrendering in Mexico that their families would be kept with them, the Cleveland administration decided instead to separate Geronimo and other "bandits" from their families and house them separately at Fort Pickens.[17]

Like Fort Marion, Fort Pickens was ill-equipped to house prisoners. The smaller number of men initially sent there were at least more easily accommodated, but since the fort had not been occupied since the Civil War, it was falling into ruin. Weeds and saplings were growing out of the masonry itself, including a pine tree peeking out of the chimney.[18] The casemates were reported to be dilapidated as well, but two of them had been "made as comfortable as they were when occupied with troops" to house the Apaches, which was probably not excessively comfortable. They slept on bunks, which

Figure 16. Photograph of Geronimo, Naiche, and Mangas
at Fort Pickens, 1886. Courtesy Western History Collections,
University of Oklahoma Libraries, Rose 874.

at least had bed sacks and blankets filled monthly with fresh straw. In contrast to relatives at Fort Marion, they were adequately clothed. A photo from the time shows Geronimo, Naiche, and Mangas posing on cannons on the grounds outside their casemates dressed in new army fatigues. Geronimo had a penchant for shaping his own image for public consumption, and it was perhaps his idea for the men to pose with the cannons, which lent the composition both martial flare and a sense of irony. On the one hand, the Apache men's lack of arms and horses and the walls of the fort behind them suggest their surrender and confinement, as does a caption added to the photograph that notes "the bent forms of former stalwart warriors, docile by compulsion." A prominent cross around Geronimo's neck might draw notice from viewers—a trophy of war, or a symbol of the warrior's reform? Geronimo's and Mangas's painted faces and the group's casual poses atop U.S. armaments of war, meanwhile, ultimately stand out most, highlighting enduring resolve over subjugation.[19]

The greatest challenge described initially at both Fort Pickens and Fort Marion was inadequate food. The quantity of the ration supplied to the prisoners was a point of controversy. The first group of Apaches to arrive at Fort Marion had received the full army ration, which was hardly generous but at least adequate to support life. It consisted of pork, beef, flour, beans, hominy, coffee, sugar, soap, salt, and some tobacco for smoking. But only days after the main group of Apaches arrived from Arizona, the U.S. Army's Subsistence Department issued a new order that the rations be reduced by half, "because the prisoners were not required to do a soldier's work and therefore should not need a full ration." As others noted, even the full soldier's ration was probably inadequate given that soldiers supplemented it by buying food with their salaries, a luxury Native prisoners did not have, at least initially. That Apaches did not eat pork meant they viewed part of the meager ration they did receive as inedible. There was a lack of fruits and vegetables, which risked scurvy. Ultimately, it was up to sympathetic local citizens and army officers to swap pork rations for boxes of potatoes, onions, and other vegetables.[20] Apaches sought to make the most of whatever limited supplies they were given. Sam Kenoi remembered the prisoners being given a little bread and meat each day and some wood for cooking. Eugene Chihuahua remembered the women preferred cooking outside, rather than in the damp casemates. "It wasn't so bad," he recalled, "except when it rained; then it was terrible. We had not had much rain in Arizona, and when our blankets and clothes got wet our food did too."[21] At Fort Pickens, one younger man in each casemate was charged with doing the cooking for the rest, as was Apache custom when separated from their wives. Here too the lack of food also was a point of complaint. Geronimo pressed the issue soon after his arrival. Sympathetic commanders at both posts responded by working to increase the ration, complaining in monthly reports that "the rations should be larger."[22]

Despite paltry rations, and contrary to the claim of the Subsistence Department that Apaches did not work, the Apache men at Fort Pickens were expected to labor. In the spring of 1887, the post commander noted that the Indians worked six hours or so per day, clearing the fort of its weeds and trees. They had also been employed in scraping and painting the inside of the fort. Because a drought had caused the water cistern to get low, the Indian prisoners had dug a well in the vicinity of the fort.[23] In sum, just like Apache foes of the Spanish had helped to renovate that empire's defenses, so too did this generation of Apache combatants for the United States. Geronimo did not remember this fondly, recalling that "for nearly two years we were kept at hard labor in this place" and noting that they did not even see their families for much of the first year, a violation of the terms of their surrender. The post commander at Fort Pickens claimed, perhaps spuriously, that he did not expect the men to work too hard. He feared that since they had lived their lives in mountain regions, they would "break down in this lower country, if kept continuously at tasks expected of white men accustomed to labor in this region."[24]

Many Apaches did break down. James Kaywaykla reportedly said that he had seen hundreds of people killed in his life up to that point, but never had seen death like this: "A girl passed away, my people said, from heartbreak and loneliness. Men took her body away in a box—a terrible thing to us. Whether she was buried, we had no way of knowing. That to us was much worse than death caused by violence; and it was the first of many, many, that were to follow."[25] Like others, Kaywaykla explained the high mortality rate as being a result of the change in climate and separation from homeland. While Apaches had, of course, experienced death from illnesses before, including smallpox and malaria, close confinement on the journey and close quarters upon arrival probably contributed to the spread of contagious diseases like tuberculosis. The death rate from such illnesses was undoubtedly raised because immune systems had been weakened by inadequate nutrition and shelter. Cases of chronic diarrhea (dysentery), tuberculosis (pulmonary consumption), and malaria (remittent fever) mounted as the weeks passed, with about twenty deaths counted by the beginning of 1887, including those of five or six children.[26]

Despite incredible obstacles, Apaches nonetheless drew upon their limited power and significant creativity to assert a future for their community. For example, they conducted ceremonies they believed were imbued with curative power to respond to the widespread death and illness. John Bourke observed four Apache medicine men perform the Spirit Dance, or Cha-ja-la, during a three-day ceremony in Florida in 1887. One of the medicine men, Ramón, explained to Bourke that the Cha-ja-la was conducted "only upon the most solemn occasions, such as the setting out of a war party, the appearance of an epidemic, or something else of like portent." In this case it was undoubtedly a response to the rampant deaths they had been experiencing, including of twenty-three children in the past year.[27] Meager rations probably played a role in such deaths, and Apaches took matters into their own hands to seek to improve this situation, especially by earning money to purchase food by selling handmade crafts. As Eugene Chihuahua later recalled, "When we were free we could always rustle food. We never went hungry till we were put in forts or on reservations. So we began making things to sell—bows and arrows, lances, moccasins, and bead work. We made anything for which we could get materials."[28] In fact, Apaches had quickly learned about their surroundings and the consumer-oriented neighbors who flocked to see them. Even as white Americans talked of sending even adult men to school for a short time to "imbibe our methods of doing business and guarding property," this education does not appear to have been needed.[29]

Despite their status as prisoners of war, Apaches were granted significant freedom of movement within the fort grounds and to travel to town to sell their wares and make purchases. While there had initially been some concern about the potential for trouble, or escape, by allowing them to travel to town, the post commander, Loomis Langdon, noted that Apaches had proved "more afraid of the whites than the whites were of them." The sheer level of interest that whites had in Apaches disinclined some of the latter to leave the fort's protective walls. Whenever Apaches left the fort, they were "swarmed about by the curious and idle . . . disinclining them often to fresh air and exercise." Yet Apaches learned that they were bothered less if they traveled in groups and soon began traveling with an interpreter in groups of about fifteen. Echoing practices from life in the North American West, it was often women and girls who went to town most frequently, "to sell their handicrafts and buy food and incidentals," and also to meet locals.[30]

Apache entrepreneurship and local business interests proved complementary from the start. In a startling contrast to white settlers in the West, who had lobbied breathlessly for years for the elimination or removal of Apache Indians, Florida cities had lobbied to be chosen to receive them. Business elites and city officials in Jacksonville, Saint Augustine, and Pensacola believed that Apache Indians, if kept under proper guard, would be a big boost to local tourism.[31]

This effort proved prescient. At Saint Augustine, adjacent to Fort Marion, and Pensacola, adjacent to Fort Pickens, tourists flocked to see Apaches. However unsettling the gaze of white Americans, Apaches exploited the opportunity to make some money. Kaywaykla explained that of the many people who came to look at them, "some of them bought trinkets."[32] While he may have exaggerated, the Indian rights activist Herbert Welsh later noted that Apaches had gleaned "a tidy profit" from their business in Apache-made goods—perhaps as much as $10,000 during their seven months at Fort Marion, which would amount to about $200,000 today. Some prisoners had also earned extra money through wage labor, having been hired by local citizens to do odd jobs.[33]

Apache leaders exploited visitors in other ways as well. They spoke eagerly about their experiences and the broken promises of U.S. officials to anyone who would listen, helping their circumstances to reach the national stage. In January 1887, a local doctor who had visited Apaches at Fort Marion, Dr. Horace Caruthers, wrote to Herbert Welsh and the Indian Rights Association

(IRA) about the condition of the captives. Welsh had founded the IRA a few years earlier, one of a growing cadre of white social activist groups concerned with U.S. treatment of American Indians. Oriented toward acculturation, the IRA's stated objective was to "bring about the complete civilization of the Indians and their admission to citizenship." As Welsh began to investigate the situation, he was joined by the Women's National Indian Association, the Boston Indian Citizenship Committee, and even sympathetic voices from within the U.S. military, such as John Bourke. After visiting Florida in March 1887, Welsh and Bourke, with the assistance of Apache prisoners, prepared and released a damning report to the public highlighting the fact that all Southern Apaches, including those who had been aiding the U.S. in pursuit of Geronimo, had been treated the same. It described in detail the shortages of food, clothing, and housing. Typical of the period, it also warned of the "lack of productive activity" for the prisoners and the lamentable moral effects that would result.[34]

In the hopes of countering this report, the War Department made its own inquiry. Yet their secret investigation, led by Colonel Romeyn Ayres, ultimately confirmed many of Welsh's findings: "Most of the [male] prisoners had at one time or another been scouts working for the government, and almost 80 percent of the women and children were families of scouts." In reporting such findings to his superiors, Ayres stressed that "care [had] been taken . . . that they be not public."[35]

Following the publication of Welsh's report, correspondence from concerned citizens flooded into Congress, the War Department, and to the U.S. president himself. A letter to President Cleveland from Pittsfield, Massachusetts, with 189 signatures, for example, pointed out the shock with which citizens there had learned that "comparatively innocent people" were being housed as prisoners. By this time, the War Department had already decided to send the families of the men housed at Fort Pickens back to them and to transfer the other prisoners from Fort Marion to Mount Vernon Barracks, Alabama. The secretary of war, William Endicott, expressed his hope that "these measures should remove all cause of complaint against the government."[36]

Moving the majority of the prisoners to Mt. Vernon Barracks in April 1887 was designed to alleviate concerns about the healthfulness of Apaches' circumstances. The post was located about thirty miles north of the Mobile, a port city on the coast of the Gulf of Mexico. The post's buildings were built on a ridge, which Apaches and white Americans alike considered to be healthier at the time. The broader military reservation stretched across a bit more than two thousand acres of pine forests and hills watered by about sixty-five inches of annual rainfall. A few log cabins bordered the post, built by poor white and black families who worked at nearby sawmills or made money gathering turpentine, a tree resin collected and used in everything from solvents to medicinal elixirs.[37]

Far from proving a solution to Apache mortality, the move to Alabama may have actually worsened it. The genocidal threats that Apaches faced in exile are illustrated visually by a notebook in which one post commander tallied the births and deaths of prisoners. Scroll through its pages, and it is impossible to escape reading it as a countdown, as the total number of prisoners gradually declines. Near the end of Apaches' internment in Alabama, a report noted 170 births compared with 270 deaths during their time in the East. A particular problem at Mt. Vernon Barracks that helps to explain this was a water supply tainted by sewage runoff from the post. Despite awareness of the problem, U.S. officials did not improve the water supply until 1892, too late to save dozens of Apaches from death from dysentery.[38]

From the time of their arrival in Alabama, Apaches were expected to work, beginning with the clearing of the forest and construction of their own accommodations. They started work on the first "Indian village" at the barracks in September 1887, and by the end of February, they had erected sixty-two tiny log cabins. Each was composed of two ten-foot-square rooms connected by a breezeway. A stove provided heat, and for ventilation a small window in each room could be opened.[39] Kenoi and other Apaches would later compare the work in building the village to slavery. "My own mother died working like a slave," he wrote, adding his usual critique of Geronimo by noting that "the very man who caused us to be slaves, didn't do a lick of work." For U.S. officials, the comparison would have been laughable—not only had slavery been abolished, but they understood Apaches to be prisoners of war being maintained at significant expense, hardly as persons being exploited to produce wealth for anyone. Yet it is understandable that for some Apaches the comparison seemed apt. Carried away to a strange land that they had not chosen, they were put to work to build their own accommodations without remuneration, under the orders and subject to the whims of others. Apache understandings of slavery emphasized labor for others, being "commanded," being "worked till death," which certainly may have seemed an apt description of life at Mt. Vernon Barracks, especially in the time before they began to be paid wages for their work around the post in 1890. Whatever freedom of movement they were allowed, whatever savings they could accrue through selling crafts or labor around the post, the larger choices about their lives and futures remained out of their hands.[40]

Figure 17. Photograph of Apache women and children at Mt. Vernon Barracks, c. 1892. Courtesy of U.S. Army Heritage and Education Center.

A photograph of women and children sitting outside their cabins at a second village of larger cabins constructed by Apaches invites layered interpretations of Apache life at Mt. Vernon Barracks. At first glance, the scene suggests the continuation of life—a family gathering, a woman's smile. Yet gaze on it longer, with knowledge of the context, and more haunting elements emerge: the space between the houses, the village "streets," cleared by Apache hands. Ostensibly for ventilation, they also enabled surveillance, to ensure that prisoners could be inspected and controlled and their belongings taken and burned if deemed unsanitary by the post surgeon. The very construction of the cabins in a spaced line evokes another regional architectural tradition: the slave cabin, also constructed by its inhabitants, also constructed with surveillance and discipline in mind. The extreme inequality of power relations between Apache prisoners and the government agents overseeing them echoed elements of these and other enslaved people's experiences, even if there were clearly important differences: Apaches' collective exile with kin, their payment for work (at least after 1890).[41]

Apaches did not remember Alabama fondly. Eugene Chihuahua noted that they had thought nothing would be worse than Fort Marion and its rain and mosquitos, but in fact they had not "known what misery was" until they arrived at Mt. Vernon Barracks. "There was no place to climb to pray," he noted, and "if we wanted to see the sky we had to climb a tall pine."[42] When General George Crook visited them in early 1890, he described their poor morale and circumstances. He noted that they were especially concerned by the high mortality rate, which as he saw it, was owing to "home-sickness, change of climate, and the dreary monotony of empty lives."[43] Crook was not alone in stressing mental health as a significant concern for Apache people at this time. Sam Kenoi later described to the anthropologist Morris Opler his attitude as a young man during this time: "You know we were prisoners of war there. Us younger fellows had nothing to look forward to. We just thought 'Aw, what the hell.'"[44]

"Dreary monotony," rampant death, "nothing to look forward to"—such descriptions perhaps help to explain numerous incidents of drunken brawls, assaults, and murders that occurred during the time in Alabama as well. Men and women alike were reported "in and out of the guardhouse." Among at least two suicides was that of Fun, who killed himself "in a fit of jealous insanity, after shooting and slightly wounding his young wife." Geronimo remembered another man shooting his wife and then himself: "He fell dead, but the woman recovered and is still living.[45]

Kenoi highlighted the influence of Apaches' status as prisoners of war in explaining the "aw, what the hell" attitude that he remembered driving his own behavior. Yet the high death rate was in and of itself a key factor shaping Apache life. As post surgeon, Dr. Walter Reed noted in July 1889 that fatalities caused mental health troubles: "anxiety and alarm amongst the Indians." He added that "mental depression" stemmed from the fact that "the Government does not propose, in the near future, to improve their condition." In July 1890, a U.S. infantry officer at Mount Vernon reported to his superiors on Apaches' poor health and the fact they were "all greatly depressed." He concurred with Apaches and other observers that Alabama did not seem to be the place for them. He described their attitude: "We are all to die here and the sooner the better."[46]

This description unwittingly evoked a past imperial agent's description of Caribbean-bound Apaches' attitude as "die first, walk tomorrow." Yet in the face of the undeniable difficulties caused by death, depression, and moments of violence, most Apaches in the past, as in the present circumstances, in fact acted to continue life. They sought to survive the threat of genocide by maintaining connections with each other in order to persist as a community despite the challenges of displacement and U.S. misgovernance.[47]

In Alabama as they had in Florida, Apaches supplemented rations and meager provisions through crafts and wage labor. Apaches sold goods to tourists traveling the railroad through the nearby town of Mt. Vernon. And just as they had in Florida, they helped bring new tourists to the area. Within a few weeks of their arrival, multiple excursions to "see the famous Apaches" in Mount Vernon had been organized. Confederate veterans in the Alabama

State Artillery sponsored an outing reportedly attended by hundreds. A little more than a week later, black churches in Mobile sponsored an expedition, which filled nine rail cars to fundraise for that city's Colored Orphan's Home. Diverse visitors continued to come in the ensuing months and years.[48]

Apaches continued to hone their trade, adapting products to market demands. They diversified their catalogue of goods, which came to include not just bows, arrows, and pottery but also cloth dolls for children, moccasins, leather belts, handbags, and water jugs, among other reportedly "very handsome and ingenious Indian curiosities." They also realized that goods sold as "Geronimo made," gleaned a higher price. Some Apache craftsmen thus gave their wares to Geronimo to sell on their behalf, and "thus many bows and articles purchasers thought were made by Geronimo [were] distributed over the country."[49] Geronimo learned that he even his signature could sell for a dollar, and one tourist reported that "a walking stick with his name upon it, he considered worth an additional fifty cents."[50]

While Apaches were initially required to do significant unpaid work in building their own village, the post commander subsequently made the decision to employ Apache men as "civilian" labor and allow them to work for wages. His aim was to improve prisoner morale and provide a sense of purpose. In July 1890, the post commander, Lieutenant William Wotherspoon, began paying Indians to split shingles for roofs, tend a community garden, and perform other odd jobs around the post for thirty-five cents per day's work. He employed women as laundresses and housekeepers for officers, and encouraged men he was not able to employ to seek work as farmhands for local farmers. A February 1891 report noted that four Apache men working at a farm fifteen miles from the post had their families with them "and were prospering."[51]

In addition to wage labor as civilians, a number of Apache men were enlisted in the U.S. Army as part of an Indian company formed at the post in May 1891. Some of these new recruits had actually served as scouts in the army in the past, including on lengthy expeditions into Mexico to track Geronimo. Yet in this case, they saw no dangerous military action, but rather maintained their uniforms, conducted drills, and otherwise helped police their own kin on the post in exchange for modest monthly salaries. For his part, Geronimo was appointed "justice of the peace" to punish minor offenses by prisoners at a monthly salary of $10.[52]

Interactions with locals provided the potential for beneficial social relations but also for conflict. Apaches gambled, drank, and hunted with soldiers stationed at the post, some of whom they came to know well. They bartered with and sometimes spent time with the residents of the cabins that dotted the boundaries of the military reserve, including African Americans whom military officials derided in racist terms as "no account niggers." Concern about interactions between Apaches, soldiers, and area residents caused the post officials to seek to restrict contact, including by establishing segregated hospital facilities and forbidding white enlisted men from gambling with Indians.[53]

The mobility afforded to prisoners to cross reserve boundaries some-times prompted concern among white landowners in the vicinity, just as it had in the Southwest. As had been true for Apaches in Arizona, it seems it was merely their presence in a place a white person did not think they belonged that was enough to elicit outrage. When an Apache hunting party with a white officer chaperone killed a few hogs running loose in October 1892, an area landowner, Dan McLeod, wrote to the post commander in a rage. "I write to make complaint of the depredations of a lot of Indians," his letter began, protesting the supposedly "wanton killing" of area residents' livestock, especially large hogs and sheep. When asked to submit a specific explanation of his losses, McLeod demurred, and the officer who accompa-nied the hunting party noted that if a few hogs had been killed, "under no circumstances could the damage be so great as Mr. McLeod would have the public believe."[54]

As Apaches adapted to life as prisoners of war, they also sought to main-tain connections with kin from whom they were separated. They sought news, provided aid, and even disputed property and money, creating net-works for survival in diaspora. Southern Apaches had lost much, including unharvested crops, when they had been captured and shipped away from Arizona, yet this did not prevent them from asking about or seeking payment for property left behind. In the summer of 1887, U.S. officials auctioned 120 horses and mules that Southern Apaches had left behind, gleaning $2,599 for the community. These funds were transferred from the National Bank at Albuquerque to the branch at Mobile, Alabama, nearest to Mt. Vernon Barracks. Individual shares of these funds were determined through a claims process at the Apache village. They were assembled and asked to attest to the number and type of animals they had owned. The amounts they were owed were totaled from the average sale price of each type of animal. Echoing the broader paternalism of U.S. Indian policy, Apaches were not simply disbursed their entire share of the sale of their property but rather were given allowances of up to $5 per month to be drawn from their account. While hardly a very

large sum, the livestock sale provided additional means for Apaches to purchase food and other supplies, including materials for their crafts business.
The Mt. Vernon Barracks post commander at the time, William Sinclair, did
not explain what he did in cases of conflict over the ownership of livestock
auctioned in the sale, but subsequent correspondence regarding funds from
the sale does suggest that conflicts had occurred.[55]

Communications initiated between Apaches in Alabama, Florida, and in
Arizona about livestock also illustrate the ways in which Apaches managed
to creatively maintain social ties in diaspora. Apaches mobilized the assistance of military commanders, interpreters, and the U.S. mail and banking
systems to settle internal community matters and aid each other, even when
separated by hundreds of miles from kin at military barracks and forts in
Alabama and Florida. In February 1888, for example, before Fort Pickens
prisoners were reunited with the bulk of Southern Apaches at Mt. Vernon
Barracks, Sinclair wrote to his counterpart at Fort Pickens enclosing a check
for $6 for the prisoner Ramón. This was payment for money owed him by
two Indians at Mt. Vernon Barracks, Not-o-gan and Bay-Koth-kay. These
men had requested through the post interpreter that Sinclair aid them in
settling their debts. A month later, Kayetena requested that a check be sent
from Alabama to his mother, Yai-e-golcho, at Fort Pickens in the amount
of $10.56. This was apparently payment for one horse. Kayetena added that
$27.70 should be sent for a mule to Non-ke-gen and Tah-sha-en, his sis-
ters. In June of that year, Nochay came forward to admit that four horses he
had claimed actually belonged to his mother. He indicated that the funds,
$42.24, should be transferred to her. Even years after Southern Apaches had
been exiled from Arizona, lost property continued to be disposed of and
funds sent across the country. In August 1889, a letter arrived at Mt. Vernon
from Fort Apache, Arizona, with $50 for Chatto "for a horse left by him."
He had left the horse in the charge of an Indian named Cooley, who had
subsequently sold the horse and honored his promise to send the funds to
its rightful owner.[56]

In short order, Apaches had learned to share resources using the U.S. military bureaucracy, mail, and banking systems. It was not just correspondence
regarding funds that Apaches asked military officials or interpreters to help
them circulate; for example, a letter arrived at Mt. Vernon Barracks in March
1888 from a father requesting that his child be sent to him at Fort Pickens.
Sinclair inquired about the child and communicated back to the father that
the boy, about four years old, was "living with a grandmother and aunt, and

that neither of them wanted to send the boy or go themselves with the boy to Fort Pickens." Sinclair added as explanation that "these women know more about the care of a child of his age [than the father]." It is not clear whether this latter comment was a direct translation of the women's or Sinclair's opinion; either way, the matter was settled.[57]

Communications were not limited to those between exiled prisoners. In September 1887, a woman named O-Neelth asked the Indian agent at San Carlos, Arizona, to write Mt. Vernon Barracks on her behalf. She wanted news of her son, Hah-skin-Kay-dze, adding a drawing of his reservation brass tag, "San Carlos D," though she could not remember the number anymore. He had been exiled because he was married to a Southern Apache woman, and they had a boy eleven or twelve years old. "Please let me hear from him," the agent noted, because "his mother is very anxious." Later that month, Sinclair responded with news about the woman's son in Alabama, noting that he was in good health. His wife had given birth to a baby at St. Augustine who had died. Their boy, Cosine, was away at Carlisle Indian School.[58]

News also was exchanged between Alabama and New Mexico. In early 1889, discussions began about returning at least seventeen Mescalero Apaches housed at Mt. Vernon Barracks to their kin in New Mexico. As was true for some Western Apaches, they had been exiled due to intermarriage with Southern Apaches. Yet correspondence over the course of these negotiations also revealed the reverse—that some Southern Apache people remained in New Mexico due to ties with Mescaleros. October 1889 correspondence from the Mescalero agency enclosed photographs and a letter from a man to his brother at Mt. Vernon. The agent noted that he believed this family was a Chihene Apache family, "but their relatives are all on this reservation [in New Mexico]." He noted that they are "anxious . . . that their friends may be returned here to them." While some Mescalero Apaches did take advantage of U.S. officials' willingness to allow them to return to New Mexico, many chose to remain with their spouses' families in Alabama.[59]

While they might seem small matters—the circulation of a few words, the sending of a couple of photographs—these various types of communication would not have been possible to the same degree a hundred years earlier. Even as new technologies aided in U.S. efforts to exile hundreds of Apaches quickly from kin and homeland, they also facilitated Apache efforts to overcome the gulf of space and time and learn about and care for relatives. "Please be kind enough to return the enclosed pictures," the Mescalero agent wrote, adding that any news about the possibility of these people being returned to New Mexico would be anxiously awaited.[60]

Perhaps no other news was awaited more anxiously than news from children at boarding schools. Apaches may have been homesick for Arizona or
New Mexico, but they also longed for relatives separated from them after they
had arrived in the East. Recall the women and children separated from the
men bound to Fort Pickens and sent to Fort Marion instead. After their arrival
at Fort Marion, Apaches began fearing new forced removals, and rightly so.
As the post commander, Loomis Langdon, reported: "A separation is what
they constantly dread . . . even a present of clothing to their more than half-
naked children excites mistrust and makes them very restless, because, it looks
to them like preparing them for a journey, a separation from their parents."
Apaches had observed the forced removal of children from the San Carlos reservation in years past, but they may have also caught wind through the interpreters of ongoing discussions to remove their children to the Carlisle Indian
School or Hampton Institute. They were right to be worried, because dozens
of Apache children would be forcibly removed in the coming months.[61]

Parents eagerly sought any news they could of their children's condition
or the possibility of their return. Routine reports from Carlisle Indian School
provided basic news not only about illnesses and deaths but also about births,
because among those sent away were a number of married couples. Typical
was an October 1887 report sent to Mt. Vernon Barracks, which noted the
deaths of male pupils Anthony and Eric and the birth of a female child to
Hilda Kinzuna. The note explained that both mother and child were doing
well and that "the other Apache youth are in good shape." Such reports also
noted the imminent return of kin, such as when Lucy Tsisnah was set to
leave Pennsylvania for Alabama in May 1890 due to poor health after two
years away. In theory sent to school at Carlisle, she had in fact spent most
of her time laboring for families in Rising Run, Maryland, and Wellsville,
Pennsylvania.[62]

Yet it was not simply through the reports of school officials that Apaches
remained connected with their children. When visitors from the Massachusetts Indian Association came to Mt. Vernon Barracks to see Apaches, they
observed reports and student letters from Carlisle and Hampton "wrapped in
pieces of cloth they had embroidered." Most prisoners of war would not have
been able to read such correspondence themselves but would have needed
some of the few literate prisoners, or an interpreter, to read it to them. More
than anything, they were likely to view the letters as symbols of those from
whom they were being kept apart, cherished reminders of loved ones they
longed for. Such affection is evoked in the care with which they decorated
and protected the documents. The exchange went two ways. At Hampton,

teachers reported seeing letters from Apache mothers bearing news of recent events, including reports about their labor around camp. These were probably written with the help of the post interpreter or a sympathetic soldier.[63]

Such correspondence between Native students and their kin helps to explain why Apaches in Alabama sometimes knew about events at Carlisle before the post commanders did. In June 1888, for example, Sinclair wrote to Captain Richard Pratt at Carlisle to acknowledge receipt of a letter with photographs of children who had recently died at the school. He noted that Apaches at Mt. Vernon had no problem recognizing them but also asked about Helen (Yot-so-ya) and Judith (Kam-kah), whom they reported they knew had also died. Sinclair explained that since no information of this had reached him, he would appreciate it if Pratt could confirm the news. He asked in the future that Pratt be sure to inform him of any death "in order that I may notify the Indians of it." At least in some cases, Apaches learned of such news through kin and without the help of school wardens or military officers.[64]

Native use of the mail system is further revealed in a startling report from April 1889. The U.S. postmaster general wrote to the War Department to complain about a recent discovery made by one of his inspectors: Apaches at Mt. Vernon Barracks had been using the government's penalty envelope system to send correspondence to their children at Carlisle Indian School, apparently with the post commander's blessing. This system allowed government business to be conducted without paying postage, and the use of it for nongovernmental business was strictly prohibited. The inspector had forwarded an envelope as evidence of the "illegal use" he had discovered, which to his dismay he had found to contain "an Indian doll and a letter addressed to one of the Indian pupils at the school . . . signed 'Salmos' mother.'"[65]

Sinclair subsequently defended his actions, and the presence of an Indian doll in a penalty envelope, by noting that he had not initiated the practice. He had first received letters from children at Carlisle addressed to their parents in a penalty envelope sent by the school's director, Captain Richard Pratt. He had subsequently learned that post commanders in Florida at Fort Marion and Fort Pickens had similarly allowed Apaches to maintain correspondence with their relatives in this fashion. When the exchange of penalty envelopes had continued without complaint, he had assumed that this was a proper use of the system. He noted that Apaches had little money, and he wondered how they were therefore expected to send letters on their own. Ultimately, the secretary of war, Redfield Proctor, stepped into defend him and ensure that Apache to Apache correspondence could continue. In a striking explanation of his reasoning, he noted in a letter to the postmaster general that "it cannot be the intention of the government to cut off its Indian captives from all communication with their children and families, which will be the consequence if they may not use penalty envelopes."[66]

This episode reveals a degree of sympathy and humanity on the part of U.S. government agents. Military officers and the secretary of war himself lobbied on Apaches' behalf to ensure they could in the very least send letters and care packages to each other. Yet Proctor was wrong when he claimed that cutting off communication between Apaches ran counter to the intentions of the U.S. government. This was precisely the intent of the boarding-school system and also was a motivating factor in other, less sympathetic officials' actions. In fact, the removal of some youths from their relatives in Florida and later Alabama was specifically motivated by efforts to sever community ties or alter Apache traditions.[67]

Months earlier at Fort Pickens, Florida, for example, Apaches had begun to plan a womanhood ceremony for a girl known as Katie. The post commander, Langdon, had first delayed the event to be sure the local tourist industry could advertise it; they billed it as a Corn Dance, which was not an Apache tradition. In the meantime, he grew increasingly concerned about Katie "in the interests of morality." There was an older, already-married Apache man named Ahandia who had expressed interest in taking her as his second wife, and Katie's family had indicated that they did not oppose the marriage. Langdon had swung into action, lobbying to prevent the marriage and get her sent to Carlisle instead. After she arrived there in April 1888, she died within about year. Undoubtedly Langdon, if he thought of her at all, managed to find a way to rationalize his role in her untimely death.[68]

A later order to remove girls from Mt. Vernon Barracks to attend boarding school was similarly motivated by concerns about marriage—and reproduction. It was also influenced by the circulation of information within the Apache diaspora. In the spring of 1894, the latest commanding officer at the post, George Russell, received an order to select five girls from among the prisoners to be sent to Hampton Institute in Virginia. Their journey and costs of education would be paid by the Massachusetts Indian Association. Initially several girls and their families had indicated a willingness to go. Several of them changed their minds, however, after three young men returned from Carlisle Indian School and told them about their experiences away from home. Oswald Smith, Leonard Kenesaw, and Knox Nostlin had each spent nearly eight years at Carlisle and were now in their early to mid-twenties. They may have been discharged from Carlisle because of their age, but Russell theorized it was because all three men had syphilis, a disease they had contracted while at school under the guardianship of the United States.[69] Whatever the precise reasons for being sent home from Carlisle, the men apparently had nothing good to say about their time there. As the infantry-man in charge of policing prisoners explained to Russell on April 6: "Yester-day a girl who had asked to go to Hampton, Va., came to me and requested that she be not sent, urging among other reasons that these Carlisle boys had told her she would be worked to death there."[70]

When Russell raised the question to his superiors of whether the girls should be sent involuntarily, an action he was reluctant to take, he was advised that the consent of the parent should be secured "if possible." He was also authorized to select two mothers to go with the girls, see the school, and stay there as long as they liked. If consent could not be secured, however, the girls should be sent anyway.[71] One military official consulted in deciding on the matter, Aide-de-Camp W. W. Wotherspoon, suggested the possibility that perhaps the mothers could be paid $15 or $20 as payment for the girls to ease parental concerns, noting that as he understood it, it was Indian custom to sell girls as brides anyway.[72]

The insistence of U.S. officials to forcibly remove the girls reflected par-ticular concerns about the Apache population in Alabama. Noting that the birth rate had finally exceeded the death rate, owing in no small measure to Apache lobbying for better conditions and Apache labor to build a new, more healthful village, officers at Mt. Vernon, and their superiors in New York and Washington, feared that the continued presence of the girls would serve to increase the Apache population. Since the girls were around fifteen years old, they believed they would become pregnant at any moment if they were allowed to stay in Alabama around Apache men. As the infantryman in charge of them in Alabama noted, "If this opportunity is not seized these five girls will in a few months be breeding more 'prisoners of war.'" As he saw it, "from a practical point of view the interests of the War Department will be best served by preventing multiplication of prisoners." Ultimately all agreed that the interests of the U.S. government were in sending the girls away, even if it was against their will—even, apparently, if it meant purchasing the girls from their mothers.[73]

These particular episodes illustrate the limits of U.S. bureaucrats and mil-itary officers' concerns about the well-being of Apache prisoners under their charge and the genocidal intentions and consequences of the U.S. treatment of Apaches during this period. Some forwarded letters and funds between

Apaches at their request, others lobbied for improved rations and living conditions. Still other agents, and the bureaucracy as a whole, was equally if not more concerned about Apache persistence, about the possibility that Apaches might thrive and multiply rather than suffer and disappear. It is impossible to quantify how much the heat and humidity— "the change in the climate"— highlighted by Apaches and non-Apaches alike, contributed to prisoners' mortality. What is clear is that U.S. supervision and decision-making on Apaches' behalf was itself deadly.[74]

Sam Kenoi summarized child separation and its implications well in his account of this time in his life. He recalled going to a little school at the barracks in Alabama, where two missionary women taught the young Apache children. At first "many of them [had] hesitated to send their children fearing that if they attended the school they would be sent to Carlisle or some other place away from here."[75] Eventually, however, Apaches came to like this local school, and even Geronimo himself attended classes regularly.[76] Kenoi contrasted his experience with local schooling to the distant boarding schools. Perhaps referring to the girls sent away to prevent an increase in the prisoner population, he explained that he remembered a few of his classmates from the "little country school" being sent to Hampton, adding that "all of them are dead now." When Kenoi got older, he was also sent away, though to Carlisle. He described his sense of the place: "In '98 I went to Carlisle. I counted in the graveyard. I counted up to one hundred and five and then I got mixed up. Very few came back."[77]

Doubly Displaced

The mortality rate for all Native students at Carlisle was high, as exemplified by the cemetery that Sam Kenoi toured that haunted his memory, but many Apaches, including Kenoi himself, did survive their time at school. For Apache youths who came of age during the Apache diaspora in Florida and Alabama, separation from kin and the experiences of boarding-school education were key life experiences. Apaches who survived and later spoke of their time away highlighted discipline, forced acculturation, and exploitation as characteristic of their time in Pennsylvania. Twice displaced, from Arizona to Florida and then from their families, these children and young adults nonetheless drew upon friendships with other students and sympathetic employees and local residents to survive their forced removal. Most important, they nearly all eventually returned to their families, bringing back with them the skills and knowledge, including of U.S. mismanagement and mistreatments, that they had gleaned while away.[78]

The first Southern Apaches to attend boarding schools had been sent from Arizona before removal to Florida. Chatto and other Apaches who traveled to Washington, D.C., in the summer of 1886 had stopped to visit these youths at Carlisle on their return trip, the trip that was ultimately rerouted to Florida. After Southern Apache prisoners arrived at Fort Marion, Richard Pratt—the founder of the school—and other interested officials began lobbying for the shipment of all "eligible" children to boarding schools. To be eligible, a child needed to be healthy and age twelve or older. In fact, "children" of nearly thirty years of age, including married couples, were sent to Carlisle, in part because of officials' ignorance of their age, in part because it was believed an industrial education would benefit adults as much as children, and in part simply because of government interest in reducing the number of prisoners they were administering at military installations in Florida and, later, Alabama. White-run Indian benevolent associations were often willing to pay tuition for students, thus relieving a perceived burden on the part of the government in feeding and clothing them.[79]

It was only about a month after the bulk of Apache prisoners of war had arrived at Fort Marion, Florida, that the shipment of youths to distant boarding schools began. The question of whether children could be taken against their parents' wishes was later raised for discussion, and as we have seen, at least one post commander in Alabama expressed discomfort with the prospect. Yet three mass shipments of 106 Apache children and young adults from Florida in November and December 1886 and April 1887 were unquestionably forced removals. The first relied on surprise. Apache children playing on the parade ground of Fort Marion were surrounded by soldiers and whisked off to a departing train. Soldiers returned for any youths missed in the first surprise roundup, holding onto them against their kicks and screams and their parents' protests. Lt. Scott Mills, an infantryman in charge of prisoner security at Fort Marion, complained that "there is no way of telling the age of the children" and noted that he had relied upon the interpreter Sam Bowman's opinion. It was perhaps for this reason that "children" nearing thirty were sent away.[80]

Jason Betzinez was sent to Carlisle in the third shipment in April 1887. He recalled the moment in his autobiography years later: "I well remember that when Captain Pratt came to me he stopped, looked me up and down, and smiled. Then he seized my hand, held it up to show that I volunteered. I only scowled; I didn't want to go at all. I was twenty-seven, too old to be at school, didn't know a word of English. This made no difference to Captain Pratt. He must have seen something in my face, sensed some future possibility in me, that I didn't know was there. At any rate this turned out to be one of the biggest events in my life."[81]

During the mass roundups of late 1886 and early 1887, young captives' journeys to school included their first long-distance ocean voyage. After traveling via railcar to Fernandina Beach, a port town near the border with Georgia, they traveled via steamship. Betzinez remembered that his journey included a stop at Charleston, South Carolina, where they docked for a day and Captain Pratt took them into town. Pratt had journeyed to Florida to retrieve the students personally. After watching a parade and spending the night, they disembarked on another steamer destined for New York. Betzinez recalled the rough sea during this longer part of the voyage and many of his companions getting sick. To escape the sound of his companions "crying in their cabins," Betzinez spent time on deck in the fresh air. He remembered feeling like he had to be strong and not exhibit any weakness, since he was a "grown man," one of the oldest to make the journey to Carlisle. After arriving in New York, they traveled across Manhattan at night in horse-drawn cabs and then were ferried across the Hudson to Jersey City to embark in railcars bound through Philadelphia to the school at Carlisle. The trip had taken about a week from Saint Augustine.[82]

They arrived midday at the station next to the Carlisle Barracks, an army installation dating to the mid-1700s that Pratt had received permission to convert into the Carlisle Indian Industrial School a few years prior. Met by a group of faculty and students, the Apache youths were assembled on the steps for photographs before being separated by gender and led to their dormitories. Betzinez recalled the boys' quarters in the old cavalry stables, where they received a bath and a haircut and then were herded to the school tailor shop to receive army-style blue school uniforms. The group would later be photographed again to generate propaganda—the famous "before and after" photographs—used by the U.S. government to document the supposed "civilizing influence" of the school.[83]

The symbolic rituals Betzinez lived through were designed to initiate Indian children into boarding-school life and also to demonstrate the efficacy of Pratt's model to outsider observers. They also were intended to make Native children legible to teachers and school officials. The renaming of Native children is particularly illustrative of the latter. In Apache tradition, it was not unusual for individuals to have multiple names—those by which they were known by outsiders and names by which they were known within the community. Such names also might change over time, based on life events or demonstrated skills. As Betzinez recalled, his childhood name had been Nahdelthy, meaning "going-to-run." After Southern Apaches were forced to the reservation at San Carlos, Arizona, his mother had changed his name to Bastinas, after an elder at San Carlos who had befriend her. At Carlisle, a teacher named Miss Low had revised this name further. She mistakenly thought the name was of Spanish origin and devised the English spelling "Betzinez" to aid her in its pronunciation. Following Carlisle norms, this teacher then gave him a new first name: Jason. This choice reflected her love of the story from Greek mythology of a hero named Jason who is sent on a quest for a golden fleece in order to claim his inheritance and ascend to the throne to rule his people. Like other youths, this new first name meant nothing to Betzinez at first, though he later came to believe that his own life paralleled that of the fable.[84]

Many Apaches received surnames during their time at boarding school that reflected important family figures—Geronimo, Chihuahua, Naiche—but others chose surnames for themselves based on their likes and experiences at school. Sam Kenoi did not recall ever having had an Apache name, hypothesizing that his first name had perhaps come from a soldier on the Arizona reservation where he had grown up. He did know how he had acquired his last name. One of his friends, Jim Miller, had known a soldier named Corporal Keno and had started calling Sam by that name. Later, at boarding school, Sam had become friends with a Pima (Akimel O'odham) boy whose name was Thomas Kenoi. He had suggested that Sam add an *i* to his name so they could have the same name, and since "he was a good friend of mine, a very good friend," Sam had agreed and went by that name at Carlisle and in the years to come. The role of an intertribal friendship in shaping Sam's name hinted at a key influence of boarding schools noted by this and subsequent generations of Native students: the creation of intertribal ties and the sense of a degree of commonality as American Indians, even given cultural diversity.[85]

These experiences of Apaches students at Carlisle were the latest iteration in a longer history of imperial efforts to transform supposedly "wild" Indians into something else. Apache children taken captive in war had similarly been reclothed, renamed, and "educated" by the United States' Hispanic predecessors in the North American West, Mexico, and the Caribbean. In those moments, as in this one, Apache children were also able to shape imperial efforts in idiosyncratic ways, including by selecting names that had some meaning to them or pressing for work or training in fields that actually interested them.[86]

The large institutional setting of Carlisle was distinct to this particular time and place, as was the emphasis on "industrial" education. Modeled after a military routine, with its highly structured schedule, the intent was to discipline children into compliance and productivity, a key skill for factory work or other manual labor that white Americans believed was the only fitting work for Indians and other nonwhite peoples in the country. Later in life, Betzinez still recalled the regimented daily life at school: "Our rising bell in the morning was at six o'clock, breakfast at six-thirty, cleaning up our quarters and other work at eight, school at nine." He recalled the strict rules against "speaking Indian," tobacco use, and profanity. He recalled the struggle of learning English but also the kindness shown to him by at least one teacher who provided encouragement.[87] Like other Native youths, Betzinez learned a trade. He had been most interested in carpentry but had been told by the school disciplinarian, a Chippewa man named W. P. Campbell, that he should learn blacksmithing instead. While disappointed at first, he later remembered with pride his skill, including an award for his welding of steel carriage axles. He noted that one axle he had welded was even sent to the Chicago World's Fair and, at least in Betzinez's recollection, "purchased by a missionary from South Africa who took it back to that country with him."[88]

The amount of time that Native pupils at Carlisle actually spent in traditional instruction was limited, and not just because of the emphasis on industrial skills. Through the so-called outing system, some girls spent months at a time as domestic workers for Philadelphia families. Boys, meanwhile, worked at area farms. While this was supposed to be summer work, some spent virtually all their time while "at Carlisle" actually working on farms in New Jersey and eastern Pennsylvania. Richard Pratt had originally viewed the outing system as key to the assimilative mission of the school. By staying with white families and attending local white public schools, Native youths would learn English and white cultural mores quickly.[89] In practice, however, some Apaches who experienced the outing system questioned its educational value. Kenoi noted that many of his peers who had gone to Carlisle could still not even read and write and that they explained it was because "they didn't have much schooling, that they were out in the country most of the time." Betzinez agreed with them. In describing his own summer work for a Pennsylvania Quaker farmer named Mr. Cooper, he noted that he valued what he learned but that this time spent farming "retarded his education." It was also potentially dangerous work. Betzinez was sent back to Carlisle after he got his hand caught in the gears of Mr. Cooper's corn-shelling machine.[90]

In theory, the outing system was carefully regulated. Homes for families that applied to receive Native youths were inspected, and expectations for salaries and room and board were spelled out in advance. In practice, however, experiences varied substantially from assignment to assignment. Sam Kenoi lived these disparities firsthand after he was sent to Carlisle. While school records indicated he matriculated at the school in September 1899, he did not remember having attended classes. There was not room at the school for the "Indians coming in from all parts of the states," he explained, and so they "began shipping some of the students out into the country to work." He was one of them, and his first country "father" in Bucks County, Pennsylvania, was a man named Charlie Henson. Henson had a big tobacco field and farmed corn, oats, onions, and other vegetables. Kenoi remembered milking cows, feeding horses, cleaning out stalls. He would then get on one of the horses he cared for and go to the local public school. Kenoi worked on the farm in exchange for schooling, room, and board. While in theory he was paid nine dollars per month for his labor, he recalled getting a dollar a week to spend. He assumed that the other five dollars was sent back to Carlisle.[91]

If Kenoi spent much of his time away from Carlisle itself, this did not mean he had no connection to the school or other students. One connection he described was the Carlisle newspaper that he received every week, which published updates on students as well as poetry, letters, advertisement, and editorials. "First they called it the Indian Helper," he remembered, noting that "sometimes I saw my report in there." Presumably he also saw the reports of other Native students, including his Apache relatives. One wonders what they made of the invitation to subscribe, which was clearly not intended for them. "THE INDIAN HELPER is PRINTED by Indian boys, but EDITED by the Man-on-the-band-stand who is NOT an Indian," it read. This was but one hint of the racial views that would shape Kenoi and other Apaches' experiences in Pennsylvania.[92]

The outing system shaped other aspects of Native life in Pennsylvania as well. Students housed at Carlisle itself, for example, spent most of their time around other Natives, including members of their own community. Such experiences educated Apaches about other Native groups' experiences and even contributed over time to a sense of shared interests across tribes and the rise of intertribal activism and organizations. Such historical influences were clearly unintended consequences of a U.S. Indian education system designed to forcibly assimilate Natives—"to kill the Indian and save the man," as Pratt famously noted.[93]

Kenoi, like others who spent their time "outing," received a different education. Pratt had envisioned that outing would promote Native students' knowledge of white society and build their affinities for it. Yet Natives also learned that many whites were troubled by their potential inclusion in that society. Kenoi learned firsthand about the racialized landscape of rural Pennsylvania and the logics of white supremacy that undergirded it. At the white country school he attended, he remembered frequent fights. The roots of this violence went beyond schoolyard quarrels and extended beyond the schoolhouse itself. As he remembered, the white boys at neighboring farms did not like to see any Indian out and about and sought to restrict their mobility. This is how Kenoi learned the concept of "white boy country": "The white boys never let the Indian go anywhere in that country. If I went to see another Indian boy six miles away, I had to go through white boy country and they would take after me and fight."[94]

Kenoi had to remain vigilant in asserting his wishes to be educated and travel and to maintain friendships with Natives and visit other displaced Apache relatives. "I wore a sling . . . as a belt," he noted, adding that he "carried two or three rocks in my pocket all the time." Years later he still remembered a time that white boys had come after him and thrown rocks at him when he had gone to see an Oneida friend he had met. He undoubtedly had this sling with him when he visited an Apache boy who had been sent to the Philadelphia Home Education School because he had been deemed "too small" to be sent to Carlisle or Hampton, and on other trips to neighboring farms where other Apache students lived with their "country" families.[95]

While Kenoi remembered his first placement fondly, his experience on his second assignment in September 1900 highlights how contingent Native youths' experiences could be based on whom they happened to be placed with. His second country master, Newt Ely, was abusive: kicking him, forcing him to sleep in an attic, working him long hours. After a particular cruel day of hard labor and beatings in October, Kenoi decided he had to make a change: "I went upstairs to the attic and dragged my trunk down. Bang, bang, bang, it came down the stairs. I told him, 'I'm going to leave.' I made him give me money. He gave me twelve dollars. I told him, 'I'm going to Trenton.'"[96] In fact, he went back to near Tullytown, the area of Bucks County where he had lived and worked before. He met up with a man whom he knew, George Peak, because he had hired other Apache boys. Kenoi's familiarity with Peak suggests that he probably had met him by visiting when other Apaches had lived with him and perhaps had also maintained a correspondence. This certainly would not have been surprising given that he noted visiting other Native friends and relatives, and given the broader evidence of correspondence maintained between Apaches during this period. He remembered feeling good that "he had pictures of [Apaches] Charlie Icti and Duncan" in his house and that he was paid well, ultimately feeling like family. "I never had better folks to stay with," he wrote, "The only thing I had to do was milk the cows and drive the [daughters]," and he managed to save around $35 by the spring, when he finally requested to go back to Carlisle since he felt like he had already spent enough of his time in the country. He remembered being asked when he got to the school to start classes what grade he was in. "I told them third grade," he recalled. He was around twenty-five years old.[97]

The end of Betzinez and Kenoi's schooling in the East reflects the range of possibilities for Native youths there. Betzinez, for example, spent more time than Kenoi at Carlisle itself. In addition to more formal classroom instruction, he had also learned construction skills, including carpentry and plumbing, because students assisted in constructing and maintaining the school buildings. Yet in 1897, after more than nine years attending Carlisle, he had not progressed beyond the eighth grade, even though he was well over thirty years old. He decided it was time he "began my life work." He was conflicted, though, because he had "established deep roots in the school at Carlisle, so that it was a real wrench to leave it." Betzinez remembered feeling deeply attached to Pennsylvania more generally and initially decided to stay there when he left Carlisle in 1897. He first went to work at a Pennsylvania steel company, exactly the kind of labor that the U.S. Indian education system envisioned for Native students. He remembered the other workers at the plant: "Many foreigners as well as native-born Americans worked in the Steelton plant." He ultimately longed to return to his people, however, and decided to leave factory work to reunite with them.[98]

Kenoi also remembered the draw of kin in his decision to leave Pennsylvania. In comparison to some, his time at boarding school involved little instruction at Carlisle and a mixed experience with white families, in which he received kindness and affection but also an education on white supremacy and exploitation. He later remembered his life in Pennsylvania as part of a broader pattern of mistreatment that he had endured since the U.S. took him prisoner as an eleven-year-old boy. Shortly after he returned to Carlisle to start classes for the first time, a letter from his aunt informing him of the death of his sister pushed him to leave the school behind for good. He took his savings from farm labor and a suitcase with all his belongings and walked to Hagerstown, Maryland, in the middle of the night. He paid rail fare to Williamsport, West Virginia, before catching a freight car and falling asleep. This began a long odyssey traveling west on the railroad in which he passed as Japanese to avoid being recognized as an Indian-school runaway. After a weeks-long adventure, he finally arrived at his father's farm in an Apache village at Fort Sill, Oklahoma.[99]

Another New Beginning

In the years since the first children had been shipped away from their families to boarding school, Southern Apaches had faced yet another forced migration at the hand of the U.S. government. While Indian rights activists, military allies, and Natives themselves had pushed for an alternative home for Apaches, as prisoners of war Apaches ultimately had no final say over the selected destination. White Americans advanced two possibilities, among many others: reservations in New Mexico, Arizona, or Oklahoma and even a scheme to obtain land for Apaches from the Cherokee in North Carolina. Yet such efforts were thwarted for years by political opposition, particularly against any proposal to move Apaches anywhere near their Southwestern homelands.[100]

Apaches said clearly to anyone who would listen that they wanted to move somewhere else, pleading with allies to find them some new home. This effort reached a fevered pitch during the summer of 1894. General Howard, who had negotiated the peace with Cochise that had led to the creation of the Chiricahua reservation, advocated sending them to back to the West: "It appears to me that the time has come for a transfer of all these Indians, not soldiers, from the status of prisoners of war to that of other Indians, not citizens, to be cared for by the Interior Department. In spite of the prejudice of Western citizens, these Indians can be sent, certainly in small parties, to different western reservations, or given land in severalty like other Indians."[101] Although Howard was correct in noting the prejudice of Western citizens, and that Apaches nonetheless could be sent to a reservation there, his suggestion of breaking Apaches up in small groups to distinct reservations reflected the same naivety of Apache affairs evident in his well-meaning but misguided negotiations with Southern Apaches twenty years earlier. His emphasis on returning Apaches to the status "of other Indians, not citizens" likewise indicated that he was hardly at the vanguard of Indian civil rights activism.[102]

General Nelson Miles, who had helped orchestrate the removal of Apaches to Florida in the first place, also decided to help pressure the War Department to find them a new home. He sent another old military acquaintance of Apaches, Captain M. P. Maus, to visit Alabama in August 1894 and discuss their situation. There was no disagreement among the Apache leaders with whom he spoke: "Young men, old men, women and children all want to get away from here—It is too hot and wet—too many of us die here." They emphasized the climate and mortality rate as a reason to be taken elsewhere. As Naiche put it, "It would be good if you could give us some good country." Geronimo felt similarly, defining more specifically that "good country" to him meant having "a farm, cattle, and cool water." For his part, Chihuahua emphasized his hope that all Apaches could be reunited, including those children who had been sent off to boarding school. He explained that wherever Apaches were sent, "I want to have all our children together where I can see them." Chatto simply wanted any decision to be made quickly: "If anything I could say would hurry up the farms I wish it would. . . . I want to hurry—I want you to tell General Miles to get them away from here in a hurry."[103]

Yet it was ultimately not up to the War Department alone to decide Apaches' fates, particularly given that military officials believed Fort Sill in the Oklahoma Territory to be the best destination. Given federal jurisdiction, the move seemed like it should be straightforward: land was available, there was a military presence for security, and the climate was believed more favorable. The Comanche, whose lands the fort was built on, had even consented to allow Apaches to be housed there. Yet there was a law on the books that prevented Apaches from being relocated to Indian Territory (now Oklahoma), an inconvenient artifact of past political machinations regarding the sites of Apache reservations in the 1870s and local opposition to sending them there then. Amid failed efforts to get this law amended, concern about Apache mortality and the imprisonment of scouts who had served the U.S. government had only grown.[104] As Congressman Joseph Outhwaite of Ohio noted amid debate in late July 1894: "We are keeping in prison . . . over 200 people because of the offenses committed by their fathers. We are keeping them also at a very great and unnecessary expense. It's time they be given an opportunity like human beings to make their own way and to establish themselves in life."[105]

Ultimately, Congress agreed to amend the Army Appropriations Act in August 1894 to allow Apaches to be transferred to any federal military installation, but it did not do so without first putting on a rhetorical circus. While many members of Congress supported Apaches being moved somewhere, most did not want them transported into their own jurisdictions. There were typical claims that Apaches were "bloody-thirsty" and "cunning" and that they would surely escape and return to Arizona, which the delegate from that territory supported by claiming inaccurately that they had "gone from Fort Sill to those [Arizona] mountains time and again." Most vehement in his opposition was the delegate from the Oklahoma Territory, Dennis Flynn. He opposed the relocation of people he termed "murderous Indians" in part by claiming that the rationale for moving them was that they were "marauding in the State of Alabama." As he saw it, "if they are marauders when confined in prison, what are they going to be when you turn them out among my settlers, scattered on tracts of a hundred and sixty acres of land?" While one Alabama rancher had in fact complained of Apache depredations after a few hogs were shot by a hunting party near his land, "marauding" was quite the stretch, and when Congressman Outhwaite challenged him on his evidence, Flynn could only muster that it was a "state secret." Delegate Smith of Arizona suggested alternative locations that drew upon long-standing critiques of government spending and "eastern" humanitarianism: "They can be kept more cheaply, every one of them, at the Fifth Avenue Hotel in New York than you will ever keep them if they get back to the military reservation," he claimed. He offered a little farm in Boston as another option, given how much "that philanthropic community loves the Indians."[106]

Accustomed to bureaucratic delays and political whims, Southern Apaches in Alabama continued living their lives, unsure when any final decision about their fates would be made. Years earlier, Britton Davis had described their attitude as "watchful waiting," and this was a key element of their status as prisoners. They were not in a literal prison, in the sense that some U.S. congressmen and senators seemed to believe, but they were not free to make basic decisions about their futures: Where should we live? How should our children be educated? How will we feed our families? Kenoi expressed this lack of self-determination in highlighting that yet another consequential decision was made for Apaches, even if some minimal efforts had been made at consultation. "All at once they said they were going to remove us to Fort Sill," he recalled. "The Indians didn't have any say about it."[107]

In early October 1894, 296 Apache prisoners embarked from Mobile, Alabama, on a special train that traveled through New Orleans and Fort Worth on its way to Oklahoma. As had been true six years earlier, crowds gathered to see their latest move. Some observers complained that an old "murderer" like Geronimo should not receive such attention, claiming that "the old devil should have been hung fifteen years ago." When they arrived at Rush Springs station in the Oklahoma Territory, wagons took them on a thirty-mile journey to the Fort Sill post. They had boxed up their possessions in trunks and boxes, along with any portable equipment from camp at Mt. Vernon Barracks, but most of it had burned in a freight shed in New Orleans that had caught fire during their stop there. Apaches were thus forced to start over again, without dogs, horses, or mules.[108]

At the station they were met by hundreds of Comanches and Kiowas. After some failed efforts at signed communication, both groups produced youths who had attended Carlisle to talk and exchange greetings in English. It was perhaps from them that they learned that there was a grove of mesquite trees about forty-five miles away. Since mesquite beans were a favorite Apache food, it did not take long for them to request permission to make a weekend journey to gather about three hundred bushels of the beans, which they hauled back to their new camp. While in Alabama, Apaches had twice built their own log cabins, but with winter on the horizon, they decided it was too late to build frame houses. Instead, drawing upon memory, they gathered brush from a nearby creek and put up wickiups, which they covered in army canvas since they did not have any animal hides.[109]

New and old, strange and familiar, mingled and merged in the latest site of the Apache diaspora: wickiups roofed in army canvas dotting a military post on the South Plains, weekends of mesquite-bean gathering, and English chats with friendly Comanche neighbors. This site would be the first home that a new generation of Apaches born in the diaspora remembered. Dan Nicholas, for example, was born in Alabama the year Apaches were sent to Oklahoma. He did not remember Alabama but heard stories about it from his family—about the trees, the heat, the deaths. Like other kids of his generation, he grew up in the Apache village at Fort Sill, which was organized by local groups and their leaders much as they would have been in the old days in Apache homelands in the Southwest. Nicholas remembered spending time at his grandmother's house while his father and other men were away on labor details doing odd jobs around Fort Sill. He remembered afternoons splashing with friends in the local creek. One time when he got sick, his family had a medicine man perform a ceremony for him. The medicine man laughed when Nicholas complained aloud that the singing sounded too sad.[110]

This generation of children was exposed from a young age to other cultures and their ways of doing things; for example, they spent many Sundays at Comanche dances, where they played baseball and pole-and-hoop games and, when they got older, started eyeing Comanche girls. Nicholas and others remembered feeling pulled between Christianity and traditional Apache beliefs. He remembered being pressured to choose between them, even though he himself believed in elements of both. In 1901, the Comanche-Kiowa reservation was allotted, and "surplus" sections of it were opened up to white homesteading by lottery. Nicholas was too young to remember this, but others recalled how "multitudes of people of every description rushed upon us in the Fort Sill area." From a young age, Apache youths encountered white and black homesteaders and soldiers, other Indians, and soldiers alike.[111]

Nicholas's father encouraged him to take education seriously, to learn how to live in a white-dominated world. When he was young, he attended the local school, which was run by the Dutch Reformed Church, and there he first started to learn English and remembered having to memorize Lincoln's Gettysburg Address. Like other Native youths in the area, he later went to Chilocco boarding school in northern Oklahoma, before spending time at Haskell Indian Institute in Kansas. He remembered playing sports and being forbidden to speak Apache. When he was away at school, his grandmother died, and years later he still felt bitter that he was not allowed to go home for the funeral.[112]

While Nicholas was away at school he missed another important event. In the spring of 1913, Southern Apaches were finally released from prisoner-of-war status. The War Department had decided to expand its use of Fort Sill for military training and testing and thus needed to remove the Apache village from its grounds. After years of lobbying by Apaches and their allies, including multiple diplomatic delegations to Washington, D.C., self-interest had finally sparked the U.S. government to act. While welcome news to Apaches, this latest imperial decision did not ultimately spell the end of the Apache diaspora but instead further divided Apaches as they weighed decisions about where to live and how to build a secure future for their families going forward.[113]

*   *   *

In the late nineteenth and early twentieth centuries, the United States orchestrated the forced diaspora of nearly five hundred Southern Apache people as a means of quelling American and Mexican complaints of continued Apache mobility in the North American West. Much as their Spanish imperial predecessors had a century before, U.S. officials contrasted the supposed "humanity" of this policy with the alternatives: genocidal wars and mass hangings. Yet in practice, genocide proved central to the U.S. management of Apache prisoners of war, as indicated by the poor conditions and high mortality rate wherever they were housed and by the separation of youths from their kin with the stated aim of preventing community reproduction.

Yet Southern Apaches survived through creative strategies of adaptation to life as a diasporic community. The very technologies that the United States relied upon to facilitate forced migration, such as the railroad, also enabled Apache communication and travel. Apaches exchanged news, sent letters of encouragement, shared monetary resources, and appealed to allies to help them find a new home or return to their Southwestern homelands. Such efforts ultimately proved successful, though the influences of this period of existential struggle in diaspora would linger in the decades to come.

Strange Places Contrary
to Their Natural Homelands

On a July morning in 1982, thirty-eight men, women, and children departed the Mescalero Apache reservation in southeastern New Mexico to connect with their people's diasporic past. They left in vans at 6:30 a.m. on July 14 in order to arrive in San Antonio by nightfall. After strolling the city's River Walk and touring the Alamo, they departed for New Orleans, where the next day they went for a boat ride on the Mississippi and explored the French Quarter before settling in at the Holiday Inn. The trip took a more solemn turn in the days that followed, when they traveled to Alabama, Florida, and Oklahoma and visited sites where the United States had housed their ancestors as prisoners of war for the twenty-seven years between 1886 and 1913.[1]

The organizers of the trip described two key goals for it. First, they hoped that traveling to important places in their people's past would further a feeling of connection with their history. After all, some of them had grown up hearing about their ancestors having once lived "in a strange place contrary to their natural homelands." They looked forward to the opportunity to see such sites firsthand. Second, they intended to "honor their Chiricahua ancestors by visiting those locations where they are buried," especially by performing dances at each site that were intended to restore balance in the world and promote healing. The dancers themselves reflected the promise of a future generation carrying on Apache traditions and history, given that they included ten-year-old Abraham Chee and eighteen-year-old Clifford Chee, Jr., among other young people.[2]

The return trip took the group through Atlanta and Nashville, where they toured Opryland, before driving on to Lawton, Oklahoma. There they visited with Fort Sill Apaches, those who had stayed in Oklahoma after the government released them from prisoner-of-war status rather than join

Mescaleros on their reservation in New Mexico. When their bus exited I-40 and turned back toward the Mescalero reservation late in July 1982, the descendants of Southern Apache prisoners of war on board reflected on their trip and the histories it had evoked. Narcissus Gayton, a descendant of Victorio whose father was born in Alabama, remembered hearing about "these different places where they were imprisoned since we were children," adding that "some of these places, especially Saint Augustine, put a lump in your throat." They also looked to the future. "As descendants of courageous Apaches," the organizing committee later noted in a pamphlet memorializing the trip, "their strength and ideals may be a source of current strength." They hoped that young people on the trip had come to see their ancestors as "real people who had mortal faults and idiosyncrasies, but also had tremendous vitality and capabilities."[3]

Similar trips to important places in Apache history took place in the coming years. In September 1986, Apaches at Mescalero and Fort Sill joined with the Arizona Historical Society and the National Park Service to commemorate the centennial of Geronimo's surrender. After dances and speeches at Fort Bowie, including a proclamation from the governor of Arizona welcoming them back to the state, a group traveled to Skeleton Canyon in the Peloncillo Mountains, the site where Geronimo made his final surrender to General Nelson Miles. Two years later, a group of thirty-six Apaches retraced the route that Apaches fleeing the San Carlos reservation in the early 1880s had taken into the Sierra Madres of northern Mexico. They were accompanied by six historians and guides, who located key historical Apache camps in Mexico in part with the help of C. S. Fly's 1886 photography. Participants reported finding meaning and hope in viewing these sites, in seeing the places their ancestors had made home. Ruey Darrow, a descendant of Mangas Coloradas and a University of Oklahoma graduate, was on the trip and reported "a nostalgic feeling." She explained that she had grown up looking at pictures, but it was something else "walking through the camp, feeling the trees, savoring the quietness. A part of me had come home."[4]

The very fact that Apache people could make such journeys, including conducting traditional dances at sites in which their ancestors had been interned, is noteworthy. For centuries, Apaches had faced captivity and forced transport all across North America into lives of bondage. Depending on the time and place, settler-colonists and their governments had contended that Apaches would be transformed into Christian farmers living alongside Spanish settlements, that their culture would be killed even if their people continued to live, or alternatively, that they would vanish "away beyond the sun" or be "colonized in a bone yard." Southern Apaches traveling freely as citizens of the United States, and also as citizens of federally recognized Apache nations, would have been unthinkable to most non-Native observers a century earlier.[5]

These pilgrimages to sites of the Apache diaspora illustrate important changes in the relationship between Apaches, empires, and nations—but also continuities. Through the twentieth century and beyond, many Apaches continued to be separated from ancestral homelands now occupied by U.S. or Mexican settler-colonists and their descendants. Knowledge of the far-flung places their ancestors had lived historically also continued to inform people's ideas of what it meant to be Apache in the present: the "strength and ideals" of kin who had persevered in difficult circumstances, the nostalgic feeling that the mountains of Mexico were home.[6]

The influence of diaspora on Apache lives continued after the United States released Apaches from prisoner-of-war status in 1913. Before this decision was finalized, they had been asked to give input on where they wanted to live in the future. Some wanted to remain in Oklahoma, some wanted to go to Mescalero, and others wanted to be granted their old reservation around Warm Springs, New Mexico. These distinct opinions reflected not only band divisions and kinships ties but also tensions and resentments heightened during Apaches' long experience of exile. Sam Kenoi was not alone in blaming what he called the "bandit faction," especially Geronimo, for the fact that Apaches had been made prisoners of war in the first place and for the many deaths that had occurred in his view as a result. Geronimo himself had died of pneumonia still a prisoner of war in 1909.[7]

Ultimately, Apaches could not agree on one new home, even after a 1911 trip to New Mexico to visit Mescalero and the old Warm Springs reservation. Jason Betzinez was on this trip as a representative of the group that wanted to remain in Oklahoma. He remembered a pleasant and hospitable visit to the Mescalero reservation, where they were greeted by some of their kin who had remained or had been able to return there due to intermarriage. All were saddened by their next stop at Warm Springs, which they discovered had been spoiled by white settlement, grazing, and mining: "The whole county, once so fertile and green, was now entirely barren. Gravel had washed down, covering all the nice valleys and pastures, even filling up the Warm Springs, which had completely vanished. The reservation was entirely ruined."[8] Based on this report, the government ultimately presented Southern Apaches with two choices in the spring of 1913: they could stay in Oklahoma and accept new eighty-acre allotments purchased for them from the government. Or they could go to the Mescalero reservation in New Mexico. In the end, 78 chose to remain, and 183 chose to go to New Mexico.[9]

Choices shaped by histories of displacement influenced the futures of each group. Apaches who remained in Oklahoma started over again, receiving allotments scattered between white and Indian-owned farms on the old Comanche-Kiowa reservation. Dan Nicholas, for example, received an eighty-acre allotment that he leased out to whites, from which he earned about $200 per year while he lived with his father on his farm and helped him grow wheat, cotton, alfalfa, watermelon, and other crops. When he was older, after a stint in the army and as a disciplinarian at an Indian boarding school, Dan grew restless and decided to go to New Mexico. He was lured by romantic ideas about the "wild West" and also by stories his elders had told him about the homeland of their people. When he arrived, he found no gunfights or fights between cowboys and Indians, but he was happy to be reunited with many of his childhood friends. He went to Whitetail on the Mescalero reservation, the place where many Southern Apaches had settled, and helped them to plant crops. He learned a new soil and a new climate.[10]

The friends and relatives he met at Mescalero had also started over. They had departed from Oklahoma on April 1, 1913, after loading their horses, mules, and other personal belongings into railcars. Betzinez remembered that before the train departed, there had been commotion because the missionary woman in charge of arrangements had seated family groups together in a way contrary to the Apache taboo against looking one's mother-in-law in the face. After that "awful situation" had been settled, the conductor realized that the group had loaded their dogs into a baggage car, leading to "quite a few lively dogfights." He ordered the dogs thrown off the train, who watched from the station grounds as the train departed without them. There was at least one exception—a savvy old woman had managed to hide her favorite pup under a blanket. Together, they had steamed toward an uncertain future, another new home.[11]

Sam Kenoi was also among them, and after settling in New Mexico, he worked as an interpreter and then as chair of the Chiricahua Business Committee. In the late 1920s and early 1930s, he worked to obtain affidavits from all living scouts and their relatives about their treatment as prisoners of war in the hopes of obtaining reparations. In addition to describing the scouts' military service on the part of the United States, most affidavits noted that their people had been farming and tending animals, gaining "a position of independence" on their Arizona reservation at the time they had been rounded up and sent into exile in Florida. The statement of Helen Chatto was particularly moving in its condemnation of genocide at the hands of the United States, although that term had not yet been coined. She was the second wife of Chatto, who had never been able to recover his first family from captivity in Mexico. Helen explained that in 1885 when Geronimo left the reservation, she had "many relatives," including six brothers, three sisters, and "four old women who were very close relatives to me." After her people were taken as prisoners of war, "most of these died in prison." She described the difficult climate; the foul water they drank—"sewer pipe water"; and the difficult labor of constructing their own villages. She appealed to white Americans' sense of justice and religiosity. "We are created by the same one the white people were created by," she stated, adding that it was "in his presence they have abused us." Reminding readers that Apaches had been convicted of no crimes, she noted that "even a horse thief gets a trial." She asked for two dollars a day for each day she was held as prisoner as some small compensation for her suffering.[12]

Apache organizing was sometimes frustrated by internal tensions related in part to the history of diaspora. In seeking the assistance of Oklahoma senator Elmer Thomas in the late 1920s, Kenoi described the divisions that stymied his efforts. "Unfortunately our little band of Chiricahua is split up into several factions," he noted in a July 1933 letter. While Kenoi preferred working directly with the senator, he explained that the Apaches in Oklahoma and a third group he called the "bandit faction," the descendants of Geronimo and his associates at Mescalero, were using attorneys. Kenoi said that he found it impossible to work with them and complained that they had stolen some of the affidavits he had helped to collect. He questioned whether those he saw as responsible for Apaches being exiled as prisoners of war—"the very bandits who have caused the rest of us so much trouble"—should be among those to receive any compensation. In 1932, Elmer introduced a bill seeking $20,000 for each claimant that was referred to and subsequently languished in the Committee on Indian Affairs.

Apaches proved more successful in later lands-claims cases. In the immediate aftermath of World War II, the United States had formed the Indian Claims Commission to adjudicate disputes between tribes and the United States. With the help of non-Native allies, including the anthropologist Morris Opler, Southern (Chiricahua) and Mescalero Apaches ultimately proved successful in prosecuting their claims. The Southern Apache judgment in August 1971 totaled a bit more than $16 million, based especially on the dissolution without compensation of the Warm Springs and Chiricahua reservations. Yet this payment of about $1 per acre, while welcome, could hardly be classified as generous.[13]

The descendants of Apaches forced into diaspora in past centuries also had mixed success in their efforts to gain recognition from outsiders and govern their own lands and communities. Three groups that included the descendants of Apaches displaced during the slave trade and interethnic conflicts of the eighteenth century secured recognition from the states in which they resided in the early 2000s, but not from the U.S. federal government: the Genízaros of New Mexico, the Lipan Apache tribe of Texas, and the Choctaw-Apache of Louisiana. The Chihene Ndé nation of New Mexico, meanwhile, which includes the descendants of Apaches who eluded the forced removals of the late nineteenth century, continues to seek recognition from both state and federal officials.[14]

Most important in explaining the mixed outcomes of Apache efforts to redress past injustices and gain recognition of sovereignty and self-determination was the U.S. government. The United States' Indian policy vacillated in the twentieth century between some recognition of Native self-governance and efforts to disperse and acculturate Natives into U.S. society. The so-called Indian New Deal of the 1930s, for example, sanctioned tribal governance, valorized Native cultures to a greater extent than ever before, and began a process of shifting limited control of internal affairs back to Native people. Yet this process proved uneven, broken by later shifts in Indian policy back to forced assimilation and the "termination" of tribal recognition. Off-reservation boarding schools continued to operate, separating children from their kin. The U.S. Indian relocation program of the 1950s and 1960s encouraged Indians to leave reservations and settle in cities, often with unfulfilled promises of jobs, although Native people also created vibrant urban communities in the process. In North America today, Native people, including Apaches, face disproportionate rates of mass incarceration and an epidemic of non-Native violence against Native women.[15]

The history of the Apache diaspora reveals the efforts of outsiders to exploit, subjugate, or eliminate Indigenous people across more than four centuries, and Natives' own determination to resist and survive wherever they have found themselves. Settler-citizens and imperial agents under Spanish, Mexican, and U.S. governments who believed themselves to be innovative often echoed one another, as they pursued failed but also destructive schemes to end Apache self-governance through enslavements and forced migrations that scattered Apaches across the continent. The ends and means of colonialism have shifted to some extent over time, but colonization and diaspora have not ended. They are ongoing, yet so too is Native resistance.

ARCHIVAL SOURCES AND ABBREVIATIONS

Archivo del Ayuntamiento de Chihuahua, Chihuahua, Mexico
Referenced as AACH, Section, Box #, Exp. (expediente, "file") #.
Manuscript Collection:
  Fondo Colonial

Archivo General de la Nación, Mexico City, Mexico
Referenced as AGN, Collection, Vol. or Box #, Exp. # (if applicable), and f.
(folio) # (when available).
Manuscript Collections:
  Alcaldes Mayores
  Archivo Histórico de Hacienda
  Carceles y Presidios
  Correspondencia de Diversas Autoridades
  General de Parte
  Historia
  Inquisición
  Provincias Internas
  Presidios y Carceles
  Indiferente de Guerra
  Indiferente Virreinal
  Reales Cedulas
  Tierras

Archivo General de Indias, Seville, Spain
Referenced as AGI, Collection, Legajo (bundle) #.
Manuscript Collections:
  Papeles de Cuba (Cuba)
  Guadalajara
  México

Nettie Lee Benson Latin American Collection, University of Texas at Austin
Microfilm Collections:

El Archivo de Hidalgo del Parral, Mexico. Referenced as AHP, Reel #, and Frame # when available.

Spanish Archives of New Mexico, Vol. II. Referenced as SANM, Reel #, and Frame # when available.

Manuscript Collection:

San Felipe y Santiago de Janos Records. Referenced as Janos Collection, Folder #, Section #.

Cornell University Library Special Collections, Ithaca, New York.
Morris Edward Opler Papers. Referenced as Opler Papers, Box or Carton #, Folder #.

United States National Archives, Washington, D.C.
Microfilm Collection:

National Archives Microfilm Publications. Referenced as NAMP, [Publication] #, Roll #, Frame #.

Publications:

T21, Records of the New Mexico Superintendency of Indian Affairs, 1849–1880

M234, Letters Received by the Office of Indian Affairs, 1824–1881

M666, Letters Received by the Office of the Adjutant General, Main Series, 1871–1880

M689, Letters Received by the Office of the Adjutant General (Main Series), 1881–1889

M1070, Reports of Inspections of the Field Jurisdictions of the Office of Indian Affairs, 1873–1900

Manuscript Collections:

Referenced as NARA, RG (record group) #, Location, Vol. or Box #.

RG 393, Records of United States Army Continental Commands, 1821–1920

RG 92, Records of the Office of the Quartermaster General, Consolidated Correspondence File, 1794–1915

University of Texas at El Paso
Microfilm Collections:

Ciudad Juárez Municipal Archives. Referenced as Cd. Juarez Municipal Archives, Part #, Reel #, Frame # (if available).

Janos Microfilm Collection. Referenced as Janos Microfilm Collection, Reel #.

NOTES

Introduction

Note to epigraph: Joy Harjo, "Anchorage," in *She Had Some Horses* (New York: W. W. Norton, 2008), 4–5.

1. "Sam Kenoi Autobiography, Part II," in Opler Papers, Box 36, Folder 4, p. 311 (hereafter cited as Kenoi Autobiography).

2. This paragraph draws from Kenoi Autobiography, 270–476, 700–704. For a brief biography of Kenoi, see Alicia Delgadillo, ed., *From Fort Marion to Fort Sill: A Documentary History of the Chiricahua Apache Prisoners of War, 1886–1913* (Lincoln: University of Nebraska Press, 2013), 149–151.

3. My formulation of these questions is influenced by Emma Christopher, Cassandra Pybus, and Marcus Rediker "Introduction," in Christopher, Pybus, and Rediker, eds., *Many Middle Passages: Forced Migration and the Making of the Modern World* (Berkeley: University of California Press, 2007), 1–19, especially their discussion of "the threefold process of violence, resistance, and creativity" characterizing forced migrations on 3.

4. This portrait draws from specific histories examined in subsequent chapters.

5. Harjo, "Anchorage"; Edward H. Spicer, *Cycles of Conquest: The Impact of Spain, Mexico, and the United States on the Indians of the Southwest* (Tucson: University of Arizona Press, 1967); Simon J. Ortiz, "Towards a National Indian Literature: Cultural Authenticity in Nationalism," *MELUS* 8, 2 (1981): 7–12; Jeffrey Ostler, *Surviving Genocide: Native Nations and the United States from the American Revolution to Bleeding Kansas* (New Haven, CT: Yale University Press, 2019); Gerald Vizenor, "Literary Aesthetics and Survivance," in *Native Liberty: Natural Reason and Cultural Survivance* (Lincoln: University of Nebraska Press, 2009), 1–14. Jace Weaver's concept of the Red Atlantic is useful in its greater attention to Native mobility, but like other framings of the Atlantic World, it is also limiting in its focus on the ocean and adjacent shores as sites for historical analysis. See Weaver, *The Red Atlantic: American Indigenes and the Making of the Modern World, 1000–1927* (Chapel Hill: University of North Carolina Press, 2014).

6. My approach to diaspora draws especially from Nancy van Deusen, "Diasporas, Bondage, and Intimacy in Lima, 1535 to 1555," *Colonial Latin American Review* 19, 2 (2010): 247–277; van Deusen, *Global Indios: The Indigenous Struggle for Justice in Sixteenth-Century Spain* (Durham, NC: Duke University Press, 2015); Rachel Sarah O'Toole, *Bound Lives: Africans, Indians, and the Making of Race in Colonial Peru* (Pittsburgh: University of Pittsburgh Press, 2012); Nancy Shoemaker, "Race and Indigeneity in the Life of Elisha Apes," *Ethnohistory* 60, 1 (2013): 27–44; Christopher Hodson, *The Acadian Diaspora: An Eighteenth-Century History* (New York: Oxford University Press, 2012); Stephanie Smallwood, *Saltwater Slavery: A Middle Passage from Africa to American Diaspora* (Cambridge, MA: Harvard University Press, 2007); James H. Sweet,

Domingo Álvares, African Healing, and the Intellectual History of the Atlantic World (Chapel Hill: University of North Carolina Press, 2013); Gregory Smithers, *The Cherokee Diaspora: An Indigenous History of Migration, Resettlement, and Identity* (New Haven, CT: Yale University Press, 2015).

7. See Kenoi Autobiography, 475; "Report of the interview remarks of the Apache prisoners of war made to Captain M. P. Maus concerning their wishes to be removed to some other locality," Mt. Vernon Barracks, Alabama, 29 August 1894, NAMP 689, Roll 197, Frames 186–198; Geronimo and S. M. Barrett, *Geronimo's Story of His Life* (Bowie, MD: Heritage Books, 1990), 215; M. Grace Hunt Watkinson, "In the Land of the Mountain Gods: Ethnotrauma and Exile Among the Apaches of the American Southwest," *Genocide Studies and Prevention: An International Journal* 10, 1 (2016): 30–43.

8. For key works on diaspora and Native mobility that have influenced my own, see note 6 above, as well as Jodi Byrd, *Transit of Empire: Indigenous Critiques of Colonialism* (Minneapolis: Unviersity of Minnesota Press, 2011); Gerald Vizenor, "The Unmissable: Transmotion in Native Stories and Literature," *Transmotion* 1, 1 (2015), https://journals.kent.ac.uk/index.php/transmotion/article/view/143/604.

While historians have examined particular moments of Apache captivity and forced migration, no monograph to date has yet focused on tracing the influence of such histories collectively. Key works that examine particular moments of Apache displacement in depth include Christon I. Archer, "The Deportation of Barbarian Indians from the Internal Provinces of New Spain, 1789–1810," *Americas* 29 (January 1973): 376–385; Max L. Moorhead, "Spanish Deportation of Hostile Apaches: The Policy and the Practice," *Arizona and the West* 17 (Autumn 1975): 205–220; Angie Debo, *Geronimo* (Norman: University of Oklahoma Press, 1976), 299–454; Anthony Turcheneske, Jr., *The Chiricahua Apache Prisoners of War: Fort Sill, 1894–1914* (Boulder: University Press of Colorado, 1997); Rick Hendricks and Gerald Mandell, "The Apache Slave Trade in Parral, 1637–1679," *Journal of Big Bend Studies*, 16 (2004): 59–81; Juliana Barr, "From Captives to Slaves: Commodifying Indian Women in the Borderlands," *Journal of American History* 92, 1 (2005): 19–46; Edwin R. Sweeney, *From Cochise to Geronimo: The Chiricahua Apaches, 1874–1886* (Norman: University of Oklahoma Press, 2010); Bud Shapard, *Chief Loco: Apache Peacemaker* (Norman: University of Oklahoma Press, 2010), 219–306; Mark Santiago, *The Jar of Severed Hands: Spanish Deportation of Apache Prisoners of War, 1770–1810* (Norman: University of Oklahoma Press, 2011); Katrina Jagodinsky, "Territorial Bonds: Indenture and Affection in Intercultural Arizona, 1864–1896," in David Wallace Adams and Crista DeLuzio, eds., *On the Borders of Love and Power: Families and Kinship in the Intercultural American Southwest* (Berkeley: University of California Press, 2012), 255–277; Lance R. Blyth, *Chiricahua and Janos: Communities of Violence in the Southwest Borderlands, 1680–1880* (Lincoln: University of Nebraska Press, 2012); Sigfrido Vázques Cienfuegos and Antonio Santamaría García, "Indios foráneos en Cuba a principios del siglo XIX: Historia de un suceso en el contexto de la movilidad poblacional y la geoestrategia del imperio español," *Colonial Latin American Historical Review*, 2nd ser., 1, 1 (2013): 1–34; Hernán Maximiliano Venegas Delgado and Carlos Manuel Valdés Dávila, *La ruta del horror: Prisioneros indios del noreste novohispano llevados como esclavos a La Habana, Cuba* ([Coahuila, Mexico]: Gobierno del Estado de Coahuila de Zaragoza, 2014); Paul Conrad, "Indians, Convicts, and Slaves: An Apache Diaspora to Cuba at the Turn of the Nineteenth Century," in James F. Brooks and Bonnie Martin, eds., *Linking the Histories of Slavery in North America and Its Borderlands* (Santa Fe: SAR Press, 2015), 67–96; Andrés Reséndez, *The Other Slavery: The Uncovered Story of Indian Enslavement in America* (New York: Houghton

Mifflin Harcourt, 2016); Jason Yaremko, *Indigenous Passages to Cuba, 1515–1900* (Gainesville: University Press of Florida, 2016), 67–91; Matthew Babcock, *Apache Adaptation to Hispanic Rule* (Cambridge: Cambridge University Press, 2016).

9. In my attention to fate of kin left behind, I draw from Smallwood, *Saltwater Slavery*, especially p. 57: "The disappearance of a community left an absence that portended consequences both for the individual and for those left behind." For the Cochise quote, see Edwin R. Sweeney, ed., *Making Peace with Cochise* (Norman: University of Oklahoma Press, 1997), 114. For an excellent overview of the debate surrounding genocide in Native American history, see Ostler, *Surviving Genocide*, 383–387; Benjamin Madley, "Reexamining the American Genocide Debate: Meaning, Historiography, and New Methods," *American Historical Review* 120, 1 (2015): 98–139.

10. On the naming and relationship between Apache bands, see Babcock, *Apache Adaptation*, especially xvii, 261–262. See also James H. Gunnerson and Dolores A. Gunnerson, "Apachean Culture: A Study in Unity and Diversity," in Keith H. Basso and Morris E. Opler, eds., *Apachean Culture History and Ethnology* (Tucson: University of Arizona Press, 1971), 7–27; Morris E. Opler, "The Apachean Culture Pattern and Its Origins," in Alfonso Ortiz, ed., *Southwest*, vol. 10 of *Handbook of North American Indians*, ed. William C. Sturtevant (Washington, DC: Smithsonian Institution, 1983), 368–392. Apache history was long primarily studied by historians of the nineteenth century, and comparatively less scholarship focused on earlier time periods or on tracing Apache history across the *longue durée*. Key exceptions include Jack D. Forbes, *Apache, Navaho, and Spaniard* (Norman: University of Oklahoma Press, 1960); Spicer, *Cycles of Conquest*; William B. Griffen, *Apaches at War and Peace: The Janos Presidio, 1750–1858* (Norman: University of Oklahoma Press, 1998). In the past decade, scholars have devoted more attention to the pre-nineteenth-century period and showing its influence on the more recent Apache past. Excellent recent works on Apache history connecting the eighteenth and nineteenth centuries include Karl Jacoby, *Shadows at Dawn: An Apache Massacre and the Violence of History* (New York: Penguin Books, 2008); Ian Record, *Big Sycamore Stands Alone: The Western Apaches, Aravaipa, and the Struggle for Place* (Norman: University of Oklahoma Press, 2008); B. Sunday Eiselt, *Becoming White Clay: A History and Archaeology of Jicarilla Apache Enclavement* (Salt Lake City: University of Utah Press, 2012); Blyth, *Chiricahua and Janos*; Babcock, *Apache Adaptation*.

11. For Apache autonyms, see Babcock, *Apache Adaptation*, especially 261–262; Opler, "Apachean Culture Pattern." See also Morris E. Opler, *An Apache Life-Way: The Economic, Social, and Religious Institutions of the Chiricahua Indians* (repr., Lincoln: University of Nebraska Press, 1996); Greenville Goodwin and Keith H. Basso, eds., *The Social Organization of the Western Apache* (Tucson: University of Arizona Press, 1969). For Cochise's local group name, see "Cochise's Group," in "Chiricahua Vocabulary I," in Opler Papers, Box 51, Carton 2. I am influenced in my description of the use of the term "Ndé" by an explanation in "Comments of Morris E. Opler on Apache Chapter, 1 December 1974," in Opler Papers, Box 37, Folder 5.

12. On "Sioux," see Jeffrey Ostler, *The Lakotas and the Black Hills: The Struggle for Sacred Ground* (New York: Penguin Books, 2010), 7; on "Comanche," see Pekka Hämäläinen, *The Comanche Empire* (New Haven, CT: Yale University Press, 2008); 24; on "Apache," see Babcock, *Apache Adaptation*, 27. For English glosses of Apache terms, see "Mexicans, na' li' ba' i," "White man, 'iná," "Navaho, Tcocta' ija," and "Pueblos, tu' he' ne," in "Chiricahua Vocabulary II," in Opler Papers, Box 51, Carton 3. For a critique of scholarly approaches to using exonyms in the broader study of Native cultures, see Chrystos, "Anthropology," in *Lesbian Ethics* 3,

3 (1989), reprinted online at "Anthropology by Chrystos," http://www.feminist-reprise.org/docs /chrystos.htm.

13. Matt Schudel, "Helen Maynor Scheirbeck, American Indian Advocate and Museum Official, Dies at 75," *Washington Post*, 25 December 2010, http://washingtonpost.com/wp-dyn /content/article/2010/12/25/AR2010122502411.html. This description of Apache mobility draws from Chapter 1 of this book and also from Forbes, *Apache, Navaho, and Spaniard*, especially 24–25; James F. Brooks, *Captives and Cousins: Slavery, Kinship, and Community in the Southwest Borderlands* (Chapel Hill: University of North Carolina Press, 2002), especially 45–62; Babcock, *Apache Adaptation*, 24–28.

14. For Apache uses of the landscape, see Opler, *Apache Life-Way*, 186–216, 370–375; Babcock, *Apache Adaptation*, 23–24; Keith H. Basso, *Wisdom Sits in Places: Landscape and Language Among the Western Apache* (Albuquerque: University New Mexico Press, 2000). My thinking about how Apache mobility challenged colonial societies is influenced by David J. Weber, *Bárbaros: Spaniards and Their Savages in the Age of Enlightenment* (New Haven, CT: Yale University Press, 2005); Lauren Benton, *A Search for Sovereignty: Law and Geography in European Empires, 1400–1900* (Cambridge: Cambridge University Press, 2010); María Josefina Saldaña-Portillo, *Indian Given: Racial Geographies Across Mexico and the United States* (Durham, NC: Duke University Press, 2016); Allan Greer, *Property and Dispossession: Natives, Empires, and Land in Early Modern North America* (Cambridge: Cambridge University Press, 2018).

15. For Apaches as "warlike" by nature, see Edwin R. Sweeney, *Cochise: Chiricahua Apache Chief* (Norman: University of Oklahoma Press, 1995), 3, 18. I am indebted to Sweeney's exhaustive research and point to him merely as an example of this widespread view. Sweeney's perspective shifted in subsequent works. In *From Cochise to Geronimo*, for example, he directly addresses this issue on p. 17, stating that he would "now argue the reverse" regarding the Apache character. In conceptualizing slavery as one extreme on a spectrum of coerced dependence, I draw from David Eltis and Stanley L. Engerman, "Dependence, Servility, and Coerced Labor in Time and Space," in Eltis and Engerman, eds., *The Cambridge World History of Slavery*, vol. 3, *AD 1420–AD 1804* (New York: Cambridge University Press, 2011); Juliana Barr, "A Spectrum of Indian Bondage in Spanish Texas," in Allan Gallay, ed., *Indian Slavery in Colonial America* (Lincoln: University of Nebraska Press, 2009), 277–309.

16. This analysis is developed further in subsequent chapters. For contemporary Apache tribal nations today, see "White Mountain Apache Tribe," http://whitemountainapache.org; "Nde-San Carlos Apache," http://www.sancarlosapache.com/home.htm; "Tonto Apache Tribe," Inter Tribal Council of Arizona, http://itcaonline.com/?page_id=1183; "Mescalero Apache Tribe," https://mescaleroapachetribe.com; "Jicarilla Agency"; U.S. Department of the Interior, https://www.bia.gov/regional-offices/southwest/jicarilla-agency; "Fort Sill Apache Tribe," https://fortsillapache-nsn.gov; "Lipan Apache Tribe of Texas," http://www.lipanapache.org /Communitypages.html; "Choctaw-Apache Tribe of Ebarb, LA," https://www.facebook.com /ChoctawApacheofEbarb. Not yet formally recognized but pursuing state and federal recognition is the Chihene Nde Nation of New Mexico: "Chihene Nde Nation of New Mexico," http:// www.chihenendenationofnewmexico.org.

17. My usage draws from Babcock, *Apache Adaptation*, 261–263.

18. Invaluable scholarly assessments of images of American Indians, including Apaches, in popular culture include Philip J. Deloria, *Indians in Unexpected Places* (Lawrence: University Press of Kansas, 2004), especially 136–169; Robert F. Berkhofer, Jr., *The White Man's Indian: Images of the American Indian from Columbus to the Present* (New York: Random House, 1978);

Sherry L. Smith, *The View from Officers' Row: Army Perceptions of Western Indians* (Tucson: University of Arizona Press, 1990).

19. The history noted here is examined in greater depth in Chapter 7 of this book. For the scene of Geronimo nursing a baby, see Debo, *Geronimo*, 326–327.

20. Camillus Sidney Fly, photographer, *Scene in Geronimo's camp . . . Before Surrender to General Crook: Group in Natches' Camp; Boys with Rifles*, 1886, photograph, Library of Congress, https://www.loc.gov/item/2005691610/. On C. S. Fly, see Thomas Vaughan, "C. S. Fly: Pioneer Photojournalist," *Journal of Arizona History* 30, 3 (1989): 303–318. My reading of his photograph and its message to contemporary audiences is influenced by Karl Jacoby, "'The Broad Platform of Extermination': Nature and Violence in the Nineteenth Century North American Borderlands," *Journal of Genocide Research* 10, 2 (2008): 249–267.

21. Louis Simonin, *Mines and Miner: Or, Underground Life*, ed. and trans. H. W. Bristow (Cambridge: Cambridge University Press, 2014), 339–341. The book was original published in 1867; for more information about the text and author, see "Underground Life," Cambridge University Press, https://www.cambridge.org/us/academic/subjects/earth-and-environmental -science/applied-geoscience-petroleum-and-mining-geoscience/underground-life-or-mines -and-miners?format=PB.

22. I build here upon other recent works challenging the idea of inherent Apache militarism. See Record, *Big Sycamore Stands Alone*; Babcock, *Apache Adaptation*.

23. See especially Chapters 1, 2, 5, and 6 of this book.

24. Key works on indigenous power include Kathleen DuVal, *The Native Ground: Indians and Colonists in the Heart of the Continent* (Philadelphia: University of Pennsylvania Press, 2006); Juliana Barr, *Peace Came in the Form of a Woman: Indians and Spaniards in the Texas Borderlands* (Chapel Hill: University of North Carolina Press, 2007); Barr, "Geographies of Power: Mapping Indian Borders in the 'Borderlands' of the Early Southwest," *William and Mary Quarterly* 68, 1 (2011): 5–46; Hämäläinen, *Comanche Empire*; Pekka Hämäläinen, *Lakota America: A New History of Indigenous Power* (New Haven, CT: Yale University Press, 2019); Brian DeLay, *War of a Thousand Deserts: Indian Raids and the U.S.-Mexican War* (New Haven, CT: Yale University Press, 2008); Natale A. Zappia, *Traders and Raiders: The Indigenous World of the Colorado Basin, 1540–1859* (Chapel Hill: University of North Carolina Press, 2014); Shawn M. Austin, "Guaraní Kinship and the Encomienda in Colonial Paraguay, Sixteenth and Early Seventeenth Centuries," *Colonial Latin American Review* 24, 4 (2015): 545–571.

For select works emphasizing settler colonialism, incarceration, or genocide, see Patrick Wolfe, "Settler Colonialism and the Elimination of the Native," *Journal of Genocide Research* 8, 4 (2006), 387–409; Ned Blackhawk, *Violence over the Land: Indians and Empires in the Early American West* (Cambridge, MA: Harvard University Press, 2006); Brendan C. Lindsay, *Murder State: California's Native American Genocide, 1846–1873* (Lincoln: University of Nebraska Press, 2012); Benjamin Madley, *An American Genocide: The United States and the California Indian Catastrophe, 1846–1873* (New Haven, CT: Yale University Press, 2016); Katrina Jagodinsky, *Legal Codes and Talking Trees: Indigenous Women's Sovereignty in the Sonoran and Puget Sound Borderlands, 1854–1946* (New Haven, CT: Yale University Press, 2016); Kelly Lytle Hernández, *City of Inmates: Conquest, Rebellion, and the Rise of Human Caging in Los Angeles, 1771–1965* (Chapel Hill: University of North Carolina Press, 2017); Douglas K. Miller, "The Spider's Web: Mass Incarceration and Settler Custodialism in Indian Country," in Robert T. Chase, ed., *Caging Borders and Carceral States: Incarceration, Immigration Detention, and Resistance* (Chapel Hill: University of North Carolina Press, 2019), 385–408.

25. I draw here upon Juliana Barr's analysis in "There's No Such Thing as 'Prehistory': What the Long Durée of Caddo and Pueblo History Tells Us about Colonial America," *William and Mary Quarterly* 74, 2 (2017): 203–240.

26. For these distinctions, see Ostler, *Surviving Genocide*, 4; Byrd, *Transit of Empire*, xiii; Lytle Hernández, *City of Inmates*, 7; Wolfe, "Settler Colonialism," 388. For North American historiography on the intersections between Indigenous and African histories—from which the West has largely been excluded—see James Brooks, ed., *Confounding the Color Line: The Indian-Black Experience in North America* (Lincoln: University of Nebraska Press, 2002); Tiya Miles, "Uncle Tom Was an Indian: Tracing the Red in Black Slavery," in Brooks, *Confounding the Color Line*, 137–160; Miles, *Ties That Bind: The Story of an Afro-Cherokee Family in Slavery and Freedom* (Berkeley: University of California Press, 2005); Claudio Saunt, *Black, White, and Indian: Race and the Unmaking of an American Family* (Oxford: Oxford University Press, 2005); Tiya Miles and Sharon Patricia Holland, eds., *Crossing Waters, Crossing Worlds: The African Diaspora in Indian Country* (Durham, NC: Duke University Press, 2006); Brett Rushforth, *Bonds of Alliance: Indigenous and Atlantic Slaveries in New France* (Chapel Hill: University of North Carolina Press, 2012); Margaret Newell, *Brethren by Nature: New England Indians, Colonists, and the Origins of American Slavery* (Ithaca, NY: Cornell University Press, 2015); Alejandra Dubcovsky, *Informed Power: Communication in the Early American South* (Cambridge, MA: Harvard University Press, 2016); Wendy Warren, *New England Bound: Slavery and Colonization in Early America* (New York: W. W. Norton, 2016); Dawn Peterson, *Indians in the Family: Adoption and the Politics of Antebellum Expansion* (Cambridge, MA: Harvard University Press, 2017). Key intersectional works in Latin American history include Matthew Restall, ed., *Beyond Black and Red: African-Native Relations in Colonial Latin America* (Albuquerque: University of New Mexico Press, 2005); O'Toole, *Bound Lives*; Tatiana Seijas, *Asian Slaves in Colonial Mexico* (Cambridge: Cambridge University Press, 2015); van Deusen, *Global Indios*.

27. For discussion of this distinction, see Lytle Hernández, *City of Inmates*, 10. See also Jane M. Rausch and David J. Weber, eds., *Where Cultures Meet: Frontier in Latin American History* (Lanham, MD: SR Books, 1994); David Weber, *The Spanish Frontier in North America* (New Haven, CT: Yale University Press, 1992); Eliga H. Gould, "Entangled Histories, Entangled Worlds: The English-Speaking Atlantic as Spanish Periphery," *American Historical Review* 112, 3 (2007): 764–786; Jorge Cañizares-Esguerra, *Puritan Conquistadors: Iberianizing the Atlantic, 1550–1700* (Stanford, CA: Stanford University Press, 2006); Cañizares-Esguerra, ed., *Entangled Empires: The Anglo-Iberian Atlantic, 1500–1830* (Philadelphia: University of Pennsylvania Press, 2018).

28. Kenoi Autobiography, 339.

Chapter 1

1. Daniel Kosharek and Alicia Romero, eds., *New Mexico's Palace of the Governors: Highlights from the Collections* (Albuquerque: Museum of New Mexico Press, 2019); Kathaleen Roberts, "New Palace Story Emerges," *Albuquerque Journal*, 16 February 2012.

2. John L. Kessell, *Pueblos, Spaniards, and the Kingdom of New Mexico* (Norman: University of Oklahoma Press, 2008), 25–50; Weber, *Spanish Frontier*, 60–91, quote on 50. For "as if they were black slaves" and "calves or colts," see Reséndez, *Other Slavery*, 119.

3. For Spanish and Native ideas of slavery, see Brooks, *Captives and Cousins*, especially 1–39.

4. This analysis emphasizing the use of the category "Apache" is my own but draws inspiration from Nancy van Deusen, "Seeing Indios in Sixteenth-Century Castile," *William and Mary*

Quarterly 69, 2 (2012): 205–234. Illustrative quotations are from Juan Manso, "Certifico a las Reales Justicias" [I certify to the royal officials], Santa Fe, New Mexico, 3 October 1658, AHP, Reel 1660C, Frame 1279. For an in-depth overview of data on Indian slavery in New Spain see Silvio Zavala, *Los Esclavos Indios en La Nueva España* (Mexico City: Colegio Nacional Luis González Obregón, 1967).

5. On Panis, see Rushforth, *Bonds of Alliance*, 173.

6. For Apache experimentation with Catholicism, see Babcock, *Apache Adaptation*, 21–24. Evidence for the larger analysis presented here is discussed and cited below.

7. I build here upon Forbes, *Apache, Navaho, and Spaniard*. See also Babcock, *Apache Adaptation*, 19–60. In noting links between Native slaves' experiences in New Mexico and slavery in other contexts, I draw from Alan Gallay, "Introduction: Indian Slavery in Historical Context," in Gallay, *Indian Slavery*, 1–32; Miles, "Uncle Tom," 137–160; Reséndez, *Other Slavery*; James F. Brooks and Bonnie Martin eds., *Linking the Histories of Slavery* (Santa Fe: SAR Press, 2015); Brooks, *Captives and Cousins*; Christina Snyder, *Slavery in Indian Country: The Changing Face of Captivity in Early America* (Cambridge, MA: Harvard University Press, 2010); Newell, *Brethren by Nature*; van Deusen, *Global Indios*.

8. Eiselt, *Becoming White Clay*, 30–42; Babcock, *Apache Adaptation*, 23–25; Catherine M. Cameron, "Captives and Culture Change Implications for Archaeology," *Current Anthropology* 52, 2 (2011): 169–209.

9. For Apache terms for captivity and slavery, see "Chiricahua Vocabulary II," in Opler Papers, Box 51, Carton 3; "Mescalero Vocabulary" excerpts from Blazer family papers, in Opler Papers, Box 9, Folder 9. On Apache captivity practices more broadly, see Opler, *Apache Life-Way*, 349–351; Goodwin and Basso, *Social Organization*, 96, 106–111.

10. Brian Fagan, *Chaco Canyon: Archaeologists Explore the Lives of an Ancient Society* (Oxford, Oxford University Press, 2005), 142–144; Stephen Plog, *Ancient Peoples of the American Southwest*, 2nd ed. (London: Thames & Hudson, 2008), 102–110; Debra L. Martin, "Ripped Flesh and Torn Souls: Skeletal Evidence for Captivity and Slavery from the La Plata Valley, New Mexico, AD 1100–1300," in Catherine M. Cameron, ed., *Invisible Citizens: Captives and Their Consequences* (Salt Lake City: University of Utah Press, 2008); Timothy A. Kohler and Kathryn Kramer Turner, "Raiding for Women in the Pre-Hispanic Northern Pueblo Southwest?," *Current Anthropology* 47, 6 (2006): 1035–1045; Daniel K. Richter, *Before the Revolution: America's Ancient Pasts* (Cambridge, MA: Harvard University Press, 2011), 19–20.

11. Archeological evidence indicates that taking captives predated the arrival of Europeans. See, for example, Kohler and Turner, "Raiding for Women"; Steven A. LeBlanc, *Prehistoric Warfare in the American Southwest* (Salt Lake City: University of Utah Press, 1999). The earliest historical evidence affirms archaeological findings; see Brooks, *Captives and Cousins*, 27–28, 45–48.

12. On Apache captivity practices, see Opler, *Apache Life-Way*, 349–351; Goodwin and Basso, *Social Organization* 96, 106–111.

13. On the relationship between kinship, slavery, and power, see Brooks, *Captives and Cousins*, 34; Snyder, *Slavery in Indian Country*, 5.

14. On the word "gotah," see "encampment, village, family cluster" in "Chiricahua & Mescalero Vocabulary (A-Z)," Opler Papers, Box 51, Carton 1. See also "Village—go ta, Informant Dan Nicholas," in Opler Papers, Box 35, Folder 3.

15. Babcock, *Apache Adaptation*, 25–26; Opler, *Apache Life-Way*, 316–400.

16. For the local group name, see "Chatto's local group," in "Chiricahua Vocabulary I," Opler Papers, Box 51, Carton 2. For band names, see Babcock, *Apache Adaptation*, 261–263.

17. Opler, *Apache Life-Way*, 186–216, 370–375; Babcock, *Apache Adaptation*, 23–24; Basso, *Wisdom Sits in Places*.

18. Forbes, *Apache, Navaho, and Spaniard*, 53.

19. Forbes, *Apache, Navaho, and Spaniard*, 62–63. For identification of these Querechos as Navajos, see Brooks, *Captives and Cousins*, 84. Given the geographic location in the mountains around Acoma Pueblo, it is equally plausible that either Navajos or Chihene Apaches could have been the group in question.

20. Forbes, *Apache, Navaho, and Spaniard*, 63. For fought "like a Lioness," see "Diego Pérez de Luxán's Account of the Espejo Expedition into New Mexico, 1582," in George P. Hammond and Agapito Rey, eds., *The Rediscovery of New Mexico, 1580–1594* (Albuquerque: University of New Mexico Press, 1966), 202.

21. For Apache approaches to outsiders during this period, see Babcock, *Apache Adaptation*, 24.

22. Kessell, *Pueblos, Spaniards*, 50.

23. Roberts, "New Palace Story Emerges."

24. Alonso de Benavides, *Benavides' Memorial of 1630*, ed. Cyprian J. Lynch, trans. Peter P. Forrestal (Washington, DC: Academy of Franciscan History, 1954); Benavides, *Fray Alonso de Benavides' Revised Memorial of 1634*, ed. Frederick Webb Hodge, George P. Hammond, and Agapito Rey, trans. Mrs. Edward E. Ayer (Albuquerque, NM: University of New Mexico Press, 1945); Forbes, *Apache, Navaho, and Spaniard*, 3–28; Babcock, *Apache Adaptation*, 27.

25. Babcock, *Apache Adaptation*, 28–31. On Western Apaches, see Record, *Big Sycamore Stands Alone*.

26. Brooks, *Captives and Cousins*, 84.

27. Forbes, *Apache, Navaho, and Spaniard*, 110; William B. Carter, *Indian Alliances and the Spanish in the Southwest, 750–1750* (Norman: University of Oklahoma Press, 2009), 151.

28. On the Plains Trade as what colonists "most hunger for," see the residencia (audit) of Governor Don Bernardo López de Mendizábal, AGN, Tierras, Section 172 (hereafter cited as Governor Mendizábal Residencia). On the Plains Indians and Native trading fairs, see also Forbes, *Apache, Navaho, and Spaniard*, 116; Eiselt, *Becoming White Clay*, 62–98. For bison hides as "dress commonly worn," see Ramón Gutiérrez, *When Jesus Came, the Corn Mothers Went Away: Marriage, Sexuality, and Power in New Mexico, 1500–1846* (Stanford, CA: Stanford University Press, 1991), 112.

29. Forbes, *Apache, Navaho, and Spaniard*, 148. The presence of Quiviras among Indians enslaved in New Mexico in discussed later in this chapter as well; for their export to New Spain see Chapter 2 of this book.

30. Brooks, *Captives and Cousins*, 29–30. For Romero's troubles with the Mexican Inquisition, see AGN, Inquisición, Vol. 586, Exp. 1; and AGN, Inquisición, Vol. 497, Exp. 16; AGN, Inquisición, Vol. 629, Exp. 2.

31. I draw here from Babcock, *Apache Adaptation*, 19–23, though I break from his analysis in seeing this as "engagement" rather than "conversion." In doing so I draw from Linford D. Fisher, *The Indian Great Awakening: Religion and the Shaping of Native Cultures in Early America* (Oxford: Oxford University Press, 2012). On the distance of a Spanish league in miles, see Ophelia Marquez and Lillian Ramos Navarro Wold, eds., "Compilation of Spanish Colonial Terms and Document Related Phrases," http://www.somosprimos.com/spanishterms /spanishterms.htm.

32. Forbes, *Apache, Navaho, and Spaniard*, 121, 133; Babcock, *Apache Adaptation*, 22–23.

33. On Navajo as targets of slave raids, see Forbes, *Apache, Navaho, and Spaniard*, 113–115, 118, 123–127, 132–136, 143–145. On Spanish challenges colonizing mobile Indigenous populations, see especially Weber, *Bárbaros*.

34. For "insatiable thirst," see Forbes, *Apache, Navaho, and Spaniard*, 131. For "as if they were black slaves" and "calves or colts," see Reséndez, *Other Slavery*, 119.

35. For the governor's salary, see Gutiérrez, *When Jesus Came*, 111. On the broader tensions between church and state and mutual accusations regarding Indian slavery, see Gutiérrez, *When Jesus Came*, 95–142; Frances V. Scholes, *Troublous Times in New Mexico, 1659–1670* (Albuquerque: University of New Mexico Press, 1942). For the first definitions of slavery, see Claude Meillassoux, *The Anthropology of Slavery: The Womb of Iron and Gold* (Chicago: University of Chicago Press, 1991), 343. The second definition is a slightly modified version of Orlando Patterson's widely cited notion of slavery as the "permanent, violent domination of natally alienated and generally dishonored persons." Patterson, *Slavery and Social Death: A Comparative Study* (Cambridge, MA: Harvard University Press, 1985), 13.

36. On Puebloan men dominating "Spanish" campaigns, see Forbes, *Apache, Navaho, and Spaniard*, 150, 153.

37. Gutiérrez, *When Jesus Came*, 105. For complaints against governor for unpaid labor, see Governor Mendizábal Residencia, ff. 168–172.

38. Governor Mendizábal Residencia, especially ff. 168–172; Frances V. Scholes, "Troublous Times in New Mexico, 1659–1670 [I]," *New Mexico Historical Review* 12, 2 (1937): 157–160. On Pueblo Indians being sentenced to convict labor, see Anton Daughters, "'Grave Offenses Worthy of Great Punishment': The Enslavement of Juan Suñi," *Journal of the Southwest* 54, 3 (2012): 437–452. European assertions of sovereignty and use of criminal punishments as a tool to acquire Native labor was evident in other colonial contexts as well. See Newell, *Brethren by Nature*, especially 211–236.

39. On seventeenth-century Spanish governance and threat of violence, see Gutiérrez, *When Jesus Came*, 111–125. See also Paul Conrad, "Captive Fates: Displaced American Indians in the Southwest Borderlands, Mexico, and Cuba, 1500–1800" (Ph.D. diss., University of Texas at Austin, 2011), 112–167.

40. Brackets in the original. Forbes, *Apache, Navaho, and Spaniard*, 132.

41. Forbes, *Apache, Navaho, and Spaniard*, 144.

42. Reséndez, *Other Slavery*, 120. For murder of Rosas due to an affair, see Gutiérrez, *When Jesus Came*, 117. For the Apache sale of Wichita [Quivira] captives, see Forbes, *Apache, Navaho, and Spaniard*, 148.

43. Rick Hendricks and Gerald J. Mandell, "Juan Manso, Frontier Entrepreneur," *New Mexico Historical Review* 75, 3 (2000): 339–367; Hendricks and Mandell, "Apache Slave Trade."

44. "Contra Andrés de Gracia y Tomas Mulato . . . haver traido indios de las salinas y vendidolos" [Case against Andrés Gracia and Tomas, a mulatto . . . for having brought Indians from the plains and sold them], AHP, Reel 1649D, Frames 2145–2174. On broader justifications for forced labor and the temporary enslavement of Indians, see also Susan M. Deeds, "Rural Work in Nueva Vizcaya: Forms of Labor Coercion on the Periphery," *Hispanic American Historical Review* 69, 3 (1989): 425–449; José Cuello, "The Persistence of Indian Slavery and Encomienda in the Northeast of Colonial Mexico, 1577–1723," *Journal of Social History*, 21, 4 (1988): 683–700.

45. For Manso's sentence of death, see Juan Manso, "Certifico a las Reales Justicias" [I certify to the royal officials], Santa Fe, New Mexico, 3 October 1658, AHP, Reel 1660C, Frame 1279.

46. For Manso's campaign against the Apaches, see Forbes, *Apache, Navaho, and Spaniard,* 148.

47. For a discussion of "legal gibberish," see Hendricks and Mandell, "Apache Slave Trade," 68. On broader Spanish practices of Indian slavery, see Reséndez, *Other Slavery,* 13–75. On the nature of law and flexibility of local authorities on New Spain's northern frontier, see Charles Cutter, *The Legal Culture of Northern New Spain, 1700–1810* (Albuquerque: University of New Mexico Press, 2001).

48. AGN, Reales Cedulas, Vol. 76, Exp. 13, 7 February 1756, "En ningun caso, lugar, ni tiempo podian sufrir Esclavitud los Indios de la America que no fuesen Caribes" [In no case, place, or time could the Indians of America who weren't Caribs be enslaved]. See also see AGN, Reales Cedulas, Vol. D30, Exp. 14, 45, 1309.

49. Other scholars have pointed to the ways in which "Apache" was used as a generic term to argue that it became a synonym for "enemy" more than a referent to specific tribal groups. In the seventeenth century, the term was certainly used to generalize, but historical evidence suggests that actual Athapaskan-speaking Ndé groups remained primary targets of the developing system of slavery. On "Apache" as a generic term, see Sara Ortelli, *Trama de Una Guera Conveniente: Nueva Vizcaya y la sombra de los apaches, 1748–1790* (Mexico City: El Colegio de Mexico, Centro de Estudios Históricos, 2007); Chantal Cramaussel, "De cómo los españoles clasificaban a los indios: Naciones y encomiendas en la Nueva Vizcaya central," in Marie-Areti Hers, José Luis Mirafuentes, María de los Dolores Soto, and Miguel Vallebueno, eds., *Nómadas y sedentarios en el norte de México: Homenaje a Beatriz Braniff* (Mexico City: Universidad Nacional Autonoma de Mexico, 2000), 275–303; Chantal Cramaussel, *Poblar la frontera: La provincia de Santa Bárbara en Nueva Vizcaya durante los siglos XVI y XVII* (Zamora, Mexico: El Colegio de Michoacán, 2006).

50. For a succinct overview of López de Mendizábal and Aguilera's histories, see Gutiérrez, *When Jesus Came,* 118–127.

51. On the journey north from Mexico City, see Scholes, "Troublous Times [I]," 153–154. On the New Mexico settlement landscape, see Kessell, *Pueblos, Spaniards,* 73–96; and Frances Levine, *Doña Teresa Confronts the Spanish Inquisition: A Seventeenth-Century New Mexican Drama* (Norman: University of Oklahoma Press, 2016), 4–5. For Governor Mendizábal's policies, see "Declaration of Fray Juan de Ramírez," September 1661, AGN, Inquisición, Vol. 593, ff. 249, 255. See also "Reply of Lopez Mendizabal to Charges," 16 June 1663, AGN, Inquisición, Vol. 594, ff. 130–131.

52. For Mendizábal statements, see Frances V. Scholes, "Troublous Times in New Mexico, 1659–1670 (Cont'd) [II]," *New Mexico Historical Review* 13, 1 (1938), 74. On captive seizure, see "Testimony of Nicolas de Freitas, Jan. 24, 1661," and "Letter of Garcia de San Francisco," in Charles Wilson Hackett, trans. and ed., *Historical Documents Relating to New Mexico, Nueva Vizcaya, and Approaches Thereto, to 1773,* 3 vols. (Washington, DC: Carnegie Institution, 1937), 3: 156, 162. On Aguilar's role in Governor Mendizábal activities, see the statement of Diego Gonsales de Apodaca, AGN, Tierras, Vol. 3268. For a summary of accusations of seizure of captives, see statement of Don Diego Dionisio de Peñalosa Brizeño y Berdugo, Santa Fe, New Mexico, 21 October 1661, AGN, Tierras, Vol. 3268.

53. Declaration of Felipe de Albisu, AGN, Tierras, Vol. 3268, ff. 168–169; Miguel de Inojos, "Memoria de las cantidades q. boy pagando" [Record of payments], AGN, Tierras, Vol. 3268, ff. 172–173. See also statement of Diego de Trujillo, Alcalde Mayor of Zuni and Moqui Pueblos, AGN, Tierras, Vol. 3268.

54. On Mendizábal's seizure of Manso's captives see Forbes, *Apache, Navaho, and Spaniard,* 148–149; on Peñalosa's seizure of Mendizábal's captives, see order of arrest, 8 February 1663, AGN, Tierras, Vol. 3268.

55. On slave trading in Parral, see Chapter 2 of this book; see also Hendricks and Mandell, "Apache Slave"; Reséndez, *Other Slavery,* especially 100–124. Governor Mendizábal's slave-trading activities were a key subject of the audit of his term in office, as well as a matter discussed in his Inquisition trial. For his audit, see AGN, Tierras, Volume 3268; see also selected transcriptions in Hackett, *Historical Documents,* vol. 3. The governor's Inquisition trial is AGN, Inquisición, Vol. 594. The inquisition trial of Governor Mendizábal's wife, Doña Teresa de Aguilera y Roche, is an especially rich source for slaves' experiences in seventeenth-century New Mexico. I originally had consulted digitized versions of the original manuscript documents accessible from the Archivo General de la Nación (Mexico). I subsequently learned that transcripts of her trial records have been created in English and Spanish by the Cibola Project at the University of California, Berkeley. Given the accessibility of these transcripts and their ease of use for any reader, all citations below are from the Cibola Project transcripts. See Magdalena Coll, Heather Bamford, Heather, McMichael, and John H. R. Polt, "Doña Teresa de Aguilera y Roche ante la Inquisición (1664), 1a parte," UC Berkeley, Research Center for Romance Studies, 2009, http://escholarship.org/uc/item/00w4c1b2 (hereafter cited as Doña Teresa Trial).

56. On the demographics of New Mexico, see Gutiérrez, *When Jesus Came,* 92, 106. On "Apacha" as an epithet, see Doña Teresa Trial, f. 67r.

57. For "all slaves are enemies of their masters," see Doña Teresa Trial, f. 152v. For "doublet" quote, see Frances V. Scholes, "Troublous Times in New Mexico, 1659–1670 (continued) [IV]," *New Mexico Historical Review* 16, 2 (1941), 190.

58. For a highly influential analysis of borderlands communities and captivity practices there, see Brooks, *Captives and Cousins,* especially 1–39 for an overview. Though Brooks notes the large concentration of Apaches in haciendas and governor's palace, he places emphasis on the numbers of households with one or two captives. See Brooks, *Captives and Cousins,* 51.

59. "Muster, September 29, 1680," in Charles Wilson Hackett, intro. and annot., *Revolt of the Pueblo Indians of New Mexico and Otermin's Attempted Reconquest, 1680–1682* (Albuquerque: University of New Mexico Press, 1942), 1: 134–153. On demographics of New Mexico see Gutiérrez, *When Jesus Came,* 92, 106.

60. Doña Teresa Trial, f. 100r. The discourse linking Christianization and the enslavement of "heathen" Indians is ubiquitous, but see especially the order of Don Juan Ignacio Flores Mogollón, 26 September 1714, SANM II, Reel 4; David M. Brugge, *Navajos in the Catholic Church Records of New Mexico, 1694–1875* (Tsaile, AZ: Navajo Community College Press, 1985).

61. This composite portrait draws from Doña Teresa Trial, ff. 82r, 87v, 101v, 119r, 119v, 131r, 150r, 151r, 154v, 157r, 159v, 161v, 173r. The presence of a significant population of servants and slaves is part of what distinguished life in the governor's palace, a hacienda, or textile workshop from the more fluid dynamics of "borderlands communities of interest" described so cogently by James F. Brooks. See Brooks, "'This Evil Extends Especially . . . to the Feminine Sex': Negotiating Captivity in the New Mexico Borderlands," *Feminist Studies* 22 (Summer 1996): 279–309.

62. Doña Teresa Trial," ff. 159v–160r.

63. For the gender breakdown of Apaches arriving in Parral, New Spain, see Chapter 2 of this book.

64. On "maidens" and broader Spanish ideologies of gender, see Ann Twinam, *Public Lives, Private Secrets: Gender, Honor, Sexuality, and Illegitimacy in Colonial Spanish America* (Stanford, CA: Stanford University Press, 1999).

65. For references to her servants or slaves as "bitch," "deceitful bitch," and "hypocritical bitch," see Doña Teresa Trial, ff. 27r, 129r, 153r, 157r, 178r. The Doña did not use the term "prostitute" in her trial records, but she does discuss her servants or slaves being "pimped" or "pimping" each other to her husband; see ff. 148, 151v, 153r, 157r. For "loved like daughters," see testimony of Juan Dominguez Mendosa, Paso del Norte, 20 November 1662, AGN, Tierras, Vol. 3268.

66. Doña Teresa Trial, ff. 152r, 153r, 154v, 157v, 159r, 191v.

67. Doña Teresa Trial, ff. 87v, 100v.

68. Doña Teresa Trial, ff. 152r, 152v, 153r, 157r.

69. Doña Teresa Trial, f. 152v.

70. On births in the governor's palace, see Doña Teresa Trial, ff. 119r, 152r. For the especially descriptive birth, see the summary of charges against Don Bernardo López de Mendizábal, AGN, Inquisición, Vol. 594, f. 62. On birth in Apache cultural context, see Opler, *Apache Life-Way*, 7–9. On slave women's challenges, I draw from Smallwood, *Saltwater Slavery*, 152.

71. Doña Teresa Trial, f. 119r.

72. Doña Teresa Trial, f. 67r. Later in the eighteenth century, the term "Genízaro" would come to occupy a similar derogatory position indicating servile status and indigenous heritage. See Gutiérrez, *When Jesus Came*, 165.

73. For "paid off his ransom" see Brooks, *Captives and Cousins*, 134n23. Many of the archival records, such as notarial records, that might help us better understand the practice of Indian slavery in New Mexico were destroyed in the Pueblo Revolt. Even where notarial records do exist, such as in Northern New Spain, there remains little evidence that masters formally tracked the terms of Indian slavery.

74. See, for example, statement of Doña Ana Munes de Rojas to the Inquisition, 3 July 1663, AGN, Tierras, Vol. 3283, Leg. 2, f. 42.

75. "Declaration of Captain Andrés Hurtado, Santa Fé, September 1661," in Hackett, *Historical Documents*, 3: 186–187. On slave prices in New Spain, see Hendricks and Mandell, "Juan Manso, Frontier Entrepreneur," 345.

76. Response of López Mendizábal, Santa Fe, Undated [October 1661 from context], AGN, Tierras, Vol.3286; see also Hendricks and Mandell, "Juan Manso, Frontier Entrepreneur," 345.

77. See the summary of charges against López de Mendizábal in AGN, Inquisición, 594. For charges against Aguilera, see Doña Teresa Trial, ff. 86v–99r. See also Frances V. Scholes, "Troublous Times in New Mexico, 1659–1670 (continued) [III]," *New Mexico Historical Review* 15, 4 (1940): 369–417.

78. For Peñalosa's life story, see Scholes, "Troublous Times (Cont'd) [II]," : 63–84; Scholes, "Troublous Times (continued) [IV]," 184–205.

79. For the fates of the women en route, see Doña Teresa Trial, f. 49r–49v.

80. On the Quiviras as likely Wichitas, see Brooks, *Captives and Cousins*, 30. For Peñalosa's "presents" and legal wrangling involved, see AGN, Tierras, Vol. 3283, Legajo 2, No. 2.

81. On the 1659 court and subsequent royal decree, see King Philip IV to Audiencia of Guadalajara, 15 April 1660, which begins with the phrase "Tocante a la libertad de los naturales," AGN, Tierras, Vol. 3286; the king summarizes here the correspondence of the governor of Nueva Vizcaya, Don Henrique Dávila y Pacheco, with the president and judges of the audiencia from October and December of 1659. On "without any charge of slavery," see the declaration

of goods, Don Bernardo López de Mendizábal, 1 September 1662, Santa Fe, AGN, Tierras, Vol. 3283. See also response of López de Mendizábal, Santa Fe, undated [October 1661 from context], AGN, Tierras, Vol. 3286.

82. Statements of Doña Ana Munes de Rojas to the Inquisition, Mexico City, 14 June 1663, 3 July 1663, 8 July 1664, 20 June 1673, AGN, Tierras, Vol. 3283, Legajo 2, no. 2.

83. Certifying statement of Don Luis Delgado to the Inquisition, Mexico City, 20 June 1673, AGN, Tierras, Vol. 3283, Legajo 2, no. 2.

84. Statement of Captain Toribio de la Huerta to the Inquisition, Mexico City, 27 June 1663, AGN, Tierras, Vol. 3283, Legajo 2, no. 2.

85. For the broader context, see Scholes, "Troublous Times (continued) [III]," 369–417; Levine, Doña Teresa, 160–164. For the fates of Doña Teresa's Apache captives, see "Querella de Doña Teresa de Aguilera y Roche" [Complaint of Doña Teresa], AGN, Tierras, Vol. 3268, Legajo 2, no. 23.

86. Statement of Doña Teresa de Aguilera y Roche to the Inquisition, 10 January 1666, Mexico City, AGN, Tierras, Vol. 3268, Legajo 2, no. 23.

87. Statement of Juana de Lancero, mulatto slave of Doña Mariana de Córdova, to the Inquisition, Mexico City, 7 February 1666; statement of Yssabel de San Miguel, an Indian from New Mexico, to the Inquisition, Mexico City, 18 February 1666, both in AGN, Tierras, Vol. 3268, Legajo 2, no. 23.

88. Statement of Gerónimo de Ribadeneira to the Inquisition, Mexico City, 18 February 1666, AGN, Tierras, Vol. 3268, Legajo 2, no. 23.

89. For a broader discussion of suicide in New Spain and its meanings, see Zeb Tortorici, "Reading the (Dead) Body: Histories of Suicide in New Spain," in Martina Will de Chaparro and Miruna Achim, eds., Death and Dying in Colonial Spanish America (Tucson: University of Arizona Press, 2011), 53–77.

90. Petition of María de la Concepción to Inquisition, Mexico City, 22 March 1673, AGN, Tierras, Vol. 3268, Legajo 2, no. 23.

91. Nancy E. van Deusen finds similar dynamics in her study of Indian enslavement in sixteenth-century Iberia. See van Deusen, Global Indios, especially 125–146.

92. On slavery as fundamentally a relation of power, I draw from Patterson, Slavery and Social Death; Smallwood, Saltwater Slavery; Vincent Brown, "Social Death and Political Life in the Study of Slavery," American Historical Review 114, 5 (2009): 1231–1249.

93. For drought and deteriorating conditions in New Mexico, see "Letter of Fray Juan Bernal to the Tribunal," 1 April 1669, Santo Domingo, in Hackett, Historical Documents, 3: 271–272; see also Forbes, Apache, Navaho, Spaniard, 156–176.

94. Fray Juan Bernal quotes, "Letter of Fray Juan Bernal to the Tribunal"; Fray Ayeta quote from Forbes, Apache, Navaho, Spaniard, 167.

95. On Apache wars for independence, see Babcock, Apache Adaptation, 29; Forbes, Apache, Navaho, Spaniard, 161.

Chapter 2

1. Statement of Don Luis de Valdés, Alcalde Mayor, Parral, New Spain, 24 March 1671, AHP, Reel 1670b, Frame 879. The larger case is contained in "Criminal, en averiguacion de una india apache que se ahorcó en la casa de Nicolas de Balderrama" [Criminal case investigating an Apache Indian woman that hung herself in the house of Nicolás Balderrama], AHP, Reel 1670b, Frames 878–883 (hereafter cited as 1671 Apache Suicide Case).

2. Previous overviews of the Apache slave trade to Parral include Hendricks and Mandell, "Apache Slave Trade"; Cramaussel, *Poblar la frontera*; Reséndez, *Other Slavery*, 100–124. I build upon this work by considering in greater depth the lived experience of Apache captives arriving in Parral, especially their interaction with servants and slaves of African descent, particularly through a systematic review of all extant Catholic Church records, including baptisms, burials, and marriage records.

3. It is possible that Apaches newly arriving in Parral had already been servants and slaves in New Mexico. This is suggested by references to them having been baptized previously or already speaking Spanish. On the deteriorating situation in New Mexico, see Forbes, *Apache, Navaho, and Spaniard*; Matthew Liebmann, *Revolt: An Archaeological History of Pueblo Resistance and Revitalization in Seventeenth Century New Mexico* (Tucson: University of Arizona Press, 2012), 29–49.

4. The "Spanish campaign" is Reséndez's formulation. His excellent global history of the subject is in *Other Slavery*, 125–148. See also Seijas, *Asian Slaves*, 212–246.

5. For the meaning of liberty for Indians, see Brian P. Owensby, *Empire of Law and Indian Justice in Colonial Mexico* (Stanford, CA: Stanford University Press, 2008), 130–166. In viewing slavery as a uniquely exploitative form of dependency and servitude, I draw from Eltis and Engerman, "Dependence, Servility"; Barr, "Spectrum of Indian Bondage."

6. My understanding of the displacement at the heart of diaspora builds from van Deusen, "Diasporas, Bondage, and Intimacy "; Smallwood, *Saltwater Slavery*, 33–64. My reference to "degree of freedom" draws from Rebecca J. Scott, *Degrees of Freedom: Louisiana and Cuba After Slavery* (Cambridge, MA: Harvard University Press, 2005).

7. Reséndez is the most recent scholar to connect the Pueblo Revolt to Spanish slaving practices in *Other Slavery*, 149–171. See also Brooks, *Captives and Cousins*, 49–57; Howard Lamar, "From Bondage to Contract: Ethnic Labor in the American West, 1600–1890," in Steven Hahn and Jonathan Prude, eds., *The Countryside in the Age of Capitalist Transformation: Essays in the Social History of Rural America* (Chapel Hill: University of North Carolina Press, 1985), 293–324. My view is that slavery is best drawn upon to explain Apache participation, whereas the Pueblo Indians had more varied motivations.

8. See Deeds, "Rural Work"; Owensby, *Empire of Law*, 130–166.

9. On the legal ability to move Indians for the public good, see Owensby, *Empire of Law*, 150.

10. Hendricks and Mandell, "Juan Manso, Frontier Entrepreneur" and "Apache Slave Trade"; see also Chapter 1 of this book.

11. My discussion of the Balderrama household, and Apache captives' experiences in Parral more broadly, builds from a review of all extant Catholic Church records from the district. Past scholars have examined these records primarily to discuss the flow of Apaches and other Indians from New Mexico into Parral. I reviewed these records in order to consider additional demographic questions, such as age and gender. In addition, I considered the qualitative data they provide, such as on godparent relationships. I consulted images of the original manuscript records available online. See "México, Chihuahua, registros parroquiales y diocesanos, 1632–1958," database with images, FamilySearch, https://www.familysearch.org/search/image/index?owc=3J1P-HZS%3A69037701%2C69037102%3Fcc%3D1521780. For the reference to Balderrama in Parral by the early 1650s, see baptism of Nicolás, Apache slave of Nicolás Balderrama, 26 August 1653, in San José Hidalgo del Parral, Bautismos, 1634–1663, 1665–1691, Image 245 of 1052, https://familysearch.org/ark:/61903/3:1:S3HT-DTCS-W7Y?cc=1521780&wc=3J1P-YWL

%3A69037701%2C69037102%2C69265301 (hereafter cited as [Name], [Date], Parral Baptismal Records). For Balderrama's birth in Mexico City, see Christening of Nicolás Fernández De La Cruz (Balderrama), 13 May 1615, in "México bautismos, 1560–1950," database, FamilySearch, https://familysearch.org/ark:/61903/1:1:N8YR-P5V. On the lure of mining in drawing people to the district, see Cramaussel, *Poblar la frontera*, 100–105; Reséndez, *Other Slavery*, 100–124; Vincent Mayer, "The Black Slave on New Spain's Northern Frontier: San Jose de Parral, 1632–1676" (Ph.D. diss., University of Utah, 1975), especially 6–19; Peter Bakewell, *Silver Mining and Society in Colonial Mexico: Zacatecas, 1546–1700* (Cambridge: Cambridge University Press, 1971).

12. Baptism of Nicolás, Apache slave of Nicolás Balderrama, 26 August 1653, Parral Baptismal Records, Image 245; baptism of Joseph, servant of Diego Pérez de Villanueva, 11 June 1679, Parral Baptismal Records, Image 665; baptism of María, servant of Don Phelipe de la Cueva Montaño, 15 December 1675, Parral Baptismal Records, Image 574; baptism of Juana, servant of Juan Luis Castelui, 21 February 1683, Parral Baptismal Records, Images 724 and 725. On childhood in Spanish America, see Ondina A. González and Bianca Premo, eds., *Raising an Empire: Children in Early Modern Iberia and Colonial Latin America* (Albuquerque: University of New Mexico Press, 2007).

13. On Manso, see Hendricks and Mandell, "Juan Manso, Frontier Entrepreneur." On the Manso Indians and the "Great Southwestern Revolt," see Babcock, *Apache Adaptation*, 36–46. On rescate, see Brooks, *Captives and Cousins*, especially 1–39.

14. On the 1648 order, see "Bando," 6 February 1648, AHP, Reel 1649D. For the request to sell Indians without having obtained titles in Santa Fe, see petition of Juan Manso, Parral, 20 December 1651, AHP, Reel 1653A, Frames 222–224. For baptismal record language, see baptism of Nicolás, Apache slave of Nicolás Balderrama, 26 August 1653, Parral Baptism Records, Image 245. The use of the term "esclavo" for Apache baptisms was actually quite rare. I have counted only four Apache baptismal records that use the term "esclavo" between 1634 and 1700.

15. "Traspaso [Transfer] of Angelina," 17 December 1654, AHP, Reel 1654B, Frame 778.

16. "Traspaso [Transfer] of Gracia," 11 July 1654, AHP, Reel 1654B, Frame 779. On the broader debates over branding Indians in Spanish America during the seventeenth century see Konetzke, *Colección de Documentos para la Historia de la Formación Social de Hispanoamérica, Volumen II, Tomo I, 1593–1659* (Madrid: Consejo Superior de Investigaciones Cientificas, 1958), 349–353.

17. See Chapter 1 of this book for the discussion of Spanish slaving practices that would have been familiar to a boy growing up during this period. On the wagon journey, see Scholes, "Troublous Times [I]," 157–160. For a broader geography of Spanish settlement during this period, see Peter Gerhard, *La Frontera Norte de la Nueva España* (México: Universidad Nacional Autónoma de México, 1996).

18. On Apache local groups, see Opler, *Apache Life-Way*, 186–216; Babcock, *Apache Adaptation*, 23–24. On Apaches being shot on sight upon reentry to New Mexico, see Hendricks and Mandell, "Apache Slave Trade," 69.

19. This view differs to a degree from Reséndez's analysis, as he stresses the openness of Apache and New Mexico Indian slave sales, noting that they were "auctioned to the highest bidder" in public auctions; see Reséndez, 106, 122. I have seen references to this practice for local Indians, such as the Tobosos, but not for Apaches, other than those convicted of crimes. For auction of a "Gavilana" Indian woman, see "Remate [Auction]," 29 May 1659, Parral, AHP, Reel 1655A, Frames 102–106. For inquiring with a friend, see testimony of Francisca de Montijos, 12 January 1665, AHP, Reel 1665C.

20. Testimony of Antonio de Villalengua, 2 March 1649, AHP, Reel 1649D, Frame 214. For "naked and maltreated," see testimony of Pedro de Andrade, 9 March 1649, AHP, Reel 1649D, Frame 217.

21. On the 1648 order, see "Bando," 6 February 1648, AHP, Reel 1649D.

22. For slave prices, see Hendricks and Mandell, "Juan Manso, Frontier Entrepreneur," 345. For an excellent overview of African slavery in Parral, see Mayer, "Black Slave." For Balderrama's possessions, see will and testament, 14 February 1672, AHP, Reel 1673A, Frames 296–298.

23. "Normales Climatológicas por Estado," Servicio Meterológico Nacional, Mexico, https://smn.conagua.gob.mx/es/climatologia/informacion-climatologica/normales-climatologicas-por-estado?estado=chih.

24. This broader investigation is in "Oficio Contra Andrés de Gracia y Tomas Mulato . . . Haver traydo Indios de las Salinas y Vendidolos" [Case against Andrés de Gracia and Tomas, a mulatto, for having brought Indians from the plains and sold them], AHP, Reel 1649C, Frames 2146–2174. My thinking about slave sales is indebted to Walter Johnson, *Soul by Soul: Life Inside the Antebellum Slave Market* (Cambridge, MA: Harvard University Press, 1999), especially 162–188.

25. Opler, *Apache Life-Way*, 36–54. My attention to the narrative rupture in Nicolás's life draws from Smallwood, *Saltwater Slavery*, especially 8. In raising questions where the archival record does not provide answers, I draw from Wendy Anne Warren, "'The Cause of Her Grief': The Rape of a Slave in Early New England," *Journal of American History* 93, 4 (2007): 1031–1049.

26. Statement of Captain Valerio Cortés, 18 October 1655, AHP, Reel 1655B, Frame 825. On the reasoning for buying silver, see testimony of Martin de Ostorga, 19 October 1655, AHP, Reel 1655B, Frame 873. The broader case is contained in AHP, Reel 1665B, Frames 823–882. For mining driving Parral industries, see Reséndez, *Other Slavery*, 106–115.

27. On the patio process, see Reséndez, *Other Slavery*, 109; Thomas Egleston, "The Patio and Cazo Process of Amalgamating Silver Ores," *Annals of the New York Academy of Sciences* 3, 1 (1883), 1–66.

28. For the industries Apaches worked, see Hendricks and Mandell, "Apache Slave Trade," 59–81; Cramaussel, *Poblar la frontera*, 194. For Apache incorporation of horse and livestock, see Babcock, *Apache Adapatation*, 28–29. In my review of seventeenth-century Parral baptismal and burial records, I found 419 Apache males and 407 Apache females, and 157 male Indians from New Mexico and 204 female Indians from New Mexico. All parish record data presented in this chapter is based on a review of all extant records from the Parral district for the seventeenth century in "México, Chihuahua, registros parroquiales y diocesanos, 1632–1958," database with images, FamilySearch, https://www.familysearch.org/search/image/index?owc=3J1P-HZS%3A69037701%2C69037102%3Fcc%3D1521780.

29. This analysis draws from Smallwood, *Saltwater Slavery*, 57; Vincent Brown, "Social Death and Political Life in the Study of Slavery," *American Historical Review* 114, 5 (2009): 1231–1249; baptism of Nicolás, Apache slave of Nicolás Balderrama, 26 August 1653, Parral Baptismal Records, Image 245. For "does know how to give account of them," see, for example, Nicolás, Apache adult servant of Manuel de Ojeda, 7 July 1670, Parral Baptism Records, Image 453.

30. On Apache engagement with Catholicism, see Babcock, *Apache Adaption*, 19–23. On the Apache cradle ceremony, see Opler, *Apache Life-Way*, 11–12.

31. This portrait draws from Cramaussel, *Poblar la frontera*, 110–116; Reséndez, *Other Slavery*, 104–113.

32. Cramaussel, *Poblar la frontera*, 110–116; Reséndez, *The Other Slavery*, 104–113. See also Mayer, "Black Slave."

33. Cramaussel, *Poblar la frontera*, 110–116; Reséndez, *Other Slavery*, 104–113. See also Deeds, "Rural Work"; José Cuello, "The Persistence of Indian Slavery and Encomienda in the Northeast of Colonial Mexico, 1577–1723," *Journal of Social History*, 21, 4 (1988): 683–700.

34. For Apache tattooing practices, see Opler, *Apache Life-Way*, 21–22. That skin color was associated with enslavement for Africans is indicated by the fact that most "mulattos" or "negros" have *libre* (free) or *esclavo* (slave) markers in their records, whereas Indians, mestizos, and Spaniards do not.

35. Kinship language is ubiquitous in Spanish discussions of Indian captivity. See Brooks, *Captives and Cousins*, especially 1–39. See also Chapter 1 of this book. For Apache captives sometimes being carried beyond Parral, see baptism of Jusepe, Apache, 8 March 1676, Santiago Papasquiaro, Durango, in "México bautismos, 1560–1950," database, FamilySearch, https://familysearch.org/ark:/61903/1:1:NPL5-P96; Cramaussel, *Poblar la frontera*, 193. Tatiana Seijas notes that a ten-year-old Apache boy was sold for eighty pesos as a "Chichimeca slave" in Mexico City in 1651. See Seijas, *Asian Slaves*, 219.

36. Opler, *Apache Life-Way*, 7.

37. Baptism of Carlos, 26 November 1656, Parral Baptism Records, Image 269; Opler, *Apache Life-Way*, 15–19.

38. On intimacy and violence in the context of slavery, I draw here from Marisa J. Fuentes, *Dispossessed Lives: Enslaved Women, Violence, and the Archive* (Philadelphia: University of Pennsylvania Press, 2018); Warren, *New England Bound*, 153–186; van Deusen, "Diasporas, Bondage, and Intimacy "; Trevor Burnard, *Master, Tyranny, and Desire: Thomas Thistlewood and His Slaves in the Anglo Jamaican World* (Chapel Hill: University of North Carolina Press, 2004); Annette Gordon-Reed, *Sally Hemings: An American Controversy* (Charlottesville: University Press of Virginia, 1997). For broader evidence of Indian women birthing children to unknown fathers in Parral, see Cramaussel, *Poblar la frontera*, 199.

39. Baptism of Carlos, 26 November 1656, Parral Baptism Records, Image 269 of 1052. In thinking about women's separation from children who remained behind, I draw from Warren, *New England Bound*, 159–164.

40. Baptism of María Balderrama Fernández, 11 February 1664, Parral Baptism Records, Image 353 of 1052; baptism of Phelipa, Apache servant of Nicolás Balderrama, 30 July 1664, Parral Baptism Records, Image 360 of 1052.

41. For Josepha's four more children, see Nicolás Balderrama, will and testament, 14 February 1672, AHP, Reel 1673A, Frame 296. On at least five more Apache women being added to the household, see baptism of Juana, Apache servant of Nicolás Balderrama, 7 August 1668, Parral Baptism Records, Image 428 of 1052; baptism of Francisca, Apache servant of Nicolás Balderrama, 18 August 1670, Parral Baptism Records, Image 456 of 1052 The additional three women are mentioned in Apache Suicide Case, Frames 878–883.

42. See Figures 4–6 for summaries of relevant Parral parish register data. In viewing baptisms as a measure of flow of arrivals, I draw from Rushforth, *Bonds of Alliance*, 397. As noted below, death records indicate that some Apaches labored and died in Parral without having been baptized. The expense of the Catholic sacraments also may have played a role in Apaches not always appearing in Catholic Church records—while baptisms were inexpensive, burials costs around seven or eight pesos, and marriages around nine pesos. Chantal Cramaussel concurs that the records represent a fragmentary tally of the actual numbers of Indians from New Mexico arriving in the district; see Cramaussel, *Poblar la frontera*, 152, 200.

43. Testimony of Diego de Tres Palazios, 28 May 1660, AHP, Reel 1660C.

44. The titles of Sebastían and Margarita are in AHP, Reel 1660C.

45. Reséndez, *Other Slavery*, 125–148. For the 1671–1672 Emancipation and references to discussion of past emancipations, see AGI, Guadalajara, 12.

46. Statement of Governor Don Joseph García de Salzedo, 17 April 1673, AHP, Reel 1671B, Frame 1303. For the spread of news of emancipation among slaves in another context, see van Deusen, *Global Indios*, 99–124.

47. For an example of a burial record indicating baptism immediately before death, see burial of Theresa, Apache servant of Juana de Avendano, 16 December 1665, San José Hidalgo del Parral, Defunciones [Deaths], 1649–1723, image 315 of 1102, FamilySearch, https://www .familysearch.org/ark:/61903/3:1:S3HT-6XH9-RJX?wc=3J1T-7M9%3A69037701%2C69037102 %2C71602501&cc=1521780 (hereafter cited as [Name], [Date], Parral Burial Records). For the cost of burial, see Cramaussel, *Poblar la frontera*, 152.

48. Reséndez, *Other Slavery*, 123.

49. Reséndez, *Other Slavery*, 141.

50. See the statements of Alonso Gracia, 17 January 1665 and 24 January 1665, in "Criminal contra el Capitan Alonso Gracia por haber traido algunas indias de la provincia del Nuevo Mexico a benderlas en este Real" [Case against Captain Alonso Gracia for having brought some Indian women from New Mexico to sell in this community], AHP, Reel 1665B.

51. Sentence against Alonso Gracia, 27 January 1665, AHP, Reel 1665B, Frame 1299. On the "forced transfer" of Indians more broadly, see also Chantal Cramaussel, "The Forced Transfer of Indians in Nueva Vizcaya and Sinaloa: A Hispanic Method of Colonization," in Juliana Barr and Edward Countryman, eds., *Contested Spaces of Early America* (Philadelphia: University of Pennsylvania Press, 2014), 184–207.

52. As noted above, in my review of Catholic Church records in the Parral district for the entire seventeenth century, I counted four Apaches or Indians from New Mexico referred to as *esclavos* [slaves] as well as two more for which titles were mentioned. On Apaches earning wages, see Hendricks and Mandell, "Apache Slave Trade," especially 69. For "having served no one," see burial of Bentura, married Apache, 13 August 1679, Parral Burial Records, Image 598; burial of Antonia, single Apache, 29 September 1681, Parral Burial Records, Image 637. For an Apache *vecino*, see burial of Luis, Single Apache citizen, 14 June 1674, Parral Burial Records, Image 479.

53. On the abandonment of Pueblos and deteriorating situation in New Mexico, see Babcock, *Apache Adaptation*, 30; Forbes, *Apache, Navaho, and Spaniard*, 156–176. On Apaches in the 1673 emancipation speaking Spanish, see the report of Joseph García de Salçedo, 17 April 1673, AHP, Reel 1671B, Frames 1303–1304.

54. On the recovery of costs, see "Civil, Por Luis de Morales contra Diego de trespalacios, por reclamo de una Yndia" [Civil case by Luis de Morales against Diego de Trespalacios complaining about an Indian woman] AHP, Reel 1660C. On haggling the price, see the testimony of Antonio de Villalengua, 2 March 1649, AHP, Reel 1649D, Frame 214.

55. On the legal distinctions between slavery and freedom, see Cramaussel, *Poblar la frontera*, 198. For a discussion of understandings of liberty among Indians in New Spain, see Owensby, *Empire of Law*, 130–166.

56. Decree of Audiencia of Guadalajara, 19 October 1671, AGI, Guadalajara, 29.

57. On the legal ability to move Indians for the public good, see Owensby, *Empire of Law*, 150.

58. For Apaches in Balderrama's household after 1666 and possessions, see notes 22 and 41. For deaths, see burial of Magdalena, Apache servant of Nicolás Balderrama, 2 March 1675, Parral

Burial Records, Image 494 of 1102; marriage of Miguel de la Cruz and Antonia Josepha, 12 May 1676, San José Hidalgo del Parral, Matrimonios [Marriages], 1632–1660, 1665–1751, Image 322 of 837, FamilySearch, https://www.familysearch.org/ark:/61903/3:1:S3HT-6FX3-LGQ?i=321&wc =3J1T-L2W%3A69037701%2C69037102%2C71777601&cc=1521780 (hereafter cited as [Name], [Date], Parral Marriage Records); death of Chatarina, Apache servant of Nicolás Balderrama, 26 June 1677, Parral Burial Records, Image 553; death of Simon, son of Miguel de la Cruz and Antonia Josepha, servants of Nicolás Balderrama, 31 October 1677, Parral Burial Records, Image 564; death of María, servant of Nicolás Balderrama, 19 March 1678, Parral Burial Records, Image 573; death of Luisa, Apache servant of Nicolás Balderrama, 24 March 1679, Parral Burial Records, Image 590; baptism of Joan, son of Miguel de la Cruz and Antonia Josepha, 5 November 1679, Parral Baptism Records, Image 671; baptism of Gregorio, son of Miguel de la Cruz and Antonia Josepha, servants of Nicolás Balderrama, 17 May 1683, Parral Baptism Records, Image 729.

59. For population estimates in Parral, see Cramaussel, *Poblar la frontera*. Balderrama's slaves are described in will and testament, 14 February 1672, AHP, Reel 1673A, Frames 296–298. For knowledge of value in a different slave context, see Johnson, *Soul by Soul*, especially 19–44.

60. Baptism of Francisca, Apache servant of Nicolás Balderrama, 18 August 1670, Parral Baptism Records, Image 456; marriage of Nicolás Fernández de Valderrama and María de Luja, 27 November 1672, Parral Marriage Records, Image 167.

61. 1672 Apache Suicide Case, Frames 878–883. My thinking about suicide is influenced by Zeb Tortorici, "Reading the (Dead) Body: Histories of Suicide in New Spain," in Will de Chaparro and Achim, *Death and Dying*, 53–77.

62. See note 58 for Catholic Church records related to Balderrama's household. Death record data is based on a review of all extant death records from the Parral district in the seventeenth century between 1640 and 1700, as explained in note 28.

63. Cramaussel, *Poblar la frontera*, 196; Reséndez, *Other* Slavery, 109.

64. Burial of María, married Apache, 11 February 1673, Parral Burial Records, Image 426; burial of Lucia, married Apache, 8 March 1674, Parral Burial Records, Image 470; burial of Lorenzo, married Apache, 26 July 1677, Parral Burial Records, Image 557; burial of Antonia, single Apache, 29 September 1681, Parral Burial Records, Image 637.

65. For the order to take Apaches beyond Parral, see Cramaussel, *Poblar la frontera*, 194. For El Tortuga's actions, see "Criminal contra un Yndio Apache llamado Francisco por robo" [Criminal case against an Apache Indian named Francisco for robbery], AHP, Reel 1672B, Frames 1293–1323. For the execution, see Hendricks and Mandell, "Apache Slave Trade," 60.

66. Statement of Diego Xorxe, defensor [defense attorney], 26 April 1670, AHP, Reel 1669B, Frame 844. The broader case is "Criminal contra unos Yndios apaches por homicidio" [Criminal case against some Apaches for homicide], AHP, Reel 1669B, Frames 880–888.

67. Sentence pronounced by Don Nicolás de Medina, 28 April 1670, AHP, Reel 1669B, Frames 886. For criminality as a tool for enslavement in colonial New England, see Newell, *Brethren by Nature*, especially 211–236.

68. On the "politics of survival," see Brown, "Social Death," 1231–1249. On the relationships between women in Balderrama's household, see 1671 Apache Suicide Case, Frames 881–883.

69. For attention to unsanctioned relationships, see James H. Sweet, "Defying Social Death: The Multiple Configurations of African Slave Family in the Atlantic World," *William and Mary Quarterly*, 70, 2 (2013): 251–272.

70. On godparenthood and compadrazgo, see Brooks, *Captives and Cousins*, especially 6, 230; See also Erika Pérez, *Colonial Intimacies: Interethnic Kinship, Sexuality, and Marriage*

in Southern California, 1769–1885 (Norman: University of Oklahoma Press, 2018); and Pérez, "Family, Spiritual Kinship, and Social Hierarchy in Early California," *Early American Studies: An Interdisciplinary Journal* 14, 4 (2016): 661–687.

71. Godparenthood data is based on a review of all extant baptismal records for people identified as "Apache" or "Indian from New Mexico." See note 28.

72. In my conceptualization of family, I draw here from Julie Hardwick, Sarah M. S. Pearsall, and Karin Wulf, "Introduction: Centering Families in Atlantic Histories," *William and Mary Quarterly* 70, 2 (2013): 205–224; Bianca Premo, "Familiar: Beyond Lineage and Across Race," *William and Mary Quarterly* 70, 2 (2013): 295–316; Warren, *New England Bound*, especially 159, 164; Sarah O'Toole, "Bonds of Kinship, the Ties of Freedom in Colonial Peru," *Journal of Family History* 42, 1 (2017): 3–21; Sweet, "Defying Social Death"; Peterson, *Indians in the Family*, especially 1–9.

73. On a suit over wedding costs, see complaint of Don Joseph Perez de Theran, 8 January 1733, AACh, Fondo Colonial, Justicia, Caja (Box) 36, Exp. 20. For the cost of the wedding and the argument that it was a tool of coercion, see Cramaussel, *Poblar la frontera*, 152.

74. Herman L. Bennett, *Colonial Blackness: A History of Afro-Mexico* (Bloomington: Indiana University Press, 2010), 86–113; Bennett, *Africans in Colonial Mexico: Absolutism, Christianity, and Afro-Creole Consciousness, 1570–1640* (Bloomington: Indiana University Press, 2010), 126–153; O'Toole, "Bonds of Kinship," 3–5

75. Premo, "Familiar," 316; Sweet, "Defying Social Death." Data on marriages is based on a review of all extant matrimonial records for the Parral district. See San José Hidalgo del Parral, Matrimonios [Marriages], 1632–1660, 1665–1751, FamilySearch, https://www.familysearch .org/search/image/index?owc=3J1P-HZS%3A69037701%2C69037102%3Fcc%3D1521780. Of seventy-six total marriages involving an Apache or Indian from New Mexico located between 1651 and 1695, fourteen were between partners both identified as Apache, six between an Apache and a black or mulatto partner, four between an Apache and an Indian from New Mexico, nine between an Apache and someone of some other ethnicity (such as "Indian"), thirteen between partners identified as Indians from New Mexico, nine between an Indian from New Mexico and someone identified as a black or mulatto, and twenty-one between an Indian from New Mexico and someone of some other ethnicity (such as "Indian"). For the specific marriages referenced, see marriage of Luis and Luiza, 8 December 1659 in "México matrimonios, 1570–1950," database, FamilySearch, https://familysearch.org/ark:/61903/1:1:JHR4-QVL (image of original in possession of author); marriage of Joan de Aguierra and María, 25 May 1676, Parral Marriage Records, Image 322; marriage of Thomasa de la Cruz and Phelipe del Santiago, 29 September 1675, Parral Marriage Records, Image 193.

76. Marriage of Francisca de la Cruz and Sebastían de Nungaras, 10 December 1668, Parral Marriage Records, Image 129.

77. On Hispanicization as a lens through which to view intermarriage, see Hendricks and Mandell, "Apache Slave Trade," especially 74–75. Nancy E. van Deusen highlights the issue of Indian slaves' deracination as a key element of their experience. I agree this was true for many, especially children, but for youths and adults, memory of their past culture and identifications would have endured. See van Deusen, "Diasporas, Bondage, and Intimacy," especially 248.

78. In emphasizing what diaspora meant for communities left behind, I draw from Smallwood, *Saltwater Slavery*, especially 57. For an excellent description of the situation in New Mexico during this period, see "Letter of Fray Juan Bernal to the Tribunal," 1 April 1669, Santo Domingo, in Hackett, *Historical Documents*, 3: 271–272.

79. On more than three hundred Puebloans killed in 1669, see Liebmann, *Revolt*, 44. For the Apache quote on horses and term "Apache war for independence," I draw from Babcock, *Apache Adaptation*, 29.

80. On the livestock trade, see Reséndez, *Other Slavery*, 123.

81. For Pueblo Indian motivations, see Liebmann, *Revolt*, 29–49; Weber, *Spanish Frontier*, 133–141.

82. For Apache participation in the Pueblo Revolt and broader rebellions of the time period, see Babcock, *Apache Adaptation*, 23–47. See also Charles Wilson Hackett, intro. and annot., *Revolt of the Pueblo Indians* (Albuquerque: University of New Mexico Press, 1942), vol. 1, especially 4, 57, 60.

83. On the Pueblo Revolt, see Weber, *Spanish Frontier*, 133–141, quote on 136; Liebmann, *Revolt*, 50–70; Forbes, *Apache, Navaho, and Spaniard*, 177–199.

84. "Opinion of Fray Francisco de Ayeta," in Hackett, *Revolt of the Pueblo Indians*, 1: 307.

85. Brooks, *Captives and Cousins*, 52.

86. Brooks, *Captives and Cousins*, 53. My argument here on the role of slavery in the revolt largely follows Brooks, though my focus is more directly on Apache motivations. This qualifies Reséndez's argument that slavery was the key cause of the revolt. For discussion of Apache participation in primary source material, see Hackett, *Revolt of the Pueblo Indians*, vol. 1, especially 4, 57, 60.

87. See Brooks, *Captives and Cousins*, 55–56.

88. Baptism of Juana, legitimate daughter of Augustín de la Cruz and Phelipa de Jesus, 9 November 1681, Baptismal Records for San Diego [Parral district] misplaced in Parral Defunciones [Death] Records, 1674–1701, Image 67 of 191; baptism of Juan, legitimate son of Juan and Juana de la Cruz, 30 July 1684, in Baptismal Records for San Diego [Parral district] misplaced in Parral Defunciones [Death] Records, 1674–1701, Image 91. Images of both records are in possession of author.

89. Seijas, *Asian Slaves*, 239–240. For the Estrada discussion, see Hackett, *Revolt of the Pueblo Indians*, vol. 1.

90. For contemporaneous worries about the "total loss" of Spanish kingdoms, see "Don Lope De Sierra Ossorio . . . informs your Majesty of the state of affairs of Nueva Vizcaya, September 26, 1678," in Hackett, *Historical Documents*, 2: 210. Baptism of Chatarina, daughter of Nicolás Balderrama and María de Luxa, 2 December 1682, Parral Baptismal Records, Image 722.

91. Baptism of Gregorio, son of Miguel de la Cruz and Antonia Josepha, servants of Nicolás Balderrama, 17 May 1683, Parral Baptism Records, Image 729; burial of Gregorio, 18 November 1683, Parral Burial Records, Image 79; baptism of Joseph, son of Miguel and Josefa, 28 August 1685, Image 765.

Chapter 3

1. Weber, *Spanish Frontier*, 137–141, quote on 139; Elizabeth A. H. John, *Storms Brewed in Other Men's Worlds: The Confrontation of Indians, Spanish, and French in the Southwest, 1540–1795* (College Station: Texas A&M University Press, 1975), 121–146; Eiselt, *Becoming White Clay*, 102–106; Brooks, *Captives and Cousins*, 55–56.

2. Quote from the Tewa Puebloans is in Sherry Robinson, *I Fought a Good Fight: A History of the Lipan Apaches* (Denton: University of North Texas Press, 2013), 30. On Plains Apaches' relative power and avoidance of mass enslavement, see Chapter 1 of this book. For slaving as an anti-colonial measure, see Rushforth, *Bonds of Alliance*, especially 197.

3. On the Comanche emergence, see Hämäläinen, *Comanche Empire*, especially 18–67; Gary Clayton Anderson, *The Indian Southwest, 1580–1830: Ethnogenesis and Reinvention* (Norman: University of Oklahoma Press, 1999), 145–165. On the interimperial rivalry and influence on intertribal politics, see John, *Storms Brewed*, 226–257; Weber, *Spanish Frontier*, 172–203; Paul W. Mapp, *The Elusive West and the Contest for Empire, 1713–1763* (Chapel Hill: University of North Carolina Press, 2011), 147–165. For Plains Apache quote, see Alfred Barnaby Thomas, ed., *After Coronado: Spanish Exploration Northeast of New Mexico, 1696–1727: Documents from the Archives of Spain, Mexico, and New Mexico* (Norman: University of Oklahoma Press, 1935), 112–113.

4. Eiselt, *Becoming White Clay*, especially 99–142; Brooks, *Captives and Cousins,* 149; Alfred Barnaby Thomas, ed., *The Plains Indians and New Mexico, 1751–1778: A Collection of Documents Illustrative of the History of the Eastern Frontier of New Mexico* (Albuquerque: University of New Mexico Press, 1940), 1–59. For Jicarilla band names, see Babcock, *Apache Adaptation,* 262.

5. On Apache history as part of the Comanche rise, see especially Hämäläinen, *Comanche Empire*; and Pekka Hämäläinen, "The Politics of Grass: European Expansion, Ecological Change, and Indigenous Power in the Southwest Borderlands," *William and Mary Quarterly* 67, 2 (2010): 173–208. Juliana Barr provides a rich analysis of Lipan Apache-Spanish relations centering on captivity and slavery, which I draw upon below while also addressing the Plains Apache groups' experiences of captivity and enslavement more broadly during the eighteenth century and their fates in the varied destinations to which they were carried. See Barr, *Peace Came*, especially 159–196; and Barr, "From Captives to Slaves." For Lipan band names, see Babcock, *Apache Adaptation*, 261.

6. Barr, *Peace Came*, 159–196; Barr, "From Captives to Slaves." See also Anderson, *Indian Southwest*, 105–127; Robinson, *I Fought*, 52–102. My analysis of the far-flung geographies of Apache slavery here is both indebted to and lends further support to Brett Rushforth and Andrés Reséndez's analyses of the intersection of Native and colonial worlds. See Rushforth, *Bonds of Alliance*; Reséndez, *Other Slavery*, especially 172–195. Map 2 is adapted from "Spanish-Franco-Indian Frontiers in the Mid-Eighteenth Century," in Weber, *Spanish Frontier*, 185.

7. Eiselt, *Becoming White Clay*, 99–117; Robinson, *I Fought*, 27–40; "The Diary of Juan de Ulibarrí to El Cuartelejo, 1706," in Thomas, *After Coronado*, 59–76 (hereafter cited as Ulibarrí Diary); "Diary of the Campaign of Governor Valverde, 1719," in Thomas, *After Coronado*, 110–132 (hereafter cited as Valverde Diary).

8. Eiselt, *Becoming White Clay*, 110–112.

9. Brooks, *Captives and Cousins*, 62.

10. Ulibarrí Diary, 72.

11. Eiselt, *Becoming White Clay*, 106–107.

12. Eiselt, *Becoming White Clay*, 68–69; see also Chapter 1of this book.

13. John, *Storms Brewed*, 121–146; Robinson, *I Fought*, 29–32; Brooks, *Captives and Cousins*, 56–57.

14. "Cuervo y Valdez to His Majesty," 18 October 1706, in Hackett, *Historical Documents*, 3: 383. See also "Governor Cuerbó Reports the Return of the Picuríes, 1706," in Thomas, *After Coronado*, 77.

15. On the Comanche-Ute alliance, see Hämäläinen, *Comanche Empire*, 24–26. The analysis of Apache and Picurís diplomacy is my own.

16. Weber, *Spanish Frontier*, 147–152; Michael Witgen, *An Infinity of Nations: How the Native New World Shaped Early North* America (Philadelphia: University of Pennsylvania Press, 2013), especially 147–156.

17. Weber, *Spanish Frontier*, 148.

18. Weber, *Spanish Frontier*, 148; see also Barr, *Peace Came*, 21–25.

19. Weber, *Spanish Frontier*, 152, 170–171.

20. Ulibarrí Diary, 65–66.

21. On homelands versus borderlands, I draw from Barr, "Geographies of Power."

22. Ulibarrí Diary, 67.

23. Ulibarrí Diary, 69.

24. Ulibarrí Diary, 70.

25. "Don Francisco Cuervo y Valdez to his Majesty," in Hackett, *Historical Documents*, 3: 383.

26. John, *Storms Brewed*, 237. For the broader implications of Spanish policy regarding presidio in Apache country, see Hämäläinen, *Comanche Empire*, 34–37.

27. Valverde Diary, 114–115.

28. Hämäläinen, *Comanche Empire*, 24–25; see also DeLay, *War of a Thousand Deserts*, 1–34.

29. On slavery as central to Comanche expansion, see Hämäläinen, *Comanche Empire*, 18–67; Conrad, "Captive Fates," 78–110; Reséndez, *Other Slavery*, 172–195.

30. "Take possession," Valverde Diary, 132; "No Longer knew," Valverde Diary, 113.

31. Anderson, *Indian Southwest*, 55–66, 105–127.

32. Anderson, *Indian Southwest*, 64.

33. Nicolás Flores y Valdéz to Aguayo, 21 October 1723, AGN, Provincias Internas, 181; see also Anderson, *Indian Southwest*, 118–122.

34. Anderson, *Indian Southwest*, 112–113; see also Barr, *Peace Came*, 160.

35. Anderson, *Indian Southwest*, 112–113; for population, 121.

36. "Diario de la campaña executada por el Govern.or de Coahuila Don Pedro de Ravago y Terran en el año de 1747" [Diary of the campaign undertaken by the Governor of Coahuila Don Pedro de Rábago y Therán in the year 1747], 1 January 1748, AGN, Historia 52, ff. 111–141 (hereafter cited as 1747 Campaign Diary).

37. 1747 Campaign Diary, f. 125.

38. 1747 Campaign Diary, f. 125.

39. 1747 Campaign Diary, f. 126b.

40. 1747 Campaign Diary. On broader Spanish inquiries into interethnic raiding activities and concerns about Apache-mission relations, see Chapter 4 of this book. On the Native peoples of present-day Texas north of the Rio Grande, see Maria Wade, *The Native Americans of the Texas Edwards Plateau, 1582–1799* (Austin: University of Texas Press, 2003).

41. Barr, *Peace Came*, 164. On the broader pattern of raiding and exchange, see Anderson, *Indian Southwest*, 112–127.

42. Anderson, *Indian Southwest*, 119.

43. Barr, *Peace Came*, 166–168, quote on 168.

44. Barr, *Peace Came*, 168–169.

45. On the Spanish generalization of Apaches in the seventeeth century, see Chapter 1 of this book. For 1729 military regulations, see Thomas H. Naylor and Charles W. Polzer, eds., *Pedro de Rivera and the Military Regulations for Northern New Spain, 1724–1729: A Documentary History*

of His Frontier Inspection and the Reglamento de 1729 (Tucson: University of Arizona Press, 1989). For the fates of Cabellos Colorados and his family and quotes, see Barr, *Peace Came*, 169–170 (brackets in the original).

46. This analysis draws from Elaine Scarry, *The Body in Pain: The Making and Unmaking of the World* (New York: Oxford University Press, 1985), 27–59; Michel Foucault, *Discipline and Punish: The Birth of the Prison* (New York: Vintage Books, 1979), 3–72; Irene Silverblatt, *Modern Inquisitions: Peru and the Colonial Origins of the Civilized World* (Durham, NC: Duke University Press, 2004), 55–76.

47. On the cycles of violence and truce that characterized Spanish-Apache relations near San Antonio in the 1740s, see Barr, *Peace Came*, 172–175.

48. David M. Brugge, *Navajos in the Catholic Church Records of New Mexico, 1694–1875* (Tsaile, AZ: Navajo Community College Press, 1985), 22–23.

49. This estimate extrapolates from Cheryl English Martin's examination of San Felipe El Real de Chihuahua (Chihuahua City) parish records during the eighteenth century. Martin notes that the bulk of adult baptisms were Apache servants or slaves. See Martin, *Governance and Society in Colonial Mexico: Chihuahua in the Eighteenth Century* (Stanford, CA: Stanford University Press, 1996), 208. My own review of the records for select years supports Martin's finding, though the total number of baptisms of "Apaches" was likely even greater than the number of adult baptisms. For the year 1725, for example, Martin lists thirty-one total adult baptisms. My review of the parish records for that year found a total of thirty-six Apache baptisms, of which twenty-one were described as adults. See "México, Chihuahua, registros parroquiales y diocesanos, 1632–1958," database with images, FamilySearch, https://www.familysearch.org/ark:/61903/3:1:S3HT-6SGR-FZ?wc=3J1R-4WL%3A69034801%2C69997001%2C69997002&cc=1521780. The descriptor "adulto/a" may have simply indicated the individual was viewed as old enough to work.

50. Catholic parish records in the Mission 2000 database for the missions and presidios of Sonora include seventy-six Apache entries between 1700 and 1760. At the presidio of Janos in Nueva Vizcaya, there are fifty-five Apache entries during this same time period. See Mission 2000 Searchable Spanish Mission Records, Tumacácori National Historical Park, http://home.nps.gov/applications/tuma/search.cfm. While many of these Apaches were from Southern and Western Apache groups targeted by presidial forces' campaigns or sold to the Spanish by Native enemies, merchant networks make it plausible that some were Plains Apaches originally purchased at New Mexico trading fairs. See David M. Brugge, "Captives and Slaves on the Camino Real," in Gabrielle G. Palmer and Stephen L. Fosberg, comps., *El Camino Real de Tierra Adentro* (Santa Fe, NM: Bureau of Land Management, 1999), 103–11; Blyth, *Chiricahua and Janos*, 23–54.

51. In Louisiana, Helen Sophie Burton and F. Todd Smith note a small but persistent Indian slave population, ranging from fourteen in 1737 to forty-four by 1776. See Burton and Smith, *Colonial Natchitoches: A Creole Community on the Louisiana-Texas Frontier* (College Station: Texas A&M University Press, 2008), 56. See also Barr, "From Captives to Slaves." For Apache slave demography in New France, see Rushforth, *Bonds of Alliance*, 243.

52. Reséndez's synthesis of this period emphasizes the role of Native slavers in the trade; my analysis emphasizes instead distinctions in servant and slave experience. See Reséndez, *Other Slavery*, 172–195.

53. Report of Reverend Father Fray Andrés Varo, 1751, as quoted in "Report of the Reverend Father Provincial, Fray Pedro Serrano, to the Most Excellent Señor Viceroy, 1761," in

Hackett, *Historical Documents*, 3: 482–496, quotes on 486. The geography of the sites of baptism supports the idea that the majority of these Apache captives were Plains Apaches, including many taken captive and sold by the Comanche. Between 1726 and 1750, which were peak years in terms of the volume of baptisms, for example, more than half of all baptisms took place in northern and eastern New Mexico. See Brugge, *Navajos*, 30. For price of slave women, see Brooks, *Captives and Cousins*, 63.

54. Brooks, *Captives and Cousins*, 121–142; Gutiérrez, "Indian Slavery and the Birth of the Genízaros," in F. Richard Sánchez, ed., *White Shell Water Place: Native American Reflections on the Santa Fe 400th Commemoration* (Santa Fe, NM: Sandstone Press, 2010), 39–57.

55. Brooks, *Captives and Cousins*, 145. See also Moises Gonzales and Enrique R. Lamadrid, eds., *Nación Genízara: Ethnogensis, Place, and Identity in New Mexico* (Albuquerque: University of New Mexico Press, 2019).

56. Order of Governor Flores Mogollón, 26 September 1714, in SANM, Reel 4, Frames 1102–1106. This order is also transcribed in Brugge, *Navajos*, xx. 1733 land petition is discussed in Brooks, *Captives and Cousins*, 145.

57. For the meaning of Apache as an exonym versus autonym, see the Introduction.

58. For Sonora history and Apache relations there, see Jacoby, *Shadows at Dawn*; Cynthia Radding, *Wandering Peoples: Colonialism, Ethnic Spaces, and Ecological Frontiers in Northwestern Mexico, 1700–1850* (Durham, NC: Duke University Press, 1997).

59. Henry F. Dobyns et al., "What Were Nixoras?," *Southwestern Journal of Anthropology* 16, 2 (1960), 230–258, quote on 249; Jacoby, *Shadows at Dawn*, 54. See also Zappia, *Traders and Raiders*; Reséndez, *Other Slavery*, 196–217.

60. Testimony of María Antonia Yslas, AGN, Inquisición, Vol. 1390, f. 230.

61. Testimony of María Antonia Yslas.

62. Complaint of Antonio Gutiérrez de la Cruz, 25 September 1724, San Felipe Real de Chihuahua, AACh, Justicia, Box 14, Exp. 4. Microfilm copies of this collection are also available at the University of Texas at El Paso; however, the microfilm has not been professionally organized or indexed. The original materials in Chihuahua are thus much more useable for researchers.

63. Complaint of Antonio Gutiérrez de la Cruz, quote on 3.

64. Complaint of Ignacio Xavier Paes de Guzmán, 12 May 1737, San Felipe Real de Chihuahua, AACh, Notaria, Box 22 bis, Exp. 8.

65. Complaint of Gaspar Macias, AACh, Justicia, Box 27, Exp. 35.

66. See, for example, complaint of Don Juan Temointe, 9 October 1747, San Felipe Real de Chihuahua, AACh, Notaria, Box 32, Exp. 5; Complaint of Doña María Ledesma, San Felipe Real de Chihuahua, 7 September 1734, AACh, Fondo Colonial, Justicia, Box 40, Exp. 23.

67. Complaint of Don Joseph Pérez de Therán, 8 January 1733, San Felipe Real de Chihuahua, AACh, Justicia, Box 36, Exp. 20.

68. Complaint of Don Joseph Pérez de Therán.

69. "Diligencias Practicadas . . . en casa de Domingo de Apodaca" [Investigations carried out . . . in the home of Domingo de Apodaca], Pueblo de Nuestra Señora de Guadalupe, Real Presidio del Paso, 9 October 1758, Cd. Juarez Municipal Archives, MF 513, Part 2, Reel 7, Paging 2, Frames 212–220. For other cases of runaways, see complaint of Francisco Antonio Martínez, San Felipe Real de Chihuahua, 8 August 1746, AACh, Justicia, Box 80, Exp. 39; complaint of Manuel Muñoz Rivera, 19 September 1749, San Felipe Real de Chihuahua, AACh, Justicia, Box 90, Exp. 21.

70. "Diligencias Practicadas . . . en casa de Domingo de Apodaca."

71. "Que a ninguno le sea licito vender ni repartir comprar o recluir Apaches en las Prov .as de Sinaloa y Sonora" [Order that no one be allowed to sell or distribute, buy or shut away Apaches in the Provinces of Sinaloa and Sonora], Count of Revillagigedo, Mexico, 30 March 1751, AGN, General de Parte, Vol. 38, Exp. 16.

72. Order of the Count of Revillagigedo, 30 March 1751.

73. Ulibarrí Expedition, 74; Barr, "From Captives to Slaves," 29; Hämäläinen, *Comanche Empire*, 41.

74. Barr, "From Captives to Slaves," 24.

75. Barr, "From Captives to Slaves," 24–25.

76. Rushforth, *Bonds of Alliance*, 240–241.

77. Barr, "From Captives to Slaves," 24–25.

78. Spaniards buying and selling slaves is evident not merely in Spanish reports from the region but also in royal decrees, such as in a 1756 order from the king liberating Indian slaves found aboard a French ship exiting the Mississippi; see AGN, Reales Cedulas, Vol. 76, Exp. 13; Spanish correspondence from Louisiana is collected in Herbert Eugene Bolton, trans. and ed., *Athanase de Mezieres and the Louisiana-Texas Frontier, 1768–1780*, 2 vols. (Cleveland: Arthur H. Clark, 1914).

79. "Fray Miguel Santa María y Silva to Viceroy, July 21, 1774," in Bolton, *Athanase de Mezieres*, 2: 74–76.

80. Barr, "Captives to Slaves," 39–40.

81. John Sibley, "Historical Sketches of the Several Indian Tribes in Louisiana, South of the Arkansas River, and Between the Mississippi and River Grande," 1806, in *American State Papers, Indian Affairs*, vol. 1 (Washington: Gales and Seaton, 1832), 723.

82. Sibley, "Historical Sketches," 723. On the Choctaw-Apache tribe of Ebarb, see Robert B. Caldwell, Jr., *Choctaw-Apache Foodways* (Nacogdoches, TX: Stephen F. Austin State University Press, 2015).

83. Brett Rushforth, "'A Little Flesh We Offer You': The Origins of Indian Slavery in New France," *William and Mary Quarterly* 60, 4 (2003): 777–808.

84. This dynamic was evident in southeastern North America as well. See Snyder, *Slavery in Indian Country*, especially 46–79; Alan Gallay, *The Indian Slave Trade: The Rise of the English Empire in the American South, 1670–1717* (New Haven, CT: Yale University Press, 2002); Paul Kelton, *Epidemics and Enslavement: Biological Catastrophe in the Native Southeast, 1492–1715* (Lincoln: University of Nebraska Press, 2007).

85. Rushforth, *Bonds of Alliance*, 186, 241.

86. Rushforth, *Bonds of Alliance*, 239. For Marie Angelique's fate in France, see Sophie White, *Wild Frenchman and Frenchified Indians: Material Culture and Race in Colonial Louisiana* (Philadelphia: University of Pennsylvania Press, 2012), 244n34.

87. Valverde Diary, 132–133.

88. On the Carlana visit, see John, *Storms Brewed*, 251–252. On the three hundred Apache families at peace, see "Thomas Vélez Cachupín, Governor of New Mexico, to Count of Revilla Gigedo, Viceroy of New Spain," 29 September 1752, in Thomas, *Plains Indians*, 124.

89. Thomas, *After Coronado*, 46.

90. Eiselt, *Becoming White Clay*, 118–122.

91. "Instruction of Don Thomas Vélez Cachupín, 1754," in Thomas, *Plains Indians*, 136.

92. Babcock, *Apache Adaptation*, 262; Eiselt, *Becoming White Clay*, 130–131.

93. Barr, *Peace Came*, 174–176.

94. Barr, *Peace Came*, 190. On Lipan-Mescalero relations, see also Anderson, *Indian Southwest*, 128–144.

95. Barr, *Peace Came*, 194–196, quotes on 194 and 195.

96. Robinson, *I Fought*, xviii.

97. Brackets in the original. Hämäläinen, *Comanche Empire*, 64.

Chapter 4

1. On the journey of three Apaches to Mexico City and surrounding context, see "Cuentas de la Collera de Apaches conducida por el Alferez D.n Miguel Diaz de Luna, 1791" [Accounts of the Coffle of Apaches transported by Alferez Don Miguel Diaz de Luna, 1791], AGN, Provincias Internas, Vol. 142, ff. 436–556. For "it would not be fair," see Jacobo Ugarte y Loyola, Chihuahua City, to Viceroy, Mexico City, 6 December 1790, AGN, Provincias Internas, Vol. 142, ff. 445–446. For Apaches' petition for captives "to live in their union," see José Tapia, Mexico City, to Viceroy, 18 May 1791, AGN, Provincias Internas, Vol. 142, f. 497.

2. On the geopolitical shifts of this period, see Weber, *Spanish Frontier*, 204–235; Delay, *War of a Thousand Deserts*, 1–34.

3. My thinking on the role of family and kinship in imperial practices is influenced here by Ann Laura Stoler, "Tense and Tender Ties: The Politics of Comparison in North American History and (Post) Colonial Studies," *Journal of American History* 88, 3 (2001): 829–865; Hardwick, Pearsall, and Wulf, "Introduction"; Dawn Peterson, "Domestic Fronts in the Era of 1812: Slavery, Expansion, and Familial Struggles for Sovereignty in the Early Nineteenth-Century Choctaw South," in Nicole Eustace, Robert Parkinson, and Fredrika Teute, eds., *Warring for America: 1808–1813* (Chapel Hill: University of North Carolina Press, 2017); Anne F. Hyde, *Empires, Nations and Families: A New History of the North American West, 1800–1860* (Lincoln, NE: University of Nebraska Press, 2011).

4. On Apache divisions and ideas about loyalty and belonging, see Daniel W. Matson and Bernard L. Fontana, eds., "Cordero's Description of the Apache—1796," *New Mexico Historical Review* 32 (1957): 335–336; Griffen, *Apaches at War*, especially 5–7; Morris E. Opler, "Chiricahua Apache," in Ortiz, *Southwest*, 401–418, 410–411; Opler, "Mescalero Apache," in Ortiz, *Southwest*, 419–439, 427–428; Opler, *Apache Life-Way*. On the relationship between kinship and power, I draw from Snyder, *Slavery in Indian Country*, 5. For the Apache term for "relatives," see Dorothy Bray, ed., *Western Apache-English Dictionary: A Community-Generated Bilingual Dictionary* (Tempe, AZ: Bilingual Press, 1998), 420.

5. For "thief . . . in the house," see Pedro Queipo de Llano, Chihuahua, to Viceroy, 23 March 1773, AGN, Provincias Internas, Vol. 132.

6. This analysis builds upon recent scholarship on Apache-Spanish relations while placing a greater emphasis on the degree of the demographic crisis that Apache groups were facing during this period, on the links between the deportation or exile policy and diplomacy, and on the causative role of kinship relations in Apaches' and Spaniards' approaches to each other. Recent interpretations of Chiricahua or Southern Apache history through the lens of violence include Blyth, *Chiricahua and Janos*; Santiago, *Jar of Severed Hands*. Alternative views stressing peacemaking and diplomacy include Griffen, *Apaches at War*; Matthew Babcock, "Rethinking the Establecimientos: Why Apaches Settled on Spanish-Run Reservations, 1786–1793," *New Mexico Historical Review* 84 (Summer 2009): 363–397; Babcock, *Apache Adaptation*; Weber, *Bárbaros*. For works highlighting Apache power and expansion or Apache relations with other

Native groups, such as the Comanche, see Barr, "Geographies of Power"; Anderson, *Indian Southwest*, 140, for "peace zones"; Hämäläinen, *Comanche Empire*, especially 18–67. Recent studies of the "deportation" or exile of Apaches south through New Spain include Santiago, *Jar of Severed Hands*; Conrad, "Indians, Convicts, and Slaves."

7. The population of Apache groups during this period is difficult to determine conclusively. The Spanish records of Apaches killed in war or exiled are also incomplete, and it is often challenging to determine conclusively the band membership of those they targeted. Such records also do not account for attacks on Apaches by Comanches or Navajos. With those caveats, Southern and Mescalero Apaches represented the vast majority of those Apaches killed in Spanish campaigns this period (more than 900) as well as the vast majority of those exiled to central New Spain and the Caribbean (at least 2,266). Given that the combined Southern Apache and Mescalero Apache population was probably no more than about ten thousand, and probably less, the estimate of one-third seems reasonably conservative. See "Sobre la Junta de Guerra celebrada en Chihuahua," 29 June 1778, AGI, Guadalajara, Legajo 276, which estimates the total number of men of arms among all Apache groups from west to east as no more than five thousand, which would have included Lipan and Western Apaches not significantly affected by forced-migration campaigns. Opler estimates the mid-nineteenth-century population of Mescaleros and Chiricahuas (or Southern Apaches) at roughly six thousand, see Opler, "Chiricahua Apache"; Opler, "Mescalero Apache." For death and exile figures, see Santiago, *Jar of Severed Heads*, 203; Conrad, "Captive Fates," 256–261; Babcock, "Rethinking the Establecimientos," 383.

My emphasis on qualifying the nature of Native versus European power in the North American Southwest builds upon Ned Blackhawk's analysis of the Great Basin in *Violence over the Land* while also drawing from David J. Weber's calls for balanced approaches to both Native and Spanish worldviews in his essay "The Spanish Borderlands: Historiography Redux," *History Teacher* 39, 1 (2005), 43–56. For the rhetoric describing Apaches as heathens or "barbarians," which is ubiquitous in Spanish primary sources in the mid- to late eighteenth century, see, for example, José Antonio Areche, Mexico City, to Viceroy, 6 September 1774, AGN, Provincias Internas, Vol. 154; Jacobo Ugarte y Loyola, Chihuahua City, to Viceroy, Mexico City, 6 December 1790, AGN, Provincias Internas, Vol. 142.

8. Brooks, *Captives and Cousins*, especially 1–39; Cramaussel, "De cómo los españoles clasificaban"; Cramaussel, *Poblar la frontera*; Reséndez, *Other Slavery*, especially 76–124; Zavala, *Los Esclavos Indios*.

9. Oakah Jones, *Nueva Vizcaya: Heartland of the Spanish Frontier* (Albuquerque: University of New Mexico Press, 1988); Peter Gerhard, *The North Frontier of New Spain* (Norman: University of Oklahoma Press, 1993); Martin, *Governance and Society*; Radding, *Wandering Peoples*; Ross Frank, *From Settler to Citizen: New Mexican Economic Development and the Creation of Vecino Society, 1750–1820* (Berkeley: University of California Press, 2000).

10. On broader Spanish descriptions of fluid relations with Apaches and their interactions with missionized Natives, see Fray José de Arranegui to Viceroy, 11 June 1715, AGN, Historia, Vol. 20; José Enrique de Cosio to Viceroy, 1 September 1744, AGN, Historia, Vol. 20; "Testimonio de los Autos que se formaron . . . s.e los Robos de los Sumas infieles y la liga que tienen con los Apaches Mescaleros, 1751" [Testimony of documents formed . . . in regards to the robberies of the disloyal Sumas and their alliance with Mescalero Apaches in 1751], AGI, Guadalajara, Legajo 191; Lorenzo Cancio to Marqués de Cruillas, 2 October 1763, AGN, Provincias Internas, Vol. 25; "Diario de la campaña executada por el Governador de Coahuila Don Pedro de Ravago

y Terran en el año de 1747 para el reconocimiento de las margenes del Rio Grande del Norte"
[Diary of the campaign completed by the governor of Coahuila Don Pedro de Ravago y Terran
in the year 1747 to explore the banks of the Rio Grande], Rábago y Therán to Güemes y Horcasitas, 23 January 1748, AGN, Historia, Vol. 52. For the 1751 order from viceroy and discussion
of collaboration between escaped slaves and Apaches, see Order of the Count of Revillagigedo,
Mexico, 30 March 1751, AGN, General de Parte, Vol 38, Exp. 16.

    11. For eighteenth-century Spanish ethnographic descriptions of Apaches, see Nicolás de
la Fora and Vito Alessio Robles, *Nicolas de la Fora, relación del viaje que hizo a los presidios internos, situados en la frontera de la América septentrional, pertenecente al rey de España* (México,
D.F.: P. Robredo, 1939; José María Cortés and Elizabeth John , *Views from the Apache Frontier:
Report on the Northern Provinces of New* Spain (Norman, OK: University of Oklahoma Press,
1994); Matson and Fontana, "Cordero's Description"; Elizabeth A. H. John, "A Cautionary Exercise in Apache Historiography," *Journal of Arizona History,* 25, 3 (1984): 301–315; Opler, *Apache
Life-Way*; Hämäläinen, *Comanche Empire*, 18–67; Anderson, *Indian Southwest*, 105–144; Blackhawk, *Violence over the Land*; John, *Storms Brewed*.

    12. For "govern[ed] themselves," see Cortés, *Views from the Apache Frontier*, 49; Opler,
"Chiricahua Apache," 411–413. On Spanish military officers and Apache language culture, see
Griffen, *Apaches at War*, especially 99.

    13. Griffen, *Apaches at War*, 1–15; Babcock, *Apache Adaptation*, 261–263.

    14. Griffen, *Apaches at War*, 5; Opler, "Chiricahua Apache," 411–413.

    15. Griffen mobilizes evidence of Apaches' raiding to suggest that Apaches did not under-
stand that when they made peace with the Spanish in one place they should maintain it elsewhere. Although Apache groups did not come to understand Spanish political systems perfectly
(just as the Spaniards did not fully understand those of Apaches), I think Apache raiding practices are better read as evidence that they did understand tthe fragmented nature of Spanish
governance and used that to their own advantage. See Griffen, *Apaches at War*, 7. My reading is
influenced by Brian Delay, "Independent Indians and the U.S.-Mexican War," *American Historical Review* 112, 1 (2007): 35–68.

    16. On the Jicarilla Apaches, see Eiselt, *Becoming White Clay*. On the Lipan and Mescalero
migrations and adaptions, see Anderson, *Indian Southwest*, 105–144; Chapter 3 of this book. On
the Comanche, see also Pekka Hämäläinen, "The Rise and Fall of Plains Indian Horse Cultures,"
Journal of American History 90, 3 (2003): 833–862; Hämäläinen, *Comanche Empire*.

    17. On the Spanish presidios and demographic expansion in Northern New Spain during
this period, see Weber, *Spanish Frontier*, 204–235; John Tutino, *Making a New World: Founding
Capitalism in the Bajío and Spanish North America* (Durham, NC: Duke University, Press, 2011),
352–402; Ortelli, *Trama de una guerra conveniente*. For "go around on horseback trading," see
"Diario de la campaña executada por el Govern.or de Coahuila," 1 January 1748, AGN, Historia,
Vol. 52, especially f. 126B.

    18. For evidence of Apache ties in Spanish communities (and the reverse), see "Vando
proclamado para que sus havitadores no vendan ni cambien semillas, ni armas . . . a los apaches,
1762" [1762 notice proclaiming that inhabitants not sell or exchange seeds or arms . . . to
Apaches], Cd. Juarez Municipal Archives, Part II, Reel 7. For "those long married among us," see
Tapia, Janos, to Muñiz, 17 January 1778, Janos Collection, Folder 3, Section 1. See also "Diario
de novedades," January 1757 to November 1758, Janos Microfilm Collection, Reel 6; Antonio
María de Daroca to Bucareli, 24 October 1773, AGN, Provincias Internas, Vol. 102; William L.
Merrill, "Cultural Creativity and Raiding Bands in Eighteenth Century Northern New Spain,"

in William Taylor and Franklin Pease, eds., *Violence, Resistance, and Survival in the Americas* (Washington, DC: Smithsonian Institution Press, 1994), 124–152.

19. On the nature of Apache raiding and trading practices, see Cortés, *Apache Frontier*, 71–72; Hugo O'Connor, Presidio de San Fernando de Carrizal, to Viceroy, 30 January 1776, AGN, Provincias Internas, Vol. 88; Pedro Queipo de Llano, Chihuahua, to Viceroy, 23 March 1773, AGN, Provincias Internas, Vol. 132.

20. Such concerns had a longer history. See Barrutia to Marqués de Casa Fuerte, 29 April 1729, AGN, Provincias Internas, Vol. 154. In 1754, a meeting of the principal citizens of Chihuahua presented a joint statement warning that Apaches threatened to "completely break the obedience of the Tarahumaras": see "Decreto de Junta, San Phelipe de Real" [Decree of the council of war, Chihuahua City], 23 August 1754, AGI, Guadalajara, Legajo 194. On the "delicate" issue of prosecuting mission Indians, see Alderete to Castilla y Terán, 15 November 1769, AGN, Provincias Internas, Vol. 231.

21. Pedro Queipo de Llano, Chihuahua, to Viceroy, 23 March 1773, AGN, Provincias Internas, Vol. 132; Merrill, "Cultural Creativity." On the fear of punishment, see Queipo y Llano to Joachin Manuel Robles, 30 April 1775, AGN, Provincias Internas, Vol. 132. On Apaches staying in Tarahumara camps and the outcome of 1770s and 1780s investigations into Tarahumara-Apache relations, see Jacobo Ugarte y Loyola to Garrido y Durán, 4 January 1787, AGI, Guadalajara, Legajo 287.

22. On Apache ideas of warfare, see Opler, *Apache Life-Way*, 370–375. For the military campaigns, see Babcock, *Apache Adaptation*, 105–140; Santiago, *Jar of Severed Hands*.

23. On the Enlightenment-era Spanish interest in categorizing and understanding Indians, see Weber, *Bárbaros*, especially chapter 1.

24. On Rubi's visit, see LaFora, *Presidios Internos*; Lawrence Kinnaird, *The Frontiers of New Spain: Nicolás de LaFora's Description, 1766–1768* (Berkeley, CA: Quivira Society, 1958). On the Bourbon reforms and colonial frontiers, see Weber, *Bárbaros*, 72.

25. LaFora, *Presidios Internos*, 83.

26. LaFora, *Presidios Internos*, 277–278.

27. On Spanish understandings of *naturaleza*, I draw here from van Deusen, *Global Indios*, 20. Such understandings also warrant comparison to what Rebecca Goetz has labelled "hereditary heathenism" in the context of Anglo North America—English creoles' visions of blacks and Indians as incapable of Christianity in early Virginia. See Rebecca Anne Goetz, *The Baptism of Early Virginia: How Christianity Created Race* (Baltimore: Johns Hopkins University Press, 2016). I draw from Wolfe's critique of the distinction between cultural genocide and genocide in "Settler Colonialism," 387–409.

28. Weber, *Spanish Frontier*, 204–212; José Antonio Areche, Mexico City, to Viceroy, 6 September 1774, AGN, Provincias Internas, Vol. 154. On the escalation of war, see Hugo O'Connor, Presidio del Carrizo, to Viceroy, 24 March 1775, AGN, Provincias Internas, Vol. 88.

29. See Donald C. Cutter, ed. and trans., *The Defenses of Northern New Spain: Hugo O'Connor's Report to Teodoro de Croix, July 22, 1777* (Dallas: Southern Methodist University Press/ DeGolyer Library, 1994). O'Connor was not alone in citing such figures, noting that they were proven "by documents" in the archives—perhaps referring to a more than 260-page file in the archive in Chihuahua filled with local reports of robberies and devastating violence attributed to a vague enemy. See AACh, Justicia, Box 14, Exp. 4. Historians, however, have tended to draw upon Spanish statistics on Apache violence uncritically: see, for example, Delay, *War of a Thousand Deserts*, 12; Babcock, "Rethinking the Establecimientos," 383–384.

30. For "windward islands," see Hugo O'Connor to Viceroy, 8 March 1774, AGN, Provincias Internas, Vol. 154. See also Conrad, "Indians, Convicts, and Slaves."

31. Conrad, "Indians, Convicts, and Slaves." On the criado system and godparenthood, see also Brooks, *Captives and Cousins*, especially 1–35. For "inhuman barbarians" and "indomitable savage,s see Unzaga y Amézaga, Governor of Havana, to Carrión, governor of Veracruz, 14 April 1784, AGI, Cuba, Legajo 1335; José Antonio Areche, Mexico City, to Viceroy, 6 September 1774, AGN, Provincias Internas, Vol. 154.

32. Weber, *Spanish Frontier*, 229.

33. For the 1786–1789 statistics, see Jacobo Ugarte y Loyola, Chihuahua, 29 May 1789, AGN, Provincias Internas, Vol. 193. Matthew Babcock rightly points out that casualties were roughly even between "Spaniards" and "Apaches" between the late 1770s and mid-1790s. I do not disagree with him but suggest that in assessing the impact of war, we should also take into account the fact that Apache populations were much smaller than the population of Spanish subjects. See Babcock, "Rethinking the Establecimientos," 383, which notes that in select years between 1778 and 1795, the Spaniards reported that Apaches had killed 1,089 Spaniards, while they reported that they had killed 929 Apaches. For Spanish population figures numbering greater than fifty thousand in Nueva Vizcaya by the mid-1700s, see Peter Gerhard, *La Frontera Norte de la Nueva España* (México, D.F.: Universidad Nacional Autónoma de México, 1996), 214.

34. Griffen, *Apaches at War*, 11. On Apache ideas of warfare and revenge, see also Opler, *Apache Life-Way*, 370–375.

35. Statistics drawn from Babcock, "Rethinking the Establecimientos," 383, though the analysis is my own.

36. On families as a means of adaptation, I draw here from Hyde, *Empires, Nations, and Families*, especially 20.

37. Paul Conrad, "Bárbaros into Soldiers: Violence, Reciprocity, and Identity on New Spain's Northern Frontier" (Masters report, University of Texas at Austin, 2007). See also Blyth, *Chiricahua and Janos*, especially 87–98; Babcock, "Rethinking the Establecimientos."

38. Jacobo Ugarte y Loyola, Chihuahua, to Tovar, 14 June 1790, Janos Collection, Folder 5, Section 2.

39. Cortés, *Apache Frontier*, 32. I build here upon Babcock's work in "Turning Apaches into Spaniards" while placing a greater emphasis on the imperial dimensions of Spanish aims, especially by emphasizing the exile of Apache people to other regions of the Spanish empire.

40. For a discussion of ideas about manhood and the raid in Apache culture, see Opler, *An Apache Life-Way*, 399. See also Babcock, "Rethinking the Establecimientos"; Conrad, "Bárbaros into Soldiers."

41. William B. Griffen, "The Compás: A Chiricahua Apache Family of the Late 18th and Early 19th Centuries," *American Indian Quarterly* 7, 2 (1983), 26; Blyth, *Chiricahua and Janos*, 96–97; Antonio Cordero, Janos, to Casanova, 4 December 1790, Janos Collection, Folder 6A, Section1.

42. Pedro de Nava, Chihuahua, to Cordero, 7 June 1791, Janos Collection, Folder 7, Section 1.

43. Cordero, Janos, to Nava, 1 July 1791, Janos Collection, Folder 7, Section 1.

44. Cordero, Janos, to Nava, 1 July 1791, Janos Collection, Folder 7, Section 1. For Southern Apache ideas about reciprocity and gift giving, see Opler, *An Apache Life-Way*, 233–237. The fact that the Spanish did not employ other Apache groups such as the Lipan as military auxiliaries in the same way illustrates a distinctive characteristic of this place and time: the subjugation

of Southern and Mescalero Apaches was a particular focus and warranted creative measures because of their proximity to Spanish population centers.

45. Cortés, *Apache Frontier*, 29–30.

46. On efforts to manipulate Apache politics, see, for example, Antonio Cordero, Chihuahua, to Don Jacobo Ugarte y Loyola, 14 October 1790, AGN, Provincias Internas, Vol. 142; Pedro de Nava, Chihuahua, to Casanova, Janos, 7 de Julio de 1791, Janos Collection, Folder 7, Section 1A. For the Apache man "worrying what others thought of him," see Juan José Compa, Carcay, to Varela, 1 May 1833; Varela to Compa, 1 May 1833: Janos Microfilm Collection, Reel 25.

47. For typical censuses, see, for example, "Padron o estado del numero de Almas que se han bajado de Paz," [Census of the number of souls who have made peace], 30 March 1787, Bacoachi, AGI, Guadalajara, Legajo 287; "Estado que manifiesta el numero de Rancherias Apaches existentes de Paz en varios Parajes," [Report on the number of rancherias (local groups) at peace in various places], Chihuahua, 2 May 1793, AGI, Guadalajara, Legajo 289; Manuel de Casanova, Janos, 1 January 1793, Janos Collection, Folder 9, Section 2L. For the purposes of this article I focus on the especially descriptive censuses of Chiricahua Apaches conducted near the Spanish presidio of Janos in April, June, July, August, and October 1794. These are found in the Janos Collection, Folder 10, Section 2E (hereafter cited as Census of Apaches at Janos).

48. Census of Apaches at Janos, April, June, July, August, and October 1794.

49. Census of Apaches at Janos, April 1794.

50. Nava, Chihuahua, to Janos Commander, 8 August 1795; Janos Collection, Folder 11, Section 1F; Nava, Chihuahua to Janos Commander, 10 November 1795; Janos Collection, Folder 11, Section 1F.

51. They did locate other Apache boys in Havana, however, who were not the immediate relatives of the Apache headman requesting the return of his kin. Governor of Havana, Havana, to Viceroy, Mexico, 5 October 1790, AGI, Cuba, Legajo 1473; "Minuta de los pricioneros," Antonio Cordero, Janos, 15 February 1791, AGN, Provincias Internas, Vol. 142.

52. On the Chiricahua Apache incorporation of captives, see Opler, *An Apache Life-Way*, 349–351. For the petition, see José Tapia, Mexico City, to Viceroy, 18 May 1791, AGN, Provincias Internas, Vol. 142, f. 497; Census of Apaches at Janos, April, June, July, August, and October 1794.

53. On the careful consideration of marriage, see Opler, "Chiricahua Apaches," 411. Anderson has argued similarly for Lipan and Mescalero Apaches, in *Indian Southwest*, 135. For Eustingé and his wife three years later, see Census of Apaches at Janos, October 1794.

54. Census of Apaches at Janos, April 1794. On Chiricahua polygyny practices, including sororal polygyny and the fact polygyny was "not widely practiced," see Opler, *An Apache Life-Way*, 13, 55–56, 151, 416–420.

55. See Babcock, "Rethinking the Establecimientos," 379–380; Conrad, "Captive Fates," 249–251.

56. "Declaraciones tomadas a dos Apaches que se huyeron de las Colleras" [Statements taken from two runaways from the coffles of captives], Roque de Medina, Janos, to commandant general of Interior Provinces, 8 June 1796, AGN, Provincias Internas, Vol. 238. On Vivora's band identification, I draw from Babcock, *Apache Adaptation*, 299.

57. On the exile of non-belligerents, or those who claimed to not be belligerents, see the case of the Genízaro scout discovered wandering the streets of Valladolid, New Spain, in 1795: AGN, Provincias Internas, Vol. 204, ff. 460–487; petition of Christian Indian exiled with Apaches prisoners, Juan Pablo Montoya, Veracruz, 8 July 1783, AGN, Provincias Internas, Vol. 92;

testimony of Apache in escape case who identified himself as having been an "Apache de paz for 11 years," Jose Antonio, Pueblo de Apan, 20 August 1801, AGN, Presidios y Carceles, Vol. 6, Exp. 11.

58. LaFora, *Presidios Internos*, 280. On natal alienation as strategy of exploitation, see Orlando Patterson, *Slavery and Social Death: A Comparative Study* (Cambridge. MA: Harvard University Press, 1985).

59. Ann Laura Stoler, *Carnal Knowledge and Imperial Power: Race and the Intimate in Colonial Rule* (Berkeley: University of California Press, 2002), 210.

60. I build here on recent critiques of Orlando Patterson's concept of social death that have emphasized that it was an existential problem more than a lived condition. See Brown, "Social Death and Political Life"; Sweet, "Defying Social Death."

Chapter 5

1. Documents related to the transport of captives aboard the *Brújula* and *Polonia* are contained in AGI, Cuba, Legajos 1716 and 1721. See especially "Relación de los presidiarios q.e conduce de transporte este Buq.e desde el Puerto de Veracruz" [Report on the convicts that this boat is transporting from the port of Veracruz], 2 August 1802, AGI, Cuba, 1716. For quotes from the announcement of Indians' arrival in the Havana newspaper, see Duvon C. Corbitt, "Immigration in Cuba," *Hispanic American Historical Review* 22, 2 (1942): 285, as cited in Jason M. Yaremko, "Colonial Wars and Indigenous Geopolitics: Aboriginal Agency, the Cuba-Florida-Mexico Nexus, and the Other Diaspora," *Canadian Journal of Latin American & Caribbean Studies* 35, 70 (2010): 182. On the broader experience of exile during this period, see Conrad, "Captive Fates," 211–247.

2. Barr, "Spectrum of Indian Bondage," 277–309; Barr, "From Captives to Slaves," 19–46. I employ the category of "bondage" here to encompass slavery, incarceration, and involuntary servitude.

3. For the broader context of Native transport to the Spanish Caribbean, see Yaremko, "Colonial Wars"; Archer, "Deportation of Barbarian Indians"; Conrad, "Captive Fates," 211–247; Cienfuegos and García, "Indio foráneos"; Venegas and Valdés, *La ruta del horror*. The Spanish convict labor system is described in Ruth Pike, "Penal Servitude in the Spanish Empire: Presidio Labor in the Eighteenth Century," *Hispanic American Historical Review* 58, no. 1 (1978): 21–40. On slavery in Cuba during this period, see especially Elena Schneider, *The Occupation of Havana: War, Trade, and Slavery in the Atlantic World* (Chapel Hill: University of North Carolina Press, 2018); Matt Childs, *The 1812 Aponte Rebellion in Cuba and the Struggle Against Atlantic Slavery* (Chapel Hill: University of North Carolina Press, 2006).

4. My approach to diaspora draws from van Deusen, "Diasporas, Bondage"; Hodson, *Acadian Diaspora*, 3. My thinking about the "mercurial" nature of categories of race and bondage is influenced by Shoemaker, "Race and Indigeneity"; Rushforth, *Bonds of Alliance*, especially 3–14.

5. Claims of "humanitarian" intentions for forced removal belied by lived experiences have been commonplace in world history. See Richard Bessel and Claudia B. Haake, eds., *Removing Peoples: Forced Removal in the Modern World* (Oxford: Oxford University Press, 2009). My attention to the carceral nature of Spanish deportation policies is influenced by Lytle Hernández, *City of Inmates*. For "by the inevitable corruption of a place," see Antonio García del Postigo, Capitan de Navio [boat captain], Veracruz, to Don Antonio de Cardenas, 10 January 1797, AGN, Provincias Internas, Vol. 208, f. 580. On the deaths of approximately 30 percent en route to Mexico, see Conrad, "Captive Fates," 256–258.

6. My approach to Apaches' life trajectories in diaspora draws inspiration from Christopher, Pybus, and Rediker, "Introduction," especially 3.

7. See Chapter 3 of this book.

8. Conrad, "Captive Fates," especially 211–220.

9. Quotes on labor markets and imperial experimentation are from Hodson, *Acadian Diaspora*, 7. On convicts, see, for example, Clare Anderson, "Convict Passages in the Indian Ocean, 1790–1860," in Christopher, Cassandra Pybus, and Marcus Rediker, eds., *Many Middle Passages*, 129–149; Pike, "Penal Servitude." On Canary Islanders, see Weber, *Spanish Frontier*, 192–194.

10. For a summary of these arguments, see Hugo O'Connor to Viceroy, 8 March 1774, AGN, Provincias Internas, Vol. 54; Moorhead, "Spanish Deportation"; Archer, "Deportation of Barbarian Indians"; Santiago, *Jar of Severed Hands*, 42. On the demographics of deportation, see Conrad, "Captives Fates," 255–260.

11. Opler, *Apache Life-Way*. On the diversity of Apache groups and their cultural traditions, see the relevant entries in Alfonzo Ortiz, ed., vol. 10 of *Handbook of North American Indians*, ed. William C. Sturtevant (Washington, DC: Smithsonian Institution, 1983). On Indian territoriality, see Barr, "Geographies of Power"; Basso, *Wisdom Sits in Places*.

12. "Padrón que manifiesta el numero de Apaches de Paz establecidos en este Puesto y su Ynmediación" [Census of the peaceful Apaches settled at this post and its surroundings], 1 January 1801, 1 April 1801, 1 October 1801, in Janos Collection, Folder 16, Section 1C. On Apache motivations for entering peace agreements with the Spanish, see Babcock, "Rethinking the Establecimientos," 363–397.

13. On leveraging the captives to bring men to the negotiating table, see Chapter 4 of this book. On daybreak raids, see Jacoby, *Shadows at Dawn*.

14. Pedro de Nava, Chihuahua, to Don José Manuel de Ochoa, 11 August 1802, Janos Collection, Folder 16, Section 2D.

15. Pedro de Nava, Chihuahua, to Casanova, 20 March 1794, and 23 September 1794, Janos Collection, Folder 10, Section 1. By 1804, 10 percent of the population of the presidio of Janos was composed of Indian "orphans," or *criados*; see "Padron que manifiesta el numero de Tropa, Imbalidos, y Vecinos de este Puesto" [Census that shows the number of troops, invalids, and citzens of this post], Janos Collection, 31 December 1804, Folder 17, Section 2. Such dynamics reflect the broader cultural convergences that help explain captive exchange complexes across the North American Southwest: see Brooks, *Captives and* Cousins; Brooks, "'This Evil Extends Especially.'"

16. On the sale of Apache children and paying gambling debts with them, see Antonio García de Aexada, Chihuahua to Viceroy, 16 April 1816, AGN, Provincias Internas, Vol. 239; Gutiérrez, *When Jesus Came*, 152–153. For the broader trafficking of children in the borderlands of the North American Southwest and the relationship between intimacy and exploitation, I draw from Brooks, *Captives and Cousins;* Jagodinsky, "Territorial Bonds"; Margaret Jacobs, "Breaking and Remaking Families: The Fostering and Adoption of Native American Children in Non-Native Families in the American West, 1880–1940," in Adams and DeLuzio, *On the Borders of Love and Power*, 19–46.

17. For the 1802 convoy makeup, see "Estado que manifiesta el numero de Piezas Prisioneras de Guerra, que ha recivido en este Quartel el Sargento Joseph Antonio Uribe p.a conducir a Mexico" [Report that shows the number of prisoners of war that Sergeant Joseph Antonio Uribe received in these barracks to conduct to Mexico], AGN, Provincias Internas, Vol. 238, Exp. 12. On the broader makeup of such convoys, see Conrad, "Captive Fates," 255–260; Santiago, *Jar of Severed Hands*, 201–203.

18. Uribe, Mexico City, to Viceroy, 7 April 1802, AGN, Provincias Internas, Vol. 238, Exp. 12. On Indian escapes, see Conrad, "Captive Fates," 225–233, 259–260. On royal decrees at the turn of the nineteenth century and officials citing such decrees, see Viceroy, Mexico, to Regente de la Real Acordada, 10 January 1798, AGN, Provincias Internas, Vol. 208, f. 490; "Que se guarde lo ordenado sobre remision de Mecos" [That what has been ordered regarding the remission of Mecos be upheld], Council of Indies, Madrid, to Viceroy of New Spain, 16 July 1803, AGN, Reales Cedulas, Vol. 188, Exp. 169.

19. This account draws from testimony in the file of investigations into this escape in AGN, Indiferente de Guerra, Vol. 77, especially ff. 8–9.

20. The voluminous file documenting this escape is housed in AGN, Presidios y Carceles, Vol. 6, Exp. 3. By April more than twenty Indian women had been recaptured: see AGN, Indiferente Virreinal, Box 4817, Exp. 50.

21. The three tried in court martials were Juan de Dios Cos, D. Pedro Paez, and González. See cases in AGN, Presidios y Carceles, Vol. 6, Exp. 11, ff. 164–243; AGN, Indiferente de Guerra, Vol. 77; and AGN, Carceles y Presidios, Vol. 6, Exp. 3, respectively.

22. Domingo Valcarcel, Mexico, to Viceroy, 4 December 1778, AGN, Provincias Internas, Vol. 146, f. 414.

23. Juan Antonio de Araujo, Mexico, to Viceroy, 30 April 1792, AGN, Indiferente Virreinal, Box 1383, Exp. 3.

24. Del Corral to Viceroy, Mexico, 14 July 1790, AGN, Provincias Internas, Vol. 155, f. 97. On the imprisonment of this particular group of captives in Mexico City in 1802, see AGN, Provincias Internas, Vol. 238, Exp. 12. For broader practices, see Conrad, "Captive Fates," 211–247.

25. For a discussion of Indians returning from the coast to their homelands, see Roque de Medina to Commandant General of Interior Provinces, 8 June 1796, AGN, Provincias Internas, Vol. 238, f. 448.

26. This analysis draws from Stephanie Smallwood's approach to the experience of African captives in *Saltwater Slavery*, especially 60–63. On Apache responses to death, see Opler, *An Apache Life-Way*, 41. For deaths in jail, see AGN, Provincias Internas, Vol. 238, Exp. 12, especially ff. 362–363.

27. On the route between Mexico City and Veracruz, see "Ytinerario que debe observar el oficial que conduce la cuerda de Mecos (1810)" [Route that the official conducting the coffle of Mecos should observe], AGN, Provincias Internas, Vol. 238, f. 285. On shackles, see, for example, "Sobre haber intentado hacer fuga en Apan 27 Indios Apaches Prisioneros de Guerra (1801)" [On having tried to escape in Apan 27 Apache Indian Prisoners of War], AGN, Presidios y Carceles Vol. 6, Exp. 11, especially f. 170.

28. Testimony of Franquilino Vitado, 20 August 1801, AGN, Presidios y Carceles, Vol. 6, Exp. 11, ff. 205–206; Testimony of D. Pedro Paez, 13 August 1801, AGN, Presidios y Carceles, Vol. 6, Exp. 11, f. 172.

29. "File: Fort San Juan de Ulúa innen.jpg," Wikimedia Commons, the Free Media Repository, https://commons.wikimedia.org/w/index.php?title=File:Fort_San_Juan_de_Ul%C3%BAa_innen.jpg&oldid=109011808.

30. García del Postigo to Cardenas, AGN.

31. See José Antonio de Ogal, Mexico, to Viceroy, 9 May 1789, AGN, Provincias Internas, Vol. 155, f. 415, for quote on scurvy being an especially common illness. For more on scurvy deaths, see a similar report in AGN, Indiferente Virreinal, Box 4848, Exp. 24.

32. Order of Antonio de Puga, Santiago de Queretaro, 5 June 1780, AGN, Indiferente Virreinal, Box 2788, Exp. 38

33. On naming difficulties, see Diego de Lasaga, Villa de Padilla, to Viceroy, 5 September 1781, AGN, Provincias Internas, Vol. 123, f. 55. On the use of numbers for prisoners, see Juan Antonio de Araujo, Hospicio de Pobres, Mexico, to Viceroy, 13 February 1798, AGN, Provincias Internas, Vol. 208, f. 525.

34. For the baptism and escape, see "Sobre haberse aprehendido en Calpulalpa dos Mecas Apaches de las que hicieron fuga en la ultima Cuerda" [On having apprehended in Calpulalpa two Apache mecas of those that escaped in the last coffle], AGN, Carceles y Presidios Vol. 10, Exp. 1 (1802), especially ff. 17–18.

35. Joseph de Carrión y Andrade, Veracruz, to Unzaga y Amézaga, 30 April 1784, AGI, Cuba, Legajo 1335.

36. Documents related to the transport of captives aboard the *Brújula* and *Polonia* are contained in AGI, Cuba, Legajos 1716, 1720, 1721, which also contain correspondence related to the transport of convicts, usually referred to as *forzados* or *presidiarios*.

37. On the Apache neighborhood in Havana, see Governor Diego José Navarro, cited in Luis Unzaga y Amézaga to Viceroy, 20 September 1783, AGN, Archivo Histórico de Hacienda, Vol. 1083, Exp. 38. For his successor's similar view, see Cabello y Robles, Havana, to Pedro Corbalan, 14 January 1790, AGI, Cuba, Legajo 1429. On the lack of sentences, see Unzaga y Amézaga, Governor of Havana, to Carrión, Governor of Veracruz, 14 April 1784, AGI, Cuba, Legajo 1335.

38. Unzaga y Amézaga to Carrión, AGI.

39. On shipments arriving in Havana, see Unzaga y Amézaga to Viceroy of Mexico, 14 May 1784, AGI, Cuba, Legajo 1335.

40. The quote from announcements is drawn from Duvon C. Corbitt, "Immigration in Cuba," *Hispanic American Historical Review* 22, 2 (1942): 285, as cited in Yaremko, "Colonial Wars," 182.

41. On the subsequent boom in chattel slavery, see Childs, *1812 Aponte Rebellion*.

42. Ana María Gamonales, Havana, to Someruelos, 4 August 1802, AGI, Cuba, Legajo 1716.

43. Lorenzo de Ávila, Havana, to Someruelos, 6 August 1802, AGI, Cuba, Legajo 1716.

44. María Josefa de Castro to Governor of Havana, 11 February 1802, AGI, Cuba, Legajo 1716; Brigadir Don Vicente Nieto to Governor of Havana, 11 February 1802, AGI, Cuba, Legajo 1716.

45. Domingo Correa to Governor of Havana, 16 March 1797, AGI, Cuba, Legajo 1516A.

46. Doña María Josefa Martely to Governor of Havana, 6 August 1802, AGI, Cuba, Legajo 1716.

47. My analysis here benefits from Nancy van Deusen's consideration of the ways in which Castillians understood Native peoples arriving in Castille in the sixteenth century by comparing them to what was familiar. See van Deusen, "Seeing Indios," 205–235.

48. Ilona Katzew, *Casta Painting: Images of Race in Eighteenth-Century Mexico* (New Haven, CT: Yale University Press, 2005), especially 120–126. Torres's painting *E yndios apaches* is in the collection of the Dallas Museum of Art, Dallas, TX. Photo of painting by author.

49. Katzew, *Casta Painting*, 120–126.

50. For the role of royal slaves in transport, see, for example, Félix González to Governor, Havana, 28 March 1791, AGI, Cuba, Legajo 1516A. On the "slaves of his majesty" more broadly,

see María Elena Díaz, *The Virgin, the King, and the Royal Slaves of El Cobre: Negotiating Freedom in Colonial Cuba, 1670–1780* (Stanford, CA: Stanford University Press, 2000).

51. For institutional settings, see, for example, Francisco José de Bassave, Havana, to Someruelos, 12 February 1802, AGI, Cuba, Legajo 1721. On the distribution by the end of August, see Manuel Cavello, Casablanca, to Someruelos, 31 August 1802, AGI, Cuba, Legajo 1721.

52. Cavello to Someruelos, 31 August 1802, AGI.

53. Cavello to Someruelos, 31 August 1802, AGI.

54. Pike, "Penal Servitude." For an example of dueling over convict laborers, see Matias de Galvez, Mexico, to Luis de Unzaga y Amézaga, 12 March 1784, AGI, Cuba, Legajo 1335.

55. On these labor tasks, see Pike, "Penal Servitude." On Native labor in Veracruz, see "Arresto de dos Indios Mecos," 24 November 1784," AGN, Archivo Histórico de Hacienda, Vol. 723, Exp. 17; Doña Beatriz del Real, Veracruz, to Viceroy, 16 February 1786, AGN, Archivo Histórico de Hacienda, Vol. 723, Exp. 28.

56. On Indians not distributed because of age or appearance see Cabello, Casablanca, to Someruelos, 31 August 1802, AGI, Cuba, Legajo 1721. For "perverse inclination," see Doña Clara María de Sierra, Havana, to Governor, Undated [March 1791 from context], AGI, Cuba, Legajo 1516A.

57. On the trafficking of Native women in the New Mexican borderlands, see James Brooks, "'This Evil Extends Especially.'" For another perspective placing greater emphasis on the coercive aspects of such trades in the Louisiana borderlands, see Barr, "From Captives to Slaves."

58. Juan Manuel del Pilar y Manzano to Governor of Havana, 28 January 1791, AGI, Cuba, Legajo 1429. Similar notices in AGI, Cuba, Legajos 1716 and 1720 describe Native life events being recorded in the ledgers of "pardos y mulatos."

59. In making these comparisons and speculations, I draw from Christopher Schmidt-Nowara, *Slavery, Freedom, and Abolition in Latin America and the Atlantic World* (Albuquerque: University of New Mexico Press, 2011); and Herbert S. Klein and Ben Vinson III, *African Slavery in Latin America and the Caribbean*, 2nd ed. (New York: Oxford University Press, 2007). See also Patrick J. Carroll, *Blacks in Colonial Veracruz: Race, Ethnicity, and Economic Development* (Austin: University of Texas Press, 1991); Bennett, *Africans in Colonial Mexico*; Jane G. Landers and Barry M. Robinson, eds., *Slaves, Subjects, and Subversives: Blacks in Colonial Latin America* (Albuquerque: University of New Mexico Press, 2006).

60. "Parrafo de la carta que el Teniente D.n Jacinto de Porras . . . escrivio a su Hermano D.n Mauricio . . . su fha 26 de Abril anterior (1799)" [Paragraph of the letter that Lietenant Don Jacinto de Porras . . . wrote to his brother Don Mauricio . . . dated 26 of last April (1799)], AGI, Cuba, Legajo 1510A.

61. For historical context and the influence of the Haitian Revolution, see Laurent Dubois, *Avengers of the New World: The Story of the Haitian Revolution* (Cambridge, MA: Harvard University Press, 2005). Several files related to the escape of these six captives are contained in AGI, Cuba, Legajos 1716 and 1720 as well as AGN, Provincias Internas, Vol. 238, especially f. 475.

62. D. Josef López Gavilán, San José de las Lajas, to Someruelos, 18 September 1802, AGI, Cuba, Legajo 1720.

63. Gavilán to Someruelos, 18 September 1802, AGI.

64. Josef de Aguilar, Pinar del Rio, to the Marqués de Someruelos, Havana, 2 April 1803, AGI, Cuba, Legajo 1720; see also report of Francisco Ramos, Pinar del Rio, to the Marqués de Someruelos, Havana, 26 March 1803, AGI, Cuba, Legajo 1720.

65. Archer, "Deportation of Barbarian Indians," 381–383. On El Chico and El Grande, see "Extracto del sumario formado por D. Josef Gavilán . . . 9 de Febrero de 1803" [Abstract of the summary created by D. Josef Gavilán . . . 9 February 1803], AGI, Cuba, Legajo 1720.

66. On the actions of Indian runaways in Filipinas, see "Noticia que manifiesta los Muertos, Heridos, Robos, destrozo de Animales, Yncendios de Casas, y demas atrosidades que han cometido los Yndios feroces en el territorio de esta Jurisdiccion de Filipina, desde el año de 1796" [Report that shows the deaths, injuries, robberies, destruction of animals, and other atrocities that the ferocious Indians committed in the territory of this jurisdiction of Filipina since the year 1796], Josef de Aguilar, Pinar del Rio, to the Marqués de Someruelos, 2 April 1803, AGI, Cuba, Legajo 1720. On the bounties for El Chico and El Grande, see Real Consulado, Havana, to Someruelos, 14 October 1802, AGI, Cuba, Legajo 1720.

67. "Extracto formado por D. Josef López Gavilán" [Abstract created by D. Josef López Gavilán], Consolacion del Norte, to Someruelos, 22 January 1803, AGI, Cuba, Legajo 1720.

68. "Extracto formado por D. Josef López Gavilán," Gavilán to Someruelos, 22 January 1803, AGI.

69. "Extracto formado por D. Josef López Gavilán," Gavilán to Someruelos, 22 January 1803, AGI.

70. "Extracto formado por D. Josef López Gavilán," Gavilán to Someruelos, 22 January 1803, AGI.

71. On the actions of Indian runaways in this district, see Rudesindo de los Olivios, Santa Cruz de los Pinos, to Someruelos, 16 Mayo 1800, AGI, Cuba, Legajo 1720.

72. "Noticia que manifiesta los Muertos," Aguilar to Someruelos, AGI.

73. "Extracto formado por D. Josef López Gavilán," Gavilán to Someruelos, 22 January 1803, AGI. On Yucatec Mayans transported to Cuba, see, for example, Yaremko, "Colonial Wars," especially 179.

74. This analysis draws from Merrill, "Cultural Creativity," 124–152.

75. See the discussion above of the experiences of Apaches in Havana households who did not escape.

76. On convicts released from jails, see D. Joséf Lopez Gavilán to Consulado, Havana, 19 November 1802, AGI, Cuba, Legajo 1720. On slaves granted to widows, see Doña María Josefa Ortega, Havana, to El Consulado del Ayuntamienta, Havana, 14 May 1805, AGI, Cuba, Legajo 1720. For the folksong, see Venegas and Valdés, *La ruta del horror*, 224.

77. "Autos crimin.s seguido de oficio contra los Yndios Rafael, Vitaque, Oste, y Cle s.re la muerte del Negro Pasqual esclabo" [Criminal proceedings bought against the Indians Rafael, Vitaque, Oste, and Cle regarding the death of the black slave Pasqual], AGI, Cuba, Legajo 1716, with additional references to the case in AGI, Cuba, Legajo 1720.

78. A fragment amid documentation related to Rafael's case in AGI, Cuba, Legajo 1720 reads "murió en hospital segun informó el alcalde" [died in the hospital according to the magistrate].

79. On Apaches remaining imprisoned in Mexico City jails, see Archer, "Deportation of Barbarian Indians," 384–385. For the request for release from bondage, see Carlos and Manuel, Mecos, to Viceroy José de Iturrigaray, 14 October 1805, AGN, Indiferente Virreinal, Box 5908, Exp. 50. Documents contained in this file reveal that their first petition arrived and was brought to the viceroy's attention in March 1805, and they petitioned again in October. While the file contains several petitions from these two Indian men and documents investigating their history, there is no evidence in the file that they were freed. For the potential 1810 shipment, see the

transportation records in AGN, Provincias Internas, Vol. 238, f. 418 and Vol. 201, ff. 3–22. For 1816, see the file in AGN, Provincias Internas, Vol. 247, ff. 226–248.

80. In stressing Apaches' varied actions and their consequences, I am influenced by Walter Johnson, "On Agency," *Journal of Social History* 37, 1 (2003): 113–124.

81. My thinking on shifting approaches to punishing people cast as deviant is influenced by Foucault, *Discipline and Punish*. On criminal punishment in colonial New Spain, see Gabriel Haslip-Viera, *Crime and Punishment in Late Colonial Mexico City, 1692–1810* (Santa Fe: University of New Mexico Press, 1999).

82. I am influenced in this analysis by Barr, "From Captives to Slaves."

Chapter 6

1. "Instruccion que han de observer los Comandantes de los Puestos encargados de tratar con los Indios Apaches" [Policy that post commanders should observe in their dealings with Apache Indians], Pedro de Nava, Chihuahua, to Viceroy, the Count of RevillaGigedo, Mexico City, 14 October 1791, AGN, Provincias Internas, Vol. 66, ff. 363–377 (hereafter cited as Nava Instructions).

2. Nava Instructions, f. 364 (no insults to troops), ff. 366–367 (travel policy), ff. 371–372 (work policy).

3. I build in this chapter upon a key argument of Matthew Babcock—that the Apache de paz program resembled U.S.-run reservations—by examining the period in which Apaches inhabited U.S.-run reservations and exploring in greater depth the similarities and differences between these reservations and the previous Hispanic-Apache peace agreements. The most thorough scholarly accounts of the Apaches de paz policy are Babcock, *Apache Adaptation*; Babcock, "Rethinking the Establecimientos"; Blyth, *Chiricahua and Janos*, especially 87–121; Griffen, *Apaches at War*.

4. Babcock, *Apache Adaptation*; Blyth, *Chiricahua and Janos*, 155–186.

5. Most English-language studies of nineteenth-century Southern Apache history have focused on warfare and the biographies of key leaders, such as Mangas Coloradas, Victorio, Cochise, and Geronimo. An important exception for the pre-1850 period is Babcock, *Apache Adaptation*. The Spanish-language historiography on Apache-Hispanic interactions in Mexico has similarly emphasized conflict and warfare in the post-1830 period. See especially Isidro Vizcaya Canales, *Incursiones de indios al noreste en el México independiente (1821–1855)* (Monterrey, Mexico: Archivo General del Estado de Nuevo León, 1995); Martha Rodríguez, *La Guerra entre bárbaros y civilizados: El exterminio del nómada en Coahuila, 1840–1880* (Saltillo, Mexico: Centro de Estudios Sociales y Humanísticos, A.C., 1998).

6. For the post-1850 period, the best accounts of Southern Apaches and U.S. reservations are Sweeney, *From Cochise to Geronimo*; and Shapard, *Chief Loco*. I build upon those works by emphasizing the role of reservations in generating new forms of mobility and tying Apache experiences during this era to the long dureé of Southern Apache history, including past experiences with Spain and Mexico.

7. Sworn Testimony of Governor Henry Connelly, Santa Fe, New Mexico, 4 July 1865, in 39th Congress, 2nd Session, Senate Report No. 156, 332. For Anglo American ideas about the Hispanic past in the Southwest, see also Weber, *Spanish Frontier*, 335–360.

8. Babcock, *Apache Adaptation*, especially 1–18; Griffen, *Apaches at War*; Delay, *War of a Thousand Deserts*, 1–34.

9. Babcock, *Apache Adaptation*; Babcock, "Rethinking the Establecimientos"; Griffen, *Apaches at War*; Griffen, "Compás." The observations about source challenges are based on my

own research in the Janos Collection at the Benson Latin American Collection in Austin, TX and in the Mexican national archives in Mexico City. Map 3 is adapted from Babcock, *Apache Adaptation*, 3.

10. Griffen, "Compás," 26.

11. Babcock, *Apache Adaptation*, 121–122.

12. Griffen, *Apaches at War*, 100–109.

13. Griffen, *Apaches at War*, 102; Babcock, *Apache Adaptation*, 155–156, 181–183.

14. Griffen, *Apaches at War*, 109–110.

15. Blyth, *Chiricahua and Janos*, 108, 112, 124–126.

16. Pedro de Nava, Chihuahua, to Manuel de Casanova, Janos, 17 May 1794, Janos Collection, Folder 10, Section 1A; Griffen, "Compas," 37; Babcock, *Apache Adaptation*, 146.

17. Griffen, "Compás," 30–32.

18. Griffen, "Compás," 33–35, though analysis is my own.

19. On the unraveling of the Apache de paz program, see Babcock, *Apache Adaptation*, 172–212. On Mexican nationalism and ideas about independent Indians such as the Apache, see Delay, *War of a Thousand Deserts*, 141–164; Saldaña-Portillo, *Indian Given*, 108–153.

20. For the records of coffles of captives in these years, see AGN, Indiferente Virreinal, Box 3920, Exp. 3 (for 1801); AGN, Provincias Internas, Vol. 238, f. 328 (for 1802); AGN, Provincias Internas, Vol. 238, f. 391 (for 1803); AGN, Provincias Internas, Vol. 208, f. 550 (for 1806 and 1808); AGN, Provincias Internas, Vol. 227, ff. 226–249 (for 1816). I thank my colleague Bradley Folsom for alerting me to the story of Rafael. For discussion and citation of sources for Rafael, see Babcock, *Apache Adaptation*, 194. For the story of José Antonio Montes and his family, see Félix María Calleja del Rey, Viceroy, Mexico, to Commandant General Antonio García de Aexada, San Felipe el Real de Chihuahua (Chihuahua City), 7 January 1816; García de Aexada to Viceroy, 16 April 1816, both in AGN, Provincias Internas, Vol. 239.

21. Griffen, *Apaches at War*, 103; Babcock, *Apache Adaptation*, 158.

22. Mariano Varela to Juan José Compá, 1 May 1833, Janos Microfilm Collection, Reel #25. On El Compá's death, see Griffen, *Apaches at War*, 78, 103.

23. Blyth, *Chiricahua and Janos*, 114–118; Griffen, "Compás," 34–38; Babcock, *Apache Adaptation*, 184–187.

24. Delay, *War of a Thousand Deserts*, 165–225.

25. Babcock, *Apache Adaptation*, 172–212; Sweeney, *Cochise: Chiricahua Apache Chief*, 15–36; William B. Griffen, *Utmost Good Faith: Patterns of Apache-Mexican Hostilities in Northern Chihuahua Border Warfare, 1821–1848* (Albuquerque: University of New Mexico Press, 1989).

26. Blyth, *Chiricahua and Janos*, 123–154.

27. Juan José Compá, Carcai, to Mariano Varela, 25 April and 1 May 1833; Mariano Varela to Juan José Compá, 1 May 1833, both in Janos Microfilm Collection, Reel #25.

28. Edwin R. Sweeney, *Mangas Coloradas: Chief of the Chiricahua Apaches* (Norman: University of Oklahoma Press, 1998), 70–73; Babcock, *Apache Adaptation*, 213–215.

29. Sweeney, *Mangas Coloradas*, 72.

30. "Periko (Sago, interp.)," Morris Edward Opler Research Note, "Chiricahua: War," Opler Papers, Box 37, Folder 34. On Periko band affiliation, see Delgadillo, *From Fort Marion*, 218.

31. Sweeney, *Mangas Coloradas*, 135; Geronimo and Barrett, *Geronimo's Story*, 110; Anita Huizar-Hernández, "'The Real Geronimo Got Away': Eluding Expectation in *Geronimo: His Own Story; The Autobiography of a Great Patriot Warrior*," *Studies in American Indian Literatures*

29, 2 (2017), 49–70; Joseph C. Jastrzembski, "Treacherous Towns in Mexico: Chiricahua Apache Personal Narratives of Horrors," *Western Folklore* 54 (July 1995), 169–196; Jacoby, "'Broad Platform of Extermination.'"

32. Ralph Adam Smith, *Borderlander: The Life of James Kirker, 1793–1852* (Norman: University of Oklahoma Press, 1999), 123. For an insightful analysis of dehumanizing rhetoric in the context of interethnic conflicts, see Emile Bruneau and Nour Kteily, "The Enemy as Animal: Symmetric Dehumanization During Asymmetric Warfare," *PLoS ONE* 12, 7 (2017), 1–20.

33. Sweeney, *Mangas Coloradas*, 291.

34. Delay, *War of a Thousand Deserts*, 160–161.

35. Sweeney, *Mangas Coloradas*, 50–51, 62, 81, 94.

36. Babcock, *Apache Adaptation*, 250–285; Jastrzembski, "Treacherous Towns in Mexico."

37. Delay, *War of a Thousand Deserts*, xiii–xxi, 274–296.

38. "Transcript of Treaty of Guadalupe Hidalgo (1848)," https://www.ourdocuments.gov/doc.php?flash=true&doc=26&page=transcript.

39. Brackets in the original. Dan L. Thrapp, *Victorio and the Mimbres Apaches* (Norman: University of Oklahoma Press, 1974), 22.

40. Thrapp, *Victorio*, 22.

41. Thrapp, *Victorio*, 23–25, quote on 24. On Apaches and the boundary commission, see also Sweeney, *Mangas Coloradas*, 227–230; Babcock, 250–260; Rachel St. John, *Line in the Sand: A History of the Western U.S.-Mexico Border* (Princeton, NJ: Princeton University Press, 2011), 12–38.

42. Thrapp, *Victorio*, 27. Calhoun's perspective is a classic example of white American notions of "defensive conquest." See Philip Deloria, *Indians in Unexpected Places* (Lawrence: University Press of Kansas, 2004), 15–21; Boyd Cothran, *Remembering the Modoc War: Redemptive Violence and the Making of American Innocence* (Chapel Hill: University of North Carolina Press, 2014).

43. "Treaty with the Apache, 1852," in Charles J. Kappler, ed., *Indian Affairs: Laws and Treaties*, vol. 2 (Washington: Government Printing Office, 1904), 598–600, https://dc.library.okstate.edu/digital/collection/kapplers/id/26940/rec/2.

44. Thrapp, *Victorio*, 28. On the longer history of Apache diplomacy and its influence on this period, see Babcock, *Apache Adaptation*, 250–260.

45. "Treaty with the Apache, 1852," Article 7, 599. My thinking on recognizing Indigenous territoriality in the archive is influenced by Barr, "Geographies of Power."

46. Shapard, *Chief Loco*, 17.

47. Sweeney, *Mangas Coloradas*, 307–314.

48. Thrapp, *Victorio*, 45

49. Quote from Cochise is from John Ayers, Tularosa, New Mexico, to Nathaniel Pope, Santa Fe, New Mexico, 14 November 1872, NAMP, T21, Roll 15.

50. Sweeney, *Cochise: Chiricahua Apache Chief*, 97–113; Blyth, *Chiricahua and Janos*, 155–186. For international cooperation between the U.S. and Mexico against Apaches, see Sweeney, *From Cochise to Geronimo*, 300–301.

51. Thrapp, *Victorio*, 56–57.

52. Thrapp, *Victorio*, 57 ("Scarcely a family"); Sweeney, *Mangas Coloradas*, 362 ("talk Greek to them").

53. Thrapp, *Victorio*, 65–66; Sweeney, *Mangas Coloradas*, 307–334.

54. Debo, *Geronimo*, 69; Sweeney, *Mangas Coloradas*, 455–465.

55. James. H. Carleton, Santa Fe, to Lorenzo Thomas, Adjutant General U.S. Army, Washington, D.C., 19 March 1863, copy in Opler Papers, Box 26, Folder 12; Reséndez, *Other Slavery*, 285–290; Traci Brynne Vyles, *Wastelanding: Legacies of Uranium Mining in Navajo Country* (Minneapolis: University of Minnesota Press, 2015), ix; Hunt Watkinson, "In the Land," 30–43; Jennifer Denetdale, *The Long Walk: The Forced Navajo Exile* (New York: Chelsea House, 2007).

56. James H. Carleton, Santa Fe, New Mexico, to Christopher Carson, Cimarron River, New Mexico, 23 October, 1864, copy in Opler Papers, Box 26, folder 17; James H. Carleton, Santa Fe, New Mexico, to Ben C. Culter, Assistant Adjutant General, Santa Fe, New Mexico, 18 February 1865, in 39th Congress, 2nd Session, Senate Report No. 156, 313. On Carleton's reservation policy, see Sweeney, *Cochise:Chiricahua Apache Chief*, 223, 240, though the analysis is my own. On influential idea of "extermination," see Jacoby, "'Broad Platform of Extermination.'"

57. Cochise, in Edwin R. Sweeney, ed., Cochise: *Firsthand Accounts of the Chiricahua Apache Chief* (Norman: University of Oklahoma Press, 2015), 32.

58. Cochise, in Sweeney, *Cochise: Firsthand Accounts*, 32; Patricia Nelson Limerick, *Legacy of Conquest: The Unbroken Past of the American West* (New York: W. W. Norton, 1987), especially 17–34, 179–221; C. Joseph Genetin-Pilawa, *Crooked Paths to Allotment: The Fight Over Federal Indian Policy After the Civil War* (Chapel Hill: University of North Carolina Press, 2012), 51–72; Richard White, *Railroaded: The Transcontinentals and the Making of Modern America* (New York: W. W. Norton, 2011); White, *The Republic for Which It Stands: The United States During Reconstruction and the Gilded Age* (New York: Oxford University Press, 2017), 103–135; Jacoby, "'Broad Platform of Extermination'"; Jacoby, *Shadows at Dawn*.

59. Shapard, *Chief Loco*, 22–23.

60. Shapard, *Chief Loco*, 24–25.

61. Brackets in the original. Shapard, *Chief Loco*, 26.

62. Shapard, *Chief Loco*, 25–27. Southern Apaches demonstrated a similar flexibility during the era of the Apaches de paz program: see Babcock, *Apache Adaptation*.

63. For the Apache name of Warm Springs, see "Place Names" in Chiricahua Vocabulary II, Opler Papers, Box 51, Carton 3. For Apache descriptions of the place and its meaning to them, see Eve Ball, *Indeh: An Apache Odyssey* (Norman: Oklahoma University Press, 1988), 34, 187 ("good country"); Eve Ball and James Kaywaykla, *In the Days of Victorio: Recollections of a Warm Springs Apache* (Tucson: University of Arizona Press, 1970), 29–30; Jason Betzinez and Wilbur Sturtevant Nye, *I Fought with Geronimo* (Harrisburg, PA: Stackpole Company, 1959), 25. See also Daniel D. Arreola, "The Chiricahua Apache Homeland in the Borderland Southwest," *Geographical Review* 102, 1 (2012), 111–131.

64. On Apache relations with Cañada Alamosa/Monticello, see Sweeney, *Making Peace with Cochise*, 138–139; Thrapp, *Victorio*, 101; Shapard, *Chief Loco*, 38–39.

65. Shapard, *Chief Loco*, 38–39.

66. Orlando Piper, Pasaje, New Mexico, to Nathaniel Pope, Superintendent of Indian Affairs, Santa Fe, New Mexico, 31 March 1871, NAMP, T21, Roll 15; Piper, Cañada Alamosa, New Mexico, to Pope, 31 August 1871, NAMP; "Council of Mimbres Apaches Held at Fort Tularosa 11 September, 1872," in Sweeney, *Making Peace with Cochise*, 113–118; Shapard, *Chief Loco*, 32–33.

67. Piper, Pasaje, New Mexico to Pope, 26 January, 31 March 1871, NAMP.

68. Piper, Cañada Alamosa, New Mexico, to Pope, 31 May 1871, 30 June, 31 July, 31 August 1871 ("for more than two years," "wish of the Indians"), NAMP.

69. Sweeney, *Making Peace with Cochise*, 13–17; Genetin-Pilawa, *Crooked Paths to Allotment*, 91; Peter Cozzens, ed., *Eyewitnesses to the Indian Wars*, vol. 1, *1865–1890* (Mechanicsburg, PA: Stackpole Books, 2001), xxi–xxii.

70. Sweeney, *Victorio*, 329 ("arable lands"); Colonel Gordon Granger, in Sweeney, *Cochise: Firsthand Accounts*, 189 ("bad whites").

71. Shapard, *Chief Loco*, 45.

72. Joseph Alton Sladen, in Sweeney, *Making Peace with Cochise*, 38 ("so long as"); Shapard, *Chief Loco*, 38–39; Thrapp, *Victorio*, 145 ("wholly under").

73. Piper, Cañada Alamosa, New Mexico, to Pope, 30 September, 19 October 1871, NAMP.

74. Cochise, in Sweeney, *Cochise: Firsthand Accounts*, 179–180.

75. Piper, Cañada Alamosa, New Mexico, to Pope, 31 October 1871, NAMP. On Cochise allowing his picture to be sent instead of going himself to Washington, D.C., see Thrapp, *Victorio*, 142. On American Indian delegations to Washington D.C., see Alessandra Link, "The Iron Horse in Indian Country: Native Americans and Railroads in the U.S. West" (Ph.D. diss., University of Colorado at Boulder, 2018).

76. Piper, Cañada Alamosa, New Mexico, to Pope, 31 December 1871, 28 March 1872, NAMP.

77. Piper, Tularosa, New Mexico, to Pope, 30 June 1872, NAMP. On the journey of forced removal, see Thrapp, *Victorio*, 147–148.

78. Piper, Tularosa, New Mexico, to Pope, 30 June, 31 July 1872, NAMP; Thrapp, *Victorio*, 148; Shapard, *Chief Loco*, 55; Sweency, *Cochise*, 336–339.

79. Ayers to Pope, 31 October, 14 November, 16 November 1872, NAMP; quote from Victorio in Sweeney, *Making Peace with Cochise*, 115.

80. Ayers to Pope, 13 December, 18 December, 23 December, 31 December 1872, NAMP.

81. Benjamin Thomas, Tularosa, New Mexico, to Edwin Dudley, Superintendent of Indian Affairs, Santa Fe, New Mexico, 11 September 1873, NAMP, T21, Roll 15; Thrapp, *Victorio*, 351n11. For "pets" language, see, for example, "Two Policies," in *Arizona Miner*, 30 March 1872. On "winter resorts," see Petition of Society of Arizona Pioneers, Tucson, Arizona, to President Grover Cleveland, Washington, D.C., 25 June 1885, in Charles D. Poston, "History of the Apaches," in Opler Papers, Box 20, Folder 16. Thrapp argues that Thomas was "one of the better agents to serve" Southern Apaches. To be sure, Thomas was in an extraordinarily difficult situation—trying to administer a reservation Apaches did not want to live on—but he repeatedly made decisions that worsened relations with Apaches and led them to flee the reservation.

82. Thomas to Dudley, 14 June, 23 June, 24 June, 26 June, 11 July 1873, NAMP, Roll 15.

83. Thomas to Dudley, 24 July, 25 July, 30 July, 31 July 1873, NAMP, Roll 15.

84. Thomas to Dudley, 15 October 1873, 5 January, 31 January, 28 February 1874, NAMP, Roll 23.

85. Thomas to Dudley, 28 February, 31 March, 3 April, 19 April 1874, NAMP, Roll 23.

86. Oliver Howard, Washington, D.C., to F. A. Walker, Commissioner of Indian Affairs, Washington, D.C., 7 November 1872, NAMP, M666, Roll 24, Frames 474–485, quote on 484. For more on Howard delegation and his biography, see Sweeney, *Cochise: Chiricahua Apache Chief*, 348–366.

87. Howard to Walker, 7 November 1872, NAMP, Frame 477; Sladen, in Sweeney, *Making Peace with Cochise*, 30–31; "General Oliver Otis Howard to His Wife From Fort Tularosa," in Sweeney, *Cochise: Firsthand Accounts*, 196; Sweeney, *Cochise: Chiricahua Apache Chief,* 348–366.

88. Sweeney, *Making Peace with Cochise*, 40–64.

89. Sweeney, *Making Peace with Cochise*, 63.

90. Sweeney, *Making Peace with Cochise*, 65–66.

91. Sweeney, *Making Peace with Cochise*, 94; "Journalists and Charles Coleman Interview Cochise," in Sweeney, *Cochise: Firsthand Accounts*, 169–170.

92. While this analysis is my own, it draws from Sweeney, *Cochise*, 79–85, 357–366. Sweeney emphasizes the tension between Chihenes and Chokonens in shaping Apache diplomacy surrounding reservation sites. Apache diplomacy emphasizing a desire to live in the "land of their fathers" and attachment to land is ubiquitous. Especially descriptive examples include Ayers to Pope, 30 November 1872, NAMP; Howard to Walker, 7 November 1872, NAMP; Piper, Cañada Alamosa, New Mexico, to Pope, 20 October 1871, NAMP.

93. Major-General O. O. Howard, *My Life and Experiences Among Our Hostile Indians* (Hartford: A.D. Worthington and Company, 1907), 208. For Cochise's use of metaphors of corrals and coyotes, see "Cochise's Talk with Special Indian Agent William Frederick Milton Arny," in Sweeney, *Cochise: Firsthand Accounts*, 139; "Verbatim Account of the Interview Between Colonel Granger and Cochise," in Sweeney, *Cochise: Firsthand Accounts*, 190.

94. Sweeney, *Making Peace with Cochise*, 160n128; Julian Lim, *Porous Borders: Multiracial Migrations and the Law in the U.S.-Mexico Borderlands* (Chapel Hill: University of North Carolina Press, 2018).

95. Shapard, *Chief Loco*, 79–80; Sweeney, *From Cochise to Geronimo*, 15–27. Thrapp, *Victorio*, 164–168.

96. "Fred Hughes's Reminiscences of Cochise and the Chiricahua Reservation," in Sweeney, *Cochise: Firsthand Accounts*, 261–270.

97. Howard to Walker, 7 November 1872, NAMP, Frame 474.

98. C. L. Sonnichsen, *The Mescalero Apaches* (Norman: University of Oklahoma Press, 1979), 157; Peter Iverson, *Diné: A History of the Navajos* (Albuquerque: University of New Mexico Press, 2002), 66; Richard J. Perry, *Apache Reservation: Indigenous Peoples and the American State* (Austin: University of Texas Press, 1993), 160–190; General Order No. 8, "To carry out the wishes of the Secretary of the Interior and instructions of the Secretary of War, relating to the southern and other roving bands of Apache Indians," James. B. Fry, Assistant Adjutant General, Chicago, Illinois, 20 November 1871, NAMP, M666, Roll 24, Frames 12–13. Map 4 is adapted from Thrapp, *Victorio*, 9.

99. "Report of William Vandever, Indian Inspector, on Conditions at the Chiricahua Reservation," in Sweeney, *Cochise: Firsthand* Accounts, 271–273; Thrapp, *Victorio*, 166 ("in a short time"). Years later, an inspector of the San Carlos reservation in April 1878 would recall critically this period in which Jeffords routinely provisioned Indians from other reservations. See Report of E. C. Watkins, San Carlos, Arizona, 13 April 1878, NAMP, M1070, Roll 2.

100. Frederick G. Hughes, "The Military and Cochise," in Cozzens, *Eyewitnesses to the Indian Wars*, 132–137 (quote on 132). Sweeney describes the use of the Chiricahua reservation for raiding into Mexico and American and Mexican responses to that in detail in *From Cochise to Geronimo*, 21–44.

101. "Indian Inspector Edward Kemble's Inspection of the Chiricahua Reservation," in Sweeney, *Cochise: Firsthand* Accounts, 292–294.

102. General Order No. 9, A. H. Nickerson, Acting Assistant Adjutant General, Prescott, Arizona, Headquarters Department of Arizona to James. B. Fry, Assistant Adjutant General, Chicago, Illinois, 20 November 1871, NAMP, M666, Roll 24, Frames 12–13.

103. "Tom Jeffords' Final Report to the Commissioner of Indian Affairs, June 30, 1876," in Sweeney, *Cochise: Firsthand Accounts*, 294–301. See also Sweeney, *From Cochise to Geronimo*, 40–44.

104. Sweeney, *Cochise: Chiricahua Apache Chief*, 386–387; "Tom Jeffords' Final Report," 295–298.

105. "Tom Jeffords' Final Report," 296. Jeffords, in contrast to Agent Thomas at Tularosa, had the good sense and knowledge of Apache culture to recognize that negotiation and reciprocity were the best management practices.

106. On the nature of U.S. Indian policy, see Cathleen D. Cahill, *Federal Fathers and Mothers: A Social History of the United States Indian Service, 1869*–1933 (Chapel Hill: University of North Carolina Press, 2011); Peterson, *Indians in the Family*.

107. James H. Carleton, Santa Fe, to Lorenzo Thomas, Adjutant General U.S. Army, Washington, D.C., 19 March 1863, copy in Opler Papers, Box 26, Folder 12.

Chapter 7

1. Kenoi Autobiography, 271 ("naked, starving"), 273 ("old people"), 275 ("attending to business"), 277 ("their land").

2. Kenoi Autobiography, 275.

3. The most thorough account of Southern Apache reservation life is Sweeney, *From Cochise to Geronimo*. As he notes, relatively little prior scholarship examined reservation life, instead highlighting raids and military campaigns. I build upon his exhaustive research by centering family and kinship in explaining continued Apache mobility after forced removal to San Carlos and how this mobility in turn led to further displacement of Apache families.

4. In thinking about borders, including both reservation borders and the international U.S.-Mexico border, I am influenced by St. John, *Line in the Sand*, especially 39–62; Kelly Lytle Hernández, "Borderlands and the Future History of the American West," *Western Historical Quarterly* 42, 3 (2011), 325–330; Alice Baumgartner, "The Line of Positive Safety: Borders and Boundaries in the Rio Grande Valley, 1848–1880," *Journal of American History* 101, 4 (2015), 1106; Mary E. Mendoza, "Treacherous Terrain: Environmental Control at the U.S.-Mexico Border," *Environmental History* 23, 1 (2018), 117–127.

5. Recent scholarship has emphasized Apache resistance to Mexican and U.S. rule as being fundamentally rooted in questions of masculinity and lifestyle—"freedom." See Sweeney, *From Cochise to Geronimo*; Robert M. Utley, *Geronimo* (New Haven, CT: Yale University Press, 2013); Paul Andrew Hutton, *The Apache Wars: The Hunt for Geronimo, the Apache Kid, and the Captive Boy Who Started the Longest War in American History* (New York: Broadway Books, 2016). The Spanish-language historiography in Mexico has similarly emphasized conflict and warfare with Apaches and Comanches more than negotiation. For a detailed bibliography, see Babcock, *Apache Adaptation*, 16n16.

6. On Apache peace diplomacy, see Chapter 6 of this book. On U.S. Indian law and treaty making, see Vine Deloria, Jr., *Behind the Trail of Broken Treaties: An Indian Declaration of Independence* (Austin: University of Texas Press, 1985).

7. David E. Wilkins and K. Tsianina Lomawaima, *Uneven Ground: American Indian Sovereignty and Federal Law* (Norman: University of Oklahoma Press, 2001), especially 98–142; Genetin-Pilawa, *Crooked Paths*, 25–26. For an insightful comparison of policing of Indigenous peoples in North American border regions, see Andrew R. Graybill, *Policing the Great Plains: Rangers, Mounties, and the North American Frontiers, 1875–1910* (Lincoln: University of

Nebraska Press, 2007); Brenden W. Rensink, *Native But Foreign: Indigenous Immigrants and Refugees in the North American Borderlands* (College Station: Texas A&M University Press, 2018).

8. James H. Carleton, Santa Fe, New Mexico, to James R. Doolittle, United States Senate, Washington, D.C., 22 October 1865, Opler Papers, Box 26, Folder 17 ("exterminated or placed on reservations"). On "concentration" policy, see Debo, *Geronimo*, 55–56, 60-61 77–79, 94–97; Shapard, *Chief Loco*, 112–113, 148–149; Sweeney, *Cochise: Chiricahua Apache Chief*, 265.

9. Sweeney, *From Cochise to Geronimo*, 28–44.

10. Sweeney, *From Cochise to Geronimo*, 45–62; quote from John Clum, "Capture of Geronimo," copy in Opler Papers, Box 11, Folder 2.

11. "Tom Jeffords' Final Report," in Sweeney, *Cochise: Firsthand Accounts*, 295–298; Sweeney, *From Cochise to Geronimo*, 45–62; Debo, *Geronimo*, 97–99.

12. I drew inspiration for my larger argument from an aside in Thrapp, *Victorio*, 180, in which he noted that "the 'removal' of the Indians from the Chiricahua Reservation had succeeded in emptying that reserve, but instead of collecting its population at San Carlos . . . it was dispersed." For events leading up to removal, including the discovery of Ju and Geronimo's flight, see John P. Clum, Apache Pass, Arizona, to General August Kautz, Commanding Dept. of Arizona, Prescott, Arizona, 8 June 1876, NAMP, M234, Roll 16; Clum to Commissioner of Indian Affairs, Washington, D.C., 10 June 1876; NAMP.

13. Thrapp, *Victorio*, 179–180; Debo, *Geronimo*, 98–99; Sweeney, *From Cochise to Geronimo*, 69–70.

14. John P. Clum, Eureka Springs, Arizona, to Commissioner of Indian Affairs, Washington, D.C., telegram, 16 June 1876, NAMP, M234, Roll 16 ("grand success," "the terrible shade"). For Pionsenay's escape and population of Southern Apaches at San Carlos, see Sweeney, *From Cochise to Geronimo*, 59–63. For making and laying adobes after arrival, see Woodworth Clum, *Apache Agent: The Story of John P. Clum* (New York: Houghton Mifflin, 1936), 185.

15. Frank S. Ingoldsby, M. Kelleher, M. R. Peel, and H. S. Crocker & Co, *Map of the Tombstone Mining District: Cochise Co., Arizona Ter.* (San Francisco: H. S. Crocker, 1881), https://www.loc.gov/item/2012586611/; Jane Eppinga, *Tombstone* (Charleston, SC: Arcadia Publishing, 2003), 19–28.

16. "Informant: Sam Haozous, Ft. Sill Apache," copy of tape made in 1956 by members of the Haozous Family, in Opler Papers, Series 1, Box 37, Folder 37, summary and pp. 1–2 (hereafter cited as Haozous Oral History).

17. Haozous Oral History, 2–3.

18. Betzinez and Nye, *I Fought with Geronimo*, 44–46; Geronimo and Barrett, *Geronimo's Story*, 131–133; Shapard, *Chief Loco*, 97–100; Sweeney, *From Cochise to Geronimo*, 84–85; Debo, *Geronimo*, 103–114.

19. On the reservation landscape, see Britton Davis, *The Truth About Geronimo*, ed. Milo Milton Quaife (New Haven, CT: Yale University Press, 1929), especially 8, 31; Charles P. Elliott, "An Indian Reservation Under General George Crook," in Cozzens, *Eyewitnesses to the Indian Wars* 405–413; Anne Orth Epple, *A Field Guide to the Plants of Arizona* (Helena, MT: Falcon Publishing, 1995), 5; Sweeney, *From Cochise to Geronimo*, 59.

20. George Crook, "The Apache Troubles"; Murat Masterson, "General Crook's Return"; both in Cozzens, *Eyewitnesses to the Indian Wars*, 311–316, quote on 316; Davis, *Truth About Geronimo*, 39.

21. Elliott, "Indian Reservation," 406.

22. Frederick Lloyd, "A Profile of the San Carlos Agency," in Cozzens, *Eyewitnesses to the Indian Wars*, 329; Barnes, "In the Apache Country," in Cozzens, *Eyewitnesses to the Indian Wars*, 617; Davis, *Truth About Geronimo*, 43.

23. Barnes, "In the Apache Country," 616–617.

24. Barnes, "In the Apache Country," 617–618; Davis, *Truth About Geronimo*, 42–44; K. T. Dodge, photographer, *Line of Apache Men, Women, and Children Outside Agency Building on Issue Day*, San Carlos, Arizona, ca. 1899, photograph, Library of Congress, https://www.loc .gov/item/95506641/.

25. "Census Roll of Apache Indians of the San Carlos Reservation," 7 July 1877, taken by Martin A. Sweeney, Acting Indian Agent, NAMP, M234, Roll 18.

26. Report of Inspector E. C. Watkins, San Carlos, Arizona, to E. A. Hayt, Commission of Indian Affairs, Washington, D.C., 13 April 1878, NAMP, M1070, Roll 2.

27. Report of Inspector E. C. Watkins, NAMP.

28. Sweeney, *From Cochise to Geronimo*, 66 ("fever hole"), 117–118.

29. Sweeney, *From Cochise to Geronimo*, 117–118.

30. Sweeney details at length the ongoing struggles with malaria in *From Cochise to Geronimo*, 121, 124–126, 128–129, 133, 156, 161–162. For settler pressure, see Watkins to Hayt, 13 April 1878, NAMP; Jacoby, "'Broad Platform of Extermination,'" 249–267.

31. Petition from Millen's Camp, Globe District, Arizona, 12 July 1877, enclosed in Inspector William Vandever, San Carlos, Arizona, to Commission of Indian Affairs, Washington D.C., 26 July 1877, NAMP, M234, Roll 18.

32. John Clum, San Carlos, Arizona, to Commissioner of Indian Affairs, Washington D.C., 25 May 1877, NAMP, M234, Roll 18; Shapard, *Chief Loco*, 101–111.

33. For slipping away weeks before, see T. C. Tupper, Camp Grant, Arizona, to Post Adjutant, Camp Grant, Arizona, 18 September 1877, NAMP, M666, Roll 366; Shapard, *Chief Loco*, 105; Sweeney, *From Cochise to Geronimo*, 93–98.

34. H. L. Hart, San Carlos Agency, Arizona, to Commissioner of Indian Affairs, Washington, D.C., 18 September 1877, NAMP, M234, Roll 19; Sweeney, *From Cochise to Geronimo*, 93–98.

35. Tupper to Post Adjutant, 18 September 1877 ("considerable panic"); D. W. Whitney, Acting Agent, Ojo Caliente, New Mexico, to E. A. Hayt, Commissioner of Indian Affairs, Washington, D.C., 30 November 1877 ("seeking a place of safety"); Lt. General P. H. Sheridan, Chicago, Illinois, to General E. D. Townsend, Washington, D.C., 30 October 1877; John Pope, Fort Leavenworth, Kansas, to R. C. Drum, Chicago, Illinois, 5 November 1877 ("unless taken by force"); Edward Hatch, Santa Fe, New Mexico, to Assistant Adjutant General, Fort Leavenworth, Kansas, 28 October 1877 ("in raiding parties"); all in NAMP, M666, Roll 366.

36. Report of William Vandever, Santa Fe, New Mexico, 23 October 1877, NAMP, M1070, Roll 2 ("unfriendliness manifested)"; Pope to Drum, 18 October 1877, NAMP, M666, Roll 366 ("these Indians").

37. E. C. Watkins quoted in Sweeney, *From Cochise to Geronimo*, 126; Whitney to Hayt, 13 December 1877; endorsement of W. T. Sherman, Washington, D.C., 6 February 1878; Pope to Drum, 5 November 1877, all in NAMP, M666, Roll 366.

38. Sweeney, *From Cochise to Geronimo*, 125. For the list of relatives, see Thomas Keam, Ojo Caliente, to A. E. Hooker, Ojo Caliente, New Mexico, 21 January 1878, NAMP, M666, Roll 366, Frame 294.

39. Sheridan quoted in E. A. Hayt, Commissioner of Indian Affairs, Washington D.C., to Secretary of the Interior, 23 July 1878, NAMP, M666, Roll 366, Frames 347–351.

40. Hayt to Secretary of the Interior, 23 July 1878, NAMP.

41. F. T. Bennet, Fort Wingate, New Mexico, to Acting Assistant Adjutant General, District of New Mexico, Santa Fe, New Mexico, 4 December 1878, NAMP, M666, Roll 366, Frames 484–494.

42. Bennet to Acting Assistant Adjutant General, 4 December 1878, NAMP, Frame 488; Bennet quoted in John S. Loud, Acting Assistant Adjutant General, Fort Leavenworth, Kansas, to Assistant Adjutant General, Chicago, Illinois, 19 October 1878, NAMP.

43. Bennet to Acting Assistant Adjutant General, 4 December 1878, NAMP, Frames 490–493.

44. Hatch to Assistant Adjutant General, 26 February 1879, NAMP, Frame 520; Hayt to Secretary of the Interior, 11 April 1879, NAMP, Frames 549–551. See also Thrapp, *Victorio*, 212–217.

45. S. A. Russell, Mescalero Agency, New Mexico, to Commissioner of Indian Affairs, Washington, D.C., 30 June 1879, NAMP, M666, Roll 366, Frames 619–620.

46. Russell to Commissioner of Indian Affairs, NAMP.

47. Thrapp, *Victorio*, 215–218; Sweeney, *From Cochise to Geronimo*, 165–167.

48. Thrapp, *Victorio*, 310–311.

49. Thrapp, *Victorio*, 311.

50. Sweeney details well the demographic consequences of flights from reservation; see especially *From Cochise to Geronimo*, 145–146.

51. Sweeney, *From Cochise to Geronimo*, 145–146, 161–166.

52. Carr quoted in Sweeney, *From Cochise to Geronimo*, 161–162. On broader ideas of Indian extermination during this period, see Jacoby, "'The Broad Platform of Extermination'"; Benjamin Madley, *An American Genocide: The United States and the California Indian Catastrophe* (New Haven, CT: Yale University Press, 2016).

53. Shapard, *Chief Loco*, 142.

54. Sweeney, *From Cochise to Geronimo*, 182–183.

55. Naiche quoted in "Notes of an Interview Between Maj. Gen. George Crook, U.S. Army, and Chatto, Ka-e-te-na, Noche, and Other Chiricahua Apaches," 2 January 1890, Mt. Vernon Barracks Alabama, copy in Opler Papers, Series 1, Box 26, Folder 20; Geronimo and Barrett, *Geronimo's Story of His Life*, 141. For territorial press coverage of Apaches during this period emphasizing "extermination" or "removal," see "Exterminate the Apaches" and "They Must Go" in *Arizona Weekly Citizen*, Tucson, 18 September 1881, in Arizona Memory Project, Arizona Historical Digital Newspapers, https://azmemory.azlibrary.gov/digital/collection/sn82015133 /id/148/rec/1.

56. Sweeney, *From Cochise to Geronimo*, 191–196.

57. Sweeney, *From Cochise to Geronimo*, 184–185, 207–229; Kenoi Autobiography, 275.

58. Sweeney, *From Cochise to Geronimo*, 224–226; Betzinez and Nye, *I Fought with Geronimo*, 56–57.

59. Sweeney, *From Cochise to Geronimo*, 231–232.

60. Hunt Watkinson, "In the Land," 30; Geronimo and Barrett, *Geronimo's Story of His Life*, 67.

61. "Statement of Mañanita, Wife of Geronimo," 1 April 1884, in San Carlos, AZ, Miscellaneous Records, 1882–1900, NARA, RG 393, San Carlos, Arizona, Box 14.

62. "Statement of Mañanita," NARA.

63. See Frederick T. Frelinghuysen, "Mexico: Reciprocal Right to Pursue Savage Indians Across Boundary Line," 29 July 1882, in Cozzens, *Eyewitnesses to the Indian Wars*, 343–345; Sweeney, *From Cochise to Geronimo*, 280.

64. Sweeney, *From Cochise to Geronimo*, 301–306.

65. Sweeney, *From Cochise to Geronimo*, 301–312, quote on 308.

66. "Statements made to Captain Emmet Crawford, 3rd Cavalry, by Five Prominent Apaches [Mañanita, Ka-e-te-na, Chihuahua, Geronimo, Natchez (Naiche)] Concerning the Migration of Indians from Casa Grande, Mexico, to San Carlos, Arizona, Nov. 1883–Mar. 1884," in San Carlos, AZ, Miscellaneous Records, 1882–1900, NARA, RG 393, San Carlos, AZ, Box 14.

67. "Statement of Chatto, Chiricahua Chief," 3 March 1884, NAMP, M689, Roll 176.

68. Sweeney, *From Cochise to Geronimo*, 319–320, 349–354.

69. Joseph C. Porter, *Paper Medicine Man: John Gregory Bourke and His American West* (Norman: University of Oklahoma Press, 1986), 164; Sweeney, *From Cochise to Geronimo*, 322 ("no one likes to see").

70. "What Will We Do with Them?" *New York Times*, 18 June 1883.

71. I am influenced in this analysis of U.S. Indian policy by Wilkins and Lomawaima, *Uneven Ground*; and Peterson, *Indians in the Family*, especially the epilogue.

72. "Statement of Geronimo," 21 March 1884, NARA, RG 393, San Carlos, AZ, Box 14.

73. "Statement of Chatto, Chiricahua Chief," 3 March 1884, NAMP, M689, Roll 176.

74. P. C. Robertson, Chairman Board Supervisors, Gila Co., Arizona Territory, to P. P. Wilcox, copy enclosed in E. L. Stevens, Washington D.C., to Secretary of the Interior, Washington D.C., 9 August 1884, NAMP, M689, Roll 176.

75. "Statement of Geronimo," 21 March 1884, NARA; "Statement of Chatto, Chiricahua Chief," 3 March 1884, NAMP.

76. Davis, *Truth About Geronimo*, 103–106.

77. Davis, *Truth About Geronimo*, 107.

78. "Statement of Kaetena," 17 November 1883; "Statement of Chihuahua," 20 November 1883; both in NARA, RG 393, San Carlos, AZ, Box 14.

79. Charles B. Gatewood, *Lt. Charles Gatewood and His Apache Wars Memoir*, ed. Louis Kraft (Lincoln: University of Nebraska Press, 2009), 75; Davis, *Truth About Geronimo*, 106.

80. Davis, *Truth About Geronimo*, 102.

81. Davis, *Truth About Geronimo*, 123; Sweeney, *From Cochise to Geronimo*, 371–373.

82. Davis, *Truth About Geronimo*, 114.

83. George Crook quoted in P. H. Morgan, Mexico City, Mexico, to José Fernández, Mexico City, Mexico, 5 August 1884, NAMP, M689, Roll 177.

84. Ignacio Mariscal, Department of Foreign Relations, Mexico City, Mexico, to P. H. Morgan, Mexico City, Mexico, 10 February 1885, NAMP, M689, Roll 177.

85. George Crook to Assistant Adjutant General, 7 April 1885, with enclosure signed by Britton Davis, "Chiricahua and Warm Spring Indians Held as Captives in Mexico," NAMP, M689, Roll 177

86. Davis, "Chiricahua and Warm Springs Indians," NAMP.

87. John Pope, San Francisco, California, to Adjutant General, Washington, D.C., telegram, 26 April 1885, NAMP, M689, Roll 177; Chief Clerk for the Secretary of War, Washington, D.C., to Secretary of Interior, Washington, D.C., 28 April 1885, NAMP, M689, Roll 177; Cyrus Swan Roberts, Fort Bowie, Arizona, to F. E. Pierce, San Carlos, Arizona, 15 August 1885, NARA,

RG 393, San Carlos, AZ, Box 1; O. D. Greene, Acting Adjutant General, Washington, D.C., to Commanding General, Department of Missouri, Fort Leavenworth, Kansas, 11 November 1885, NARA, RG 92, Records of the Office of the Quartermaster General, Consolidated Correspondence File, 1794–1915, "Indian Trouble to Indians, Yuma, Box 905, Entry 225, "Indian Women (Canada Alamosa, NM) (1885)."

88. Sweeney, *From Cochise to Geronimo,* 401.

89. Brackets in the original. Sweeney, *From Cochise to Geronimo*, 402.

90. Sweeney, *From Cochise to Geronimo*, 403; Kenoi Autobiography, 275.

91. Public meeting reports in "Apaches Must Go," *Arizona Weekly Citizen*, 20 June 1885, in Arizona Memory Project, Arizona Historical Digital Newspapers, https://azmemory.azlibrary .gov/digital/collection/sn82015133/id/1118/rec/223.

92. Public meeting reports in "Apaches Must Go."

93. Public meeting reports in "Apaches Must Go"; "bone yard" quote in *Clifton Clarion*, 10 June 1885, in Arizona Memory Project, Arizona Historical Digital Newspapers, https:// azmemory.azlibrary.gov/digital/collection/sn94050557/id/79/rec/16.

94. On the 1879 law, see Debo, *Geronimo*, 272–273. For a discussion of removal sites, see Nelson Miles, Fort Apache, Arizona, to Assistant Adjutant General, San Francisco, California, 7 July 1886, NAMP, M689, Roll 184, Frames 230–235; Loomis Langdon, St. Augustine, Florida, to R. C. Drum, Washington, D.C., 24 August 1886, NAMP.

95. The most thorough and accurate scholarly account of this campaign is Sweeney, *From Cochise to Geronimo*, 429–551.

96. Bourke quoted in Porter, *Paper Medicine Man*, 193.

97. Porter, *Paper Medicine Man*, 193, 197–198.

98. "Conference held March 25 and 27 1886 at Cañon de los Embudos," transcript reprinted in Davis, *Truth About Geronimo*, 200–212.

99. Porter, *Paper Medicine Man*, 210–211.

100. George Crook, "The Apache Problem," copy of article from *Journal of the Military Service Institution of the United* States (September 1886) in Opler Papers, Series I, Box 11, Folder 12.

101. For Chatto's visit to Washington, D.C. see Shapard, *Chief Loco*, 219–225; Porter, *Paper Medicine Man*, 210–219; "Transcript of Stenographer's Notes of a Conference Between Honorable William C. Endicott, Secretary of War, and Chato, Chief of the Chiricahua Apache Indians, Held at War Department Building, Washington, D.C., 26 July 1886," copy in Opler Papers, Series I, Box 26, Folder 20.

102. "Transcript of Stenographer's Notes."

103. A. F. Randall, photographer, *Chatto, Apache Chiricahua Chief*, United States, ca. 1884, photograph, Library of Congress, https://www.loc.gov/item/2002715253/.

104. Sweeney, *From Cochise to Geronimo*, 552–581; Debo, *Geronimo*, 281–312.

105. For voices against removal, see Shapard, *Chief Loco*, 219–220.

106. Kenoi Autobiography, 293–294.

107. Kenoi Autobiography, 294–295.

108. Unknown artist, *Chiricahuas Preparing to Board Trains at Holbrook, Arizona Territory*, drawing, ca. 1886, https://azmemory.azlibrary.gov/digital/collection/ahsger/id/31/

109. Kenoi Autobiography, 295.

Chapter 8

1. Kenoi Autobiography, 295–296; Betzinez and Nye, *I Fought with Geronimo*, 141–146, quote on 146. Image of Fort Marion is by an unknown photographer, *Birds-Eye View of Fort*

Marion, Saint Augustine Florida, photographic print, 1920, Library of Congress, https://www
.loc.gov/pictures/item/2013645404/.

2. Betzinez and Nye, *I Fought with Geronimo*, 145.

3. For descriptions of tourist interest in Apaches during their journey and the history of
Fort Marion, see Shapard, *Chief Loco*, 219–232, 250.

4. Shapard, *Chief Loco*, 225–231; Debo, *Geronimo*, 316.

5. Debo, *Geronimo*, 299–312, 321.

6. One hundred and seventy-seven Southern Apache students are documented to have
enrolled in boarding school or day school at some point between 1886 and 1913; see Debo,
Geronimo, 317–320; Shapard, *Chief Loco*, 265–266; Delgadillo, *From Fort Marion*, especially
xxxvi–xxxvii.

7. For an excellent scholarly account of health conditions in Florida, see Shapard, *Chief
Loco*, 250–258.

8. Betzinez and Nye, *I Fought with Geronimo*, 146.

9. On the "smallness of the ration," see Loomis Langdon, Fort Barrancas, Florida, to Assistant Adjutant General, Headquarters Division of the Atlantic, Governor's Island, New York, 7
January 1887, NAMP, M689, Roll 188, Frames 8–12. My use of the phrase "survive genocide"
draws from Ostler, *Surviving Genocide*.

10. This approach builds upon recent works in Native American studies emphasizing
Native American life over death. Particularly influential for my thinking have been David
Treuer, *The Heartbeat of Wounded Knee: Native America from 1890 to the Present* (New York:
Riverhead Books, 2019); Alejandra Dubcovsky, "Defying Indian Slavery: Apalachee Voices
and Spanish Sources in the Eighteenth-Century Southeast," *William and Mary Quarterly* 75,
2 (2018), 295–322; Jean M. O'Brien, "Historical Sources and Methods in Indigenous Studies:
Touching on the Past, Looking to the Future," in Chris Andersen and O'Brien, eds., *Sources and
Methods in Indigenous Studies* (London: Routledge, 2017), 15–22; Link, "Iron Horse in Indian
Country." I also draw significantly upon Apache oral histories and autobiographies in this chap-
ter. Particularly useful are two autobiographical accounts collected by the anthropologist Morris
Edward Opler in the 1930s from Sam Kenoi and Dan Nicholas, manuscript versions of which
are extant in Opler's papers housed at Cornell. Opler used the collection of autobiographies as a
device for obtaining the ethnographic material that informed his seminal book *An Apache Life-
Way*. See also Betzinez and Nye, *I Fought with Geronimo*; Ruth McDonald Boyer and Narcissus
Duffy Gayton, *Apache Mothers and Daughters* (Norman: University of Oklahoma Press, 1992).
Consulted but used more sparingly are Eve Ball's oral histories, which are particularly (if not
uniquely) problematic in the degree to which Ball's rhetorical flourishes shaped and stylized the
reflections of her informants. See Ball and Kaywaykla, *In the Days of Victorio* and Ball, *Indeh*.

11. Shapard, *Chief Loco*, 227–230; Kenoi Autobiography, 295–296; Betzinez and Nye,
I Fought with Geronimo, 140–146.

12. Kenoi Autobiography, 295; Shapard, *Chief Loco*, 229;

13. Kenoi Autobiography, 296; Shapard, *Chief Loco*, 229–231, quotes on 231; analysis is
my own.

14. Colonel Romeyn Ayres, Saint Francis Barracks, Florida, to Assistant Adjutant General, Governor's Island, New York, 31 May 1886, NAMP, M689, Roll 184, Frames 10–11; Debo,
Geronimo, 316–317; Shapard, *Chief Loco*, 250–258.

15. Ayres to Assistant Adjutant General, 20 August 1886, NAMP, Frames 441–444.

16. On interpreters and their role, see George Wratten, San Antonio, Texas, to General Nelson
Miles, Albuquerque, New Mexico, 23 September 1886, in Opler Papers, Box 14, Folder 2, "Research

Items–Gatewood, C. B. Papers"; Kenoi Autobiography, 305–306; William Sinclair, Mt. Vernon Barracks, Alabama, to Assistant Adjutant General, Governor's Island, New York, 25 May 1887, NARA, RG 393, Part V, Mt. Vernon Barracks, Alabama, Letters & Telegrams Sent, Entry 2, Vol. 4.

17. Debo, *Geronimo*, 299–312, 325 ("roman holiday"). Map of Florida is adapted from *Detail-Military Map of the United States & Territories . . . ,1861*, Maps Etc., http://fcit.usf.edu /florida/maps/pages/9400/f9473/f9473.htm.

18. Loomis Langdon, Fort Barrancas, Florida, to Assistant Adjutant General, Governor's Island, New York, 7 January 1887, NAMP, M689, Roll 188, Frames 8–12.

19. Debo, *Geronimo*, 321–323.

20. Shapard, *Chief Loco*, 256; Debo, *Geronimo*, 317, 323.

21. Kenoi Autobiography, 298; Ball, *Indeh*, 137.

22. Shapard, *Chief Loco*, 256; Debo, *Geronimo*, 317, 323, 336–337.

23. Langdon to Assistant Adjutant General, 25 April 1887, NAMP, Roll 189, Frames 227–230.

24. Geronimo and Barrett, *Geronimo's Story*, 177; Langdon to Assistant Adjutant General, 23 June 1887, NAMP, Frame 332.

25. Ball and Kaywaykla, *In the Days of Victorio*, 197.

26. Ball and Kaywaykla, *In the Days of Victorio*, 197; Major General George Crook, Washington, D.C., to Secretary of War, 6 January 1890, Opler Papers, Box 26, Folder 20, p. 31; Kenoi Autobiography, 300.

27. Porter, *Paper Medicine Man*, 196–197.

28. Ball, *Indeh*, 137.

29. John G. Bourke, Washington D.C., to Adjutant General, U.S. Army, Washington D.C., 19 April 1887, NAMP, M689, Roll 189, Frames 142–146.

30. Quotes in Shapard, *Chief Loco*, 259-260; see also Loomis Langdon, Saint Francis Barracks, Florida, to Assistant Adjutant General, Governor's Island, New York, 1 October 1886, in Opler Papers, "Gov't-Congress-Senate Documents, 1851–1887," Box 26, Folder 19. On relations with Apaches and town citizens, see C. B. Agnew, Enterprise, Florida, to John B. Riley, Superintendent of Indian Schools, 24 December 1886, in Opler Papers, "Gov't-Congress-Senate Documents, 1851–1887," Box 26, Folder 19.

31. Shapard, *Chief Loco*, 251–252.

32. Ball, *In the Days of Victorio*, 137.

33. Shapard, *Chief Loco*, 262.

34. For the aims of the Indian Rights Association, see *Brief Statement of the Aims, Work, and Achievements of the Indian Rights Association* (Philadelphia: Indian Rights Association, 1886). For an assessment, see Vine Deloria, Jr., "The Indian Rights Association: An Appraisal," in *Aggressions of Civilization: Federal Indian Policy since the 1880's*, ed. Sandra L. Cadawalader and Vine Deloria, Jr. (Philadelphia: Temple University Press, 1984), 3–18. On the broader reform organizations related to Indian affairs that Welsh was a key figure in, see David Wallace Adams, *Education for Extinction: American Indians and the Boarding School Experience, 1875–1928* (Lawrence: University Press of Kansas, 1995), 5–27. For Welsh's report on Apaches, see his *Apache Prisoners in Fort Marion, St. Augustine, Florida* (Philadelphia: Office of the Indian Rights Association, 1887); Shapard, *Chief Loco*, 267 ("lack of productive activity").

35. Quotes in Shapard, *Chief Loco*, 267–268. See also Debo, *Geronimo*, 324; David Michael Goodman, "Apaches as Prisoners of War, 1886-1894," (Ph.D. diss., Texas Christian University, 1969), especially 75–98.

36. Petition from citizens of Pittsfield, Massachusetts, to President Grover Cleveland, Washington, D.C., 4 April 1887; petition from citizens of New Haven, Connecticut, to the President of the United States, Washington, D.C., 5 April 1887; both in NAMP, M689, Roll 189, Frames 182–186 and 177–179; Secretary of War to P. H. Sheridan, 22 April 1887, NAMP, M689, Roll 189, Frame 187.

37. Debo, *Geronimo*, 334.

38. "Roster of Indian Prisoners, 1889–1894," Mt. Vernon Barracks, Alabama, NARA RG 393, Part V, Entry 13, Vol. 1; Aide-de-Camp, Mt. Vernon Barracks, Alabama, to Major General Nelson Miles, Chicago, Illinois, 1 September 1894, NAMP, M689, Roll 197, Frames 161–177. On water problems at Mt. Vernon, see Shapard, *Chief Loco*, 284–294.

39. Shapard, *Chief Loco*, 273.

40. Kenoi Autobiography, 300. For Apache terms for captivity and slavery, see "Chiricahua Vocabulary II," in Opler Papers, Box 51, Carton 3; "Mescalero Vocabulary" excerpts from Blazer Family Papers, in Opler Papers, Box 9, Folder 9.

41. I am indebted to my colleague Delaina Price for a timely conversation in my office that helped me think through this photograph and my broader analysis in this chapter. On slave cabin architecture and surveillance, see John Solomon Otto and Augustus Marion Burns III, "Black Folks and Poor Buckras: Archeological Evidence of Slave and Overseer Living Conditions on an Antebellum Plantation," *Journal of Black Studies* 14, 2 (1983): 185–200. The photograph is from the Wotherspoon Collection at the U.S. Army Heritage and Education Center, Box 1, Folder 38. I first came across the photo in Shapard, *Chief Loco*, 245.

42. Ball, *Indeh*, 139.

43. George Crook, Washington, D.C., to Redfield Proctor, Secretary of War, Washington, D.C., 6 January 1890, in Opler Papers, "Series I: Apache Indian Tribe: Research," Box 26, Folder 20.

44. "Sam and the Attitude of Prisoners of War," Morris Edward Opler research note, in Opler Papers, Series I "Chiricahua: Sam Kenoi Materials," Box 36, Folder 8.

45. Aide-de-Camp, Mt. Vernon Barracks, Alabama, to Major General Nelson Miles, Chicago, Illinois, 1 September 1894, NAMP, M689, Roll 197, Frames 161–177; Debo, *Geronimo*, 354; Shapard, *Chief Loco*, 291–292; Geronimo and Barrett, *Geronimo's Story*, 178.

46. Debo, *Geronimo*, 343–344 ("Government does not propose"); Major H. A. Theaker, Mt. Vernon Barracks, to Assistant Adjutant General, Governor's Island, New York, 13 July 1890, NARA RG 393, Mt. Vernon Barracks, Letters Sent, Part V, Entry 2, Vol. 5, Letter No. 133 ("We are all to die here").

47. For this comparison, see Chapter 5 of this book.

48. Shapard, *Chief Loco*, 278–279.

49. Eugene Chihuahua, in Ball, *Indeh*, 153.

50. Shapard, *Chief Loco*, 278–279. See also Erika Bsumek, *Indian-Made: Navajo Culture in the Marketplace, 1868–1940* (Lawrence: University Press of Kansas, 2008).

51. Samuel Breck, Acting Adjutant General, Washington, D.C., to Commanding General, Division of the Atlantic, Governor's Island, New York, 18 July 1890, NAMP, M689, Roll 197, Frames 73–75; Shapard, *Chief Loco*, 279–280.

52. Delgadillo, *From Fort Marion*, xxxviii; Debo, *Geronimo*, 349–350.

53. On the local population as "no account niggers," see Report of T. F. Forbes, Captain of Infantry, Mt. Vernon Barracks, Alabama, to Post Adjutant, 3 July 1891, NARA, RG 393, Part V, Mt. Vernon Barracks, Letters & Telegrams Received, Box 4. On gambling, see

W. W. Wotherspoon, Mt. Vernon Barracks, to Post Adjutant, 22 June 1890, NARA, RG 393, Part V, Mt. Vernon Barracks, Letters & Telegrams Received, Box 4.

54. Dan Mcleod, Leaksville, Mississippi, to George W. Russell, Mt. Vernon Barracks, 2 November 1892, NARA, RG 393, Part V, Mr. Vernon Barracks, Letters & Telegrams Received, Box 5.

55. Sinclair to Assistant Adjutant General, 27 August 1887, NARA, Letter No. 169.

56. W. Sinclair, Mt. Vernon Barracks, Alabama, to L.L. Langdon, Forts Barrancas and Pickens, Florida, 6 February 1888, NARA, RG 393, Part V, Mt. Vernon Barracks, Letters & Telegrams Sent, Vol. 4, Letter No. 35; Sinclair to Assistant Adjutant General, 9 March 1888, NARA, Letter No. 64; Sinclair to Assistant Adjutant General, 4 June 1888, NARA, Letter No. 123; J. W. Jones, Fort Apache, Arizona, to Commanding Officer, Mt. Vernon Barracks, Alabama, 15 August 1889, NARA, RG 393, Part V, Mt. Vernon Barracks, Letters & Telegrams Received, Box 4.

57. Sinclair to Assistant Adjutant General, 26 March 1888, NARA, letter unnumbered but located on p. 188 of volume.

58. F. Pierce, San Carlos, Arizona, to Commanding Officer, Mt. Vernon Barracks, Alabama, 17 September 1887, NARA, RG 393, Part V, Mt. Vernon Barracks, Letters & Telegrams Received, Box 3, Letter No. 441; W. Sinclair, Mt. Vernon Barracks, Alabama, to F. Pierce, San Carlos, Arizona, 28 September 1887, NARA, RG 393, Part V, Mt. Vernon Barracks, Letters & Telegrams Sent, Vol. 4, Letter No. 194.

59. J. Bennett, Mescalero Agency, New Mexico, to Commanding Officer, Mt. Vernon Barracks, Alabama, 2 October 1889, NARA, RG 393, Part V, Mt. Vernon Barracks, Letters & Telegrams Received, Box 3; on issue of spouses returning to the Southwest or to remain in the Southeast, see Geronimo and Barrett, *Geronimo's Story*, 178–179; Debo, *Geronimo*, 342

60. Bennett to Commanding Officer, 2 October 1889.

61. Loomis L. Langdon, St. Francis Barracks, Saint Augustine, Florida, to Assistant Adjutant General, Governor's Island, New York, 23 August 1886, NAMP, M689, Roll 184, Frames 568–574.

62. R. H. Pratt, Carlisle, Pennsylvania, to W. P. Howe, Mt. Vernon Barracks, Alabama, 7 October 1887, NARA, RG 393, Part V, Mt. Vernon Barracks, Letters & Telegrams Received, Box 3; A. J. Standing, Carlisle, Pennsylvania, to W. L. Kellogg, Mt. Vernon Barracks, 5 May 1890, NARA, RG 393, Part V, Mt. Vernon Barracks, Letters & Telegrams Received, Box 4; Standing to Kellogg, 5 May 1890, NARA. For her domestic labor, see "Lucy Tsisnah," in Delgadillo, *From Fort Marion*, 261.

63. Debo, *Geronimo*, 339.

64. W. M. Sinclair, Mt. Vernon Barracks, to R. H. Pratt, Carlisle, Pennsylvania, 18 June 1888, NARA, RG 393, Part V, Entry 2, Vol. 4, Letter No. 133.

65. Jno. Wanamaker, Postmaster General, Washington D.C., to Secretary of War, Washington D.C., 11 April 1889, NARA, RG 393, Part V, Mt. Vernon Barracks, Letters & Telegrams Received, Box 4; "What Is Official Mail (Penalty Mail)?" https://faq.usps.com/s/article/What-is-Official-Mail-Penalty-Mail.

66. Redfield Proctor, Secretary of War, Washington D.C., to Postmaster General, Washington D.C., 22 March 1889, NARA, RG 393, Part V, Mt. Vernon Barracks, Letters & Telegrams Received, Box 4.

67. David Wallace Adams, *Education for Extinction: American Indians and the Boarding School Experience, 1875–1928* (Lawrence: University Press of Kansas, 1995), especially 28–59.

68. Debo, *Geronimo*, 330.

69. G. W. Russell, Mt. Vernon Barracks, Alabama, to Department Headquarters, Governor's Island, New York, 9 April 1894, NAMP, M689, Roll 197, Frames 104–105.

70. C. C. Ballou, Mt. Vernon Barracks, to Commanding Officer, Mt. Vernon Barracks, 6 April 1894, NAMP, M689, Roll 197, Frame 114.

71. Joseph B. Doe, Acting Secretary of War, Washington D.C., to Commanding Officer, Mt. Vernon Barracks, Alabama, 9 May 1894, NAMP, M689, Roll 197, Frame 107.

72. W. W. Wotherspoon, Aid-de-Camp, Governor's Island, New York, to Assistant Adjutant General, Governor' Island, New York, 13 April 1894, NAMP, M689, Roll 197, Frame 105; Adjutant General, Washington D.C., to Commanding General, Department of the East, Governor's Island, New York, 14 May 1894, NAMP, M689, Roll 197, Frames 115–116.

73. Ballou to Commanding Officer, 6 April 1894, NAMP; Joseph B. Doe, Acting Secretary of War, Washington D.C., to Commanding Officer, Mt. Vernon Barracks, Alabama, 9 May 1894, NAMP, M689, Roll 197, Frame 107. The whole exchange of correspondence regarding this case runs from Frames 104 to 120.

74. For the varied sympathies and ideological viewpoints of U.S. Indian agents, see Cahill, *Federal Fathers and Mothers*. Particularly influential in my analysis of U.S. imperial ideas here are Wolfe, "Settler Colonialism"; Roxanne Dunbar-Ortiz, *An Indigenous Peoples' History of the United States* (Boston: Beacon Press, 2014); Peterson, *Indians in the Family*.

75. W. L. Kellogg, Mt. Vernon Barracks, Alabama, to Adjutant General, U.S. Army, Washington D.C., 17 November 1889, NARA, RG 393, Part V, Entry 2, Vol. 5, Letter No. 146.

76. Debo, *Geronimo*, 341.

77. Kenoi Autobiography, 311. Note that Carlisle records indicate that it was actually 1899 that Kenoi matriculated. See "Samuel Keno Student File," *Carlisle Indian School Digital Resource Center*, http://carlisleindian.dickinson.edu/student_files/samuel-keno-student-file.

78. On the high death rate and challenges of calculating it precisely, see Adams, *Education for Extinction*, 130. For an encyclopedic overview of Apache prisoners of war's fates at boarding school and their return to kin, see Delgadillo, *From Fort Marion*.

79. Shapard, *Chief Loco*, 225: Debo, *Geronimo*, 317–319.

80. Miriam Perrett, introduction to Delgadillo, *From Fort Marion*, xxxv–xxxvi; Shapard, *Chief Loco*, 265; "Case for Information Concerning Apache Indian Children Now Prisoners in Florida," 20 October 1886, NAMP, M689, Roll 186, Frames 516–518.

81. Betzinez and Nye, *I Fought with Geronimo*, 149.

82. Betzinez and Nye, *I Fought with Geronimo*, 151–152.

83. Betzinez and Nye, *I Fought with Geronimo*, 152–153. On the origins of the Carlisle School and its curriculum, see Adams, *Education for Extinction*, 28–59.

84. Betzinez and Nye, *I Fought with Geronimo*, 154. On the broader patterns of renaming at boarding schools, see Adams, *Education for Extinction*, 110–112; Barbara Landis, "The Names," in Jacqueline Fear-Segal and Susan D. Rose, eds., *Carlisle Indian Industrial School: Indigenous Histories, Memories, and Reclamations* (Lincoln: University of Nebraska Press, 2016), 88–105.

85. Kenoi Autobiography, 314–315.

86. This analysis draws from Chapters 1–5 of this book, as well as Babcock, *Apache Adaptation*, especially 141–171. On one Apache educated at the presidio school in Northern New Spain, see also Griffen, "Compás."

87. On routine and structure of classroom instruction and daily life, see Adams, *Education for Extinction*, 136–163; Betzinez and Nye, *I Fought with Geronimo*, 153.

88. Betzinez and Nye, *I Fought with Geronimo*, 154–155.

89. On the ideology of the outing system, see Robert A. Trennert, "From Carlisle to Phoenix: The Rise and Fall of the Indian Outing System, 1878–1930," *Pacific Historical Review* 52, 3 (1983): 267–291.

90. Kenoi autobiography, 311; Betzinez and Nye, *I Fought with Geronimo*, 156–157.

91. Trennert, "From Carlisle to Phoenix," 273–274; Kenoi Autobiography, 339–341. Kenoi remembered his first father as "Charlie Hansard." I have corrected the name based on school records. See "Samuel Keno Student File," *Carlisle Indian School Digital Resource Center*, http://carlisleindian.dickinson.edu/student_files/samuel-keno-student-file. See also "Kenoi (Samuel)" in Delgadillo, *From Fort Marion*, 149–151.

92. Kenoi Autobiography, 341. On boarding-school newspapers and the connective role of student writing, see Jacqueline Emery, ed., *Recovering Native American Writings in the Boarding School Press* (Lincoln: University of Nebraska Press, 2017), especially 1–34. Quote is from *Indian Helper*, 14, 12 (1899), [p, 2], Carlisle Indian School Digital Resource Center, http://carlisleindian.dickinson.edu/publications/indian-helper-vol-14-no-12.

93. Adams, *Education for Extinction*, 335–338.

94. Kenoi Autobiography, 342.

95. Kenoi Autobiography, 309, 341–342.

96. Kenoi Autobiography, 344. The names and locations of Kenoi's first two placements track with school records, though Kenoi recalls spending a much longer time with the "Hansard" (Henson) family than the three months indicated in his student file. His recollection of a lengthy period in the employ of the Peak family after escaping his second abusive "outing" assignment also is not indicated in Carlisle records, but this would not be surprising given that it was not an official assignment. Note that school records also indicate that Kenoi was 18 years old, though he was in fact significantly older. See "Samuel Kenoi Student File"; See also "Kenoi (Samuel)" in Delgadillo, *From Fort Marion*, 149–151.

97. Kenoi Autobiography, 345–346.

98. Betzinez and Nye, *I Fought with Geronimo*, 158–162, quotes on 158, 162, 160.

99. The odyssey of Kenoi's escape and journey on the railroad is described in Kenoi Autobiography, 347–374.

100. John Anthony Turcheneske, Jr., *The Chiricahua Apache Prisoners of War: Fort Sill 1894–1914* (Boulder: University Press of Colorado, 1997), 15–40; Shapard, *Chief Loco*, 295–302.

101. General Howard endorsement on report of Captain Wotherspoon, dated 14 December 1893, Headquarters Department of the East, Governor's Island, New York, 26 December 1893, NAMP, M689, Roll 197, Frame 223.

102. Discussion of breaking Apaches up into small groups was not new. See Chapters 5 and 7 of this book.

103. "Report of the Interview Remarks of the Apache Prisoners of War Made to Captain M. P. Maus Concerning Their Wishes to Be Removed to Some Other Locality," Mt. Vernon Barracks, Alabama, 29 August 1894, NAMP, M689, Roll 197, Frames 186–198.

104. On the 1879 law, see Debo, *Geronimo*, 272–273.

105. Congressional Record, House of Representatives, 27 July 1894, copy in NAMP, M689, Roll 197, Frames 226–232, quote on 229.

106. On the amendment to the Army Appropriations Act on 2 August 1894, see Turcheneske, *Chiricahua Apache Prisoners*, 37. Quotes from Congressional Record, 27 July 1894, in NAMP M689, Roll 197, Frames 228, 229, 231.

107. Davis, *Truth About Geronimo*, 43; Kenoi Autobiography, 323.

108. Debo, *Geronimo*, 364–365.

109. Debo, *Geronimo*, 365; Shapard, *Chief Loco*, 300–301.

110. Morris Edward Opler papers, Box 36, Folder 1, Dan Nicholas Autobiography, 1, 5–8, 13, 33 (hereafter cited as Nicholas Autobiography).

111. Nicholas Autobiography, 47, 62, 69, 72, 98–99; quote from Betzinez and Nye, *I Fought with Geronimo*, 185.

112. Nicholas Autobiography, 6, 43–46, 90–92.

113. Perrett, introduction to Delgadillo, *From Fort Marion*, xlii–xliii; Debo, *Geronimo*, 445–454.

Epilogue

1. Keith Kolb, Portales, New Mexico, to Morris Edward Opler, Norman, Oklahoma, 18 June 1982, Opler Papers, Box 37, Folder 1. On the Apache period of exile, see Shapard, *Chief Loco*, especially 219–306.

2. "A Historical Trip Covering the Chiricahua Apache Imprisonment, 1886–1913," pamphlet produced by Wendell Chino, Freddie Kaydahzinne, and Narcissus Duffy Gayton for the Mescalero Apache Tribe of New Mexico, July 1982, copy in Opler Papers, Box 36, Folder 23.

3. Morris Edward Opler, Norman, Oklahoma, to Keith Kolb, Portales, New Mexico, 11 February 1982, Opler Papers, Box 37, Folder 1; "Historical Trip Covering the Chiricahua Apache Imprisonment," Opler Papers.

4. On the Mexico pilgrimages, see Arreola, "Chiricahua Apache Homeland," 125–127; 1988 photograph by Karen Hayes in Arreola, "Chiricahua Apache Homeland," 127.

5. See especially Chapters 6 and 7 of this book for discussion of these non-Native visions.

6. Quotes from "Historical Trip Covering the Chiricahua Apache Imprisonment," Opler Papers; Arreola, "Chiricahua Apache Homeland."

7. Sam Kenoi, Mescalero, New Mexico, to Senator Elmer E. Thomas, Medicine Park, Oklahoma, 6 February and 17 July 1933, Opler Papers, Box 36, Folder 25; Betzinez and Nye, *I Fought with Geronimo*, 98.

8. Betzinez and Nye, *I Fought with Geronimo*, 195.

9. Debo, *Geronimo*, 448.

10. Nicholas Autobiography, 97, 107–140; Turcheneske, *Chiricahua Apache Prisoners*, 177–180.

11. Betzinez and Nye, *I Fought with Geronimo*, 198.

12. Copies of affidavits in Opler Papers, Box 36, Folder 25. See especially "Affidavit of Mrs. Helen Chatto," undated but c. 1929 based on adjacent affidavits.

13. For Chiricahua and Mescalero land claims, see Ball, *Indeh*, 290–291.

14. Gonzales and Lamadrid, *Nación Genízara*; "Chihene Nde Nation of New Mexico," http://www.chihenendenationofnewmexico.org.

15. On these broader trends in Native American history, see Treuer, *Heartbeat of Wounded Knee*, 233–280; Farina King, *The Earth Memory Compass: Diné Landscapes and Education in the Twentieth Century* (Lawrence: University Press of Kansas, 2018); Douglas Miller, *Indians on the Move: Native American Mobility and Urbanization in the Twentieth Century* (Chapel Hill: University of North Carolina Press, 2019); Miller, "Spider's Web."

INDEX

ACKNOWLEDGMENTS

I should have kept a list of everyone who crossed my path and helped me to write this book over the years. For a historian, however, I am not a very good record keeper, so I am left to my hazy memory to thank those who helped me along the way.

I start with those who set me on my career path when I was an undergraduate at Stony Brook University. Little acts of kindness can have a huge impact. I thank Richard Gerrig for going out of his way to help a college student find his way. For inspiring me to become a historian, I thank Brooke Larson, who in the fall of 2001 captivated me in her introductory course on Colonial Latin American history and continued to inspire me in future courses. I also thank Alix Cooper, who shaped my thinking on intercultural interactions and environmental history and read my papers with a critical but helpful eye. A dear friend, Maggie Sturm, deserves special mention for the adventures that made the academic work possible.

As a graduate student at UT-Austin, I benefited from the sage advice of Erika Bsumek, the encouragement and practical feedback of Jim Sidbury, and the push to think big of Jorge Cañizares-Esguerra. A course with Ann Twinam brought me to tears, but with years of hindsight I see now that it was also beneficial. More than anything, I am grateful for the comradery of fellow graduate students, especially Leah Deane, Jessica Luther, Claire Gherini, Renata Keller, Cameron Strang, Jessica Rae, Claudia Rueda, and Juandrea Bates. For fifteen years, Ann Cooper has been a listening ear as we both managed to write dissertations, took new jobs, and more. I am forever grateful, buddy! I also made a dear friend in Bradley Anderson, a grad student in the math department, who occasionally listened intelligently to my thoughts on history but more often encouraged me to have a good time. During my initial research trip to Mexico City during 2008, I met and learned a lot from Zeb Tortorici. He was among the first people to read any of the writing that eventually became this book, and he helped to make it better. While I wish I had written down the names of every archivist who helped me in Mexico, Spain, and the United States in this and subsequent years, I did not. Thank you to all of you for your help and professional guidance.

I wrote my dissertation while in residence at the McNeil Center for Early American Studies in Philadelphia between 2009 and 2011. While I always struggled to find the right words to say to Dan Richter, the director, he influenced me in other ways, especially by pushing me to present a seminar paper during my year as a fellow and with kind notes of encouragement in subsequent years. While it's been nearly a decade since I lived in Philadelphia, the people I met there have continued to influence me, especially Joe Rezek, Dawn Peterson, Cassandra Good, Alyssa Mt. Pleasant, and Elena Schneider. Dawn deserves special mention for always pushing me to be a better scholar and for her reading multiple chapters of this book over time (though existing faults are all my own!). While in Philadelphia I also met Bob Lockhart, an editor at Penn Press, who continued to be a cheerleader and mentor for the project for the next decade. He may never have thought I would actually finish, but I thank him for his generous guidance all along the way.

I also met Yanni Kotziagkiaouridis in Philadelphia in September 2009. More than a decade later we live in Dallas with our two sons, Luka and Niko. A lot has changed but a constant through almost all the time we've known each other has been my work on this book. When I recently told him my ideas for a new book, he said "You mean you are going to write another one of these things?" His reaction speaks to the many sacrifices he's made for me along the way. I love you and our boys like the moon, stars, clouds, sun, sky, and rainbows, as Luka would say!

After finishing my dissertation in the summer of 2011, I started a position at Colorado State University–Pueblo. The first year was trying but magical as I joined a cohort of incredible scholars and friends: Juan Morales, Kristen Epps, Scott Gage, Alegría Ribadaneira, Fawn Amber-Montoya, and Audrey Dehdouh-Berg in particular. In 2012–2013 I benefited from a fellowship at the Clements Center for Southwest Studies at SMU. Sherry Smith, Andy Graybill, Ruth Ann Elmore, and my fellow fellows, especially Tyina Steptoe, helped make this year productive and enjoyable. I also participated in a symposium that year organized by James Brooks and Bonnie Martin, which proved incredibly stimulating, especially because of fellow participants like Mark Goldberg, Nat Zappia, and Calvin Schermerhorn. In 2015, while still writing this book (it has been a long process), I joined the faculty at the University of Texas at Arlington. While everyone has been welcoming, I want to especially thank Cristina Salinas, Erin Murrah-Mandril, Delaina Price,

Robert Caldwell, Ken Roemer, Chris Morris, Sam Haynes, and Stephanie Cole for their camaraderie, conversations, and advice. I thank my colleague Charles Travis for stepping in at the last minute to help me prepare maps. I also want to thank my chair, Scott Palmer, for his support.

Other institutions not yet named that have provided financial support for my research along the way include: the Mellon Institute (for an invaluable Spanish paleography course), the Phillips Fund for Native American Research, the Lozano Long Institute for Latin American Studies at UT-Austin, and UT-Arlington's Center for the Study of the Greater Southwest for a generous subvention.

This book would not have come to fruition without generous people who have given me copious feedback along the way. Non-academics who have expressed interest in my work deserve special mention, especially Siggy Jumper who shared his own stories from the Apache diaspora. Thanks too to public audiences at El Pueblo Museum and the Louisville History Foundation for giving me the opportunity to test out still nascent ideas. Brian Delay was among the first scholars to comment on my project back in 2009, when he agreed to read a lengthy conference paper I had written despite the fact that he was not the chair or commentator of the panel in question. He also provided much feedback on my dissertation when I was a fellow at the Clements Center, and then again on the book manuscript. I cannot thank him enough for both his line edits and big ideas. Juliana Barr has also been a key mentor for me as we have crossed paths over the years—at numerous conferences and at a Newberry symposium that became an edited volume. She also read the entire manuscript and provided insightful feedback. I thank Andrés Reséndez as well for reading carefully the first chapters of the book and encouraging me to keep going. I probably would not have finished this book without the encouragement of Mary E. Mendoza, whom I met years ago but got to know better in 2018–2019, when she was in the Dallas area as a Clements fellow. Her enthusiasm helped me to buckle down and finally finish the writing. Robert Caldwell and Juan Albert Nungaray generously read and commented on the Introduction, helping me to clarify my ideas. Other scholars who deserve special mention for their useful comments include: Cynthia Radding, Christina Snyder, Farina King, Alejandra Dubcovsky, Stephanie Smallwood, Celia Naylor, Jennifer Morgan, Sarah Keyes, Alessandra Link, James Brooks, Joaquín Rivaya-Martínez, and Karl Jacoby. I also could not have written this book without the prior scholarship of Matthew Babcock and Lance Blyth.

Through it all two things were constants: my parents and my cocker spaniel Kong. Kong died a few weeks before I sent off the manuscript to peer review, but he was by my feet through essentially all of the writing. My parents have been believers and cheerleaders from the beginning, my dad among the few people to have actually read most of the words I have written. I am so grateful and love you both!